PORT OF
NO RETURN

PORT OF NO RETURN

Enemy Alien Internment in World War II New Orleans

MARILYN GRACE MILLER

LOUISIANA STATE UNIVERSITY PRESS
BATON ROUGE

Published by Louisiana State University Press
www.lsupress.org

Copyright © 2021 by Louisiana State University Press
All rights reserved. Except in the case of brief quotations used in articles or reviews, no part of this publication may be reproduced or transmitted in any format or by any means without written permission of Louisiana State University Press.

LSU Press Paperback Original

DESIGNER: Mandy McDonald Scallan
TYPEFACE: Whitman

Portions of the introduction first appeared, in somewhat different form, in "Lessons for the Present from the Alien Enemy Act and the Deportation of Latin Americans to the United States during World War II" / "Lecciones para el presente que deja la Ley del Extranjero Enemigo y la deportación de latinoamericanos a Estados Unidos durante la Segunda Guerra Mundial," *Tabula rasa* 33 (2020): 201–24.

Cover photo: Building at the former Camp Algiers. Photo taken in 2017. David Bulit / Shutterstock.com.

Library of Congress Cataloging-in-Publication Data

Names: Miller, Marilyn Grace, author.
Title: Port of no return : enemy alien internment in World War II New Orleans / Marilyn Grace Miller.
Description: Baton Rouge : Louisiana State University Press, 2021. | Includes bibliographical references and index.
Identifiers: LCCN 2020039701 (print) | LCCN 2020039702 (ebook) | ISBN 978-0-8071-7527-9 (paperback) | ISBN 978-0-8071-7535-4 (pdf) | ISBN 978-0-8071-7536-1 (epub)
Subjects: LCSH: Camp Algiers (Algiers, New Orleans, La.) | World War, 1939–1945—Concentration camps—United States. | World War, 1939–1945—Prisoners and prisons, American. | World War, 1939–1945—Louisiana—New Orleans. | Aliens—Louisiana—New Orleans. | Algiers (New Orleans, La.)—History—20th century.
Classification: LCC D805.5.A425 M55 2021 (print) | LCC D805.5.A425 (ebook) | DDC 940.53/1776335—dc23
LC record available at https://lccn.loc.gov/2020039701
LC ebook record available at https://lccn.loc.gov/2020039702

Contents

Preface: *A Surprising Piece of the City's Past* | ix

Acknowledgments | xv

Introduction | 1

CHAPTER 1.
New Orleans's (Mostly) Secret Internment History | 25

CHAPTER 2.
The Quandaries of Classification | 52

CHAPTER 3.
Incarceration or a Welcome Refuge? *The Panama Jews at Camp Algiers* | 89

CHAPTER 4.
Professor, Spy, Confidant: *Three Notables Interned in New Orleans* | 122

CHAPTER 5.
Royals and Nobles behind Barbed Wire | 159

CHAPTER 6.
Aid Organizations, Diplomatic Efforts, and Community Allies | 189

Epilogue | 207

Notes | 217

Selected Bibliography | 251

Index | 263

Illustrations

1.1. "Plague of Japanese Beetles," *Kansas City Star* cartoon | 3
1.2. Argentines celebrating Hitler's annexation of Austria, 1938 | 7
1.3. "Peace is spelled with a swastika" | 8
1.4. The "secret map" FDR referred to in his October 1941 "New World Order Speech" | 10
1.5. Gertrude Harten with her children, 1944 | 17
1.1. US Quarantine Station–New Orleans, circa 1930s | 26
1.2. Floor plan for the first floor of Building 13 | 27
1.3. Building 13, US Customs and Border Patrol Headquarters, 2017 | 28
1.4. Telegram announcing the opening of the Algiers site as a wartime detention station, 1941 | 29

1.5. Plans designating the use of Building 5 for detention | 33
2.1. Ship manifest of the SS *Florida,* April 8, 1942 | 54
2.2. Ship manifest of the SS *Cuba,* October 4, 1942 | 55
2.3. A page of the November 1944 list of enemy aliens interned at the Algiers detention station | 57
3.1. "Enemy Aliens Leave Panama for the U.S.," April 6, 1942 | 90
3.2. Death certificate for Martin Kallman | 101
4.1. Studio portrait of Hermann Beyer | 123
4.2. Hermann Beyer's Nazi-era passport | 125
4.3. Hermann Beyer's alien enemy personnel record | 132
4.4. Jacket for John Roy Carlson's *Under Cover,* published in 1943 | 144
5.1. Death certificate for Count Axel Wachmeister | 167
5.2. Nazi Golden Party Badge | 174
5.3. Schloss Leopoldskron, confiscated by the Gestapo and used as an event venue for elite Nazis | 175
5.4. Major Lemuel Schofield, Solicitor General Francis Biddle, and Attorney General Robert Jackson, 1940 | 179
6.1. The *Serpa Pinto* | 192

Preface
A Surprising Piece of the City's Past

On November 9, 2016, the day after the 2016 presidential election, I stood with producer Laine Kaplan-Levenson just outside the locked security gates of a border patrol station in the Algiers neighborhood on the West Bank of the Mississippi River in New Orleans, Louisiana. After learning of the station's use as an Immigration and Naturalization Service–administered enemy alien detention camp during World War II, I had contacted Kaplan-Levenson about creating a segment on the site for the series *TriPod: New Orleans at 300*. Airing weekly on local public radio station WWNO from October 2015 to October 2018, *TriPod* offered "fresh" radio history about New Orleans in the lead-up to its 2018 tricentennial. Each *TriPod* segment moved beyond the familiar themes of New Orleans history "to focus on forgotten, neglected, or surprising pieces of the city's past, and to enrich understanding of its present and future."[1] It seemed the perfect venue for the weird, incredible tale of enemy aliens being housed in the Crescent City during wartime.

Kaplan-Levenson and I had studied anecdotal references to the Algiers Detention Station in accounts by historians such as Max Paul Friedman and Harvey Strum.[2] I had already compiled a starter bibliography and brought with me copies of local news articles from 1943 to 1946 that referred to the detention station, one of which even featured a photo taken soon after its decommissioning as an internment station. That photo, which ran on the front page of the *Times-Picayune* on March 30, 1946, with the headline "Close Pal of Hitler Held in Algiers Detention Unit," confirmed we were, in fact, standing at the very spot on the Mississippi River levee from which the site had been photographed for posterity seventy years earlier. The photo and accompanying headline also posed some big questions. Was someone from Hitler's inner circle in fact detained at the Algiers facility during World War II? If so, who was this mysterious person whose name was not revealed in the article? Why was he held here? Such details suggested a vital if buried episode in the city's rich and complex history. The celebration of New Orleans's tricentennial in 2018 provided an opportune moment for uncovering this shadowy chapter of a global story from a local vantage point.

When we requested entry to the facility in order to investigate further, there was a pregnant pause from the voice on the other end of the Customs and Border Patrol intercom; you could almost hear the head scratching. Referred to the US Border Patrol's information officer, Robert Rivet, we later found that neither he nor anyone else then working at the former quarantine station knew of this episode in the facility's past or had even *heard* of it. In the face of their skepticism, we might have given up. Hadn't reputed historians already done admirable scholarship on the broader topic of World War II enemy alien internment across the United States, though none had focused in particular on New Orleans? Nonetheless, we agreed the Camp Algiers story merited further attention, perhaps even more so, given the aura of mystery and secrecy surrounding it and the fact that topics such as the "enemy" nature of aliens seeking asylum and New Orleans's role as a sanctuary city were much in the news.

Kaplan-Levenson produced two segments that first aired on *TriPod* on January 12 and 19, 2017, and on many subsequent occasions as well. Part 1 provided the general history of the Department of State's Enemy Alien Control Program, implemented immediately after the bombing of Pearl Harbor. That first segment included audio commentary from Friedman, Strum, myself, and Nancy Cortés Reinbold, a Honduran whose German-born grandfather, Fritz Reinbold, was detained in Tegucigalpa and deported to New Orleans for US internment. He was later confined at a camp in Crystal City, Texas, along with his wife and children, including Nancy's mother, Ingrid, less than a year old at the time. An employee of the German embassy when apprehended, Reinbold had likely been named an enemy alien "because he was rich" rather than for any political activity, his granddaughter told Kaplan-Levenson. The deportation allowed for the Honduran government's appropriation of Reinbold's property and assets.

This material injustice was layered with another tragic loss that I later uncovered in my research. The Reinbolds' three-year-old son, Edgar, born in Honduras in 1941, died at the Crystal City internment camp of internal injuries after being hit by a truck there in May 1944. His gravestone at the Edgewood Cemetery in Crystal City bears the inscription "In Liebe deine Eltern," or "With love, your parents."[3] Learning of personal experiences like those of the Reinbolds spurred me to look for the human stories at the heart of this history, to flesh out, as it were, the decisions, policies, events, places, and paperwork that governed the operation of the Enemy Alien Control Program at the local level.

Part 2 of the *TriPod* podcast on Camp Algiers served as a kind of teaser for this approach by focusing on everyday life for the internees in New Orleans. The podcast remarked on the station's erstwhile designation as a "Camp of the Innocent," thanks to the arrival in 1943 and after of many anti-Nazi detainees, including about sixty Jewish men, women, and children who were transferred from camps where they faced harassment and violence from pro Nazi, pro-Fascist and/or antisemitic detainees. Discovering that about eighty Jews were among the enemy aliens apprehended in Latin America as Nazi or Axis sympathizers (or at least potential subversives) was a veritable assault to credulity, but learning these individuals and families were ultimately congregated at Camp Algiers further piqued my curiosity and compelled me to continue the research.

Energized by the ways in which the radio format had given the topic of an old immigration station new life, I ventured forward in search of sources pertaining to Camp Algiers and New Orleans's role in wartime enemy alien internment more broadly. The National World War II Museum in New Orleans seemed a likely repository for this information, but colleagues there were unable to provide information on Camp Algiers. In fact, three-quarters of a century after the end of the World War II, I was increasingly realizing how little knowledge there was, even in the halls of museums, academia, and government itself, of the United States' internment of German, Italian, and Japanese noncitizens at Algiers and other camps located in Texas, Tennessee, Oklahoma, Georgia, and elsewhere.

There appeared to be even less awareness of the Latin American component of this internment effort, in which some fifteen cooperating countries identified and arrested Axis nationals who could potentially pose a threat to hemispheric security, holding them in internal facilities or aiding the US military in deporting them to the United States. As the point of delivery for many of the ships carrying enemy aliens and the family members who voluntarily accompanied them from ports in Panama, Peru, Ecuador, Belize, and other countries, New Orleans functioned as a threshold from which named aliens would be dispatched to a network of internment facilities. It was in New Orleans, frequently, that Latin American detainees were stripped of their passports and other documentation and then charged with entering the United States illegally. It was in New Orleans, the same US port inextricably tied to the trade in enslaved human beings in the nineteenth century, where another kind of forced displacement played out after the United States' entry into World War II. Though a certain percentage of the people who passed through the Crescent City as enemy aliens would finally return through it en route to the countries where they were detained, New Orleans nevertheless represented a "port of no return," a brink that, once crossed, could not be traversed in reverse.

Albeit overshadowed by the case of Japanese "relocation," which affected some 112,000 people, the majority of them American citizens, the internment of German, Italian, and Japanese noncitizens from across the Americas is a crucial aspect of the United States' management of wartime fears of insecurity, conspiracy, and invasion. The Crescent City's role was clearly significant, but the program's secret status meant the research demanded the skills of a dogged detective. I scoured the files at National Archives sites I and II in Washington, DC, and College Park, Maryland, respectively, and studied other records at Tulane University Archives and Special Collections, the YIVO Institute for Jewish Studies, and the American Jewish Historical Society in New York, and the New Orleans Public Library. Reference archivist William Creech, a specialist at the National Archives on the internment camps operated by the Immigration and Naturalization Service, warned me that I was unlikely to find much of a paper trail for Camp Algiers, as it was only a small and arguably insignificant camp alongside mammoth operations like Camp Crystal City, Camp Seagoville, and Camp Kenedy, all located in Texas. Sometimes the only information for "minor" sites such as Algiers was how many potatoes per week they ordered, he cautioned. Creech was right—to an extent. The records were incomplete for the Algiers station, with the most glaring gap the absence of full lists of internees throughout the years of its operation.

Ultimately, though, there was enough information in the combined archival records and relevant bibliography to reconstruct this strange historical episode, one that begins with the role of the Enemy Alien Control Program in the broader story of World War II detention and internment and then continues with the specific part New Orleans played in that drama. The heart of this chronicle, though, is the human story. How and why were people of varied political and religious persuasions named "alien enemies"—a label that led to forced displacement, indefinite detention, separation from family members, loss of property, and long periods behind bars or fences—based solely on the question of where they were born? What were their individual backgrounds? What baggage, other than their strictly regulated single suitcase, did they bring with them into the camps? What conditions did they find there? What were the gains and losses of the program, both collectively and individually?

This book argues for the value of asking these questions today, even when the answers are troublesome or incomplete, and the human stories fragmented. Aspects of the United States' Enemy Alien Control Program have been held up for examination by many fine scholars. This volume, however, focuses on the men, women, and children caught up in the wartime program's operation from the unlikely viewpoint of a single city, one known more for its laissez-faire attitude than for the restrictions, controls, and dubious outcomes of a wartime internment program directed at its Latin American neighbors. My hope is that this book can serve as a memorial to those who experienced injustice and to those who helped them in their plight, while providing a provocative viewpoint for reflection and reassessment of our contemporary responsibility toward and together with our noncitizen neighbors.

Acknowledgments

I am grateful for the generous assistance and wise counsel of many individuals who helped advance this sometimes quixotic project from start to finish. Early in its gestation, Eve Abrams of the *Unprisoned* series on New Orleans public radio station WWNO introduced me to Laine Kaplan-Levenson, who was producing *TriPod: New Orleans at 300*, also for WWNO. Kaplan-Levenson provided the first media venue for this lost story, a version of which later aired on *Latino USA* as well. Along the way, I profited from the work of many outstanding historians and archivists, especially Max Paul Friedman and Harvey Strum, whose studies undergird this effort. Greg Robinson proved to be a savvy interlocutor on the topics of internment history and New Orleans food. Joseph Page and Gunter Bischof invited me to present the research in their respective centers. Many archivists, especially William Creech at National Archives I and Hayley Maynard at National Archives II, helped me access key records for Camp Algiers and those detained there. Staff members at the Historic New Orleans Collection, the YIVO Institute, and the American Jewish Historical Society helped with archival materials. Seale Paterson at the New Orleans Public Library deserves a special mention. Robert Rivet of the Customs and Border Patrol facility at the former Camp Algiers guided a site visit and pointed me to additional government documents. Historical preservationists Kelly Calhoun and Kate Clark met with me and Algiers historian Donald Costello at the site to exchange expertise and local knowledge. Heidi Gurke Donald shared the resources of the German American Internee Coalition and put me in touch with Grace Shimizu and Karin Harten Schramm. Filmmaker Abby Ginzberg and journalist Andrea Pitzer took time from their own internment-related projects to show an interest in mine. Intellectual kin at other institutions, including Esther Allen, Robert McKee Irwin, Jacqueline Loss, Michaela Raggam-Blesch, Fernando Rosenberg, Jonathan Sarna, Maximilian Strnad, Estelle Tarica, and Nicaso Urbina aided this endeavor in myriad ways. Luisa Campuzano, a veritable encyclopedia of Cuban cultural history and scholarship, helped me investigate the Cuban case of World War II–era alien detention, a topic I hope to return to in later research. I am also enormously grateful to the capable leaders and diverse fellow scholars whom I joined for *After Evil: The Ethical Dynamics of Addressing the Past*, the 2018 Annual Seminar on Religion, Ethics, and the Holocaust held at the US Holocaust Memorial Museum.

So many colleagues at Tulane University lent a hand that I hope to have recalled all those to whom I owe a debt of gratitude. Emily Clark blessed me with helpful advice throughout the process, beginning with the suggestion to query Margaret Lovecraft at Louisiana State University Press about the project. I thank Margaret, Jenny Keegan, and the other members of the Press's editorial staff for their support of this book and its many pieces. Sylvia Frey not only recognized the value of the topic but also understood why I would set aside other important projects for this one. Lawrence Powell recommended tactics for tracking down buried threads of New Orleans Jewish history. Hortensia Calvo, Rachel Stein, Christine Hernández, and Verónica Sánchez in the Latin American Library at Tulane expertly guided me to the many wonders of the LAL collections. Eric Wedig provided punctual, friendly help at Howard-Tilton Memorial Library as well. Ann Case shared her formidable knowledge of the university archives. Several colleagues in the Department of Spanish and Portuguese cheered me on, especially Jean Dangler, Kathleen Davis, and Christopher Dunn. John Charles provided steady and timely sources of encouragement and enlightenment. Rosanne Adderley, Carolina Caballero, Marcello Canuto, Michael Cohen, Brian Edwards, Holly Flora, Brian Horowitz, Jana Lipman, Frances Simon, and Justin Wolfe all contributed directly or indirectly to this book's successful completion as well. I am thankful for the multitasking expertise of Claudia DeBrito and Terry Spriggs in the Department of Spanish and Portuguese. Certain Tulane students who developed an interest in this story also deserve thanks, including the trio of Mira Kohl, Joseph Hiller, and Jack Collins, who produced the documentary *Camp of the Innocents* for Justin Wolfe's seminar on Historical Documentary Filmmaking. Oswaldo Vargas Díaz, who took a summer course at Tulane, became a zealot for the topic as well, unearthing fresh materials from the New Orleans Public Library. Funding from the Sizeler Family Professorship in Judaic Studies, the School of Liberal Arts, and the Stone Center for Latin American Studies at Tulane contributed to the research and compilation of this material.

Recognizing those who have helped in the completion of this book also brings into view a whole network of supporters from outside the halls of academia and the institutions where I conducted research. Ana Serra and the Dreissen-Serra family generously housed me during long stints in Washington working in the National Archives. Kristi Drake and the Drake family helped me decompress on their deck overlooking Puget Sound and in the restaurants of Rome. Suzanne Stone carefully read several chapters of the manuscript for clarity and flow and refused to accept any form of payment. Joan Kay, Jane Guild, and the other wise women of the Rayne Covenant Group offered affirmation and good humor throughout the book's development. Sharon London reminded me I was providing a voice for the voiceless. Reverend Callie Crawford and Rabbis Alexis Berk and Katie Bauman exemplified the interconnectedness of intellectual projects, personal convictions, and community engagement I hope to have modeled in these pages. The unexpected discovery of, and subsequent friendships with, my vibrant and accomplished cousins Joanna Miller Bukszpan, Judith Miller Zachs, and Stephen Miller provided a connection to the family legacy of my father, Rudolph Miller, whom I never had the chance to meet.

Chief among all my supporters and collaborators is without doubt Eduardo Alvelo, who accompanied me on each step of this peripatetic journey with the repeated reassurance *siempre con vos*.

PORT OF NO RETURN

Introduction

Retrofitting the Alien Acts

In 1941, when Franklin D. Roosevelt implemented the Enemy Alien Control Program in response to World War II security concerns, legislation controlling and criminalizing noncitizens had been in force in this country for almost a century and a half.[1] In 1798, little more than a decade after the drafting of the Constitution, the Fifth Congress passed the Alien and Sedition Acts. Signed by President John Adams, these laws made it more difficult for immigrants to become citizens and set an ominous precedent by pejoratively coupling the terms "alien" and "enemy" in American political and cultural discourse. Among other provisions, the Alien and Sedition Acts invested the president with the power to imprison and deport noncitizens the state deemed dangerous or who had arrived in the United States from a hostile nation.

These measures conceived in the nation's infancy "are seen as the forerunners of such modern abuses of American rights and liberties as twentieth-century immigration quotas, the Red Scare, Japanese internment camps, and minority voter suppression," notes historian Carol Berkin in her 2017 study *A Sovereign People*.[2] Recognizing the challenge they presented to the nascent democratic ideals of the United States, John Miller titled his 1951 study of these acts *Crisis in Freedom*, commenting, "In enacting the Alien and Sedition laws, the Federalists professed to act upon this premise: that a dangerous French faction was at work in the United States and that the survival of the Republic required that it be stamped out."[3] Even in the eighteenth century, according to Miller, "abusing foreigners was the road to political favor," although it was the

Irish and the English who served as the primary targets of opprobrium at that moment. The alien bills granted the president "virtually unlimited power over all aliens in the United States," creating a lasting effect on noncitizens' personal liberties. *Liberty's First Crisis* was the title Charles Slack similarly chose for his twenty-first-century examination of these laws.[4]

However broad the powers against aliens were at the time of the alien laws' inception, nonetheless, FDR would significantly expand their application in the context of World War II, first through the 1940 Alien Registration Act, which for the first time in history required every alien living in the United States to register and be fingerprinted, and then through internment. As Francis Biddle later wrote regarding the first of these measures, "The very word *alien* suggested those who had been estranged and excluded"; with the passage of the Alien Registration Act, "The beginning of the witch hunt was on."[5]

This study focuses on the internment of named alien enemies as a tool for managing perceived security threats both within and beyond US borders during World War II. It summarizes how an apparatus of dubious effectiveness became a fundamental—though officially secret—element of the war effort. It asks what this internment initiative meant at the local level, focusing on a quarantine station in New Orleans that was used as an internment facility from 1941 to 1946 and on the city itself as a port of entry for the human traffic of internment. While internment camps have been a widespread feature of protective policies in many parts of the world, especially in wartime, the United States' operation of such sites on its own soil and in other parts of the Americas is a chapter of US history rarely taught and little known. Contemporary questions concerning the appropriate policies and conditions of noncitizen detention signal the need for a fuller awareness of this earlier internment history.

The limited contemporary knowledge of US internment history has been compounded on the one hand by the secrecy deemed necessary for the program's efficacy and on the other by the fact that—as with the story of World War II itself—few of the key characters in that drama are still alive to attest to it. Were it not for the historical materials examined here that document the rehabilitation of the immigration station on New Orleans's West Bank as a detention unit, the local story of internment might be passed off as an urban myth. These pages reveal that not only did the Crescent City play a pivotal role in the massive matrix of World War II internment, but also that this role, like the city itself, was utterly unique. This small slice of World War II history is, then, an "only in New Orleans" story as well.

FIGURE I.1. "Plague of Japanese Beetles" shows Uncle Sam conducting pest control on the enemy alien problem in California. *Kansas City Star*, March 9, 1942. Reprinted by permission of the *Kansas City Star*.

Internment and Relocation

The confinement in so-called relocation camps of some 112,000 men, women, and children of Japanese descent, two-thirds of them US citizens, is a widely known aspect of the United States' efforts to bolster domestic security after it entered World War II.[6] Now recognized as a tragic abrogation of personal rights, this episode represents a contradiction of America's claims to equality and protection for all its citizenry. The removal of the Japanese from their homes in Pacific Coast states and other regions, first to assembly centers and then to internment facilities, should not be conflated, however, with the enemy alien internment program. Forced displacement of Japanese Americans was triggered "by order of the President" when Roosevelt signed Executive Order 9066 on February 19, 1942, authorizing the secretary of war to designate certain areas of the country military zones, thus clearing the way for the removal of Japanese Americans from these restricted areas.

INTRODUCTION | 3

The deep racism informing the order was starkly exposed in the words of General John De Witt, who asserted in his February 14 recommendation to the secretary of war, "Racial affinities are not severed by migration. The Japanese race is an enemy race and while many second and third generation Japanese born on American soil, possessed of United States citizenship, have become 'Americanized,' the racial strains are undiluted."[7] The misrepresentation of American citizens of Japanese descent as enemy aliens is graphically portrayed in a cartoon that ran in the *Kansas City Star* on March 9, 1942, in which a plague of Japanese beetles constitutes the "enemy alien problem" (figure I.1). DeWitt later told the *Washington Post,* "A Jap's a Jap. It makes no difference whether he is an American citizen or not."[8] As Greg Robinson explains, "While Executive Order 9066 did not specifically mention Japanese Americans, it was intended to apply to them exclusively."[9]

New measures affecting noncitizen populations born in countries rendered enemy antagonists by the US entry into the war, on the other hand, had already been announced prior to Executive Order 9066. Proclamation 2525 (Japanese), signed on December 7, 1941, and Proclamations 2526 (Germans) and 2527 (Italians), signed the following day, authorized the apprehension and internment for the duration of the war of an alien enemy "deemed *potentially dangerous* to the peace and security of the US" (my emphasis).[10] The Special War Problems Division of the State Department was created to deal with matters of civilian internment of enemy aliens. While the proclamations following Pearl Harbor in December 1941 and Executive Order 9066 announced in February 1942 were both unilateral presidential directives that led to forced displacement, family separation, community disintegration, job and property loss, and even public repudiation, they targeted distinct populations and functioned differently, as the following pages show.

The larger scale of Japanese American internment may explain, at least in part, why the fates of alien enemy internees of German, Italian, and even Japanese descent, apprehended in the United States or in Latin America, have often been ignored in our collective reckoning with America's history of wartime detention. Nevertheless, both groups and their fates are crucial parts of the internment story. More than two decades into the twenty-first century, and three quarters of a century after the official end of World War II, some of that story is still waiting to be told.

Available records indicate that few if any Japanese Americans passed through the gates of the New Orleans internment facility at the center of this study. The majority of persons confined inside its fence were Axis nationals deported from Latin America to the United States, some of whom had only recently found a haven in Central or South America after fleeing war-torn Europe.[11] A small percentage of the internees held at Camp Algiers were German-born alien enemies apprehended in the United States, as chapter 4 demonstrates. Representing a broad range of nationalities, languages, professions, cultures, and even religions, these diverse internees' experiences are unified by the common themes of despondency and indignation, countered by hope and the dogged pursuit of personal and/or collective justice.

Officials and lawmakers had begun to plot the contours of alien enemy internment well before the US entry into the war. Some pointed to the disquieting relationship new internment policy might bear to similar policies in Germany under Hitler. In May 1939, a vigorous debate ensued in Congress over the so-called Hobbs Bill, under which "subversive" aliens could be detained in the United States. New York congresswoman Caroline O'Day was provoked to comment, "I can imagine with what satisfaction Hitler will learn that his emissaries in this country have so influenced Congress that it is following his example in setting up concentration camps during peacetime."[12] Indeed, the network of facilities that housed alien internees during the war would crisscross the United States from Honolulu to Ellis Island and from North Dakota to southern states such as Texas and Louisiana. In its own overview of the World War II Enemy Alien Control Program, the US government concluded that by the end of the war, "over 31,000 suspected enemy aliens and their families, including a few Jewish refugees from Nazi Germany, had been interned at Immigration and Naturalization Service internment camps and military facilities throughout the United States."[13]

Heightened Security Measures

The stated purpose of the United States' program of naming, apprehending, and detaining "alien enemies" was to enhance national and hemispheric security. Though unimpeachable in the abstract, the program was deeply flawed in practice. "While the identification of potentially disloyal noncitizens would certainly seem prudent during wartime, the program was created during peacetime, secretly, and gave those so labeled no right to confront their accusers," notes historian Arnold Krammer.[14] Even before the bombing of Pearl Harbor, President Roosevelt set out to convince both his domestic constituency and his southern neighbors of a concerted Nazi push for control of the entire hemisphere. Largely successful in that effort, the president would seek and receive the cooperation of most Latin American countries (Mexico, Brazil, and Argentina were notable exceptions).[15] The Roosevelt administration was thus able to implement its Enemy Alien Control Program inside its national boundaries, in spaces such as the Panama Canal Zone, where the United States exerted substantial political control, and in more than a dozen other sovereign republics. The push to uncover and debilitate pro-Nazi and pro-Fascist forces would constitute, in theory at least, an unprecedented example of intra-American cooperation.

Paradoxically, a Good Neighbor Policy less than a decade old that vowed noninterference in the other nations of the Americas provided the background for the United States' deployment of the Latin American internment initiative.[16] Armed with its own Alien Enemy Act renovated for the twentieth century, the US government tasked officials in Latin America with drawing up lists of potential enemies of the United States residing in their countries, often supplying them with intelligence gathered by the FBI in their regions. In many cases, European and Japanese-born residents in Latin America were deemed a threat based solely on their country of origin, regardless of any political or criminal activity—or lack of it. Thousands were summarily subjected to US-sponsored surveillance and seizure outside its borders and became part of a new, specious wartime commerce in which officials in Latin America frequently demanded bribes from those who hoped to avoid internment or deportation under the US program, appropriated properties and businesses of those who were detained, and improved their countries' standing with the powerful neighbor to the north by swelling the ranks of potential enemy aliens.

How real were the dangers the United States claimed were lurking south of its borders? As early as 1932, adherents had organized the first Nazi party in Latin America in the unexpected location of Paraguay.[17] Champions of Hitler and the Nazis existed in many parts of the region, including Argentina, Uruguay, Colombia, Bolivia, and Mexico.[18] On April 10, 1938, thousands filled Buenos Aires's Luna Park stadium to celebrate Hitler's annexation of Austria (figure I.2); police outside reportedly suppressed those opposing the rally.[19] That same year, Uruguayan politician and journalist Adolfo Tejera published *Penetración nazi en América Latina* (Nazi penetration in Latin America) and in 1940, an anonymous pamphlet titled *La "quinta columna" en las dos Américas: La conquista de la América Latina es el objectivo final de Hitler* (The "fifth column" in the two Americas: the conquest of Latin America is the final objective of Hitler) appeared.

FIGURE I.2. Thousands of Argentines fill Buenos Aires's Luna Park stadium on April 10, 1938, to celebrate Hitler's annexation of Austria. Photo courtesy Rare Historical Photos.

A May 25, 1940, issue of the Guatemalan journal *Resumen de las actualidades* (Summary of current events) celebrated Hitler's official visit to Italy and meeting with Benito Mussolini with a series of photos, waxing poetic with these lines accompanying a picture of the two leaders together:

> The army that marches under your upraised arm is Latin
> it is the friendship of one of our own peoples
> it is our Roman culture on the defense
> Here for your heroic struggle, oh Führer,
> is the fraternal support of our eternal lineage.[20]

The photo-essay included a final image that declared, "Paz se escribe con swástica" (Peace is spelled with a swastika) (figure I.3). In Panama, where 250 Jewish refugees were rounded up and detained at the Balboa Internment Camp in the Canal Zone just two days after the bombing of Pearl Harbor, the operation was overseen by the country's antisemitic president, Arnulfo Arias, "whose ideas were in line with Nazi ideas and compounded U.S. suspicion of his administration."[21]

INTRODUCTION | 7

FIGURE 1.3. "Peace is spelled with a swastika." Image from Guatemalan journal *Resumen de las actualidades*, May 25, 1940. Photo courtesy Latin American Library, Tulane University.

Episodes and anecdotes such as these exacerbated external qualms about Nazi inroads in the Americas. The clandestine US Office of Strategic Services had been investigating the level and commitment of pro-Nazi sentiment since 1941; its "alarming reports fill ten reels of microfilm."[22] But as Max Paul Friedman notes, the Germans in Latin America were targeted differently from their counterparts in North America "because of an essential aspect of US–Latin American relations that went back to the Monroe Doctrine and forward to the present day: many in the United States thought Latin American countries could not manage their own affairs without paternal guidance from Washington, and assumed that the hidden hand of a European power lay behind any significant unrest or discordance with U.S. plans."[23] Britain was also keen to accentuate the possibility of a Nazi incursion. A July 25, 1941, article in the *Spectator* ("The Nazis in Latin America") claimed, "The intensity of Nazi activity in Latin America has reached a point when it constitutes a grave danger to certain Governments" and noted that twenty Germans who had arrived in La Paz, Bolivia, with diplomatic passports were described in a Bolivian newspaper as "agents for the Nazi invasion."

Thomas Leonard and John Bratzel's volume *Latin America during World War II* offers insights on the depth of the Axis presence and influence in specific countries during this tense period, warning against facile overgeneralization of the region as a whole. Its introduction, however, judges US reports and analysis of the Axis threat as on the whole marked by "incredible overstatements and puffery."[24] It notes that most existing scholarship on subversion in Latin America focuses on the sizable populations of Germans then living in Argentina, Brazil, Chile, and Mexico; several of these hot spots in fact refused to collaborate in the US detention and internment program. "In a very broad sense the Abwehr (German military intelligence) did not have very ambitious goals for Latin America," Peru specialists Daniel Masterson and Jorge Ortiz Sotelo conclude.[25] Still, Roosevelt "sought evidence to prove that Hitler planned to attack the Americas" and continued to promote "Naziphobia."[26] Ultimately, along with assessing the supposed construction of a Nazi "fifth column" in its midst, "each nation had to respond to the U.S. desire to control these populations, or to at the very least break their power."[27] Thus Latin American nations, especially contributors to the internment effort, had to negotiate undue influence from both Germany *and* the United States, which had only recently promised nonintervention. This juggling act was especially difficult after July 1941, when President Roosevelt announced the Proclaimed List of Blocked Nationals or "Blacklist," affecting the American republics' economic interactions with Germany.

The Secret Map

On October 27, 1941, a few weeks before the bombing of Pearl Harbor, Roosevelt delivered a National Defense Day address in which he claimed that he had in his possession a secret map (figure I.4) proving Adolf Hitler planned to establish a new world order in the Americas: "It is a map of South America and a part of Central America as Hitler proposes to reorganize it. The geographical experts of Berlin, however, have ruthlessly obliterated all existing boundary lines and have divided South America into five vassal states, bringing the whole continent under their domination. And they have also arranged it that the territory of one of these new puppet states includes the Republic of Panama and our great lifeline—the Panama Canal."[28] Both the source and veracity of this map were questioned; Berlin insisted it was a forgery, and the president refused to produce it for reporters, citing security concerns. He urged his aides to read a British intelligence Secret Service report that ominously predicted German takeovers in Argentina, Brazil, Chile, Peru, Colombia, Venezuela, and Ecuador and recommended preemptive coups against all seven governments.[29]

FIGURE 1.4. The "secret map" FDR referred to in his October 1941 "New World Order Speech." President's Secretary's Files: Safe Files: Germany, July 1941–1944. Image courtesy the FDR Presidential Library and Museum.

In spite of these heightened alarms, some historians argue that "the Roosevelt administration never obtained evidence to prove that Germany was trying to foment revolution in the Americas."[30] David Haglund wrote that "Washington's fascination with subversion in Latin America quickly became annoying to most governments below the Rio Grande, who argued that the real menace was the 'Sixth Column' of people who believed in the Fifth Column."[31] Nonetheless, even in the abstract the secret map was a convincing tool for rallying support both at home and in the countries that agreed to cooperate with Uncle Sam to defend the hemisphere.[32] However real or exaggerated, FDR's fears of a "Fifth Column" in the Americas informed many wartime policies, including the expansion of existing federal legislation regarding enemy aliens that dated back to the late eighteenth century. This time, though, the government called for surveillance and control of alien persons it considered a threat both inside *and outside* its national borders.

Governmental policy and actions spurred by fears of Nazi and Fascist gains in the Americas assumed thoroughly different forms north and south of the Rio Grande. Despite the complete lack of evidence that Germans, Italians, and other Axis nationals living in Latin America "outdid their fellow citizens in the United States in their support for Hitler," their treatment was very distinct. Germans taken into custody in the United States were granted hearings, and less than 1 percent of German citizens entered internment, whereas in Latin America, as many as half of all German residents of some countries, such as Honduras, were detained and interned.[33]

Officials in cooperating countries received US funds and other forms of support for naming and detaining suspected enemy aliens. Eager to comply with (and benefit from) northern fears, they also operated or allowed US officials to operate internment camps at sites such as the Isle of Pines in Cuba, Camp Empire in the Panama Canal Zone, and prisons in Managua and San José.[34] In many cases, "internment facilities" were no more than requisitioned sections of their own jails and prisons.[35] Many enemy aliens recounted how paying a "fee" to law enforcement and internment personnel could allow them to avoid detention or lessen their time behind bars. This under-the-table commerce obviously compromised the very nature of the hemispheric security initiatives, as the most hardened Nazis and Fascists with the necessary funds could avoid detention, while impoverished and vulnerable refugees had no recourse to release.

The United States' counterparts in Latin America also took advantage of the enemy alien directive to target noncitizens with valuable businesses, properties, or other goods for detention; once listed for deportation, such individuals were forced to sell their holdings at a fraction of their worth or abandon them completely. After they were deported, such assets could be further appropriated without the owners' knowledge and without leaving them any recourse.[36] Ted Eckardt, interned with his family at Crystal City, Texas, at age eight, reflected, "Personally, I believe the Panamanian government went along with the deportation so that they could then confiscate our property."[37] The detention and deportation drive might have been both politically and economically advantageous to the Latin American countries that collaborated in it, but the "national" assets acquired were rarely if ever distributed equitably. Scores of enemy aliens caught up in the process lost their properties, businesses, and households in Latin America; many lost their faith in the goodwill of their adopted countries and in the United States itself.

As more internees told their stories, government officials overseeing the

Latin American internment program became increasingly aware that foreign leaders and their police forces were using the alien enemy apprehension mandate to line a few select pockets, acquire valuable properties and businesses, and neutralize political antagonists. Ultimately, the United States would seize on the multiple inefficiencies of Latin American cooperation as a pretext for transferring Axis nationals to its own custody. But even before Pearl Harbor and the signing of Proclamations 2425, 2526, and 2527, its defense planners were looking to parlay the Good Neighbor Policy into a plan for deporting aliens to the United States, and by December 20, 1941, two months before Executive Order 9066 was announced, a policy of urging Latin American governments to send their Axis nationals north was in place. Even then, some US officials could see that these machinations in Latin America ultimately might have a negative effect on US–Latin American relations. John Moors Cabot gave voice to such misgivings, warning: "I think it is undesirable for the written record to show that the initiative came from us. . . . I fear that in the post-war period, unfriendly leaders in the other republics may use incidents such as this to demonstrate that behind the façade of Good Neighborship the US was really interfering in the internal affairs of the other republics . . . the kind of thing . . . which in my opinion may well rise to damn us when the present crisis is over."[38]

Protecting itself and its neighbors to the south from potentially dangerous aliens and their susceptibility to Nazi propaganda and other nefarious influences—however real those threats—was likely the United States' principal motive for apprehending and interning Axis nationals beyond its borders. Some scholars also point to "the idea that the United States might assure the good treatment of U.S. citizens caught behind enemy lines by a reciprocal policy toward Axis civilians in this country," a policy that ostensibly prompted the State Department to "develop a plan in which these individuals might be used as hostage exchanges for Americans held overseas." According to Karen Riley, the Justice Department's logic was simple: "The United States could not easily deport enemy aliens who were parents of U.S. citizens; however, it could exchange Latin American enemy aliens not protected by U.S. laws for Americans held overseas."[39] Drawing on internal State Department memos, including one from Cordell Hull to President Roosevelt and records of the Special War Problems Division, Bat-Ami Zucker concludes, "The issue of hemispheric security aside, America's intention was to build up a reserve of internees to trade with the enemy."[40] But as Max Paul Friedman points out, however ambitious the United States' plans for repatriating Germans in order to liberate US nationals in Europe—plans written into its arrangements with several Latin American governments—the exchanges proved less advantageous than its officials had hoped. The ships brought back "many undesirable people," leaving American officials dissatisfied with the "quality of the human material they . . . received" and leading to a halt in the exchanges after the arrival of just two voyages.[41]

How did those of Japanese descent fit into the Roosevelt administration's fears of a Nazi-engineered fifth column in Latin America? Whereas German and Italian populations in the region were widely targeted for real or imagined anti-American political activities and allegiances, proving the subversive character of the Japanese would become a moot point. As the United States' string of defeats in the Pacific theater grew following its entry into the war, it looked for ways to bargain with Japan for the return of American prisoners of war, diplomats, and other US citizens in the region. While the United States could not use its own citizens of Japanese descent for exchange (though it could deprive them of their homes, properties, livelihoods, etc.), it argued noncitizen Japanese persons from Latin America could serve as barter. In August 1942, after estimating that there were more than three thousand American citizens in China alone anxious to return home, Secretary of State Cordell Hull told President Roosevelt, "In exchange for them, we will have to send out Japanese in the same quantity." Hull then called for the enemy alien program to "remove all the Japanese from these American Republic countries for internment in the United States."[42]

Despite the brash calculations of Hull and others, some in the administration realized that exchanging Latin American deportees for US war detainees was ethically, morally, and politically questionable—or at the very least, damning to the United States' reputation. John K. Emmerson of the US diplomatic service in Lima would later admit that the embassy staff "found no reliable evidence of planned or contemplated acts of sabotage, subversion or espionage."[43] Japanese assets were frozen, Japanese businesses blacklisted, and lists of prospective detainees drawn up in Peru and elsewhere with the dubious blanket classification "believed to be dangerous." With these restrictions, the plight of the Japanese detained in the other Americas mirrored the situation of US Japanese herded into horse corrals and other substandard buildings at so-called relocation camps. But perhaps the situation of the Japanese Latin Americans was even more precarious, due to their heightened exchange value as "pawns in a human traffic."[44] "About two thousand" Germans picked up in Latin America were also shipped back to Germany, some willingly, deciding a return trip to

Germany at US expense was a better alternative than blacklisting and impoverishment in Latin America or indefinite detention.[45] In any case, the German cases demonstrated that the predicament of repatriation without a trial was not only a Japanese problem.

New Orleans Traffic

With the varied motivations and concerns of enhanced security and exchange in mind, Washington ultimately determined it could best monitor potentially dangerous aliens by detaining them on its own turf for the "duration," that is, until the war ended. In early 1942, US personnel began using army vessels manned with military police to move named enemy aliens from points in Latin America to New Orleans and other US ports. The trips were long, the boats were often overcrowded, and sanitation and other conditions were often insufficient and insalubrious.

Though not the first internment destination of many deportees arriving from Latin America, New Orleans nonetheless thus figured into many of their stories, as their first contact with the United States was through the mouth of the Mississippi River and the port of New Orleans. By the middle of June 1942, several big, slow ships had transported thousands of persons of German, Italian, and Japanese descent from Latin America to the United States. Many of these vessels docked in New Orleans. For example, after a twelve-day journey, the *Acadia* arrived in the Crescent City with over six hundred German, Japanese, and Italian aliens aboard. Though all were sent on to other camps, for some of the Japanese, their US internment would be brief, as they "would soon board the *Gripsholm* on its repatriation voyage to the Far East."[46]

In total, about twenty-three hundred Latin American Japanese were sent to the United States, some 80 percent of them from Peru, according to congressional testimony.[47] Figures regarding the fates of Germans and Italians apprehended in Latin America are still uncertain. Lists from the National Archives show 1,813 prisoners were sent directly on to Germany prior to internment in the United States. The US government tallies a total of 4,058 Germans, 2,264 Japanese, and 287 Italians deported from Latin America to the United States with their families and housed in internment camps administered by the Immigration and Naturalization Service (INS), of whom 3,317 Latin American internees of German ethnicity were eventually sent to Germany.[48]

Named alien enemies, the vast majority of them males, were not the only ones aboard the big vessels. Hoping to avoid family fragmentation, many wives and children also opted to accompany their loved ones into internment as "voluntary detainees." For wives and children of those rounded up in the earliest apprehension sweeps, this decision often entailed spending several months in internment in the Canal Zone with the detainee or in another Latin American port awaiting space on a transfer vessel. And sometimes the family unity that motivated their decision was denied them upon their arrival in the United States. For example, when the SS *Florida* arrived in New Orleans in April 1942, only to discover there were insufficient family internment facilities to receive those aboard, some of the men aboard were sent on to Camp Livingston, Louisiana, or Fort Sill, Oklahoma, while women and children went on to Seagoville, near Dallas, Texas.[49]

As a principal port of entry for the Latin American deportees, New Orleans was the stage on which many internment procedural protocols played out. On one hand, Department of Justice personnel reviewing the paperwork of the recent arrivals expressed shock at who had been deported and on what grounds and "immediately threatened to refuse to take custody of at least a third of the group against whom there was no evidence or even any suspicion of activity sufficient to have warranted deportation."[50] On the other hand, though, were those officials who, following orders, further violated the aliens' individual rights by stripping them of their passports and other documents in order to subsequently charge them with illegal entry into the United States. The distress of being torn from families, homes, communities, and businesses—many of whom or which they would never see again—was "compounded when the deportees reached their debarkation location at New Orleans. Their passports were taken from them and never returned. They were thus declared illegal enemy aliens and were subject to deportation when their confinement in the United States came to an end," testified Professor Daniel Masterson in a 2009 hearing.[51] Travel-tired detainees "stood before Immigration and Naturalization Service (INS) officials, who solemnly requested that they present their visas for entry into the United States. Some of the new arrivals thought it was a joke. 'What visa—I was kidnapped!' was a typical reply."[52]

Being stripped of one's *documents* was only one of the indignities the Latin American deportees experienced upon arrival at New Orleans. When the *Cuba* sailed from Peru in March 1944, it took twenty-one days total to reach New Orleans; on board were 339 Peruvian Japanese along with a few Peruvian Germans and Italians. Kunikichi Matsuda recalled that all men and boys were forced to stay below deck for most of the voyage, so after three weeks of seasickness in cramped and fetid quarters, the fresh air of the Mississippi River was a welcome relief. But the subsequent INS processing included entering a large shower room with hot water running. "If we had known then what had happened at the camp in Auschwitz, the simple mention of 'shower room' would have made our blood freeze," recalled Matsuda.[53] He and fellow Latin American Japanese deportee Seechi Higashide reported their subsequent "baptism" with the pesticide DDT in powdered form.[54] The procedure was apparently used on both the alien enemies themselves and the family members who chose to accompany them as voluntary detainees: "At the Port of New Orleans, the women and children were marched to a warehouse, forced to strip, and made to stand in line naked. 'Then we were all sprayed with insecticide that stung our skin,' remembered Carmen [Higa Mochizuki]."[55]

Even the option to voluntarily accompany a loved one on the alien enemy list into US internment was not available to all. Many detainees were forced to leave spouses and children behind, not knowing where they were headed and in some cases not even having the chance to say goodbye; in other situations, those apprehended believed their detentions would be short-lived. Most spouses and children left behind soon found their prospects for survival were grim, however, as the (generally male) detainee's absence led to a drop in family income as well as ostracism and isolation in their communities. Efforts to later join a family member often involved waiting for weeks or months in a Latin American port before boarding a transport vessel. Gertrude Harten's story of trying to manage on her own with three small children, including a perilously sick baby (figure I.5), after her husband was deported from Ecuador, is no doubt representative of the trials and challenges many spouses of detainees faced. On October 9, 1944, Harten and others watched as a "huge American war vessel" came into port; after a medical examination, 156 women and 47 children, Japanese and German, were "allowed" on board. They were taken to hatchways "where we had to sleep in hammocks which hung one above the other. We were allowed to go on deck only 2 hours per day in order to get fresh air. And during the crossing of the Panama Canal not even that! Still to this day, I feel indignation when thinking of that trip. Karin became dangerously ill with gastroenteritis and was not given any medicine. She almost died. . . . I prayed and prayed that, upon arrival in New Orleans, I could deliver my little daughter into her father's arms." Upon the family's arrival in the Crescent City, a scene painted by other Latin American detainees is repeated: "The first thing the American

FIGURE I.5. Gertrude Harten with her children, Alke, Karin, and Wolf, 1944. Photo courtesy Karin Harten Schramm.

authorities did to us was to 'clean' us, *putting us into hot water and disinfecting us using DDT!* They did not consider Karin's grave health situation at all. I was exhausted from the long trip, taking care of Karin all the time, without proper medicine and possibilities to nurse her. Both of us fainted for a long time."[56]

Government officials in the United States became increasingly aware that family separations like that of the Hartens was an unpopular consequence of the enemy alien deportations. A telegram sent to the US embassy in Lima on January 22, 1943, signed by Cordell Hull, noted, "The Department [of State] in principle does not approve of the separation of families, particularly where the families themselves or Axis sympathizers make use of their situation to attempt to arouse public opinion against this Government on grounds of needless suffering of women and children separated from wage earners."[57] Once more, though, it seemed the country's reputation, and the damage it might sustain at the hands of the families affected and other "Axis sympathizers," was of more concern than the possible "needless suffering" the alien control program produced.

Motley Krewe of Algiers

Port of No Return uncovers how New Orleans's Camp Algiers came to house an increasingly diverse assortment of German, Italian, and Japanese aliens along with Austrians, Czechs, Poles, and even a few citizens of Latin American countries. Among its internees were those who had arrived in Central or South America in the early part of the twentieth century and had lived peacefully alongside their fellow immigrants and native neighbors until late 1941; others had fled from Europe in the years, months, or even days preceding the United States' entry into the war. A few individuals who spent time at the Algiers Detention Station were apprehended within the United States, such as Hitler's "pal" Kurt Ludecke (chapter 4). The incredible tales of three titled Europeans interned in other camps appear in chapter 5 in an attempt to show that even counts and princesses were not exempt from the internment initiative. The sundry backgrounds and experiences of those who passed through Camp Algiers and other internment hubs provide us with a fuller understanding of the extent and influence of the US internment program.

In the chapters that follow, the lives of these individuals come into view at the moment of their apprehension, their transport to US internment facilities, their stays in the camps and movements between them, their release to "internment at large," and, where possible, their reintegration into society after finally shedding the status of enemy alien. Government memos, decrees, orders, lists, and interagency administrative documents; reports of those who worked at the camps or visited them; internee correspondence that passed through censors' hands; first-person accounts; ship logs; news articles; naturalization records; aid organization paperwork; even death certificates help us to better comprehend what US wartime internment was like. Together these documents suggest that whether or not a given alien detainee made the return journey *physically* through the port of New Orleans after the war's end, he or she to some extent had arrived at a point or port of no return; at the very least, the internment experience left an indelible mark on one's sense of self and community.

The fates of a small group of Jews deported from Latin America to internment camps in the United States and later gathered at Camp Algiers receive special attention in this study for several reasons. First, as targets *of* the Nazis, these Jews' internment *as* Nazis or *together with* Nazis remains a particularly confounding element of the enemy alien operation. For the first year and a quarter of the war, these Jews agonized alongside their enemies in the same camps; even when they were able to convince camp personnel to segregate their sleeping quarters, they were compelled to listen to Nazi internees sing fight songs and rehearse victory speeches.[58] Ironically, many Jews held as enemy aliens in US internment had hoped to reach North America as refugees from Europe but settled for South or Central America when they were unable to obtain entry visas for this country. At least eleven internees held at Algiers had spent time in Nazi concentration camps before stepping onto US soil. Their internment points to the antisemitism of the Washington brass and the North American populace as a whole during wartime.[59]

European-born Jews' stateless condition at the moment of their apprehension and internment as enemy aliens poses a uniquely thorny legal and ethical challenge to the presuppositions and protocols undergirding Roosevelt's control program. How could Jewish refugees born in Germany or territories held by Germany by 1941 be held as German aliens when the Nuremberg Laws of 1935 had revoked their German citizenship and defined them as a separate and inferior race to "true" Germans? Had they not been cast as the *enemy* of the United States' enemy? Didn't these Jews constitute a particularly vulnerable population, given the use of genocide already practiced on their population and other non-Aryan populations by the German government? The Roosevelt administration was clearly aware of the problem statelessness presented to its control program, as Proclamation 2537, dated January 14, 1942, defined alien enemies in two categories: (1) all aliens aged fourteen years or older on December 7, 1941, who were citizens or subjects of Germany or Japan and (2) all aliens aged fourteen years or older *who at present are stateless but who at the time they became stateless were citizens or subjects of Germany or Japan* (my emphasis).[60] Jews and other stateless aliens were thus subject to restrictions on their movements and rights to own property, while they were required to carry and present on demand certificates of identity.

The National Refugee Service estimated "about 200,000 Jewish refugees throughout the United States were affected" by these regulations on their daily movements, but more injurious still "was the shocking realization that they were being classified as enemy aliens together with fascists and Nazis—the very people at whose hands they had suffered untold hardships, indignities and insult." Jews' sense of betrayal was only heightened when Attorney General Frances Biddle removed Italian Americans from the stigma of the enemy alien label on October 19, 1942, but left it in place for stateless refugees.[61] Under pressure, the Justice Department weeks later added "refugees—driven from their countries for religious, ethnic, or racial discrimination, or because of their activity against political systems abhorrent to Americans" as the fifth category of aliens declared exempt from arrest, but that exception did not affect those already in internment or those apprehended outside US borders.[62]

Some political elites believed Jewish aliens posing as refugees were actually acting as spies as part of their persecution by the Nazis. A year and a half before the United States entered the war, Roosevelt stated in a June 1940 press conference: "Now, of course, the refugees has [sic] got to be checked because unfortunately, among the refugees there are some spies, as has been found in other countries. And not all of them are voluntary spies—it is rather a horrible story but in some of the other countries that refugees out of Germany have gone to, especially Jewish refugees; they have found a number of definitely proven spies . . . it is something we have got to watch."[63] Jews apprehended in the United States as enemy aliens were subject to such suspicions as well. When FBI agents picked up Eddie Friedman in his San Francisco apartment and his wife protested, saying he might be German but he was also a Jew, they told her, "Mrs. Friedman, many German Jews have left relatives over there. They are compelled now to work for the Nazis or their relatives will be killed."[64] Despite evidence gathered from within the State Department itself that "the most dangerous place for a spy to be was in the refugee stream," personnel throughout the internment system continued to act on this theory, and it was incumbent on every Jewish internee to disprove its validity as a condition for his or her possible release.[65]

The irony of being labeled a Nazi sympathizer or collaborator, even an unwilling one, was made more bitter by the knowledge that many dangerous Nazis were released from custody, while refugees were not. Julius Maier, a German Jew who fled to Holland, England, and finally Belize, explained, "The real Nazi sympathizers were warned and given a chance to get out of Belize and into Panama or some other adjacent country, whereas the Belize people and Jewish refugees were given no chance to escape. . . . Then we heard that we were accused of spying." In describing his voyage from Panama to New Orleans aboard the *Cuba,* Maier described a level of antipathy so high among the military personnel on board that he feared the detainees might be thrown into the ocean.[66]

Once interned, Jews in the United States had to struggle with the "ironic senselessness" of being confined "with the very jackbooted Nazi element" they had fled from in Germany, Austria, France, Italy, and other countries. Whereas in Great Britain, Jewish refugees were held separately from so-called Aryan Germans, the US camps forced them to share spaces with inmates who greeted each other with the Hitler salute and decorated their rooms with swastikas.[67]

Though never wholly Jewish, the internee population at Camp Algiers did at one point become a haven for about sixty of the eighty-one Jews deported to the United States, contributing to its unique status as an "anti-Nazi" camp. There they joined others who wanted out of camps where pro-Nazi internees had both clout and control. At Camp Kenedy, Fritz Sauter, a nineteen-year-old deportee born in Costa Rica to German parents, so staunchly defended his loyalty to Costa Rica that a pro-Nazi group attacked him, leading to his transfer to Camp Algiers.[68] Camp Kenedy was a Civilian Conservation Corps site in rural south-central Texas that had been repurposed as an internment camp earlier that year. Designated a men's facility, Camp Kenedy was considered a "temporary" site for holding Germans and Japanese, most of them originating from Latin America, who were to be exchanged for soldiers and other US citizens held in camps in Axis-controlled territories.

New Orleans thus became the final stage on which the "Jewish problem" of Latin American alien enemy internment played out, as it was at Camp Algiers that Jewish deportees from Panama and elsewhere in Latin America were congregated in early 1943, and it was there where most finally received hearings in the early summer of that year and where the great majority were released a few months later. Even then, though, they were not at full liberty, as they were freed only conditionally to "internment at large," a parole-like status in which they were closely monitored and subjected to numerous restrictions in their actions and movements. The Roosevelt administration balked at removing them from this parole "because it would establish a precedent for other Jewish refugees."[69]

One overlooked consequence of designating Algiers an anti-Nazi camp, sometimes dubbed the "Camp of the Innocent," and transferring Jews and other anti-Nazi detainees facing harassment in other facilities to Algiers, is that with this gesture the government acknowledged, if only implicitly, many of the shortcomings of its alien control program. It acknowledged the faulty nature of blanket characterizations of national origin groups such as "Germans" or "Japanese." It revealed the diversity and complexity of the populations it had conglomerated under the label "alien enemies." And it acknowledged, however implicitly, that it was falling short of its own pledge of humane treatment for the internees, laid out in Instruction No. 58 of the Rules for Detainees: "Detainees must at all times be protected against acts of violence, insults, and public curiosity."[70]

On Balance

What were the real benefits of the United States wartime internment program, both at home and in Latin America? What were its true economic and human costs? What insights does this history offer for our own time? On the positive side, the number of internees (at least for those apprehended in the United States) was small compared to the multitude who "continued their lives unhampered by the authorities"; the "general levelheadedness" of officials such as Francis Biddle, Earl Harrison, and a few others kept excesses to a minimum, though the "relatively small number of victims lessens neither their humiliation nor their lost years." From a less rosy perspective, though, mass evacuation, deportation, and internment left a dangerous legacy for America's future, causing "a crack in the Constitution that allowed McCarthyism and the communist witch hunts of the late 1940s and early 1950s."[71] To be clear, internment of a country's own residents was legal and constitutional in the United States as in other countries that engaged in the practice during the war. What was not legal or constitutional—or widely practiced—was the apprehension, arrest, and forced displacement of people in other countries. Arnold Krammer argues that public tolerance of the wartime internment and mass relocation programs served as a prequel to the FBI crackdown on the antiwar and civil rights movements in the second half of the twentieth century.

Even if all its consequences cannot be empirically measured, lingering questions remain regarding the efficacy of the methods used and the results obtained in the United States' internment initiative. Eugene Rostow, a Yale law professor who worked in the State Department during the war, claimed at the program's end that the community hearing boards responsible for determining an arrested alien's loyalty or disloyalty "were smoothly conducted, and they did nothing to lower prevailing standards of justice."[72] For hundreds of arrested aliens who criticized the boards' slipshod interrogation methods, things looked very different. The Justice Department was known to remove hearing officers who were too lenient, under pressure from the FBI. The volunteers who constituted the hearing boards "often had to make difficult (and arguably illegal) decisions based on little more than informants' hearsay, heavily accented testimonies that were difficult to understand or evidence made through translation."[73] A respected US attorney in the North Dakota district where the Fort Lincoln internment camp was located, P. W. Lanier "privately confessed that the FBI agents who did the investigation work for the [alien enemy] case files were young, over-zealous, self-important hot-shots."[74]

Some who study outcomes of the Latin American arm of the Enemy Alien Control Program conclude it "did not contribute to U.S. national security and actually represented a net loss to national goals, even setting aside questions of justice and individual rights."[75] When Raymond Ickes and James Bell were sent to Central America in 1943 to investigate the cases of Latin Americans being held at Algiers and elsewhere, Ickes noted, even then, that "experience has indicated that in too many instances we have had to accept for internment an inordinately large number of apparently harmless individuals disliked for one reason or another by the local governments, in order to get a very few persons who can properly be considered dangerous subjects." This outcome was harmful to the United States' standing in Latin America, he believed, as it tended "to create a feeling in the Central and South American Republics that the United States Government is bungling its share of the internment program and that it is doing exactly what it condemns in its enemies by interning those inconsequential individuals who have no influence, while the rest escape."[76]

Even the assistant to alien internment program architect Earl Harrison, an Italian American named Jetre Mangione, described the program as an "international form of kidnapping" and admitted he and many others in the INS opposed the arrest of Latin Americans.[77] In hindsight, then, Washington's ability to pressure its Latin American counterparts to name, detain, and deport German, Japanese, and Italian Latin Americans was arguably more a loss than a gain for inter-American collaboration, as this pressure violated both the letter and the spirit of the Good Neighbor Policy, signaling its ultimate demise. In addition, the Latin American control program's most troubling features, such as underlying beliefs in Latin American inferiority, prejudices based on country of origin, and political expediency driven by economic opportunism, all continue to characterize volatile relationships between the United States and its southern neighbors today.[78]

The very reticence of governments and former detainees to broach the subject of internment hints at its high toll on individuals and institutions. Experts list embarrassment, fear of violent reprisals, event-induced depression and behavior disorders, and the inability to navigate everyday life without suppressing the past as reasons many people choose never to discuss their internment experiences.[79] Tetsuden Kachima, a sociology professor whose family was held at a camp in Topaz, Utah, believes such imprisonments "created a social amnesia in which there was an effort, conscious or otherwise, to suppress 'less than pleasant memories.'"[80]

Despite these silences and the reasons for them, the documents cited in this volume still speak volumes. Even three-quarters of a century later, they reveal how the Alien Enemy Act of 1798 was recalibrated for the heightened fears of World War II and how that wartime recalibration led to highly questionable protocols for the treatment of aliens inside and outside the United States' boundaries. The following chapters open a porthole on how those protocols played out in New Orleans, at its Algiers detention camp, and across the country and the hemisphere, leaving in their wake troublesome policies adversely affecting noncitizens even today. The personal stories of those affected by that program expose the fissures in the image of the United States as a safe harbor for all. Acknowledging the historic significance of this legislation, especially its broad identification of aliens as enemies early in the nation's history and in subsequent moments of national "crisis" helps us better see where we stand, and why, on related issues in our own time.

CHAPTER 1

New Orleans's (Mostly) Secret Internment History

Three Miles from the Foot of Canal Street

The arrest and internment in the United States of thousands of German, Italian, and Japanese nationals as dangerous "alien enemies" during World War II is also a New Orleans story, a tale with local twists that reflects the unique nature of the Crescent City and its storied port. Touted in the mid-twentieth century as a "Gateway to the Americas," the city served as a vital conduit to inter-American internment traffic.[1] The city's proximity to the mouth of the Mississippi and the Gulf of Mexico, as well as to the Canal Zone and other Latin American ports, made it a principal point of entry and departure for enemy aliens headed to or from internment in the United States, as well as for those bound for repatriation or exchange. Thousands of people were processed by the Immigration and Naturalization Service in New Orleans before being sent on to camps throughout the United States, particularly in the South.[2] The role of an alien detention station on the West Bank of the Mississippi in the Algiers neighborhood was also significant.[3] The old US Quarantine Station–New Orleans (figure 1.1), rechristened as Camp Algiers, would gain (and then arguably lose) a reputation as a refuge for internees facing or fearing violence in other camps, promising—like the city itself—a unique, less stressful atmosphere than elsewhere in the country.[4]

25

FIGURE 1.1. US Quarantine Station–New Orleans, circa 1930s, soon after its completion. Photo courtesy The Historic New Orleans Collection, acc. no. 1995.19.

While enemy alien detention didn't shift into full gear in the United States until after the attack on Pearl Harbor, the government was already on alert and preparing for possible scenarios in anticipation of its implementation. A primary question was who would be responsible for monitoring alien enemies. On October 10, 1941, Eugene Kessler, district director of the INS in New Orleans, reported, "It has been tentatively decided that the temporary detention phase of the alien enemy program to be followed in the event of a declaration of war will be under the jurisdiction of this Service, and that this Service is to be responsible for providing facilities for the maintenance of alien enemies arrested, pending the decision of boards as to whether the alien is to be interned or paroled."[5] The INS would thus play a key role in detaining and interning these noncitizens, though the Department of Justice, Department of State, War Department, FBI, Office of Naval Intelligence, several branches of the US military, and even the US Postal Service would also collaborate in the effort. A letter directed to the special assistant to the attorney general ten days later

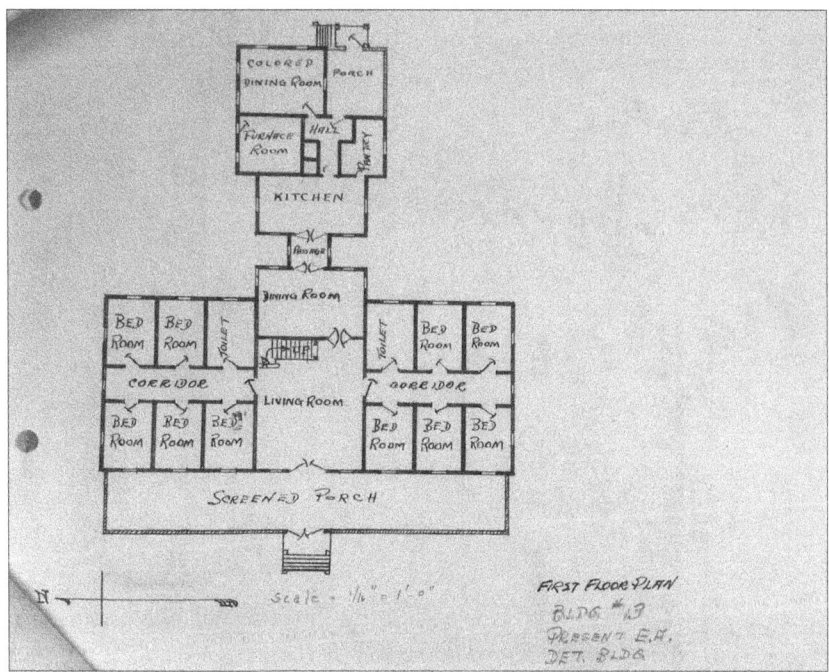

FIGURE 1.2. Floor plan for the first floor of Building 13, used to house enemy aliens. National Archives, used with permission.

notes, "Consideration might also be given to the Old U.S. Immigration Station on the Lower Coast, Algiers, 3 miles down the river from New Orleans."[6] The US Quarantine Station–New Orleans, located at 3819 Patterson Road along the Mississippi River levee, was established in 1934 with eighteen buildings, only a few of which would be used for the detention station. The site was described as "ideal as a detention headquarters if modernized," better suited than any other location in the area for that purpose.[7]

A survey showed that the buildings set aside at the quarantine station could provide detention facilities for an estimated 30 detainees, although the camp's director, Raymond Bunker, would later reveal that more than 250 detainees at a time were held at the site at the height of the war.[8] Surveyors described the spot as being three miles from a railroad station and four miles from a local bus route but reachable from downtown New Orleans only by ferry, as the bridge known as the Crescent City Connection had not yet been built.[9] A memo sent to the attention of Joseph Savoretti, deputy commissioner in the attorney general's

NEW ORLEANS'S (MOSTLY) SECRET INTERNMENT HISTORY | 27

FIGURE 1.3. Building 13, US Customs and Border Patrol Headquarters, 2017. Photo by Eduardo Alvelo, used with permission.

office, also presented the quarantine station as the best available option, given its location "about three miles from the foot of Canal Street."[10] The grounds comprised a total of about eight acres. Floor plans of the first and second floor of Building 13 were provided with the memo (figure 1.2), along with an estimate from a contractor for erecting fencing and window guards around the facility. Though Building 13 was later modified to serve as offices for a Border Patrol Headquarters Station active on the site until late 2018, its exterior still looked very much as it did while serving as a detention facility (figure 1.3).

A November 5, 1941, communiqué specified that "approximately 23,000 potential alien enemies have registered as residing in the States of Louisiana, Mississippi and Arkansas, and the bulk of these are in Louisiana, for which reason it is deemed necessary to establish a temporary detention facility at New Orleans, which has been determined to be most centrally located with respect to the geographic distribution of the majority of the persons concerned."[11] This suggests that early on, the Algiers station was planned as a temporary holding facility for enemy aliens apprehended domestically rather than a site concentrating detainees from Latin America, as it would become later. On December 8, the day after the bombing of Pearl Harbor, a memo to Major Lemuel B. Schofield, special assistant to the attorney general, confirmed "the Public Health Service has now informed this office that they will permit the use of Building No 13 at the New Orleans Quarantine Station during the present National emergency."[12]

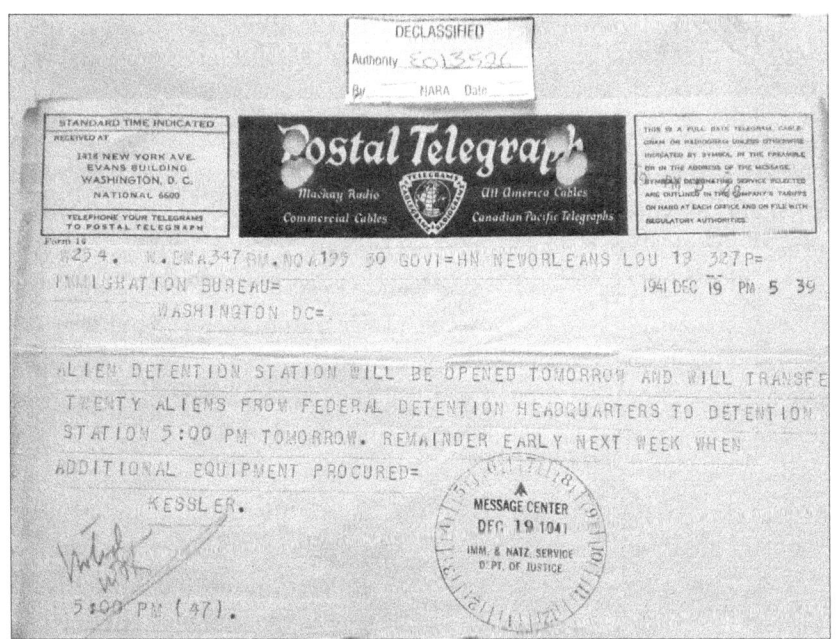

FIGURE 1.4. Telegram dated December 19, 1941, announcing the opening of the Algiers site as a wartime detention station. National Archives, used with permission.

Kessler's telegram to the Department of Justice, dated December 19, 1941 (figure 1.4), indicates it took less than two weeks after the US entry into the war to get the Algiers site up and running: "Alien detention station will be opened tomorrow and will transfer twenty aliens from federal detention headquarters to detention station 5:00 p.m. tomorrow. Remainder early next week when additional equipment procured." The files do not tell us who these twenty people were or where, why, or by whom they were detained or how long they remained in detention at Algiers. Nor do we know what persons constituted the "remainder" set to follow them into detention. But for the next four and a half years, the station would intern hundreds of "dangerous" alien enemies, right in the "backyard" of the French Quarter, as it were.

Actually, it would be some time before the quarantine station would become "Camp Algiers," that is, a full-fledged internment facility where men, women, and children resided for significant periods of time. For the first year of the war, it appears it was mostly used on an occasional basis for a variety of temporary detention needs. A memo indicates that in April 1942, Alicia Klemm and Elida

NEW ORLEANS'S (MOSTLY) SECRET INTERNMENT HISTORY | 29

Levigon, who had arrived from Panama aboard the *Florida*—probably as voluntary internees accompanying their deported husbands—were detained at the station with their small children en route to Texas's Camp Seagoville, due to their advanced pregnancies. Levigon may have even delivered a child in New Orleans, as the memo claims she "gave birth on the 9th instant" and was ready for discharge, while hospital authorities confirmed Mrs. Klemm was not ready to deliver her baby and could be removed to Seagoville without danger, though they requested the services of a matron and a nurse during the transfer.[13]

Even if the part Camp Algiers would play in the internment drama was still in development, New Orleans itself was from early 1942 serving as a primary hub for transport vessels leaving for Latin America and for people arriving en route to US detention centers.[14] For example, an April 1942 Department of Justice memo from Willard Kelly warned that it would not be possible for twenty patrol inspectors to satisfactorily guard the *Acadia* against sabotage and asked for increased security personnel on board. That ship was scheduled to leave New Orleans on May 1 and to return on May 16, after picking up four hundred Axis aliens in Colombia and two hundred in Ecuador. As noted in the introduction, with cabin space for only two hundred passengers, the *Acadia* ultimately boarded more than three times that number. Max Paul Friedman calculates 675 Axis nationals from Peru, Ecuador, and Colombia created a scene of "unimaginable overcrowding," severe shortages of food and water, and insufficient bathing facilities for the New Orleans–bound detainees. The transports were staffed with inexperienced army and marine personnel who reportedly stole liquor and valuables from the detainees' luggage.[15]

Whereas there was significant internment traffic through the port of New Orleans in the first half of 1942, the limited use of the Algiers facility in that period presented a red flag to administrators. Kessler noted in a May 1, 1942, letter to the deputy commissioner of the INS in Philadelphia, "the total personnel of the Alien Detention Station at Algiers as of May 1st is ten, i.e., the Officer in Charge, seven Guards, one Cook and one Janitor-Fireman," adding, "There are in detention at the Station at this time but ten enemy aliens, all males (not counting one female at the Convent of the Good Shepherd and one male at the Marine Hospital). This makes one employee for each detainee, which naturally renders the cost of detention per alien exceedingly high to say the least."[16] Given this unfavorable cost-benefit ratio (even for government work), Kessler had a suggestion: "It occurs to me that possibly the Central Office might wish to give consideration to using the facilities of the station . . . for such aliens ordered interned who express a desire in writing to remain there rather than to be transferred to a permanent detention camp, as well as for aliens ordered paroled who are unable to secure sponsors. The station might also be utilized for aliens arriving from abroad destined to a permanent internment camp whose repatriation at an early date is contemplated."

Apparently, these suggestions met with approval; the station's use expanded steadily, allowing for Bunker's later claim of servicing 250 internees at a time. However, as there is no complete set of records for the facility, it is difficult to generalize regarding its population beyond the fact that it fluctuated. For example, Italian names constituted the majority of the list of those held at the alien detention station in a September 25, 1942, memo to Savoretti. Eleven Italian citizens were awaiting transfer to a camp in Fort Missoula, Montana, and three more were detained under "internment proceedings," along with five German citizens and one Japanese citizen.[17]

A letter from Kessler to the INS commissioner in mid-June 1942 alludes to yet another proposed use for the Algiers site. "The local United States Army Provost Marshal has requested permission to lodge small groups of alien enemies in the Detention Station at Algiers, Louisiana. As the Provost Marshal had explained, "Occasionally the Army transport service lands groups of alien enemies here at times when it is not convenient or practicable to remove them from the vessel and ship them out immediately by train." The army promised not to hold the alien enemies at the detention station for more than twenty-four hours, and the provost marshal was willing to offer as many soldiers as might be needed as additional guards. This would prevent holding enemy aliens in the local (federal) jail—a fate many coming from Latin America had already experienced. A pencil-written message on the letter shows it was approved.[18]

Under the umbrella of the INS, much of the operation of the Algiers camp would fall to the Border Patrol itself. The Border Patrol was entrusted with this job "because of their long and successful record of work with aliens," a local news story explained.[19] Eleanor Nicholson began her article titled "What's That Uniform You're Wearing?" with the observation:

> In a uniform conscious world where Canal street [sic] often resembles a League of Nations, few people recognize the uniform of the Border Patrol of the United States Immigration and Naturalization Service. But this department of justice agency is performing two big wartime jobs—the

detention of enemy civilians and keeping the vessels of the allied nations plowing the seas with their wartime cargoes. . . . Whether it's looking for hidden meanings of love letters of German internees, ordering food by the ton, or supervising the education of the internees' children the Border Patrolmen are not stumped by the job.[20]

Nicholson's article explained that the country's ports—New Orleans included—presented "miles and miles of unfenced frontier, land and sea" to the Border Patrol, whose "constant vigilance provides the fences." The news story spoke of the extensive training employees received at the Border Patrol school in El Paso, where, in addition to Spanish, "which every inspector must speak," and the handling of firearms, the trainees studied five volumes of immigration and naturalization laws and operation manuals.

As the chief officer at the Algiers Detention Station, Border Patrolman Bunker described his duties to Nicholson as "much more than surveillance. . . . We are more social workers than jailers and have a wonderful opportunity to show these people what the American way of life is. Life in the camp is governed by three principals [sic]—the regulations of the Geneva convention, reciprocity and the belief in humanity." Internees and administrative personnel at Algiers saw Bunker's commitment to these lofty aims in action and on the whole welcomed his presence at the camp's helm. A July 1942 report from the Swiss consulate in New Orleans, representing German aliens, cited a detainee who commented after Bunker's arrival at the station: "All the tension which caused so much mental strain upon all of us in here has ceased and everybody feels satisfied. We get the maximum outdoor exercise, granted by the federal authorities, have access to the tennis court which we use freely, and our food is good, sufficient and excellently prepared, so everybody is happy and tries to forget the hardship of the Detainment."[21]

In October 1942, Paul V. McNutt, chief administrator of the Federal Security Agency in Washington, responded to the attorney general's request to utilize the New Orleans station to detain passengers and crew members under investigation, as space at central INS facilities was insufficient. A prominent politician, professor and diplomat who had hoped to become president, McNutt was buttonholed by Roosevelt in April 1942 to chair the War Manpower Commission, a post that he held until the war's end. McNutt's response to the attorney general shows how officials across several agencies were pressed to prioritize war-related efforts among other needs. His letter

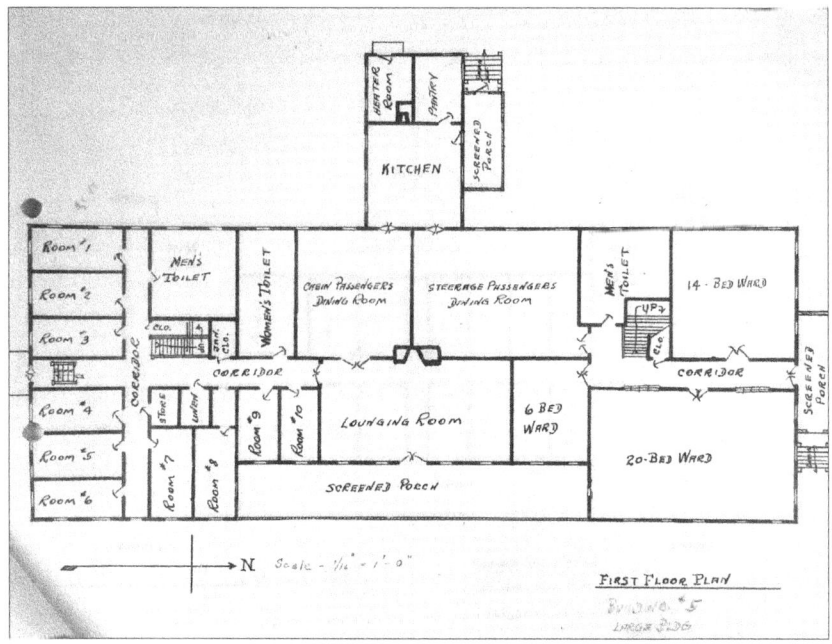

FIGURE 1.5. Plans designating the use of Building 5 for detention. National Archives, used with permission.

also contains an unexpectedly broad use of the term "detention": "This office has made arrangements for the use of Building No. 5 at the New Orleans Quarantine Station as a detention home for venereally infected prostitutes, but in view of the more imperative demands of your Department, we feel that Building No. 5 should be made available for the above-mentioned purpose. It is recommended that your local representative at New Orleans . . . complete the necessary arrangements to use Building No. 5 in the same manner as Building No. 13 is now being used."[22] Thus Building 5 was incorporated into the detention operation (figure 1.5), initially designated for persons who would stay there only on a short-term basis.

As time went on, the New Orleans facility became increasingly associated with specialized populations remaining for longer periods. A news article later explained, "The station was started a few days after Pearl Harbor as a temporary affair, but was later made permanent as some of the more troublesome aliens in other stations were sent to Algiers."[23] Included in these "troublesome" cases were most of the approximately eighty Jewish refugees deported to the United

States from several countries in Latin America as well as several "former" Nazis whose professed change of heart allegedly made them targets of violence in other camps as well.

Camp of the Innocents

On August 18, 1942, the Jewish Telegraphic Agency in Washington, DC, published an article with the headline "Jews, Nazis Fight in U.S. Internment Camps; Separation Asked by Jewish Internees." Reports such as these in the Jewish press point to conditions in which Nazis subjected Jewish prisoners in the alien detention camps to insults, refused to serve them in mess halls, paraded Nazi flags and other symbols, and published newspapers with Fascist and antisemitic content.[24] But Jews weren't the only ones suffering this abuse. Despite the fact that avowed pro-Nazis constituted a small minority of German aliens detained, this more extremist contingent was given substantial liberty to exert power in many camps, complicating life for compatriots who felt differently. Gunter Lisken, deported from Ecuador, was told at Crystal City in Texas, "In this camp we're all Nazis and anyone who doesn't agree, we'll break his skull." On April 20, Hitler's birthday, Lisken and other Latin American deportees were "shocked to see fellow inmates, mostly longtime US residents, parading through the camp in brownshirts and singing Nazi songs all the way to the assembly hall, where they held a celebration under a huge portrait of Hitler."[25]

In late 1942, the Justice Department began reviewing the cases of those who protested their internment based on their identity as Jews or anti-Nazis. Beginning in early 1943, all Jewish internees and many anti-Nazis who feared violence—or had already suffered it—at the hands of detainees in other camps, were transferred to Camp Algiers for their protection, earning it the moniker "Camp of (or for) the innocents."[26] Francis Biddle was intent on securing the Jewish detainees' release, even claiming that budget cuts made it necessary to close Camp Algiers and disperse its internees.[27] Despite his efforts, some in the group would wait several months longer for their provisional release under "internment at large," an arrangement in which internees could move to another community in the US heartland with the support of a sponsor and report regularly to an INS official until the internment at large status was lifted. Others would wait several more years to leave Camp Algiers. After a Department of Justice employee returned from Central America, where he reviewed their cases, more than fifty Jews were released from

Camp Algiers in the summer of 1943; six remained interned for the duration of the war.[28]

Continued internment was an especially bitter pill for Jewish aliens detained in Latin America, many of whom had been told deportation offered them a longed-for ticket to the United States and believed the government would release them soon after their arrival.[29] Thanks to appeals from the National Refugee Service and other agencies, many family members were eventually reunited, and most Jewish detainees were given living quarters separate from their Nazi persecutors—at least for a period of time. A list of thirty-one Jewish internees who arrived at Algiers on February 11, 1943, showed they were housed in Building 5, suggesting that even at Algiers, they were segregated from other alien detainees. That list included persons ranging in age from the two-year-old Joan Loewenthal to the sixty-five-year-old Jeanette Wolff; the "German" group also contained five Poles, three Austrians, and a Czechoslovakian.[30] Twelve more Jewish internees from Camp Kenedy were transferred to Algiers on February 13. By the end of March, there were seventy-nine aliens at the station, including the entire Jewish contingent, a single Japanese detainee, and two Frenchmen.[31] As time went on, conditions and populations at Camp Algiers further fluctuated as administrators of other camps sought to unload a variety of "problem" detainees there.

In April, a memo from assistant commissioner for alien control Willard Kelly to the INS district director in New Orleans directed him to have the Jewish detainees fill out an I-55 immigration form and send it on to his office posthaste. Those forms would provide necessary background for arguing for their release to internment at large, a process that would finally begin on August 20, when several dozen detainees would leave Algiers for such cities as Minneapolis, Pittsburgh, Cincinnati, Milwaukee, Memphis, Chicago, and Cleveland.[32]

The New Orleans press documented this large release in several buoyant stories. The *New Orleans Item* titled an August 19 story "Freedom Soon for 50 'Enemy Alien' Refugees at Algiers," using quotation marks for the dubious label in the body of the story as well: "The New Orleans committee for refugee service announced today that 50 refugees formerly detained as 'enemy aliens' at the Algiers immigration detention station would leave soon for locations in cities where they may become successfully adjusted."[33] The article noted, "Most of the men are young and formerly were engaged in business and professions in Latin America. The majority speak English fluently. They are originally from Germany where they left to get away from the Nazis. Most of them are Jewish." The next day, the *Times-Picayune* put "50 Refugees Long Interned Here to Be Released Soon" on its front page with the second head "Aliens Get Chance to Make Homes, Support Selves."[34] "Fifty men, women, and children, all refugees from Hitlerism, who have been interned at the Algiers immigration detention station for many months," the article explained, "will be released in the near future under 'internment-at-large' regulations of the justice department, allowing them to establish their own homes, earn a livelihood, and in general, lead a normal existence." Dr. David Fichman of the National Refugee Service (NRS) had helped make this happen, as well as refugee aid committees in the fourteen communities to which the "refugees" would travel. The article claimed the group had been segregated from known Nazi and Fascist internees at the request of the NRS: "Upon their release, several of the young men in the group intend to join the armed forces to fight the oppression which drove them from their homelands." Heavily vetted for their loyalty and trustworthiness, the soon-to-be-released internees "possess in the aggregate an impressive array of skills useful to warring America," the article added.

The *Item* addressed the story again on August 21 in a page 4 story titled "Democracy at Work," judging, "This will be a memorable season for some 53 internees classified as 'enemy aliens' who, after nearly a year of representations by the Jewish Federation, will be released from the former Quarantine Station at New Orleans, with permission to live inland in the United States, under 'internment-at-large.'"[35] Which part of the story did the writers or editors intend to associate with "democracy at work"? Were these internees finally seeing democracy at work in the decision to release them from the questionable category of "enemy alien"? Or should readers assume that the enemy alien program itself was a good example of democracy at work, just as another article that same day celebrated the "welcome" a German violinist and his mother would receive in the United States as newly released alien enemies?[36]

A Special Hearing

While internment seemingly ended well for the large group of detainees released in August 1943, the outcome of long-sought hearings and rehearings was not always positive. This was true for those detained at Camp Algiers as well as for some who traveled there for hearings that would determine their fate. Otto Trott was in the latter group. Trott had earned his medical degree at the University of Freiburg in 1936. He emigrated from Germany to the United States in 1937 to escape persecution after being denied a medical license due to the fact that he was partially Jewish. After completing a residency in Syracuse, New York, Trott moved to Seattle in 1939 and worked for the King County Public Health Department. He joined Seattle's mountaineering community and became a founding member of the Ski Patrol on Mount Baker, where he kept a cabin. The ski area's "Ottobahn" run still bears his first name.

But things went downhill for Trott after he complained that his hospital needed better equipment and refused to support hospital employees' efforts to unionize. Soon after, he was arrested as an alien enemy, apparently due to a tip provided to the FBI by hospital colleagues. When a friend of Trott's later wrote to Edward Ennis about his case, he asserted that after Trott's arrest, "an order had gone out at the hospital that any staff who visited him or testified for him 'would be in danger of losing his or her job.'"[37] After spending time in an "immigration prison," Dr. Trott was transferred to the custody of the US Army at Fort Lewis; from there he traveled to Angel Island, where he boarded a prison train with other Germans and Japanese detainees, the latter of whom he watched, after eight sweltering days on the train, descend at an unnamed internment camp in the desert. Dr. Trott himself was interned at Camp Forrest, Tennessee. There he complained about the mail delays, poor clothing, filthy mattresses, concrete floors, and "indescribable" latrine. More serious still was his assessment in a letter to his girlfriend that "eighty percent of all arrests are simply extreme misjudgments which will ever be a mark . . . on the United States."[38] As the camp doctor at the Tennessee facility, Trott treated his fellow internees for diseases such as malaria and syphilis and even developed an antivenom serum for black widow spider bites. Camp Forrest's officer in charge described him as "above reproach."[39]

Trott was finally granted a rehearing on his case at New Orleans's Camp Algiers in February 1943. The board included Allan Pomeroy, an assistant US attorney from Seattle who would later become the mayor of that city. The first questions the board posed to Trott were about his Jewish ancestry, about which they expressed skepticism. Then came Pomeroy's "BIG question. He said: 'Dr. Trott, if Germany were completely devastated, would you like that?'" Trott answered that having been born there and loving the country of his birth, of course he wouldn't like it, and that no one could sincerely respond to such a question about their homeland in any other way. Trott's honesty would cost him dearly; his was described as a "close, difficult and borderline" case, and the majority recommended his continued internment.[40]

"Aliens Live Well at Algiers Base"

What can we know about daily life for those interned at Camp Algiers? The few historians to document conditions there often note unusual freedoms the detainees enjoyed at the station, such as sending their children to local schools outside the gates or being permitted to shop off base, accompanied by a guard. Reportedly, some were even allowed to participate in Mardi Gras. Frank Meyer, who spent some of his high school years at the camp, recalled, "Can you imagine? . . . Kids from both our groups were bused daily to the same schools. All the same we managed to have fun, and I was the class valedictorian of 1945. Man, the Nazi side was furious!"[41] But by granting freedoms such as attending school and religious services off-site, administrators at Algiers acknowledged that many of those interned posed little verifiable danger to US security.

In September 1945, as the last of the internees at the camp awaited departure, the headline of a story in the *Times-Picayune* assured New Orleanians that "Aliens Live Well at Algiers Base." The short article included an image of chief officer Bunker and cited him saying, "It's not so dull as you might think. There's always something doing. We want to keep their minds occupied so they won't dry out."[42] Dismissing rumors that internees were filling up on steaks while the regular populace suffered through wartime shortages and rations, Bunker assured that meals were wholesome but not fancy; internees were not provided with butter or the better cuts of meat. Though it was still too early to reveal their identities, the group included a former city attorney from one of Germany's largest cities, a doctor from a renowned German university specializing in tropical medicine (likely Frank Meyer's father, Siegfried), and a former language professor from a leading university.

Of course, the quality of life for internees at the Algiers station depended on one's point of view, and on when one passed into and out of its gates. While the reports of visitors to Camp Algiers provide valuable firsthand information about everyday life for the internees, their observations and assessments vary widely. Those who observed the Algiers facility throughout the years of its operation do concur, though, that it was more than just a "transit camp," unappealing for both the climate and the living conditions, as Arnold Krammer describes it.[43] Observers' field notes speak of ups and downs in the morale of the internees, tales of corruption and mistreatment during their apprehensions, political differences among detainees, and over and over again, requests from internees to know why they were locked up and when they would be set free.

Jules Seitz with the National Refugee Service visited the station on February 23, 1943, filing a field report that same day that reflected his interviews with individuals and his address to the group as a whole.[44] Several Jewish internees had recently been transferred to Camp Algiers from Camp McAlester in Oklahoma and Camp Seagoville in Texas. Those seeking a transfer from Camp Kenedy, where tensions between pro-Nazi and anti-Nazi factions were reportedly at dangerous levels, still had not been integrated into the New Orleans population, and it was not known when they would arrive. But Seitz's encounters with certain internees mentioned elsewhere in these pages offer insights into the corruption that plagued the apprehension and detention of alien enemies in the Latin American countries from which they were deported to the United States.

Ernst (Ernesto) and Clotilde Gerothwohl (discussed further in chapter 2) were the only couple at the New Orleans site from Costa Rica at the time of Seitz's visit and told him, "The Litwins remained in Costa Rica. . . . The others on the Costa Rican list are all Nazis."[45] Whether or not this was in fact the case, the deportation of the Gerothwohls along with a group of avowed Nazis may have been retribution for Ernesto's whistleblower tendencies, explored further in chapter 2. Seitz's report noted that Simon Gunther, one of several Algiers internees who would later serve in the US armed forces, "was one of the men who paid for his freedom from Panamanian internment on three occasions and was always rearrested until he requested transfer to U.S." Simon had arrived on the same boat as the Gerothwohls.

Under a section titled "Morale," Seitz reported, "The morale of the individuals is very low, since they couldn't understand the reason for their transfer and are getting tired of doing nothing." Since the internees were not allowed to work except at the base, boredom was a perpetual malaise. As Stephen Fox notes in *America's Invisible Gulag,* "The internees found conditions at Algiers a definite improvement, but they still considered it a prison."[46] Although Seitz did not witness open fights, the field reporter "noted an undercurrent of resentment of some by others and there are petty jealousies."[47] He also noticed that a twelve-year-old girl from an internee family was permitted to attend school in Algiers, but two other children aged four and two lacked company their own age. Seitz spoke with Superintendent Bunker about the need for occupational therapy, as gardening and light maintenance were the only options then offered, and he described Bunker's response as "definitely concerned about the loss of valuable manpower to the country which the internees are capable of contributing." He arranged with Mrs. Kahn of the local chapter of the Council of Jewish Women to organize classes for the internees in English, history, and "Americanization." David Fichman, also of the NRS, would arrange for visits from a rabbi.

Seitz's report also touched on matters of financial assistance to the internees and the individual hearings camp personnel anticipated would start in mid-March, less than a month in the future. He closed by recommending that Earl Harrison, the director of alien registration, and Willard Kelly, the assistant commissioner for alien control, "be told that they have a very cooperative, progressive, and understanding group of administrators in Raymond Bunker, Neely and Peoples. They were very helpful to me."

Aside from a few cases, Seitz reported "the internees are much more satisfied with the physical comforts of the Quarantine Station than they were at Seagoville and the other camps and feel easier mentally since they have been separated from the Nazis and Italian Fascists." But would the security for Jews at Algiers last? Or would one historian's characterization of Algiers as "equally dangerous for the Jews" prove true?[48]

As the war continued and internees' stays in the camps lengthened, individuals from aid organizations visited more frequently and made efforts to improve conditions for internees languishing at Algiers. Paul Schnyder of the International Red Cross visited on April 19, 1944.[49] Since his report indicates it is a translation, Schnyder likely wrote it in German, the primary language of most of the detainees at the time. "The climate is semi-tropical and the residence building is surrounded by magnificent gardens planted with palm trees," he observed. There were only twenty-two internees at Algiers as of that date: four couples, six children, two unmarried women, and six bachelors. Friedrich Karl Kaul was their designated spokesman. "The internees are of different nationalities, and with few exceptions, are all Jews from South America," Schnyder wrote. These characterizations were not entirely precise, as most of the internees had been apprehended in Central America, and non-Jew Kurt Ludecke had been arrested in the United States. Schnyder also specified that most of the detainees had been at the camp since March 1943, but Ludecke had arrived in October 1943, after the majority of the Jews were released. Horst von der Goltz (discussed in chapter 4) would arrive a month later. These and other changes in the camp's internee population would upset the balance and call into question its "anti-Nazi" label.

Regarding the buildings, Schnyder reported, "The internees are lodged in a pretty red brick house, quite large and spacious; this house is built like a hotel and each internee has his room and bath." He remarked on the ground-floor lounge area where adults could gather for "moving picture presentations" or indoor games and where children could also play. According to Schnyder's observations, internees had sufficient clothing and access to laundry facilities, were cooking their own good-quality food in a kitchen in their building, and could read books from the camp's library or obtained by an aid organization at the public library. They had access to sports equipment, attended religious services at the camp or elsewhere, and were even "permitted to go into town to make purchases accompanied by a guard in plain clothes." Most engaged in small tasks around the station for which they received eighty cents a day; "all the women and even a few men" also passed the time knitting items for babies and children that were sold in stores in New Orleans. The internees had access to their mail and were in touch with their families in the United States and other countries. "The camp makes a very good impression," Schnyder concluded. "All the internees are satisfied with the way they are treated." He closed his report by acknowledging, however, "they are thinking and hoping to be set free soon."

It appears there was less bonhomie at the station by the end of 1944. Albert Greutert, the Acting Swiss consul in New Orleans, filed a December 29 report.[50] The German internees he spoke with complained that they did not have sufficient winter clothing and their food rations were barely sufficient. Beyond these creature comforts, a changed social landscape was weighing even more heavily on some. By this point they had no designated spokesman, and "unanimously declared" this was an urgent need. Greutert seemed to agree, noting, "The fact that there is no spokesman is working in the long run to a disadvantage for all concerned, especially for the internees, as the officials in charge at the Camp cannot always readily see the side of the internees." The more important change, though, was in the composition of the internee population itself: "The members of the 'Refugee Group' said that since there have been so many 'Nazis' transferred to the Algiers station, they now suffer some kind of a mental torture, which Dr. Kaul described as 'destructive' for their well-being. . . . The logical conclusion is that the members of these different groups should also be segregated in different camps. However the speakers for the Refugee Group say that they were first here in the Algiers Station, and that, therefore, the others should be sent away."

From Greutert's report, it would seem Camp Algiers's period as an "anti-

Nazi" facility had passed or at the very least was in jeopardy. A June 1944 letter to officer in charge Bunker with eleven detainee signatures shows just how much the situation had deteriorated. Jewish internee Friedrich Karl Kaul, the first signatory to the letter, was likely its author. He began by reminding Bunker, "This detention station Algiers-La. is by the authorities designated as a strictly Antinazi camp. In summer 1943 the well-known Nazi Kurt Ludecke life-long member of the Nazi-party and the confessed official organizer of Nazis in USA was transferred to this camp, under the pretense, that he wanted to live and work here quietly and alone." Nonetheless, as soon as other Nazis arrived at the station, Ludecke had organized a campaign to become camp spokesman, and the election had taken place the very day of the letter. Kaul wanted to clarify several internees' dissent with this decision:

> We, the undersigned 11 people have all cast our vote against this Nazi, who however won the election with 15 votes of those people who are set to fight the American administration on all issues. Five of those people are going to be repatriated. The outcome of this election shows that the caracter [sic] of this station as an Anti-Nazi-camp has entirely changed due to the fact that some Nazis have temporarily been transferred here. We the undersigned, respectfully beg that the administration does not recognize any spokesman until the Nazis, who do not belong into the antinazi station, have been removed.[51]

How Bunker or anyone else responded to Kaul and the rest of the signers is not clear, but he was careful to maintain an upbeat attitude regarding the internment operation with the press. The friction Kaul and his cosigners expressed does help explain a list drafted in November 1944 categorizing internees as "Pro-Nazi," "Anti-Nazi," or "Jew."[52]

Several reports from 1945–46 complete a picture of the camp as seen by its official visitors. Frank Stoltzfus with the YMCA reported on February 6, 1945, that there were about eighty "persons of enemy alien connections" at the Algiers station when he visited, and "all but two or three of the persons of Jewish blood have been set at liberty." Nevertheless, "being anti-Nazi in mind, the representatives here believe that German films would not be well received."[53] Perhaps if the internee population was no longer decidedly anti-Nazi, the staff was?

Paul Schnyder of the International Red Cross returned to Camp Algiers in early February 1945, this time accompanied by Max Zehnder. Schnyder acknowledged that not much had changed in the ten months since his last visit except that now a team of internees—Horst von der Goltz, Wilhelm Huper, Kurt Ludecke, Friedrich Karl Kaul, and Jakob Christian Paulsen—had "formed a committee of 5 spokesmen to carry out justice for everyone."[54] Taking into account the earlier letter from Kaul and ten other signers, as well as the varied backgrounds and points of view of the group of five, together with the explicit call for "justice," tensions apparently were running high at Camp Algiers by this point, especially as some of the detainees' internments had dragged on for several years. Schnyder finished his report with this summary: "The officer in charge of the camp does his best to satisfy the internees; but because of the mixture of political opinions which one finds among these internes, the work of the American Authorities is very difficult. The internees are so divided that there are many misunderstandings, and for that reason they have formed a committee of 5 which represents all their opinions. Many of them are apprehensive over what will become of them when they leave the internment camp, as all their resources have been confiscated."

In late May 1945, Olle Axberg of the War Prisoners Aid unit of the YMCA showed up at the station. He described the internee population as "Germans, Austrians and Italians," and later specified there were "11 ladies, 23 bachelors, 6 couples, 6 children," most of whom were Germans.[55] Axberg met Bunker and his assistant, Colonel Edmund Levy, and noted, "Mr. Bunker welcomed a visit from War Prisoners Aid very much, and he himself was kind enough to show me around this Station, which reminded me more of a tourist court than a prisoner's camp." Axberg noted the magnolia, olive, cedar, myrtle, cypress, orange, and banana trees that populated the "small park" on the property and wagered "the beautiful subtropical birds should be some solace for the internees." He observed, "Most of the people here speak good English as they have been for a very long time in USA or South America."

Axberg observed conditions regarding religious observance, educational opportunities, library holdings, music, movies, sports, art, and handicrafts. Protestants at Algiers were served by a Baptist preacher who held services every Sunday in the camp's large reception room; Catholics could attend a church close by, and "the Jewish people [were] taken to New Orleans for services," he indicated. Axberg reported that children attended public primary and secondary schools nearby. He assessed the variety of books in the camp library (three hundred texts in German, fifty in Spanish, thirty in English) and noted the need for additional literature in English. There was no orchestra at Algiers, and the music-making resources were "poor"; the lack of a piano was especially evident, as there were three pianists in residence at the time (the German conductor and multi-instrumentalist Siegfried Wolff, discussed in chapter 3, had been released to internment at large almost two years earlier). Axberg believed something needed to be done so that the internees would have more access to movies; he ordered them a few tools for the small workshop they had set up; and he noted they hoped to get some additional rackets, balls, and nets for the tennis court. Finally, he admired the handiwork of the unnamed librarian, who asked that his hobby of making baby booties not be advertised in Germany, as this was "not the job for a professor in jurisprudence."

When Axberg returned to Algiers with Louis Phillipp of the State Department in October 1945, the latter wrote to Bunker in a cover letter for their report, "I am convinced that you are carrying out your duties with respect to these internees in complete harmony with the highest ideals of the Immigration and Naturalization Service."[56] There were then thirty-seven internees, thirty-five of them Germans and the other two Austrians. "Their chief concern was over the uncertainty of their fate," Phillipp wrote. Horst von der Goltz (discussed in chapter 4) claimed he had not had a hearing since being detained. Kurt Ludecke "delivered a short Anti-American harangue and demanded that he be permitted to take along his typewriter, reference books, letters, and manuscripts, upon his return to Germany." The sixty-seven-year-old Hans Rucker, at Algiers with his Bolivian wife, had been detained and deported as the former German consul of the Andean country. Rucker "had spent two-thirds (46 years) of his life in Bolivia and desired to return there for the remainder of his life." The Jewish refugee Ernst Blumenthal had by that date been interned for forty-six months after being detained in Nicaragua; he and his wife, Anneliese, were still waiting for official confirmation of their release. "Since most of these internees were picked up in South American countries, their plan is to be allowed to return to their former residences and businesses," Phillipp noted. But would those houses be empty and waiting for them? Would their businesses still figure in their names?

Reverse Orders

If the Enemy Alien Control Program was officially a secret program during its operation—despite local news stories in 1943 celebrating the release of a large group of Jewish refugees from the detention station at Algiers—the end of the war signaled a softening of the pretense of secrecy and mystery. "Distinguished Enemy Aliens N.O. Neighbors for 4 Years," proclaimed the *New Orleans States* on August 31, 1945.[57] After listing once again the professions of several esteemed internees, author Cope Routh wrote, "For nearly four years these men and their families and scores of others like them have lived in complete anonymity to the outside world, within the confines of an eight-acre plot of ground that is the Enemy Alien Detention Station at Algiers." "It hasn't been the best kind of life, of course," he admitted, noting that reporters had only then been allowed a "first peek" into the operation, following the relaxation of wartime controls. Names and other information about the internees were still protected under the Geneva Convention, but Bunker was now free to elaborate on the station's operation: "Most people get the wrong idea about this station. . . . It is not a correctional institution but only a detention station. The internees are free to spend their days as they please. . . . Our idea is to maintain the family group as much as possible and have no disruption of family life." Routh's story suggests the secrecy around the operation of a detention station three miles from the foot of Canal Street had some negative effects: "There has been so little information made available about the station since it opened December 19, 1941, that rumors have periodically swept the city, exciting some citizens with tales of steak dinners, luxurious living, and other things that were being denied by wartime shortages to the average American citizen." Instead of this plush panorama, "there were full days of activity, simple, comfortable quarters in which to live" and just "adequate" food. Routh's article described camp administrator Bunker as "pretty proud of the program which once cared for as many as 250 of the nation's worst enemy aliens." Of the forty-eight internees still at the site as of that date, most wished to remain in the United States. Nevertheless, arrangements were then being made to repatriate them to their native countries.

Plans to finally close Algiers and other camps posed complex problems. Just as Proclamations 2425, 2526, and 2527 and Executive Order 9066 had authorized the forcible displacement of alien enemies and many citizens during the war, a proclamation signed by President Truman on September 8, 1945, authorized the secretary of state to order the repatriation of "any person who appears to be so clearly dangerous as to make his repatriation desirable." This mandate presented a new host of uncertainties and obstacles for those interned: many German and Japanese aliens arrested in the United States fought their repatriations, having lived outside their birth countries for decades and feeling no connection to them politically or socially; other alien internees were barred from entering the Latin American countries where they were apprehended; still others faced logistical or economic difficulties in returning to those homes, as properties and businesses were now in other hands. The US government's assistance in funding aliens' returns did not always extend to the family members who had accompanied them voluntarily, making some wonder how they would now get the whole family "home." All detained aliens, whatever their financial circumstances, faced uncertainty as to what they would find upon their "repatriations."

These questions were still pending for the ten German adults and one child still at Camp Algiers as of late February 1946, several months after the official end of the war. Most of their fellow internees had been released as of December 31, 1945, and all those remaining were anxiously awaiting decisions regarding their own fates. Following his visit there on February 25 and 26, Van Arsdale Turner of the Special Projects Division of the Department of State filed a report detailing the status of each individual or family.[58] Apprehended in Costa Rica, Guatemala, Ecuador, Peru, and Bolivia, the remaining internees were hoping Turner could tell them when they would be released. Most were anticipating returning to their adopted countries in Latin America, not as they had come to the United States, via a lengthy, overcrowded sea voyage, but by air.

The difficulties in following through on Truman's proclamation are apparent in the time it took to close Camp Algiers, not only because of the internees still held there but also because it continued to function as a temporary facility, this time for those arriving from other camps who were on their way to repatriation to Germany, Japan, or Latin America. On March 30, 1946, Marjorie Roehl wrote another story for the *New Orleans Item*, which ran with the headline "Alien Detention Camp in Algiers to Close."[59] "The work of the alien detention station at Algiers, which once held a Nazi party organizer, German industrialists, lawyers and beachcombers, Japanese and Italians, is almost finished," the article began. Camp Algiers was scheduled to close on May 15. Of the thirty-three people still at the station, only three were still categorized as enemy aliens; the others "had been released from that category" and were awaiting transportation to Central and South America, Bunker informed the reporter. He said about 1,000 persons had been interned there since the station's opening in December 1941, the majority of them Germans, though the figure also included about 250 Japanese and 50 Italians. "At one point in time, the camp held misfits and malcontents," the article stated. Though some had supported Germany openly or surreptitiously during the gains and losses of the war, Kurt Ludecke was the only one whose Nazi allegiance outlasted the allied declaration of victory in Europe. "Within one hour after we got V-E Day news, everybody else was loudly anti-Nazi," Bunker reported.

Now that Algiers was about to close, Bunker could also be more forthcoming about some of the "passive resistance" that occurred under his watch. Once he had to break up a kitchen strike, and on another occasion, someone mowed a large swastika into the grass at the station, making it necessary to cut the grass close enough to mow under the offensive symbol. Political arguments between anti-Nazis and pro-Nazis had produced "considerable heat." Nevertheless, the camp "never knew violence" nor births nor deaths, and another 250 aliens were scheduled to pass through it en route to their homes. The buildings used for detention would then return to the service of the Public Health Service Quarantine Station.

An interesting photo accompanied the *Item* story. With a caption titled "Waits to Go Home," it showed a person facing the camera with a large book in his hands that completely obscured his face. To whom did the obscured face belong? Perhaps it was that of Ludecke himself, as "All but three of the more than 50 persons in the alien detention station at Algiers, are no longer considered enemy aliens. They are merely awaiting transportation home. One enlivens the waiting period by reading one of the 700 books in the camp library," the photo caption read. The book in question was the *Neues Wilhelm Busch Album*, a collection of texts and illustrations by the celebrated nineteenth-century German humorist, poet, and painter Wilhelm Busch. Known as an early virtuoso of illustrated stories and a pioneer of the comics genre, Busch was enormously successful both in Germany and internationally. His most popular works, such as *Max and Moritz*, were translated into English, Danish, Hebrew, Japanese, Latin, Polish, Portuguese, Russian, Hungarian, and Swedish.[60] The *Neues Wilhelm Busch Album* was translated into English as *Helen Who Couldn't Help It* or *Hypocritical Helena: Plus a Plenty of Other Pleasures*. Though universally acclaimed, Busch was charged with being susceptible to antisemitic stereotypes, evident, for example, in a passage from *Die fromme Helene* or *Pious Helene*: "And the Hebrew, sly and craven, Round of shoulder, nose, and knee, Slinks to the Exchange, unshaven And intent on usury."[61] The masked model's choice of the text was most likely deliberate, a coded gesture perhaps of the very debates that had brewed at the Algiers station in previous years.

The *New Orleans States* and *Times-Picayune* probably got the same information from Bunker and the INS on the detention site's imminent closure as did the *Item* but chose a very different focus for their stories also published on March 30, 1946: that of Ludecke himself—though still incognito. "Friend of Hitler in Algiers Camp," ran the headline for a small story on page 5 of the *New Orleans States*.[62] "According to Raymond E. Bunker, officer in charge, all shades of 'isms' were represented in the camp, but in general it was sharply divided into Nazi and anti-Nazi," the reporter noted. Bunker stated, "The war was over on the morning of May 8 and by 10 o'clock within the hour, there was only one Nazi left in the entire camp the man who was Hitler's friend and a leader in the party inner circles."

The *Times-Picayune*, however, deemed the story worthy of the front page, and chose the headline "Close Pal of Hitler Held in Algiers Detention Unit" with a photo of the camp and arrows indicating the buildings at the site used for detention. Author Ken Gormin used the phrase "guests of the United States" in quotation marks as he described the newly revealed function of the quarantine station as a detention facility for alien enemies.[63] Besides housing "one of Hitler's closest friends and confidants," Algiers was home for a time to "a leading German industrialist, a man with a name known the world over." This was likely Fritz von Opel, the grandson of the German carmaker. And there was Mr. ———, who in excellent English, told the assembled reporters of his early history in Germany, his service with the German cavalry during World War I, his migration to Ecuador, and his internment. The unnamed internee also recalled the time some Nazis demanded a swimming pool be installed at Algiers. "Such trash," Gormin quoted him as saying, "they had never seen a swimming pool. Or such good food or such clothes that they gave us."

The late date of the speaker's internment and the reference to his migration to Ecuador suggests the man reporters spoke with at Algiers that day was Friedrich Paul Partmuss, also known as Federico Pablo Partmuss. Partmuss was an engineer for Ecuapetrol whose name shows up in the "FBI Files on Communism in Ecuador in the 1940s," despite his identification by the FBI as a Nazi, not a Communist.[64] The German-born Partmuss and his Chilean wife and two daughters appear on the November 1944 list classifying alien internees by political persuasion as "Anti-Nazi," though officials were clearly befuddled, adding a question mark right next to the "X" on the chart that identified him as such.

According to the FBI report, Partmuss had been the nominal head of the Nazi Party in Quito. "Although he is intelligent and could be dangerous, there is no proof as to his having engaged in Nazi activities," the confidential memo stated. In any case, "Partmuss expressed a fear to the Ecuadorian foreign office that his return to Germany would mean his death," and "it was not the intention of the government to send any man to his death." In fact, the Partmusses were spared such a fate, and their file shows they departed from New Orleans for Ecuador—rather than Germany—on April 1, 1946.[65]

Two other news stories mentioned the Algiers camp the following month. The *New Orleans Item* published "Aliens to Leave by Air" on the front page of its April 24, 1946, edition. "Eighty-five former enemy alien internees in the next two days will be flown from New Orleans to South America at a cost to the Federal Government of between $195 and $266 a person, it was learned today."[66] The article claimed, "Planes are being used for their removal because there is no available shipping space." Detained at the alien detention station in Algiers, the group was "composed mostly of German nationals and includes a few Japanese." The aliens "began to stream into this country in early 1942. Several thousands passed through New Orleans and were confined to internment camps in Crystal City, Kenedy and Seagoville, Tex.; Fort Lincoln, N. Dakota; Santa Fe, New Mexico, and other places." Over two hundred internees had recently been sent to the "Algiers evacuation center" from Crystal City, en route to the countries in Latin America where they were apprehended.

A couple of inches of newsprint buried on page 15 of the April 26, 1946, *Times-Picayune* is apparently the last mention of Algiers as a detention station in the New Orleans papers: "A Pan American Airways plane bearing approximately 40 former enemy alien internees to their prewar Central and South American homes took off early this morning from Moisant Airport. A second carrying about 40 others is scheduled to leave at 7 P.M. today."[67] The story provided a condensed history of the entire enemy alien operation, now playing out in reverse: "The group, composed mostly of Germans and a few Japanese, was part of a contingent of several thousand aliens rounded up in Latin-American countries during the war. They were then placed in internment camps in this country. The Algiers detention station is being used an as assembly point to which aliens are shipped for deportation." The majority of the Latin American detainees thus endured not one but two deportations, one to the United States and the other away from it.

While there are almost no government records that tell us what happened to enemy aliens after being slated for this second, reverse deportation, Gertrude Harten wrote about it in her diary, and her daughter assured those recollections would be available to the public.[68] "Once again we were behind barbed wire," Harten noted, recalling being sent from Crystal City, Texas, to Algiers in May

1946. "We were desperate, food and lodgings were miserable. We stayed three weeks in that prison and only a few times we were allowed to go to New Orleans. But when we could do that, it was wonderful. Once we took the children to the zoo, another time we saw the great Mississippi, where big and impressive paddle steamers crossed." Finally, word came that Ecuador was willing to receive Germans who had lived there before the war and had been in the internment camps, and on May 29, 1946, the Hartens were taken to the airport, boarding their flight for Panama after many hours of waiting. Gertrude's separation from her husband, once in Panama, suggests the internment program was not entirely over for Panama, however:

> And what happened there was unconceivable! Right away they separated Wolfgang from us and we were not allowed to approach him. We were kept under armed surveillance, even when we were eating and sleeping. We lost all hope of returning to Ecuador within a short time. We had to eat and sleep separated from our husbands. Only at 7 P.M. we were allowed to go near the barbed wire to talk 20 minutes with them. The children asked me whether war had started again. After 8 interminable days we were informed that we could travel to Ecuador and that we had only been "under quarantine"! But why had they separated us from our husbands? We were never told.

Even at the airport, the returning internees could not move freely but were always accompanied by soldiers. Finally, the family landed in Guayaquil, Ecuador. It was July 1946, more than a year after World War II had ended.

Preservation and Gentrification

After the Algiers site's closure as a detention station an entire year after the end of World War II, the quarantine station continued to function until the 1970s. The government then determined some of the buildings were unnecessary, and Building 5 was demolished. A New Orleans Police Department station, built on adjacent property in the 1970s, was abandoned in 2012. Until late 2017, the remaining buildings of the old quarantine station were used as a headquarters station by the US Border Patrol (USBP), most recently under the auspices of the Department of Homeland Security.[69]

In October 2018, USBP Headquarters were relocated to the French Quarter, and the quarantine station was officially closed. The government then listed the site for public auction, and it was sold to a team of private investors for $750,000. The new owners' plans to develop the station for private residences, taking advantage of its proximity to the riverfront levee and downtown New Orleans, suggest a rather extreme case of gentrification: from internment camp to upscale condominiums. Nonetheless, the sale of the property has also encouraged both government and private entities to reconsider the historical significance of the US Quarantine Station–New Orleans. Efforts by historic preservation consultants Kelly Calhoun and Kate Clarke of Calhoun Preservation, LLC, led to the property being listed in the National Register of Historic Places in December 2019. Perhaps this designation will serve as a prompt to preserve not only the buildings themselves but also the little known history they contain.

CHAPTER 2

The Quandaries of Classification

Classified Information

Persons labeled "enemy aliens" by the United States or the Latin American governments it cooperated with were categorized by name, age, sex, marital status, calling or occupation, ability to read and write, languages they spoke, nationality, "race or people," and city and country of birth. All of these designations appear on the manifests of ships that passed through the port of New Orleans, such as the *Florida* (figure 2.1). While such administrative documents offer a significant amount of information, they tell us very little about any given individual's political stance, activities, or affiliations. In addition, government paperwork was by no means uniform; a ship manifest from the army transfer vessel *Cuba*'s arrival in New Orleans on October 4, 1942, classifies several of its passengers as "Jewish" under the category "race or people" (figure 2.2), while the manifest for the overloaded April 1942 arrival of the *Florida* did not, though it carried a large percentage of the Jewish refugees who would later be congregated at Camp Algiers.

For both the enemy aliens and those classifying them, answers to basic questions such as country of birth, nationality, or religious affiliation were less straightforward than they might appear in this paperwork. In the mid-1930s, the Nazi leadership drafted new laws that declared Jews and other non-Aryans stateless noncitizens, leaving them with no nationality they could claim. Earlier wars had changed boundary lines of several countries, so that a person born into one nation near the turn of the twentieth century by the 1940s might belong to another. While many people targeted as alien enemies in Latin America had emigrated to the region in the late 1930s, others had arrived early in the twentieth century; some had married citizens of their adopted countries, had children born in Latin America who were thus Latin American citizens, or had lived long enough outside their birthplace that they had assumed a new national identity in practice if not in fact.

Though religion was not a standard category of classification, it was sometimes confused with "race or people." As Jewish identity was usually associated with religious practice, secular, nonpracticing Jews were at pains to confirm their place within this category, as were Jews who had converted to Christianity; the latter encountered distrust from members of their own "race or people" as well as from government officials convinced that devious pro-Nazis were playing the "Jewish refugee" card.

The confiscation of documents of enemy aliens from Latin America upon arrival in New Orleans or another point of entry for the purpose of then charging aliens with entering the United States illegally further muddled citizenship inquiries and, more crucially, demonstrated the government's violation of the right to any citizenship, even a previous one, for many of the deportees arriving from Latin America. Annoyed at a request for hearings from interned Jews who had been declared stateless by Nazi decree only to find themselves accused of pro-Axis activity and in danger of repatriation to Germany or other Nazi-held territories, Assistant Secretary of State Breckenridge Long objected, "I do not see that we have to be concerned about the *citizenship* of these people."[1]

And even when national origin was more easily determined, enemy aliens were subject to sweeping stereotypes and blanket characterizations. While the excoriation of the Japanese in the United States and elsewhere in the Americas has been documented by many scholars and is known to the general public, German nationals in these territories were also subject to stereotypes espoused in the media that "titillated suspicions" and "fanned the flames of prejudice and xenophobia."[2] In fact, German-born persons became such a ready target of criticism and distrust in the media and popular culture in the United States, the Senate held hearings in September 1941 regarding the role of propaganda in representing that population in American motion pictures.[3] Classification on the basis of a sole aspect of one's identity (such as being born in Germany or being of Japanese descent, even if born in the United States) in effect subjected all members of these groups to guilt by association until they could prove their innocence—an impossible task in some cases and a long-winded one in others.

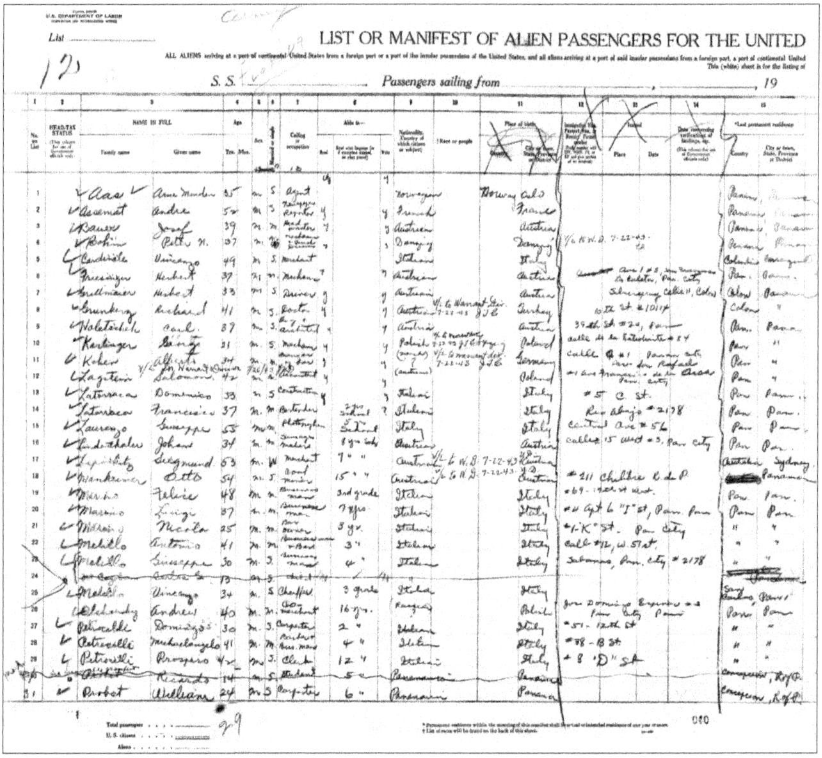

FIGURE 2.1. Ship manifest of the SS *Florida,* which arrived from the Panama Canal in New Orleans on April 8, 1942. New Orleans Passenger Lists, 1820–1945. Records of the Immigration and Naturalization Service, National Archives.

However reassuring to US citizens such measures seemed in the moment, wartime apprehension by the police based on little more than one's place of birth and indefinite detention, at times without access to a hearing, were elements of US enemy alien protocols that bore certain disturbing resemblances to policies and actions of the Fascist states against which America was purportedly securing itself. After 1933, the German state had shifted the basis of citizenship to an imagined ethnic one; in September 1935 German Jews and other "Non-Aryans" were deprived officially of their citizenship under the Nuremberg Laws, an "essential prelude for later persecutions." Viewed alongside the Nazis' end goal of annihilation for its own internal "aliens," the American government's dismissive attitude toward citizenship assumes a more

PORT OF NO RETURN | 54

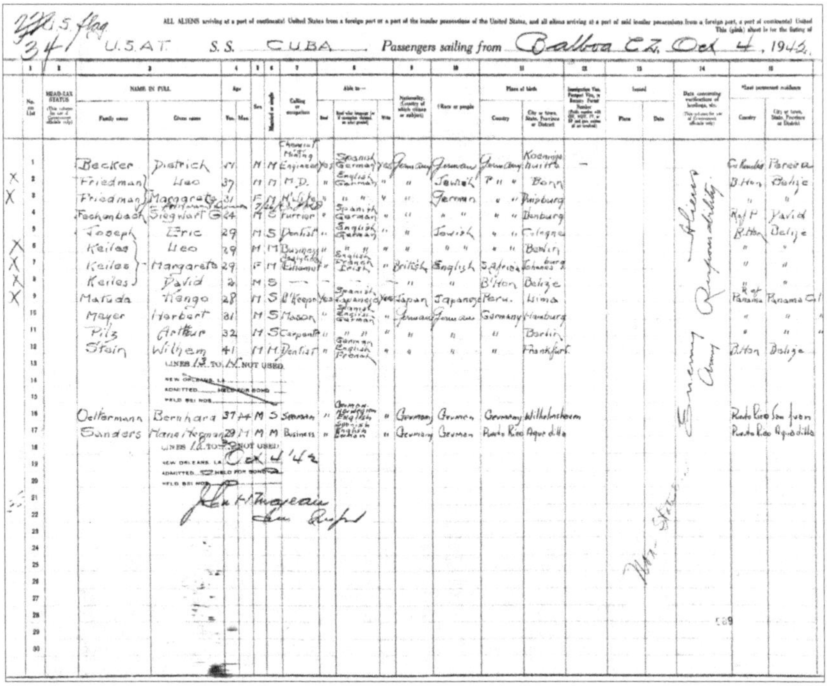

FIGURE 2.2. Ship manifest of the SS *Cuba*, sailing October 4, 1942, from the Canal Zone to New Orleans, identifying some passengers as Jewish under the heading "Race or People." New Orleans Passenger Lists, 1820–1945. Records of the Immigration and Naturalization Service, National Archives.

sinister face, even if it did not result in the same horrific levels of genocide. As Holocaust scholar David Gushee urges, "Let us declare a principle here that extends far beyond Nazi Germany: once it is 'open season' on any outcast social group in a society, the preferred groups collectively, and many individuals, will quickly join in on the fun and quickly take advantage of their neighbors' powerlessness."[4]

Enemy alien internees sometimes pointed to these ways in which their US detention did not seem so different from policies and practices implemented by the United States' declared enemies, even if conditions of everyday life in detention on American soil were in general much better and did not include starvation, torture, medical experimentation, or death by execution or the gas chamber or the infamous *Gnadenschuss*, the single shot to the back of the neck.[5]

THE QUANDARIES OF CLASSIFICATION | 55

Nonetheless, nationality-, race-, or religion-based discrimination were inherent parts of the internment apparatus from its beginning, even prior to its implementation. As Duncan Ryūken Williams has shown, as early as 1936—five years prior to the attack on Pearl Harbor—President Roosevelt endorsed a plan to maintain a secret list of Japanese to be detained. By 1940, FBI director J. Edgar Hoover warned his colleagues in military intelligence that those most likely to be disloyal included "Buddhist and Shintoist priests, the Japanese-language schoolteachers, consular agents, and a small percentage of prominent alien Japanese Businessmen."[6] Cultural markers such as language and religion were conflated with "race" and in turn equated with disloyalty.

Such stereotypes were often left over from World War I or even earlier. Historian Gary Okihiro discovered a 1919 report on the Japanese population in the United States in which "Christians showed 'an independence of thought' and were imbued with 'more of the ideals of American democracy,'" while the large majority of non-Christians in that population were believed to worship the emperor.[7] In the later context of World War II, the same War Relocation Authority responsible for assembling and confining tens of thousands of Japanese Americans similarly ranked their access to release from this incarceration with a loyalty questionnaire that granted two extra points to anyone identifying as "Christian," reducing one's loyalty score one point for those calling themselves "Buddhist" and automatically rejecting those checking the option "Shintoist."[8]

At Camp Algiers, the extant document trail of such classification processes focuses heavily on suspected "German" alien enemies detained in Latin America, even if roundups in Latin America and the Caribbean also reaped deportees from Austria, Poland, Czechoslovakia, and in at least one case, Sweden (see Axel Wachtmeister's story in chapter 5).[9] Thus, while "German" itself was a slippery category, internment administrators and officials were hard put to sort out who was a Nazi, who was pro-German but anti-Nazi, and who was a refugee. Few of these determinations were self-evident, and many government officials brought to their task a legacy of bias. They worried that those who claimed to be Jewish refugees were wolves in sheep's clothing, only pretending to be victims in need of aid and assistance as they conspired to build a Nazi fifth column in the Americas. Differentiating between who was pro-Axis and who was loyal to the United States proved to be a fraught task with unreliable results at every juncture of enemy alien internment, from the moment of adding a name to a list of "possible" threats and through to the internee's eventual release, repatriation, or in a few cases, death.

```
                    ALIENS AT ALGIERS, LA.

                                    Pro-Nazi  Anti-Nazi  Jew
        German - Detained
Steiner, Carl Offerman       39/10518        X
        Germans Interned
Barber, Harold               56176/788                          ?
Blumenthal, Annaliese Gaertner 56162/820               X
Blumenthal, Ernst            56125/317
Hoffmann, Franz              56176/552        X
HUMPER, Wilhelm L.D.C.       56125/789        X
Ising, Friedrich Wilhelm Hermann
                             56176/901                          ?
Jacobi, Arthur               56125/462
Jacobi, Erna Frieda          56125/388                 X
Jacobi, Herta                56125/388
Jacobi, Manfred              56125/388
Jacobi, Ursula               56125/386
Johanning, Friedrich         39/7162          X
Kaul, Fritz Karl, Dr.        56125/318                 X
Kolb, Gertraude Rose         39/7694
Kolb, Heide Marie            39/7694          X
Kolb, Karl                   39/9042
Kolb, Klaus Peter            39/7694
Kuhne, Werner Gerhard Otto   56176/856        X
Loewenthal, Emil             56125/459
Loewenthal, Hilda            56125/384
Loewenthal, Joan             56125/384
Ludecke, Kurt George V.      39/3087                  X?
Meyer, Irmgard Martha        56162/33                           X
Meyer, Siegfried Bernhard, Dr.
                             56125/320
```

FIGURE 2.3. A page of the November 1944 list of enemy aliens interned at the Algiers detention station, categorized as "Pro-Nazi," "Anti-Nazi," or "Jew." National Archives, used with permission.

The political classification of named enemy aliens proved to be so indeterminate that as late as November 1944, less than a year before the official cessation of World War II, and almost three years after many persons had been identified and detained as enemy aliens following the bombing of Pearl Harbor, officials were still trying to sort it out at Camp Algiers and elsewhere. That month, S. W. Anderson, assistant supervisor of the Detentions Unit, sent a letter to Willard Kelly, assistant commissioner for alien control under Edward Ennis, explaining he had reviewed the files of the men, women, and children detained at the Algiers Detention Station, and had classified them as either "Pro-Nazi," "Anti-Nazi" or "Jew": "There is attached a list of these individuals from which it will be seen that I have classified twelve (12) men, women and children as members of the pro-Nazi group, twenty-two (22) men, women and children as the anti-Nazi group, and fourteen (14) men, women and children as Jewish. In addition, there are two, who on the basis of their files, I was unable to classify in any one of these categories."[10] A page of this document indicates Anderson's designations and even suggests some of his reservations (figure 2.3).

Kurt Ludecke, whose story is further explored in chapter 4, was one of the internees who gave Anderson pause. An early member of Hitler's inner circle, Ludecke's professed repentance from his pro-Nazi stance was doubted before, during, and after his long internment, both by internment custodians and his fellow internees. Anderson's ambivalence is evident in his conclusion that Ludecke's file contained some evidence that he might be anti-Nazi, but "it does clearly indicate that he is pro-German, and my classification of him as a member of the anti-Nazi group was made hesitantly." Three other internees were marked as anti-Nazi with some hesitation, Anderson wrote, as the records did not leave him "thoroughly satisfied" as to their appropriate classification.

Such a list reveals several interesting details about the composition of the Algiers population at that time, as well as some of the changes that had already taken place there during the years the site was used as an internment facility. First, it shows that even if the pro-Nazi contingent was the smallest of the three groups at Algiers in late 1944, the function of the station as an "anti-Nazi camp" was by then open to debate.[11] Its previous designation as a site where "Jewish internees and others who could prove their anti-Fascist credentials were . . . segregated for their own protection" seemed to have changed.[12]

Anderson did acknowledge counting several individuals as pro-Nazi "purely on the basis of their outstanding petitions for repatriation to Germany," a sorting tool that, as we soon discover, did not leave much room for the politics of someone like Friedrich Karl Kaul, a Jew and anti-Nazi who requested repatriation, saw his request granted, and rose to become a leading political star of the German Democratic Republic. Anderson's classification reveals other pitfalls as well. For example, he typically counted all members of a family within a single designation, assuming a uniform political stance among husband, wife, and children, whatever their age. Anderson himself admitted the fallibility of this method when he called attention to the cases of Humberto Plath and his seventeen-year-old son, August Wilhelm Plath, "as it appears the father is pro-Nazi and the son is anti-Nazi."[13]

Agitation and Ambiguity

Even before Anderson set about to sort pro-Nazis from pro-Germans and Jews at Algiers, the internees' files were already significantly if not hopelessly tainted by hearsay and dubious intelligence work. Identity problems for Ernst (Ernesto) Blumenthal, whom Anderson appears to have left without any classification at all, began when "evidence" from a Honduran functionary suggested he was a Gestapo agent; his State Department file reveals other suspicions that he was a "dangerous totalitarian agent" and that he and his friend Kaul were "professional spies or agitators." Thus, though his FBI file begins, "Ernst Blumenthal, a Jew, was born in Berlin, Germany on May 29, 1903," authorities were never certain of Blumenthal's loyalties throughout his long internment.[14]

Blumenthal had been apprehended by the Nicaraguan government on December 19, 1941, and arrived at Camp Kenedy in Texas on May 30, 1942. From there, he wrote to the Swiss legation representing German interests in the United States in the hopes he could be reunited with his wife, "left behind" in Barranquilla, Colombia, when he was apprehended in Nicaragua. In his missive to the legation, Blumenthal was at pains to establish his and his wife's status as political refugees trying to survive in a precarious economic situation. Calling her physical condition "as low as possible," he warned that Anneliese was on the point of starving in the hot, tropical climate of the Caribbean coast of Colombia and as "the wife of me, a Jew, does not get one cent of relief from the German Representative in Columbia."[15] In a letter Ernst included in his missive to the legation, his wife spoke of her loneliness and misfortune and wondered, "How long will it last until mankind is freed from the leprosy in human form?"[16]

For Ernst, the expression of such sentiments made it "heedless to stress the mental depression under which [her letter] was written." He asks if the diplomatic liaison is himself a married man, hoping to establish common ground and arouse sympathy in him. When Blumenthal some days later received a letter from a Central American acquaintance warning that internees' wives and families in Latin America would be repatriated to Germany on December 21, 1942, he wrote to the legation again, pleading, "My wife is as much a political refugee as I am. . . . Her repatriation to Germany would have exactly the same consequences for her as my repatriation for me, mind you under the present political doctrine in Germany."[17]

While the Algiers Detention Station's chief officer Raymond Bunker would characterize Ernst as a "whiner," the Blumenthals' anxieties had a backstory. Both had spent time in European concentration camps due to their "hostility toward the Reich," and their worries doubtless redoubled when the very "crime" that put them in the European camps, the mere fact of being Jewish, was cast into doubt. Nonetheless, Blumenthal's behavior in internment did not ingratiate him to the authorities:

> There is no evidence referred to prove the accusations that Blumenthal was a Gestapo agent and perhaps too much was made from the fact that he and his friend sailed up and down the coast of Central America trying to get a country that would admit them. In any event now Blumenthal, who made something of a nuisance of himself for several years in an effort to get released from confinement, states that he wants his name and honor cleared and wants a thorough investigation and a clean bill of health. He does not want to go to Germany nor does he want to return to South America, and really there is no country there which wants him or to whom he belongs.[18]

However peevish Blumenthal's character, this account suggests that even efforts to seek release from internment and recuperate one's honor, reputation, or health could render an internee a "nuisance" and negatively impact his or her prospects for a hearing, improved conditions, or release.

In fact, it took a long time for Ernst and Anneliese Blumenthal to be excised from the lists of alien enemies. A note stapled to a confidential memo in their State Department file dated January 4, 1946, concluded, "The difficult problem in his case will be to find some one who will take him, since I am sure that no country who has already had the pleasure of his presence will want him again. Perhaps in the long run Germany will be the only place he can go. That, however, is a problem for Immigration. For our purposes Blumenthal is not dangerous within the meaning of our standards, and I recommend his release." Despite the ominous mention of Germany, naturalization records created in Brooklyn, New York, in the 1950s exist for both Anneliese Blumenthal (1954) and her husband (1955), a full two decades after a run-in with the Gestapo landed him in the Lichtenburg concentration camp.

The files of several Algiers detainees demonstrate that the imminent dangers faced by the Jewish population in the region under the control of the Third Reich provided an insufficient reason for the US government to clear the names of such individuals from the charge of "dangerousness." Agents from the FBI and other US entities repeatedly failed to deduce that as the default enemies of Nazism, Jews were unlikely supporters of Hitler and other Fascist leaders. Sometimes, though, European refugees in Latin America acted in ways that invited distrust or confusion, confounding efforts to sort out allegiances. Siegwart Fechenbach, born in 1918 in Eilenburg, Germany, claimed, like others, to be stateless because of his Jewish descent.[19] After working as a furrier in Colombia from September 1938 to January 1940, Fechenbach was jailed in Panama for illegal entry and after two unsuccessful attempts to enter Costa Rica was sentenced by the Panamanians to two years in jail.

A November 15, 1945, confidential memo in his file refers to a source who "said he was pure German and not Jewish." Other documents state that in May 1940, Fechenbach himself confessed to American officials that he had been a member of the German Gestapo in Colombia and offered his services to US intelligence. He was described at that time as being very emaciated from lack of food and "gave the impression that he was somewhat mentally deranged." His file claims "Fechenbach served a two year sentence at the Penal Colony of Coiba for violation of a deportation order" and upon his release was removed to the United States. The head of the Panama National Police even described him as a "screwball."[20]

When later interviewed in the United States, however, Fechenbach explained he had purposely made the false confession of his membership in the Gestapo in an effort to get himself arrested by U.S. authorities and thus avoid serving a two-year sentence in the Panama Canal Colony. On American soil, he denied ever having worked for the Germans in Colombia, raising the question of whether he was in fact politically untrustworthy or just hungry, or whether he even served two years at Coiba. Described as Panama's own "Devil's Island," Coiba was one of "history's most nightmarish penal colonies," a prison that would later become notorious for torture and disappearances under the presidency of Manuel Noriega.[21] It seems likely that almost anyone, but especially a down-on-his-luck foreigner, would have gone to extreme ends to avoid a prolonged stay there. At the very least, descriptions of the young man's mental and physical state at that time suggest the ravages of a harsh existence.

Fechenbach's file contains other unusual elements as well, including an undated letter he wrote to the king of England volunteering to fight against

Germany. In another missive intercepted by censors, this one dated October 17, 1942, he "indicated anti-Nazi feelings."[22] Interviewers at Algiers trying to piece together his true story even inquired about his conversion to Catholicism; one account claimed he had converted in order to marry a Catholic girl, while his sister explained in an affidavit that he converted because only Catholics could work at that time in Colombia. Ultimately, Fechenbach's strained circumstances and changes of face recall the subterfuge Jews found themselves obligated to turn to in other moments of intense persecution or uncertainty, such as the late fifteenth century, when Spain demanded that all subjects convert to Catholicism or leave the region, backing up its demands with sinister Inquisitional surveillance and security forces aided by complicit citizens.

Eventually, Fechenbach was interned at large on the grounds that there was no evidence he had ever engaged in subversive activities. The hearing board still described his mental state as "poor" but approved his release from Camp Algiers in 1943 to facilitate his induction into the US Army. His draft registration card is dated August 28, 1943, and as of November 29, 1945, his address was listed as the 106th Infantry Regiment in San Francisco. Finally, in mid-March 1946, the authorities determined he was "not to be subjected to any further restraint under the Alien Enemy Act."[23]

Pro-Nazi, anti-Nazi, or Jew: which category to check? Fechenbach seems to have attempted to "pass" as pro-German and perhaps even pro-Nazi to avoid incarceration in Colombia or Panama (or both), but he also expressed his anti-Nazi sentiments in writing. Did his apparent conversion to Catholicism, especially if chosen to allow him to work or marry, erase his identity as a Jew? As to his true attitude toward the United Sates, he apparently served honorably in the armed forces, made a home in the St. Louis area, and is buried in Missouri's Jefferson Barracks National Cemetery.

The Harm in Speaking Out

In certain Latin American territories, expressing one's hatred of Hitler and the Nazis outright could even backfire against a detainee. Such appears to be the case of Ernesto Gerothwohl (sometimes Gerothwol), deported from Costa Rica to the United States with his wife, Clotilde, accompanying him as a voluntary detainee.[24] A confidential memo in Gerothwohl's State Department file, dated January 18, 1946, well after the war's end, reiterated that he was born on December 12, 1904, in Frankfurt, and considered himself stateless as a result of the Nuremberg Laws, since both he and his wife were Jewish. The memo adds, rather curiously, "but this is doubtful as well as irrelevant." How was Gerothwohl's Jewish identity "irrelevant," given he "had fled Germany during *Kristallnacht* in 1938 with four dollars and a few clothes"?[25] By the 1946 date of the memo, US and Russian soldiers had already liberated the Nazi work and death camps, revealing in personal testimonies and photographs the genocide they had found. Under the heading "Activities," the writer of the memo clarified, "There are no allegations whatsoever of pro-Nazi activity or sympathy on the part of either Gerothwol. It seems evident that they were deported because Gerothwol was a constant thorn in the side of the Costa Rican government, *urging stronger action against the Nazi element in the country*" (my emphasis). It is noteworthy here that speaking out against Nazism and its dangers seems to have worked *against* Gerothwohl, who after he arrived in Costa Rica as a refugee in 1939 "persistently needled the authorities about the Nazis" and "gave them valuable information regarding dangerous ones." He also "wrote articles in the local newspapers and open letters criticizing the Chief of Police for his lenient attitude."[26] A December 22, 1942, aerogram from San José to the US secretary of state included in their file notes that the Gerothwohls, "now in concentration camp in San José," were "considered dangerous," and were being deported at the request of the Costa Rican government.[27] Officials in the United States accepted the pernicious characterization of the Gerothwohls and others based on what amounted to *anti*-Nazi activity, raising disturbing questions as to how "dangerous" alien enemies were identified, apprehended, and deported in each participating Latin American republic and who ultimately made those decisions.

In fact, while many Latin American countries considered Jews "undesirable" immigrants during periods of the nineteenth and twentieth century, the fact that the Gerothwohls were able to enter legally was itself a sign of unusual good fortune, given that "Costa Rica was guilty of extraordinary hostility toward Jewish victims of the Nazis, and did nothing to rescue them."[28] Was their deportation to the United States another stroke of luck, or at least a dark cloud with a silver lining? Arriving in California aboard the *Puebla* in February 1943, the Gerothwols were interned at the Algiers Detention Station in New Orleans a few days later. Harold Ickes and James Bell, after interviewing the couple at Algiers on June 29 of that year, recommended internment at large; after their eventual release, the couple settled in St. Louis.

But Mr. Gerothwohl had a hard time keeping quiet during the parole-like period of internment at large, too. His Department of Justice file notes that subsequent to his release, he responded to advertisements placed by the United Fruit Company, offering a reward for information on enemy activities in Costa Rica. Despite rules forbidding those under internment at large from sending international correspondence, Gerothwohl "sent a long letter, describing himself as a German Jewish refugee interested only in doing as much as possible against the enemy." Once more, it seems, adopting the role of a whistleblower got Gerothwohl into trouble, as "since being paroled in this country Gerothwol has demonstrated the same lack of caution or restraint and has continually violated correspondence regulations, as a result of which he has almost been re-interned."[29] Finally, though, the couple was released from internment at large. Both have death records in Dade County, Florida, Ernesto's dated 1968 and Clotilde's 1970.

Dubious Deportation

Born in Poland in 1897, Leo Hamermann had left Austria for Bolivia in 1938; he wasn't deported from the Andean country to the United States until 1944, and the government itself recognized the rationale for his deportation as dubious. His State Department name file indicates: "The Embassy at the time reported that it was 'doubtful' about the case and had never been notified that he was listed for deportation. The Legal Attaché did not then have, and still does not have, any derogatory information regarding Hamermann and the Bolivian Police as of June 1945 had failed to produce any such information, despite several requests."[30] Notwithstanding a "Basic Personnel Record" that identified Hamermann as Protestant, a January 2, 1946, memo classified him as a Polish Jewish refugee whose name was not among those "whose deportation was desired" and who did not know he was being deported "until a few minutes prior to the time the plane left the airport at La Paz." Hamermann (also spelled Hammerman in some documents) had been targeted by La Paz police chief Captain José Escobar as a "dangerous Nazi," though the Bolivian police could supply no evidence for this claim and never replied to repeated requests for information. Efforts to deport as many Axis nationals as possible in order to make a good showing with the American government, combined with retribution from local authorities for a letter Hamermann wrote expressing his dislike for the country, likely provided the background for his being aboard the *Florida* when it arrived in New Orleans on July 2, 1944.[31]

The US Office of Censorship got involved in his case as well, intercepting a letter from Jacobo Kramer in La Paz to Isidore Hamermann at 353 Hearn Avenue, Cincinnati, postmarked June 16, 1944, with the subject "Interested Party in La

Paz Urges U.S. Individual to Assist in Obtaining Release of Latter's Relative Who Has Been Erroneously Deported from Bolivia for Internment Camp in the U.S." In the censor's translation, Kramer laments the "misfortune of our poor Lunek," who on May 18 of that year had been "deported with his worst enemies, the Nazis."[32] The American legation in La Paz had assured Kramer that the "error" would be quickly rectified and Hamermann would be released immediately on his arrival. Hearing of no such outcome, Kramer had appealed to the American Jewish Joint Distribution Committee and the National Refugee Service. These anxious interventions on his behalf meant that Hamermann only had to spend a few weeks in detention. He was interned at large on August 29, 1944, and other INS records indicate he successfully petitioned for naturalization in 1951. Hamermann died on April 19, 1975, and is buried in Mt. Hebron Cemetery in Queens, New York.

Kafkaesque Scenarios

Professing innocence before the authorities in their adopted countries was usually futile for the Latin American internees, unless they accompanied that protest with a monetary incentive. While enemy aliens detained within the United States were entitled to a hearing, and in many cases also had rehearings, few alien enemies from Latin America received such an opportunity. An accusation of collusion with the Nazis was especially exasperating for Jews, who found their situation absurd as well as unjust. Wilhelm Heinemann's case brings to mind Harvey Strum's contention that "only Franz Kafka could have created a tale of German Jews being arrested as pro-Nazi enemy aliens and then being sent to the United States for internment with real Nazi sympathizers. Once caught in the bureaucratic web, the Jews found it difficult to escape the absurdity of their situation."[33]

A restaurant manager in David, Panama, Heinemann was accused of being a Nazi spy when Lieutenant Jules Dubois, chief of intelligence with the US Army's Panama Canal Department, found a bent piece of straw or wire in the bottom of his coffee cup in Heinemann's restaurant and interpreted it as secret code. Convinced that Germany had a grand plan to "acquire the Republic of Panama, and with it the vital link in the defense of the United States and the American republics,"[34] the lieutenant was unmoved by Heinemann's story of flight from Hitler's Germany, Franco's Spain, and Mussolini's Italy before finding a fragile refuge in Central America.[35]

THE QUANDARIES OF CLASSIFICATION | 65

Heinemann's sense of humiliation and injustice mushroomed when his wife Marta refused to join him for voluntary internment, and he wrote a letter from his internment camp "blaming his Aryan wife for getting him into trouble and stating that she was dangerous to the United States."[36] Later he admitted such statements were untrue and explained he had written the letter out of anger at her reluctance to accompany him. As for Marta Heinemann, though Wilhelm's ship had sailed without her, her respite—whether from internment or from an angry husband—was short-lived, as "four months later, in June 1942, Mrs. Heinemann's mind was made up for her when she was apprehended by the U.S. Army."

Born in 1892, Wilhelm Heinemann had first married in Germany in 1920, moving to Guatemala with his first wife in 1926 and then spending some time in Mexico. When his wife left him, he returned to Germany to obtain a divorce and in 1938 set out again for Latin America, marrying Marta, also German-born, in Bogotá. The couple spent time in Mallorca and then San Remo, Italy, until Heinemann was expelled from that country "on racial grounds" in 1939. He finally obtained a visa for Panama, but this new refuge also proved temporary when Heinemann was apprehended by Panama police the day after the bombing of Pearl Harbor. Wilhelm was aboard the *Florida* when it entered the port of New Orleans in early April 1942; he then spent time at three camps—Blanding, Stringtown, and Seagoville—before arriving at Algiers in February 1943.

A censorship intercept of a letter Wilhelm Heinemann wrote from Camp Blanding to Leo Marchowsky in Panama includes a note that reads, "This Jewish Internee is suffering extreme mental anguish due to fear of being returned to Germany." In the letter itself, Heinemann had written,

> I am suffering very much mentally. I have an urgent request to make, and please attend to it immediately because it is a question of life and death. . . . A rumor is circulating here in camp that we will be considered as exchange prisoners irrespective of race and religion. I am living in constant fear, because if this is true I can be sure of a death sentence in Germany. Through devastating articles in the "Eco de Valle" and the "Renovación" I openly expressed my abhorrence against the murderous Nazi Government, and besides I am a Jew.[37]

Alongside this paragraph, someone in official quarters wrote in pencil, "Is this true?" It's hard to know if the reader's question refers to Heinemann's Jewish identity, his outspoken criticism in the Panama newspapers, the impending prisoner exchange, or perhaps all three. In any case, Heinemann wanted his wife's help in preventing this outcome: "My wife should with your assistance . . . immediately make a petition to the President of the U.S.A. in Washington asking to free me or at least for God's sake not be considered for exchange, because, my dear Mr. Marchowsky, I rather take my own life than to go to this beast Hitler. Please Mr. Marchowsky send this petition immediately. I cannot bear it much longer, my old heart ailment brings me to the verge of desperation." Indeed, a memorandum for the chief of the Review Section of the Immigration Service later characterized Heinemann as "harmless but close to a mental and nervous breakdown and approaching insanity," perhaps due to "Heinemann's very real fear in the early stages of his internment that he would be rapidly deported to Germany."[38]

For better or for worse, the Heinemanns would be reunited. Like most of the wives among the internee population, Marta's paperwork merited less time and attention from the officials than her husband's (documents relating to wives are usually part of the male internee's file). A confidential memo states that she was born in Aachen, Germany, in 1907 but claimed to be "stateless" on the grounds that if her husband had lost his citizenship, she also lost hers, although she was "Aryan." She was picked up by police in December 1941 but apparently let go; she was again apprehended on June 3, 1942.[39] Her name appears on the manifest for the Army transport vessel *Evangeline*, arriving in Tampa, Florida, from Trinidad, Cuba, on June 24, 1942. Mrs. Heinemann was received by the INS there and sent across the country to Camp Seagoville, where she stayed until arriving with a large group at Camp Algiers in February 1943.

Ultimately, after a long process of considerations and reconsiderations, the Heinemanns were released from alien enemy proceedings on the grounds of "insufficient evidence of dangerousness" in January 1946. A pair of reports titled "Death of American Citizen Abroad" show that they were both finally naturalized in the United States in 1955, making their home in Chicago. One of those documents also shows the couple was still together—or at least in the same country—at the time of their death. Wilhelm's report attributes his December 1973 death at age eighty to old age, heart failure, and mental disorientation; a heart attack was responsible for Marta's death at sixty-six a few months earlier that same year, according to the other report. Both Heinemanns were buried in the same field—though not the same row—of the beautiful Waldfriedhof Cemetery in Aachen, Germany, where many soldiers, citizens, and victims of concentration camps are also buried.[40]

Confounding the Categories

Friedrich Karl Kaul presented a particularly bewildering case to Anderson and other government officials trying to determine each Camp Algiers detainee's political stance and loyalty to the United States. Born in 1906 in Posen, Germany, Kaul would arrive at Algiers on March 13, 1943; more than two years later, as of August 25, 1945, he was en route to Ellis Island for repatriation to Germany.[41] Though Kaul was an important figure in the history of Algiers and other US internment camps, even serving as spokesman for the Jewish group for a time, the most intriguing parts of his story for many will be first, his desire to be repatriated to the same country that had sent him to two concentration camps and, second, his subsequent rise to prominence as a star lawyer and ideological standard-bearer for the German Democratic Republic.[42] He even represented East Germany at the trial of Nazi henchman Adolf Eichmann in Jerusalem in 1961, bringing with him his experiences of exile as an alien enemy both in Nazi Germany and in the United States.

In his own personal account composed during US internment and included in his State Department file, Kaul detailed how he studied law at Heidelberg and Berlin, working afterward with the "administration of justice in Berlin" and as an assistant to the law faculty at the University of Berlin. But these occupations ended in 1933 due to new Nazi laws, "because I was a Jew."[43] From 1935 to 1937, Kaul was interned (his word) at the Lichtenburg and Dachau concentration camps, charged with high treason. In June 1937, he was released on the condition that he leave Germany immediately for Colombia.

Arriving in Bogotá with $2.50 and no knowledge of Spanish, Kaul worked in a series of odd jobs in that city and elsewhere in the country, including a stint with an architect who was also a Jewish refugee. The latter apparently aided him in arranging for his parents' travel to Colombia. Though they arrived penniless and Kaul's own finances were precarious, the elder Kauls subsequently received papers to immigrate to the United States, settling in New York. This allayed Kaul's primary worry and would constitute the single source of his subsequent gratitude to the United States.

Kaul's situation was more complicated, however, as laws restricted him from doing any work besides the occupation listed on his papers, "scientist of law." Under this restriction, "it was impossible to me to earn my bread," Kaul stated. He was apprehended in Nicaragua on December 19, 1941, and received by the INS at Camp Kenedy on May 30, 1942. He was likely the sole Jewish internee there or elsewhere in the internment apparatus to request repatriation. A May 1942 memo in his State Department name file explains, "Since being in detention in the United States, the subject has consistently maintained an anti-Nazi but definitely pro-German attitude." He was seen as associating mostly with pro-German sympathizers, and "it is his claim that the only salvation of Germany lies in the formation of a central government strong enough to wage another war in a few years in order to obtain for Germany the things to which, according to his belief, she is justly entitled. Subject is a Jew."[44]

By the time Kaul's requested repatriation became a reality, besides the time already spent in concentration camps in Europe, he

> had spent four years as a US captive, being interned first in Texas, then in New Orleans. Upon his arrival back in Germany, he was interned, again, by US occupation authorities and went on to spend six months in the Asperg prison, in Baden-Wütteberg [sic]. It is not hard to see why he would later become such a vehement critic of the United States, and of the Western bloc, while working for the East German regime. . . . Indeed, the fury that characterized his attacks against the Western superpower may well have been linked to the traumatic memories of his long years of captivity.[45]

Despite the bitterness he expressed in the wake of these experiences, Kaul remade his life, rising to prominence as a star lawyer of the Socialist Unity Party in the German Democratic Republic (GDR). In that role, he traveled to Israel in 1961 to take part in the trial of Adolf Eichmann, a principal organizer and facilitator of the Holocaust. The presence of a high-profile East German representative in Israel in that era was unprecedented: "At the time, the GDR had no official relations with the State of Israel (nor would it have any by the time of its collapse, in 1990). And while West Germany had agreed, in 1952, to pay restitutions to the Jewish State in an attempt to atone for the Nazi persecution of the Jews, the GDR had never agreed to such a commitment."[46]

In the 1970s, Kaul was also called on to represent "the most extravagant and all-encompassing example of unity between East Germany and a Black American," the GDR's solidarity campaign for the African American communist Angela Davis.[47] Demonstrating East Germany's solidarity with the Free Angela Davis movement and other African American civil rights issues, Kaul wrote a letter to the judge in Davis's case, explaining why he believed she could not and would not have a fair trial: "The President, public opinion, the prosecutor, the judge and the jury, are against Angela Davis, even before a verdict has been returned. The designation of the case 'United States versus Angela Davis,' has thus taken on a different, a terrible meaning. It is the American ruling circles who have put Angela Davis on trial. If they have their way, they will make short work of her."[48]

Wielding substantial influence in both East and West Germany and beyond, Kaul also authored some thirty-five books and sixty screenplays, including a 1959 fictionalized memoir titled *Es wird Zeit, dass Du nach Hause kommst* (published in Spanish in 2015 as *Iba siendo hora de que volvieras a casa*). In that text, as Max Paul Friedman shows in a close reading of the German original, Kaul offers readers a notably revised version of his own wartime experiences under the guise of a protagonist named Günther Karst. Karst embodies Kaul in the best possible light as a devoted German loyal first and foremost to his nation, rather than to any other identity marker, such as his Jewishness. In this way, Kaul, through his protagonist, sought to embody Victor Klemperer's contention that it was the Nazis who were un-German, not he himself. At one point in the pages of Kaul's memoir, his alter ego Karst ends up in an anti-Nazi camp very much like Camp Algiers, though it has been fictionally relocated to Norfolk, Virginia.[49] Upon his own return to Germany, Kaul himself made almost a complete circle, making good on his insistence during US internment that one could be pro-German and anti-Nazi, even in the 1940s. He died in 1981; his tombstone can be found in Friedrichsfelde Central Cemetery, also known as the Memorial to the Socialists, in Berlin.

Stating the Obvious

Some of the decisions as to how to classify alien enemies' political leanings did seem rather obvious. Karl Kolb was transferred to the Algiers station with his family from the Crystal City camp in Texas as a "disciplinary measure."[50] At Crystal City, Kolb had been elected spokesman of a pro-German contingent so hostile to the United States that on April 21, 1943—the day after Adolf Hitler's birthday—some of its members removed the US flag from the recreation hall, hoisting in its place the red, black, and white German flag, adorned with the swastika.[51] American guards arrived and removed the German flag, tearing it to shreds, but a few days later, a squad of Germans exacted their revenge by cutting down the American flag from a pole on the grounds in the middle of the night, retaining their anonymity. Five Germans wrote a letter to camp officials, with copies to the Swiss legation and the International Red Cross, stating, "We believe that the flag of the Detaining power does not belong inside of an enemy alien internment camp."[52] The INS commissioner, Earl Harrison, compromised by seeing that one US flag was removed from the recreation hall while another was moved outside the camp fence.[53]

Kolb was one of the signers of the complaint about the Stars and Stripes. At the time of his arrest he was living with his family in New York City, where he was an executive with Zeiss Ikon. First interned at Ellis Island, he was later reunited with his wife and daughter at Crystal City in the summer of 1943, after which he was elected spokesman for the German group. Under a laissez-faire policy adopted by camp administrators, Kolb and other pro-Nazi internees seized substantial power over camp life, including authority over job assignments for both German and Japanese internees. He also helped organize strikes among the German workers. In her study of Crystal City, the US government's "flagship" family internment camp, Jan Jarboe Russell describes escalating tensions under Kolb's leadership, to the point that "organized bands of agitators roamed the camp, many of them brandishing clubs," some greeting each other with the raised arm of the Hitler salute.[54]

In February of 1944, Berlin and Washington completed their negotiations for a prisoner exchange of more than six hundred Germans and German Americans interned at Crystal City, among them two of the most outspoken Nazi sympathizers in the camp.[55] After their departure, Joseph O'Rourke, the officer in charge, was eager to rid himself of Karl Kolb as well, and once more, Camp Algiers served as a place to dispose of a "problem" internee. By that date, a majority of the Jews who had arrived at Algiers in February 1943 had been released. Nonetheless, when Kolb and his family were transferred, he telegrammed the INS headquarters in Philadelphia, protesting that his transfer was "unacceptable" due to the "racially mixed couples" still at the New Orleans facility, a term which could have applied to the remaining Jews as well as other Germans married to Jews and other non-Aryans, among them Latin Americans.[56]

There were, in fact, many such "mixed marriages" among the internees at Algiers and other US detention facilities across the country, including that of Rodolfo Manzoni and his Nicaraguan-born wife, Eva Velázquez.[57] Although the details in Manzoni's file are few, we know he was born in Orleans, France, in 1899 and was an Italian citizen, one of the approximately fifty Italians who joined the ranks of German and Japanese enemy aliens from Latin America held at Algiers. Manzoni was a pianist and the director of an orchestra in León, Nicaragua, birthplace of the famed Latin American *modernista* poet Rubén Darío.

Picked up by Nicaraguan police on December 11, 1941, Manzoni was likely held along with other German and Italian nationals at the notorious "El Hormiguero" jail until a concentration camp could be established. *La Prensa* and other Nicaraguan newspapers covered the story of their apprehension on the front page.[58] A detention facility was later established at Quinta Eitzen by the country's president, Anastasio Somoza García, who had seized the property from its elderly German-born owner, Ulrich (Ulrico) Eitzen.

Manzoni's State Department file shows he wasn't processed by the INS at Camp Kenedy until May 25, 1943. His wife, Eva, from Diriamba, Nicaragua, was twenty-two at the time of her husband's apprehension, about half his age. From Camp Kenedy, Manzoni wrote to Eva in Managua with a furious tale of how he ended up in internment, rendered into English by a government censor:

> I was on my way toward San Rafael del Sur when I fell into the hands of a Curate without soul and not worthy of belonging to the Catholic Church. Father Obando, abductor of women, has abandoned the Cassock for a woman of evil life. This priest, who was pardoned by Monseñor, went to San Rafael del Sur. It is obvious to all that this woman moved into his house pretending to be his sister. The Curate, who calls himself a liberal, conspired with the Conservatives in order to get what he wanted from Mr. Gral. Somoza. Personal vengeance caused him to denounce me for something I never committed.[59]

As in Eugenia Mateju's story below, Manzoni's missive claims that his internment was the result of a personal vendetta, resulting from his outing of a corrupt priest looking for favors from Somoza rather than any political activity on his part. Despite his indignant protest, Manzoni found himself incarcerated first in Nicaragua and then in the United States. He requested his wife join him in detention, and she arrived at Camp Seagoville on October 28, 1943.

Things didn't seem to improve for the maestro after his wife joined him in internment in Texas, however. Assistant commissioner for alien control Willard Kelly wrote to Albert Clattenburg Jr. of the Special War Problems Division explaining, "A report received from the Officer in Charge at Seagoville indicates that this couple desires to separate, that a reconciliation appears to be hopeless and that Mrs. Manzoni desires to be returned to her home in Nicaragua. Their marital difficulties have become so acute, that it has been necessary, in order to restrain Mrs. Manzoni from assaulting her husband and other internees, to confine her in the quarantine building at Seagoville, and she is presently to be transferred from there to our station at Algiers, Louisiana."[60] While we know Kelly sought help in arranging for Eva's return to Nicaragua, what happened to Rodolfo or Eva afterward is not entirely clear. The American embassy in Managua indicated in a September 1944 memo that it had started deportation proceedings to return Mrs. Manzoni to Nicaragua, but according to the INS, she was by then refusing to leave the United States. Though Rodolfo Manzoni had signed a draft card at Camp Seagoville in March 1944, his documents show he was deported in May 1945—whether to Nicaragua or Italy is not evident. One final curiosity in his case is his appearance on a Registration of Foreigners and German Persecutees list dated 1947 in Salzburg. That document gathers the names of "all allied nationals and all other foreigners, German Jews, and stateless, etc., who were temporarily or permanently stationed in the community, but are no longer in residence."[61] Did Manzoni end up in one of the five displaced persons camps in Salzburg? Or was he in Salzburg of his own volition, perhaps in an attempt to return to his life in music?

Reluctantly "German"

Well before the United States entered World War II, it had agents on the ground in Latin America identifying individuals they believed might pose a threat, however threadbare the evidence. Colorful characters seemed to attract an extra measure of suspicion. Volatile or indignant reactions seemed to only make thing worse for such people. For example, Eugenia Mateju, apprehended in Quito, Ecuador, on January 19, 1944, was born in Vienna in 1904 but claimed to be Czech and had traveled to Ecuador on a Czech passport in 1936.[62] Identified as a "merchandise agent," Mateju's enemy alien name file indicates she was deported from Salinas, Ecuador, aboard the army transfer vessel *Madison* on January 21, 1944, and received by the INS in New Orleans on February 10 of that year. A manifest record for the port of New Orleans shows her arriving, nonetheless, aboard the SS *George Washington*, sailing from the Canal Zone, and lists her occupation as "domestic." In the confusion that frequently accompanied the identification of an enemy alien, officials listed her nationality as Czechoslovakian on the manifest but classified her "race or people" as German. On this question, as on finding herself interned, Mateju was adamant: "What right have they, or who has the right to put me out of Ecuador? I am not German, my country is not at war either with Ecuador or the U.S.A."[63]

Suspicions about Mateju show up in the "FBI Files on Communism in Ecuador in the 1940s" under the heading "Other Individuals whose Expulsion would be Desirable." That now declassified report bearing FBI director J. Edgar Hoover's name (there is no visible date on the document, but it likely dates to 1942 or earlier) acknowledges, "This list is incomplete at the present time, but it is meant to include those, not thus far proved especially dangerous, whose expulsion would be an advantage. The enlarging of and proving of this list, is, of course, the work of the immediate future."[64] To Mateju's chagrin, that "work" was apparently accomplished to the FBI's satisfaction, though the tale she told of how she became an enemy alien suggests she was apprehended on the basis of a personal matter involving yet another corrupt official.[65]

After entering the port of New Orleans, Mateju was sent to Camp Seagoville, Texas; at some later point she was transferred to Algiers, making her one of the few single women and one of the last detainees to be held there. In the spring of 1944, she wrote to no less a personage than the Ecuadorian president at the time, Dr. Carlos Arroyo Del Río. In the English translation of that missive, which passed through the censors' hands on March 21 of that year, Mateju dramatically declared,

> Just as Zola in the case of Dreyfuss, some years ago, shouted to the whole world demanding justice do I call out with my utmost strength: Help me, I am innocent! Believe my friends but not my enemies. About two years ago, Mr. IGNACIO DAVALO, who had seen me at the Government Palace, called me ten times on the telephone warning me that Your Excellency had left my case entirely under his supervision. Since he could not obtain that which he sought from me as a woman—and he went about it in a low and detestable way . . . he became my enemy, and together with other enemies placed me in my present position.[66]

Mateju's not-so-subtle hints that her failure to perform sexual favors was the cause for her enemy alien status is unusual in the documented testimonies of internees, though perhaps less rare in practice. Ignacio Davalos is in fact named in the aforementioned FBI report as "Chief of the Secret Police" in the country. Nonetheless, it seems Mateju and her pre-#metoo complaint weren't taken very seriously. Officials in the United States summarized her case by saying, "The alien is a gushy, protesting and slightly psychopathic woman judging from reports as well as the tenor of the mass of letters she has been writing. She is single but has a fiancé in Ecuador concerning whom she gets rather flowery."

Although her file does not indicate if Arroyo Del Río actually received her letter, Mateju continued to protest her internment vociferously all the way to the top, both in Ecuador and in the United States.

Proof of this is provided in the July 19, 1945, letter Mateju wrote to Edward Ennis, chief of the Enemy Alien Control Unit, inquiring "when you intend to send me back to my second homeland, my beloved Ecuador. It is already two months since the war ended and my nervousness has reached the highest point." Mateju believed she had been removed "by force and without any right," and admonished Ennis, "Let me remind you, Mr. Director, that I am a Czechoslovackian [sic] democrat; I am forced to live with my enemies, with the enemies of my country, and I who have never known a Nazi in my life, am thrown among them by force!" Defending her honor, drawing on her faith, and even making a case for the sacrament of matrimony, she declared:

> My honor as a democrat and a Czech must be vindicated. I repeat a thousand times: I am innocent! And my unshakeable faith in the justice of the Lord is the foundation of my conscience, which is clear. Our merciful God has all of us in His hands: the innocent and the guilty.... I am the fiancée of a noble, honest and highly democratic Ecuadoran, and he also has all his Ecuadoran papers in order, just as I have my Czechoslovakian papers in order. Can there be anybody or anything that can prevent the sacred sacrament of matrimony?[67]

This emotional appeal did not have its intended effect, however. Officials did not trust Mateju's anti-Nazi stance, as she was ostensibly "known to have close friends among Nazis." Whether this was true or not, her file also raises other uncertainties regarding her politics, as she reportedly "became openly and violently anti-Jewish although she was stated to be of half Jewish blood." Ultimately, though, the United States found the evidence insufficient to continue holding her, and Mateju was released from alien enemy proceedings in January 1946. The INS reported her departure from the United States for her "beloved Ecuador" on April 3 of that year.

The question of "German" citizenship was a problem in the case of Gustavo Mathies, too.[68] Born in Santa Ana, El Salvador, in 1901, Gustavo had, at his father's insistence, attended high school in Germany from 1913 to 1919 and then returned to a rural life as a coffee grower in his country of birth. Married to a Salvadoran woman and the father of eight daughters, ranging from one to eighteen years of age, he was deported to the United States from El Salvador on October 25, 1943, processed at Algiers on November 12 of that year, and sent on to Camp Kenedy.

Despite spending several of his formative years in Germany at his father's insistence, Mathies found it difficult to deal with the Nazi culture some in the US camps espoused. In a censored letter written in Spanish dated January 24, 1944, directed to a contact in El Salvador, he wrote:

> The American authorities are very nice to us, so we are very thankful to them. The difficulty is this, living among the race of Germans, they think they are our gods and look upon those who aren't pure Germans with contempt, thus making life hard for them. These sons of —— don't realize that we are suffering because of them. I have never hated my fellow-men, but today I'm very sorry I'm living among this condemned race who can only be ranked among the devils. The bad part is that they don't want us to work. Since I need a few cents, I worked several days. They consider this wrong and call us traitors.[69]

Although interned at large from Camp Kenedy, Mathies's paperwork finds him back at Camp Algiers in December 1944, where the government had plans to repatriate him to Germany. In fact, his file indicates he was "en route to Ellis Island for repatriation," but that he requested in a September 4, 1945, telegram that "his deportation be cancelled in view of his being a Salvadoran by birth and having a family in El Salvador."[70] Mathies finally departed by air for El Salvador on December 9, 1945, more than two years after he was deported, according to his State Department records, long enough for the youngest of his eight daughters to have had her third birthday.

Contemporary *Conversos*

Besides the difficulty in determining who was a Nazi, or even a German, questions arose around who among the internees was a Jew. Those born into Jewish families who had converted to Christianity and other religions, often referred to in Spanish as *conversos*, were subject to distrust from Jews and non-Jews alike.[71] Ironically, some internees whose Jewishness was in doubt in the Americas had only recently escaped Nazi Europe, where they had suffered persecution and in some cases imprisonment as Jews, regardless of whether they practiced Judaism or were married to Jews. Siegfried Meyer, apprehended in the Dominican Republic, was a German physician born in Posen, Germany, in 1898. According to a confidential memo dated February 21, 1946, Meyer claimed that "he was deprived of German citizenship in February 1940 because of his Jewish descent," that he came to the Dominican Republic as a refugee from Germany in 1939, and once in the Caribbean, operated a photography shop, until he received permission in February 1941 to practice as a doctor.[72]

On the surface, Meyer's story is much like that of other internees at Algiers, featuring forced displacement from a site in Latin America that had recently become a new home for a family fleeing war, the discouraging prospect of detention for the duration of the war upon arrival in the United States, initial separation from family members followed by a later reunification with them in internment, attempts to demonstrate the injustice of one's detention to government personnel and aid organizations, eventual release to internment at large, and finally, removal from the status of enemy alien. But underneath this by now familiar narrative, the details of Siegfried Meyer's situation were unique on several counts. For one thing, he was the one deported to the United States in March 1942, even though the embassy suspected his wife, Irmgard, to be the member of the family most actively involved in pro-Nazi activities in the Dominican Republic.

Picked up by police on December 11, 1941, Meyer spent time in Dominican detention before traveling to the United States aboard the army transfer vessel *Algonquin*. He was processed by the INS in New Orleans on May 24, 1942, and sent to Camp Kenedy, where after several months, he sent a request to the Swiss legation, the diplomatic entity representing German enemy aliens, asking it be forwarded to the American Committee for Christian Refugees: "Please, inform the committee that Rev. H. Singer from the American Board of Missions to the Jews, Station A, Box 10, Brooklyn, NY, certainly will collaborate as to the financial assistance of my family so that the expenses might be splitted [sic]."[73] It appears the Meyers had been helped by both Jewish and Christian relief organizations, and Siegfried thought it judicious for the two organizations to jointly help his family still in the Dominican Republic while he was interned. With this aid, Meyer hoped to keep his family in the Caribbean rather than in US detention, even though his wife, after a yearlong separation, felt conditions for her and the family were unbearable: "In her last letter, dated Nov. 22, my wife wrote that after all the miseries she had to endure during this year of my detention she feels unable to continue, so that she is determined to quit and to follow me to the Detention Camp. I prefer to have my family left in Santo Domingo. The only possibility to avoid the transfer of my family is to grant a permanent assistance which, of course, I shall pay back as soon as I can." Whatever happened after that, Meyer's wife, Irmgard, joined him in 1943. The couple was interned at Camp Algiers until early 1945 along with their two teenage children, Francis Ludwig, born in 1926, and his sister, Ursel-Renate, born in 1928.

The most troubling aspect of the Meyers' case for US officials was not any behavior or political stance on Siegfried's part but rather Irmgard's connection with Karl Hertel, "the leading Dominican Nazi and one of the stalwarts of the German Colony."[74] Exactly what was the relationship between Mrs. Meyer and Hertel? Was it chiefly political or economic? Born in 1901 in Bernstadt, Schlesien, Irmgard Meyer claimed Aryan blood but asserted she was deprived of German citizenship by a February 3, 1940, decree criminalizing her marriage to Siegfried. Though Siegfried had converted to Christianity in 1929, theirs was still considered a "mixed" marriage, a case of *Rassenschande*. Conditions for the family disintegrated rapidly in the 1930s: "She admitted having joined the Arbeitsfront in Germany while her husband was in concentration camp and explains she had to do that in order to obtain a job with which she could support herself and her children. She also admitted the truth of the report that her son had been a member of the Hitler Youth. She explained that he joined in 1934, and was forced out of the organization by the middle of the next year."[75]

As Evan Bukey notes in his 2011 study *Jews and Intermarriage in Nazi Austria*, "Stigmatized by neighbors, Aryan relatives, and Nazi activists, those families found it hard to cope with capricious intrusions that severely disrupted family life, pitted relatives against each other and raised unanswerable questions about religious, racial, and national identity." Many Jewish mothers were obliged to watch as their "sons became enthusiastic members of the Hitler Youth and later the German Wehrmacht, especially those who distinguished themselves in combat." Both Jewish spouses and those married to them were dismissed from civil service and public-sector jobs; subsequent regulations prohibited these persons from pursuing careers in medicine, law, and journalism. "Worse, the regime harassed children in schools, interfered in custody disputes, and put pressure on Aryan partners to divorce their Jewish wives or husbands."[76]

Indeed, according to Irmgard Meyer's own account preserved in her husband's State Department name file, she was approached by the Gestapo to divorce Siegfried but refused to do so, instead leaving Germany in 1939 and rejoining her husband who had been "kicked out after a two-year [prison] term for 'racial contamination.'" With the assistance of the Christian Refugee Commission, the family left for the Dominican Republic in July 1939. It was on the transatlantic voyage that they met Hertel, who offered Mrs. Meyer a job as a secretary in his export-import business, pointing out how hard it would be for her husband to establish himself professionally in their new home. "She claims that she worked for Hertel because she did not speak any Spanish when she arrived in the Dominican Republic, and would have had great difficulty in obtaining any other sort of job."[77] Thus, although Irmgard "learned Hertel's true position" four or five months later, she continued to work for him for an additional thirteen or fourteen months, claiming her husband was ill and had to wait until February 1941 to receive a license to practice medicine. When he did, she reportedly quit her job the following day, suggesting the arrangement with Hertel was chiefly a matter of economic survival.

Even after leaving the position, though, Irmgard's reputation remained tainted by her association with Hertel, and that stain extended to her person as well. "It is the impression of the Board that there was more between Mrs. Meyer and Hertel than business and Nazi party interests, and this may have had a good deal to do with her continuing her work for him and her willingness to do Nazi party work," documents in her husband's file explained. Thus, when Mrs. Meyer and her children joined Siegfried in detention, her very status as an enemy alien or voluntary internee remained in question. A handwritten note in her INS paperwork signed in Miami on Mar 16, 1943, clarified that she "is a deportation case, not a voluntary detainee," though other forms identify her as choosing internment to join her husband.

Was Mrs. Meyer pro-Nazi, having joined the German Labor front, having allowed her son to join the Hitler Youth, and having worked for Karl Hertel? All these elements constituted black marks for US government personnel, as well as for many of the internees at Algiers. Her husband's file quotes a 1946 letter from the National Refugee Service saying, "The Jewish refugees resented the presence of the Meyers, being convinced that the son had been in the Hitler Jugend. They also knew of the reports that Mrs. Meyer was rather pro-Nazi in sympathies."[78] Given this distrust, things weren't easy for Siegfried, either: "Meyer's adoption of the Christian faith in 1929 might have been the reason for the Jewish refugees at least to have it in for him. He apparently was definitely not welcome among the Jewish refugees at Algiers." Nonetheless, camp personnel were eventually convinced of Meyer's anti-Nazi stance and remarked on his good behavior, as he "was at first something of an agitator on behalf of the 'rights and privileges' of the internees at Algiers, but later discontinued such practices. His associates were without exception pro-Allied and the reporting officer believed that Meyer was himself sincerely anti-German and pro-Allied."

Thus, "After an initial period of friction with the Jewish refugees at Algiers and of agitation with the camp authorities, the Meyers succeeded in impressing the immigration officials in contact with them of their true devotion to the cause of the United Nations," their file states. In December 1944, a reporting officer—probably Raymond Bunker—confirmed he was also convinced from many conversations over a period of twenty-one months that Mrs. Meyer was "truly opposed to everything German," held a "bitter personal enmity towards the Nazis and Germans," and was "very happy" about her son's induction into the US Army. The officer added that other internees from the Dominican Republic had confirmed that Mrs. Meyer had been forced to continue working for Hertel because of the family's scant economic resources.[79]

The Meyers were held at Algiers Detention Station from March 1943 until March 1945, giving son Francis ("Frank") time to graduate from high school in New Orleans. A Special War Problems file on Irmgard Meyer contains a summary of the hearing that took place in New York on March 5, 1946, prior to her eventual release from enemy alien proceedings. The members of the hearing board included Louis Henkin, Daniel G. Tenney, and James D. Bell. Meyer was represented by George G. Dix, who began by stating:

> The alien submits to this hearing without conceding that this Board has any jurisdiction to hear or determine the merits of the issues alleged to be pending before this Board, and without conceding that the Secretary of State of the United States has any jurisdiction over her or any right in law or otherwise to determine the issues in this proceeding; and without waiving any rights that the alien has, either in a proceeding now pending in the United States District Court for the Southern District of New York or in any subsequent proceeding which the alien may be advised to institute in such court; and insisting that the only competent tribunal which has the right to hear or determine any charges against her are the duly constituted courts of the country of Santo Domingo [sic].[80]

The interchange between the board and Mrs. Meyer offers us an unusual opportunity to "hear" her perspective of the events that transpired from the moment of her emigration from Europe to the Caribbean to her eventual deportation to internment in the United States, beginning with her husband's case:

> *Hearing Board:* Was he charged with any crime?
> *Irmgard Meyer:* Rassenschande.[81]
> *Hearing Board:* Were you ever in prison in Germany?
> *Meyer:* No.
> *Hearing Board:* Didn't they consider it a crime for you to marry your husband?
> *Meyer:* We married in 1925.[82]

When asked how her son Frank—now in the US Army—could have joined the Hitler Youth, she replied, "My husband was the only Jew in that little village at that time. . . . You see, that was in January, 1934. We thought we might have the biggest difficulties if we said no."

> *Hearing Board:* After you learned that Hertel was leader of the Nazi Party, did you continue to be on good terms with him socially, as well as working for him?
> *Meyer:* Yes, I was, because he always was kind to me and he helped my family.
> *Henken:* I assume you were opposed to the racial laws of Hitler?
> *Meyer:* Yes, I am.
> *Hearing Board:* What do you think of the rest of National Socialism?
> *Meyer:* It was just a gathering of Germans.
> *Hearing Board:* I am talking now about Germany; leaving aside what Hitler had done to the Jews. What do you think of Hitler?
> *Meyer:* Hitler was, so far as I understand, an insane man.
> *Hearing Board:* Did you think so when you were in Germany?
> *Meyer:* Yes.
> *Hearing Board:* Then you did not approve of his regime?
> *Meyer:* No, I did not.
> *Hearing Board:* You didn't realize that it was rather strange that the wife of a man who had been in concentration camps in Germany and forced to leave the country would get work for the Nazi Party in Central America?
> *Meyer:* I felt very bad about it, and in fact, I had a breakdown in 1940.

Hearing Board: *But you continued to work?*
Meyer: No, after this, I didn't write any more letters.
Hearing Board: After your breakdown.
Meyer: Yes.

Irmgard Meyer's hearing prior to her release from enemy alien proceedings reveals the extreme turmoil experienced by individuals and refugee families interned as part of the Enemy Alien Control Program in Latin America. It shows that turmoil was both external and internal, encompassing practical issues of everyday survival as well as deeper emotional and moral struggles. In the case of the Meyers and many others, questions about who was an ally and who an enemy were not as clear-cut as the orders for apprehension, deportation, and detention would suggest, and the burden of proving one's allegiance seemed always to fall on the internee, whereas declaring someone an alien enemy occurred quickly and often arbitrarily, based on rumor or innuendo or a perceived opportunity to profit from another's detention.

In the Meyers' case, the recommendation for internment at large "included detailed information about Meyer's desire to serve the United States in his capacity and his delight that his son was being inducted into the United Sates Army."[83] For the US government, another essential proof of the family's allegiance was the "Routine Inquiry Concerning Wish to Be Repatriated" forms on which both Siegfried and Ingmar indicated their desire not to be repatriated. Frank Meyer was drafted into the army on January 11, 1945, perhaps before finishing high school in the spring. His parents were released from Camp Algiers that same year. A city directory for 1945 lists his father as a resident bacteriologist in a hospital in Logansport, Indiana, where the couple was finally released from enemy alien proceedings on April 18, 1946. What happened to Siegfried Meyer after that date is not apparent. In any case, his record suggests that his flight to the Dominican Republic, and even his subsequent internment in the United States were preferable alternatives to incarceration or death, both common fates for intermarried Jewish men at the hands of the Nazi terror apparatus between 1938 and 1945. His *Mischlinge* or "mixed-race" children also avoided an assault from the Nazis that ranged from excluding them from schools and universities to expulsion from the workplace, arguing for mass sterilization, and in some cases, deporting them to extermination centers.[84]

Irmgard Meyer remarried and became a US citizen in 1954; she is buried at Woodlawn Cemetery in Santa Monica, California, under a tombstone that reads,

"In Memory of our Most Beloved Mother, Grandmother and Great-Grand mother."[83] High school class valedictorian Frank Meyer reenlisted after his initial release from the US Army in 1946, later establishing a practice as a physician in California, where he died in 1989.[86]

Suffering the Consequences

However bright the final outcome of the Latin American enemy alien program for individual detainees and families, their stories reveal an embarrassing degree of inefficiency and incomprehension in the selection process and unnecessary suffering as a consequence of that process. As Friedman notes, while the policy was based on a genuine desire for security against a real enemy, in practice "the expulsion and incarceration of Germans from Latin America neither hurt Nazi Germany nor helped the U.S. war effort. Its lack of effectiveness was due to two fundamental and familiar flaws: inadequate understanding of this region of the world, reflected in poor intelligence; and the use of ethnic or national identity, rather than individual actions, as a marker to establish dangerousness and threat."[87]

Olaf Mueller, born in Altenburg in 1905 to a German father and American mother, had lived for many years in Canada when he and his wife, Theodora, left Vancouver in August 1939 aboard the Hamburg-America line on a trip to Germany.[88] En route to their destination, the couple was removed from the ship at a port in El Salvador, where they remained and a child was born to them. In October 1943, however, Mueller was apprehended by Salvadoran authorities after his wife and child decided to return to Germany. He disclaimed membership in any political organization and executed a petition for nonrepatriation, "giving as his reasons that he has been on the Continent for 16 years, his mother was born here and he likes freedom and does not care for the European form of government. He states that he would be subject to persecution if he were now in Germany for the reason that he does not believe in the present form of government in Germany and would not hesitate to say so."[89]

Mueller also protested his detention on the grounds that he and his wife were Mennonites, a religious group espousing nonviolence and pacifism.[90] None of this appeared to sway the authorities, however. He was accused of being an associate of the German consul, of meeting with Germans in his home, of being "an oral propagandist in El Salvador" and of being paid by the German government. Ultimately, though, a hearing at Camp Kenedy in February 1944 acknowledged that "the only evidence of pro-Nazi activities or sympathies on the part of subject is contained in the Embassy report and the source is not shown."[91] Mueller's Department of Justice file is thus marked by unsubstantiated accusations and darkened by his subsequent poor health, perhaps exacerbated by mental or emotional trauma. For in a letter dated May 25, 1945, sent from the Algiers station to Willard Kelly, supervisor of the INS camp system, Mueller refers to a "breakdown" he suffered in October 1944 in Akron, Ohio, after he was interned at large there, ostensibly due to cardiac disease. At the time he composed the letter, he had been recuperating for the last five months at Camp Algiers. In other words, it seems that Mueller returned or was returned to internment from internment at large, presumably for violating the terms of this parole-style arrangement. The available documentation does not reveal the circumstances of Mueller's breakdown, but Kelly subsequently wrote to Edward Ennis, requesting he be reinstated as an internee at large and rereleased from Algiers.

Some internees put a name on the malaise of indefinite detention itself: *Gitterkrankheit* or "fence sickness." As German Americans at Fort Lincoln, a Department of Justice detention camp in Bismarck, North Dakota, explained to John Christgau, "After you've been behind barbed wire for a long time, even if you know you've done nothing wrong, a part of you begins to feel like a criminal. Once you get out, it's not something you want to talk about."[92] Eddie Friedman, a German Jew picked up in San Francisco and interned at the Fort Lincoln detention facility, said it was the same thing he had felt inside the German prison camp Sachsenhausen.[93] The US government downplayed such maladies, however. A World War II–era film praising the Crystal City internment camp in Texas as a showpiece of the successful internment effort described the hospital built there, stating, "Ills were often imaginary, traceable to detention . . . the fence . . . the loss of freedom."[94]

As might be expected, official internee records are generally mute on the causes of a documented emotional illness or distress; it's easy to see that recognizing "fence sickness" as a *real* ill would expose prickly ethical or moral issues of the internment program. But perhaps it was this condition that troubled María (Emma Marie) Paschka, born in Germany in 1906. She boarded the *Cuba* with her eight-year-old daughter, Gudrun, in a location identified only as a "Central American port," arriving in the United States on November 12, 1943.[95] Her husband, Max Richard Paschka, apprehended by the government of Costa Rica in February 1942, had arrived in New Orleans nineteen months earlier aboard the bulging *Florida*, proceeding to camps in Fort Blanding, Florida, and Kenedy, Texas. Max apparently was transferred to Crystal City in anticipation of his wife and child joining him, and it seems the family was together there until they were transferred to Camp Algiers in 1944.

No reason is given in an October 4, 1945, report indicating that Maria had been taken from the Algiers Detention Station to the US Marine Hospital, where her condition was diagnosed as "Psychoneurotic Reaction, Anxiety State, Class 'A.'"[96] What was the cause of Mrs. Paschka's breakdown? While post-traumatic stress disorder did not exist as a clinical diagnosis in the 1940s, Mrs. Paschka's case might now be viewed as such. In the early twentieth century, Swiss researcher Eduard Stierlin, considered the first researcher of "disaster psychology," had concluded, "Doctors are not sufficiently aware that emotions can give rise to serious psychoneurotic long-term effects, while laymen as a rule equate psychic causes of illness with simulation. Patients thus not only receive inadequate treatment but also have little chance to get adequate compensation."[97] The government records provide no further information on María Paschka's condition or recovery, indicating only the family's May 22, 1946, departure date for Costa Rica, when her daughter, Gudrun, was about ten years old.

Rocket Fritz

Though Jews on the run from Nazism and individuals without access to economic resources may have felt the most vulnerable within the US internment apparatus, wealth and status (and even a royal or noble title, as we will see further in chapter 5) were no safeguards against internment or a long detention for enemy aliens deemed dangerous. Among an internee population that included physicians, lawyers, writers, a musician, a butcher, and a statistician, Baron Fritz von Opel left behind a high-profile life as a pioneer inventor, sportsman, and yachtsman before ending up at Algiers.

Born in 1899 in Rüsselsheim, Germany, and heir of the Opel carmaker family (his grandfather was known as the "Henry Ford of Germany"), Opel was the first person to travel in a rocket-propelled car in 1928, earning him the nickname "Rocket Fritz." But that life ended, or was at least interrupted for several years, when he was arrested by the FBI on February 26, 1942, along with his wife, the German actress Margot Sellnick, and two unnamed Hungarians, at his Palm Beach residence. According to news stories, the agency found guns and ammunition in Opel's possession, a violation of wartime policy on the basis of which agents declared the group potentially dangerous alien enemies.[98]

Before traveling to the United States in 1940, Opel and his wife had secured passports from the tiny country of Liechtenstein, nestled between Switzerland and Austria. The US government looked askance at this, assuming the couple had bought their citizenship in the neutral country. In May 1940, they had been detained by the British in Gibraltar for sixteen days, another black mark against them. Privilege and affluence were of little help, and press accounts from the era declared that the Baroness von Opel suffered a nervous breakdown after the couple's apprehension in Florida.

While a 2017 retrospective in *The Palm Beach Post* claimed the Opels would wait out the war in a New Jersey camp, Anderson's list of pro-Nazis, anti-Nazis, and Jews at Algiers shows that Fritz von Opel was in New Orleans, not New Jersey, as of late 1944.[99] And though Anderson appears not to have checked any of the columns for Opel, a letter Opel wrote at Algiers after a nasty spat with Kurt Ludecke left few doubts as to how he felt about being summarily clumped or dumped with pro-Nazis, if only on the basis of suspicion.

On August 1, 1944, Opel sent a letter from the alien detention station in New Orleans to his representative at the legation of Switzerland in Washington, DC, hoping to provide the background for an altercation he had recently had with Ludecke "so that you don't gain the impression that my prison psychosis get the better of me and made me loose [sic] my usual attitude."[100] He described his antagonist as "a Nazi party member for 15 years" and the "official organizer of the Nazi party in USA," explaining, "After the nazis had come to power he returned to Germany, for no other reason but to share in the loot and spoils. However his way of extorting money from several Jewish people mispleased even the not too soft hearted nazis and they put him twice in a concentration camp." Opel assessed Ludecke's 1937 book *I Knew Hitler* as "in its essence . . . open praise of Hitler and nazism, though somewhat sarcastic towards Goering, who had thrown him in the concentration camp." He explained how Ludecke had been elected spokesman at Camp Algiers after the arrival of "4 fullfledged nazis" who enlisted the help of "two jewish families, who were debased enough to kiss the boot who had kicked them out of their country. As I and our minority group of 11 people refused to cooperate with this nazi gangster, he started to make speeches insult me [sic]." When Opel sought the help of camp administrator Raymond Bunker to quell the verbal abuse, Ludecke reportedly took his vituperation to a baser level, and Opel admitted he retaliated and "slapped him right and left, unfortunately as it otherwise only happens in comedies."

Opel's chief concern in the letter, as it turns out, was not resolving the conflict with Ludecke, as that had been "settled in all fairness," but rather making clear to officials that he refused to be represented by a Nazi and, finally, to clear his name in advance of a pending decision regarding his case. His wife had ascertained in a recent conversation that she had made an August 12 appointment with Edward Ennis, "who promised a definite action of his department for this date." The last two sentences of Opel's letter put the issue of classification even before that of release itself: "I have informed Mr. Ennis already several weeks ago, that I am less interested in a release than in a complete statement containing the reasons for my detention. It is more than unbearable for me to be in any way connected with Nazism, what is implicitly done by judging a person potentially dangerous." While Opel was finally released in 1945, presumably with the Department of Justice's endorsement, Ennis, for his part, would apparently continue to wonder about the enemy alien classification protocols and Opel's case in particular for decades to come.

For on December 20, 1972, Miriam Feingold sat down with Ennis in his New York law office to conduct an interview. While the topic was Japanese American relocation, Feingold also asked Ennis about the criteria used to name enemy aliens in general, to which he replied,

> The evidence which was used in these alien enemy hearings were really the reports of the Federal Bureau of Investigation upon the enemy associations of a particular enemy. . . . But the kind of evidence—take, for example, German army officers, like a man who later after the war became a friend of mine, Fritz von Opel of the Opel Motor people. . . . I happened to know Mr. Opel very well after the war, and I think we may have made a mistake, that his sentiments, in spite of the fact that he was a visitor here, were not with the German Nazis. But it is very difficult to determine those things in time of war.[101]

As in many other cases, eventual release from detention was not the end of the story. Opel's property holdings in the United States had been confiscated as part of his detention, leading to a prolonged battle to recuperate them in which the former detainee claimed that the US government had seized about $2.6 million in gold coins from a New York safe deposit vault in 1936. In 1950, Florida senator Claude Pepper introduced a bill to block Opel's deportation, portraying the former internee as a victim of the Nazis and a refugee in the United States. Regarding his potential danger as a Nazi or pro-Nazi during the war, one of the attorneys, George A. Salley, retorted that "Fritz Von Opel is about as much a Nazi as Franklin Roosevelt."[102] Author Scott Nehmer paints Fritz as an "anti-Nazi pacifist," in contrast to his brother Wilhelm, who had received an award from Hitler in May 1941 for his service to the war economy.[103] Senator Pepper's bill ultimately failed and Opel was deported, spending the remainder of his life in St. Moritz.

The consequences of declaring persons "alien enemies" based on superficial factors and flimsy evidence multiplied as named enemies' family members were caught up in the internment saga, usually as voluntary internees. By the middle of the war, certain government officials recognized that the initial classification systems responsible for shuttling men, women, and children into internment— whether in the United States or the other American republics—were hopelessly flawed. In July 1943, Attorney General Francis Biddle issued a "stinging memorandum" to J. Edgar Hoover, directing the FBI to cease using its detention lists and danger classifications. "It is now clear to me that the classification system is utterly unreliable," Biddle wrote, and "the evidence used for the purpose of making these classifications was inadequate, the standards applied to the evidence for the purpose of making the classification were defective; and finally, the notion that it is possible to make a valid determination of how dangerous a person is . . . without reference to time, environment, and other relevant circumstances is impractical, unwise, and dangerous."[104] Given Biddle's own lack of confidence in the process of assessing loyalty or disloyalty before internment, it's clear that the job of determining the allegiances and potential danger of an internee *behind* the fence, as Anderson sought to do in November 1944 at Algiers, was also inevitably subject to error. As explored in the next chapter, perhaps no aspect of the Latin American enemy alien control program better highlights governmental agents' misplaced zeal, on the one hand, and lack of historical and cultural knowledge, on the other, than the inclusion of approximately eighty Jews among the ranks of German nationals suspected of pro-Nazi allegiance and activities. In 1943, Camp Algiers would become the temporary home to the majority of those Jews (some of whose stories are featured in this chapter), even if its reputation as an "anti-Nazi" camp would later come into question.

CHAPTER 3

Incarceration or a Welcome Refuge?
The Panama Jews at Camp Algiers

Camp Stories

Benno Ascher was the first name on the list of a large group of Jewish detainees who arrived at Camp Algiers, Louisiana, on February 11, 1943. He was accompanied by his wife, Clara, and their daughter, Steffi, born to the couple in Germany in 1922.[1] Like many others in the group who arrived in New Orleans on that date, Ascher had been apprehended in Panama in the second week of December 1941, immediately following the attack on Pearl Harbor. Records from the Departments of State and Justice show that after a stay at Camp Balboa, Ascher, then fifty-six years old, was just one of the many detainees to board the US Army transport *Florida*, which left Colón, Panama, on April 2, 1942. Ascher's wife and daughter were also on board as "voluntary" deportees. As the caption from an Associated Press photo from that period documents, enemy aliens boarded the *Florida* and other ships under the supervision of US military police and the ships' movements were kept a close secret, ostensibly "to protect the enemies from their own submarines" (figure 3.1).

The Aschers were processed through the Algiers immigration station on April 9, 1942; Benno went from there to Camp Stringtown, a subprison of the Oklahoma State Penitentiary, while his wife and daughter traveled west to an intern-

FIGURE 3.1. "Enemy Aliens Leave Panama for the U.S." Photo dated April 6, 1942, shows people leaving the Canal Zone under the watchful eye of military police, "to protect the enemies from their own submarines," according to the original caption. Associated Press photo, used with permission.

ment facility at Seagoville, Texas.[2] The family was finally reunited in September of that year at Seagoville, where they would remain until their transfer to New Orleans in the winter of 1943. None of these sites was the setting of Ascher's first experience of "camp" life, however. That occurred before his arrival in the United States. Documents in his files indicate that in early 1939, he was released from Buchenwald with the stipulation that he leave the country immediately.

Like several other Algiers detainees, Ascher was a European concentration camp survivor who ended up in Panama when it was the only country to provide him with a visa and a way out of his homeland when he became stateless under Nazi racial laws. As we picture him confined once again, this time on US soil, many questions emerge. How could refugees who had fled persecution under Hitler be suspected of supporting the Nazis and placed in detention based on that suspicion? What role did antisemitism play in the apprehension and detention of the small contingent of Jewish refugees deported from Central and South America? How could they be incarcerated in Latin America or in the United States alongside fellow European nationals who openly supported the Third Reich and its Final Solution? If US officials recognized the special status of such refugees, even recording their Jewish identity on some ship manifests of the enemy alien transports, why did they make no provision for that distinct status in the administration of the internment process? Why did most of the Jewish detainees (as well as non-Jews) never receive an explanation for their arrests, even after months or years behind barbed wire? Why was there space for Jewish refugees in enemy alien internment camps but not in refugee camps in the United States, with the sole exception of Fort Ontario, a camp in New York State, where over a thousand Europeans fleeing Nazi-occupied territories finally found a haven in 1944?[3]

Underlying these confounding queries is another more central question that relates to the larger story of global Jewish survival in the World War II era: Did the Latin American component of the US enemy alien internment program present detained Jews with a welcome refuge and a path to US citizenship, as some newspapers of the era proclaimed? Or did it unjustly subject to a form of incarceration many individuals already traumatized by their own displacement and that of their loved ones still in danger in Axis-held territory? The life stories that emerge from the paper trail of apprehension and internment suggest the program ultimately signified *both* an experience the Jewish detainees considered an irrational and unjust form of imprisonment *and* an eventual throughway to a new life in the United States.

Certainly, the United States was by no means the only country to enact wartime policies that enfolded Jews into programs controlling enemy aliens. Thousands of Jews were sent to internment camps in parts of the world far from Nazi-controlled Europe, including Great Britain, Australia, and Canada.[4] The scale of the Jewish internees' story must also be taken into account: the small number of Jews from Latin America—only about eighty in total—is dwarfed by the thousands of Japanese (some 112,000 in the United States alone), Germans (probably 11,000 at most), and Italians (more than 1,800) the United States housed behind barbed wire as civilian detainees during World War II.

But what the story of Jews sent from Latin America to US internment camps lacks in numbers it makes up for in paradox and contradiction. The centerpiece of the limited bibliography on the topic is Harvey Strum's essay "Jewish Internees in the American South, 1942–1945," published in the *American Jewish*

Archives in 1990. Max Paul Friedman's *Nazis and Good Neighbors,* based on research in several Latin American countries as well as the United States and Germany, also includes details of the Jewish internees within the larger narrative of the Latin American Enemy Alien Control Program. News articles published in wartime by the Jewish Telegraphic Agency occasionally mentioned aspects of life in the camps for the Jewish cohort, such as conflicts with pro-Nazi internees, opportunities for religious observance, and eventual release. Archives for aid organizations such as the National Refugee Service and the Joint Distribution Committee (JDC), explored further in chapter 6, also help us put a face on the Jewish internee experience, especially in these NGOs' lists of individuals and families it helped with camp transfers, hearings, release petitions, and parole or "internment at large." While the absence of a full list of internees at Camp Algiers through the entire period of its operation limits avenues of research regarding the entire population that passed through its doors, lists from the NRS and the JDC provide resources specific to Jews interned there.

The surprisingly prominent role of the Algiers quarantine station in the unusual story of the Jewish Latin American detainees emerges in many of these primary and secondary documents. For example, a Jewish Telegraphic Agency news bulletin from April 15, 1943, notes: "A group of Jewish refugees from Axis countries who reached British Honduras and were sent from there to the United States for internment as enemy aliens, have now been released from the internment camp in Seagoville, Texas, through the efforts of the National Refugee Service, it was announced here today. . . . Another group of fifty refugees still confined in Camp Algiers, an alien detention station near New Orleans, will observe Passover in their camp at services arranged by the National Refugee Service."[5] The congregation of fifty Jewish detainees at Algiers in spring of 1943, constituting more than half of all those deported from Latin America, points to the camp's erstwhile reputation as a "Camp of the Innocents" where Jews and anti-Nazis were sent for their protection when they suffered abuse in other camps.[6] While, paradoxically, the Algiers station would later house several prominent figures with close ties to the Nazis, the convening of the Latin American Jewish group there in the spring and summer of 1943 was a clear indication that the government finally recognized their status and history as different from those of the general European-born internee population. At Algiers, Benno Ascher would have found some sense of community, despite frustrations with an internment scheduled to last through the duration of the war.

Born in 1886 in Posen, Germany, Ascher hailed from one of the many territories that would change names, presiding governments, and allegiances during the first half of the twentieth century. These upheavals caused confusion around questions of country of origin and national status for wartime officials in the Americas, especially with regard to Jewish "alien enemies." The province of Posen was part of the German empire from 1871 until 1918, but Germany was obliged to return most of it to the Second Polish Republic under the Treaty of Versailles. Then, following the Nazi decree of November 25, 1941, that stripped Jews living outside Germany of their citizenship, Ascher lost his claim to nationality of any kind and was declared stateless. Luckily, he had reached Panama in May 1939 on a passport issued in Breslau, Germany, and his wife Clara, also of Posen, arrived in Panama in November of that year with their daughter.

The charge against Ascher, or more concretely, the *lack* of any specific charge, was typical of the Jews detained in Panama who ended up in detention in the United States. "No charges" is written in red ink across an August 1943 Department of Justice summary of his case, archived in his State Department name file.[7] The DOJ acknowledged his previous imprisonment at Buchenwald as well as his release from that camp. In Panama, Ascher had opened a store, hoping to generate a new source of livelihood for his family, but in 1941, a law was passed there making a five-year residence in the country necessary for owning a business. Faced with that complication, Ascher took a job as a butler while he waited expectantly for an immigration visa to the United States that never materialized.

When later questioned by the authorities, Ascher denied knowing any Nazis in Panama, except by hearsay, and insisted repeatedly that he was Jewish and therefore anti-Nazi. Five relatives and a friend in New York presented sworn affidavits in his favor. Indeed, the Justice Department summary admitted, "The only indication of any charges against Ascher is the report in the Justice file that he denied knowing the German Consul in Panama or any Nazis." How a *denial* that Ascher knew the German consul in Panama or other Nazis could be construed as a charge of subversion is one of the frustrating anomalies of his and many similar cases.

After a year and some months in camps in the United States, including a final stop at the Algiers Detention Station in New Orleans, the Aschers were released to internment at large in August 1943. The task of clearing Benno Ascher's name from the ranks of "enemy aliens" still under suspicion would take nearly two and a half years longer. The family declined voluntary departure to any other country; the Justice Department summary indicates that Benno was "very anxious to legalize his status in this country and to acquire U.S. citizenship," noting, "One acquaintance has reported that he is rather worried about the possibility of being sent out of the United States after the war is over."

Benno's fears were allayed and the proceedings against the Aschers were finally terminated on February 11, 1946, some seven years after the family left Europe for Panama. Benno Ascher was sworn in as a US citizen on May 4, 1956, in Chicago. One of his witnesses was none other than Walter Wolff, another member of the Jewish contingent at Camp Algiers and the brother of the musician Siegfried Wolff, to whose stories we return at the end of this chapter. Clara Ascher's petition for naturalization was granted in June 1956. Benno Ascher died in 1969, his wife, Clara, in 1984.

The Good Neighbor Policy Gone Awry

While Ascher himself was a concentration camp survivor, many other Jewish internees who had not spent time in the European camps had close family members who had been deported to work camps or those that came to be known as death camps, accelerating their anxious efforts to flee Nazi-controlled territories. Peter Martin Bohm was one such individual; his file shows that several close family members who had remained in Europe suffered significant persecution before the US entry into World War II. Born in Danzig, Bohm lived in Germany until 1937, except between 1924 and 1926, when he lived in Brazil.[8] He had married a Czech woman in 1936 but divorced in Berlin in 1939. A March 1941 marriage to a German woman in Panama didn't last either, and at the time of his apprehension, he was separated. But marital troubles were not his only problem, as the US Office of Naval Intelligence also believed his second wife to be a Nazi spy.

Bohm claimed not to know his estranged wife's politics and pointed out that he had traveled to Panama on a visa acquired through the efforts of a Jewish organization in Amsterdam; he assured authorities that he attended services at the synagogue regularly and wasn't engaged in any political activity. His landlord also considered him to be anti-Nazi. In Panama, he had worked as a mechanic, a carpenter, an attendant and manager at a gas station, and a chauffeur. His G-2 files, prepared by US Army military intelligence, "reveal nothing derogatory according to a memo from Major Bristol to the Panama Police." But the unsupported characterization of dangerousness in the report filed by the Office of Naval Intelligence was seemingly sufficient cause for apprehension, and "as of Nov. 28, 1942, he was interned because of his German nationality."[9]

Like that of many other internees who identified as Jews, Bohm's claim to being a stateless refugee was treated with skepticism. "He says he lost his citizenship—Danzig—by an act of German government, Nov. 25, 1941," the Justice Department summary sheet in his name file notes. But Bohm's Department of Justice file also includes his I-55 immigration form, in which fear emerges as a motivating factor for his move to Panama. To the question, "Have any of your relatives been imprisoned or persecuted for racial, religious, social, or political reasons by any foreign government, foreign government official, or foreign political party or organization?" Bohm replied, "My brother-in-law Sally Rosenbaum spent in 1939 5 months in the dreaded concentration-camp Dachau, for no other reason as being a Jew. His son, my nephew Walter Rosenbaum was likewise for the same reason arrested by the Nazis in 1939, brought to the concentration-camp Dachau and has not been released according to my last received information."[10]

Bohm's file specifies that he was apprehended by Panamanian police and delivered to the US Army on December 9, 1941, just two days after Pearl Harbor, that he was later received by the INS at New Orleans upon his entry into the United States, and that he was in detention at Algiers as of February 19, 1943. He was interned at large in July of that same year, but it took until January 31, 1946, for the Department of State to declare that "no fault has been found with his conduct." In February of that year, Jonathan Bingham of the Alien Enemy Control Section finally wrote that he was "not to be subjected to any further restraint under the Alien Enemy Act," as his case showed "insufficient evidence of dangerousness."[11]

Peter Bohm's Tennessee naturalization record shows that he married Harriet Peiser in August 1950, died on May 24, 1982, and is buried at Temple Israel Cemetery in Memphis. His name is etched in glass alongside those of other Memphis-area Holocaust survivors on a sculpture created by artist Brian Russell, displayed in the lobby of the Memphis Jewish Community Center. The Memphis Jewish Federation uses the US Holocaust Memorial Museum's definition of "Holocaust survivor," as including all who fled their homes as a result of Nazi persecution and/or occupation, not just those who experienced it firsthand.

Refugees from Oppression

Stories of numerous internees' eventual success in acquiring US citizenship, even if it took many years, suggest that the enemy alien detention program ultimately served as a form of American aid for European Jews fleeing Nazism. But the detainees had no guarantee of this outcome during their internment; in fact, most had no information as to why they had been apprehended in the first place. Named spokesman of the Jewish group at Camp Algiers, Dr. Erwin Frankel, for example, did not mince words regarding his opinion of US internment. After a visit to Camp Algiers on April 15, 1943, by Evelyn Hersey, assistant to Earl G. Harrison, director of alien registration, Frankel was emboldened to write a letter to Cordell Hull, the secretary of state. Hersey had told the group that Edward Ennis, director of the Alien Enemy Control Unit, categorized the question of the Jewish detainees' release as "extremely doubtful."[12] This gloomy forecast seems to have propelled Frankel to direct his appeal to the top brass. Speaking for "our group of 60 Jewish refugees at this station, detained upon request by 4 Latin-American countries," he wrote, "after 17 months of undeserved internment, which has been serial [sic] of humiliating experiences, the final 'formula' seems now to have been invented." Comparing the United States' enemy alien program to Hitler's final solution of total extermination of the Jewish people may seem an exaggeration in hindsight, but Frankel was convinced of the parallels: "Though refugees from oppression, racially the deadliest enemies of Nazism, morally untouchable, ideologically devoted to the aims of your government and people and politically an unwritten sheet of paper—you are determined to punish us with a penalty of agony for the duration."

The "duration" referred to was that of the war itself, which would end at some point, though Frankel and others had no clear view of that end in 1943. "The fact that 60 proven innocent people should be locked up for years, in contradiction to the pledges of your nations [sic] leading personalities only for the sake of prestige—is far beyond the human imagination," he protested. Frankel was not unaware of the complexities of the "entangled diplomatic life"; his letter to Hull even recognized "the delicacy of your position with regard to the newly created Good Neighbor Policy" and further surmised that the lack of such a policy in Europe could be a core cause of the tragedy of world war that was then unfolding. "But the Good Neighbor Policy must turn out to become a failure, if used to camouflage a violation of the primitive human rights," he prophetically judged.

After almost a year and a half in detention, Frankel addressed Hull as the representative of "the greatest democracy in the world, fighting a deadly struggle for the survival of decency and human rights." "It depends on you," he admonished, "to determine whether 60 innocent people—among them 25 women and children—shall live or perish." The reference to life or death suggests detainees were still worried about repatriation, as did the signed declarations of almost all Jewish detainees refusing repatriation to Germany.

Frankel's letter to Hull also suggests that one of the worst aspects of detention was unstructured time itself. He asked the secretary of state to consider changing the detainees' status to a limited restriction so that they might be able to work in some capacity; indeed, as the war wore on and time in detention lengthened, levels of frustration and in-fighting increased. Frankel ended the letter by vowing, "We cannot give up our fight for our freedom and will carry on this fight in the knowledge that our conscience is clean and in confidence to the sense of rightness heretofore attributed to the American people." The man repeatedly accused of being a Nazi operative signed off with "Your obedient servant" above his signature and name and "Spokesman of the Jewish group" under it.

Apprehended by the Panama police the day after the bombing of Pearl Harbor, Frankel was aboard the *Florida* when it sailed from Colón, docking in New Orleans on April 8, 1942. The ship manifest identifies him as a forty-eight-year-old doctor who spoke German, English, Polish, Spanish, and Portuguese. From New Orleans, Frankel was sent to Camp Blanding in Florida, then to Stringtown, in McAlester, Oklahoma, in April 1942, and from there to Seagoville, Texas, in September. In February 1943, he arrived at the Algiers Detention Station with his wife Toni, a voluntary internee. When provided the chance to describe his apprehension, Frankel explained how he was rounded up and brought by US Army truck to the rail station in Colón, Panama, and from there traveled by train to the Balboa Internment Camp in the Canal Zone. He stated for the record, "There was neither a hearing nor an investigation." Despite these breaches of basic human rights and a lack of evidence in general, Frankel's file contains a crudely written police memo describing the subject as "very pro-Nazi." "Possible that subject is cover up. . . . Opinion of Canal Zone police is that subject or brother want to be trouble makers. Suspected of activities on behalf of German gov't," the memo claimed.[13]

Like those of other Jewish detainees he spoke for in his letter, Frankel's efforts to clear his name had fallen on deaf ears for a long time. It proved to be much easier to acquire a damning record as an enemy alien, however questionable, than to rectify one's reputation and establish loyalty to the United States. Frankel's case is just one example; long before his impassioned plea to Cordell Hull, the United States had gathered "intelligence" that he was a Nazi and perhaps a Gestapo agent as well. His Department of Justice file contains an FBI form dated August 28, 1940—well before the bombing of Pearl Harbor and the United States' official entry into the war—in which a Richard E. Smith claims Frankel was operating the New Cristobal Garage in Panama, having purchased it from a "known Nazi" and that, furthermore, he was known to intelligence officers in the Canal Zone as being definitely pro-Nazi and a German nationalist. An intelligence memo dated April 3, 1941, quoted an informant who accused Frankel of being a "Gestapo agent." Another report, dated April 10, 1941, and directed to the director of the FBI, claimed, "Dr. Hubert Erwin Frankel has boasted about the easy way in which Germans can secure jobs in the United States and can seriously hamper defense preparations through sabotage."[14] However trustworthy or spurious the claims in these documents, they indicate that Frankel and other European nationals were already being watched and labeled by the FBI well before the United States entered the war fray directly.

Only in subsequent documents in Frankel's file does the government acknowledge that most of these accusations were provided by Henry Grunberg, a former US Treasury agent in Cuba who had swindled Frankel out of over $800 by falsely stating he could obtain Panamanian visas for his relatives in Europe. Frankel explained to government personnel that as a result of that deal gone wrong he had lost not only the $1,226 he had paid out for steamship reservations on a ship sailing from the Netherlands but also the relatives whom he was trying to save, since he had not heard from them since.[15] Raymond Ickes and James Bell, investigators for the Department of Justice, ultimately termed all charges by Grunberg as "unreliable." They clarified that Frankel acquired the garage in Colón when Carl Westermeier, the German owner, couldn't keep up with the rent and was evicted; they reported that when Westermeier subsequently met Frankel on the street, he greeted him as "you dirty Jew."[16] Adding injury and apparent corruption to this insult, the files note that "just before Mrs. Frankel left Panama to join her husband in internment an official of the Panamanian Tax Office tried to buy for $500 Frankel's garage which netted $300 monthly. Although Mrs. Frankel turned down the offer, she was forced to sell the day before she left for $250."[17]

Another confidential memo, this one from February 28, 1945, suggests that anyone apprehended in Panama as an alien enemy could make that charge disappear and return to society if enough money changed hands. "Fraenkel was arrested on December 9, 1941. While he was in detention in Balboa a number of persons suggested to Mrs. Fraenkel that for a 'fee' they could obtain her husband's release; the figure of $2,000 was named by a member of the Criminal

Court of Colon." Paying off officials sometimes worked, as we see in the case of the Swedish Count Axel Wachtmeister (chapter 5), who reportedly bought his release from his first detention in the Dominican Republic for a mere hundred dollars. But such an arrangement could also be used against a named alien enemy, as happened when Wachtmeister was picked up a second time and then sent to the United States, where the payment of one hundred dollars for his freedom was considered proof of his untrustworthiness.

Both of the Frankels' responses on INS paperwork also clarified their status as Jewish refugees, despite FBI reports identifying them as pro-Nazi. To the question concerning persecution of their relatives, Toni Frankel responded on her I-55 form, signed November 4, 1942, "Jenny Englander, my sister, was persecuted by Germany. They took all of her fortune, her home, her clothes, everything, and forced her to live in a ghetto in Poland. Mrs. Helene Fischer, my sister, was persecuted in the same manner by Germany. My sister, Mrs. Rebecca Pick, was persecuted by Germany in the same manner. My brother, Siegfried Arian, was persecuted by Germany also. He had to leave Germany, his home, and go to Poland. All this happened when Germany took over Poland in 1939." Responding to the question "Do you wish to be repatriated?" she answered, "No. I am Jewish and would like to remain in the United States if possible and become a naturalized citizen."[18]

The Frankels were interned at large from Camp Algiers in August 1943, the same month the majority of the other Jewish detainees were also released. They and several other couples and families created a small enclave in the Chicago area. A letter three years later recommending his eventual release from internment at large reports that Frankel served as a staff physician and surgeon at Jackson Park Hospital, was interviewed four times by military intelligence representatives, and confirmed his willingness to serve in the armed forces, though he was by then approaching fifty. And despite Frankel's characterization by the FBI and other governmental operatives as "pro-Nazi" both before and during the war, "he impressed the superintendent of his hospital and also several of his neighbors with his loyalty to the U.S. and anti-Nazism."[19] Furthermore, as of September 1945, Frankel had purchased $5,700 in war bonds, a sum equivalent to over $84,000 today.

This favorable evidence was enough, finally, to garner the couple's release from enemy alien status on the grounds of insufficient evidence of dangerousness. A lengthy memorandum in Erwin Frankel's DOJ file includes "the informal opinion that the Frankels are not and never have been Nazis and that they perhaps have been the victims of not too well considered judgment on the part of our agents in Panama who were overly anxious to submit reports regarding all natives and citizens of Germany and Italy who were in that country when World War II got under way."[20] Thomas M. Cooley II, then director of the Alien Enemy Control Unit, prepared a memo on July 31, 1946, for the attorney general in which he said of the Frankels, "They were initially brought here in a very general round-up which sent to the United States for internment substantially all aliens as to whom a breath of suspicion existed. Any attempt to detail the conflicting reports thought to cast suspicion on these individuals would require more discussion than is justified here. I think it sufficient to say first, that these people are plainly Jewish Refugees, and second, that the specialists appointed by this Unit, Mr. Bell and Mr. Ickes, established to their own satisfaction that there was nothing substantial in the rumors concerning these people."[21] And so it was that finally, after leaving Germany for Poland, Poland for Czechoslovakia, Czechoslovakia for Hungary, then on to Yugoslavia and after that Italy, and then finally leaving Italy for Panama, the Frankels' long journey toward a safe haven reached its end in the United States. Dr. Frankel died in 1968 as a US citizen.

Matters of Life and Death

Many in the Jewish group apprehended by Panamanian police in the wake of Pearl Harbor told a similar tale: on the one hand they were given little or no reason for their arrest and on the other they were repeatedly assured that deportation to the United States was in their best interest, and they would be placed at liberty soon after their arrival. For many—especially those who had hoped to immigrate from Europe to the United States but were diverted to Panama—boarding a vessel bound for the United States no doubt seemed a better option than remaining incarcerated at detention facilities in the Canal Zone. But intimations that the Jewish detainees would quickly find refuge and relief from persecution and prejudice in the promised land of the United States—even if it meant leaving family members, businesses, and property behind in Panama—soon proved overly optimistic.

Some cases are particularly tragic. The Panamanian police picked up Martin Kallman, born in Poland in 1894, on December 10, 1941.[22] He spent several months at Camp Empire in the Canal Zone, where in March 1942 his wife, Lucy, and daughter, Lieselotte, presented themselves as voluntary internees rather than separate the family. The Kallmans traveled together to the United States

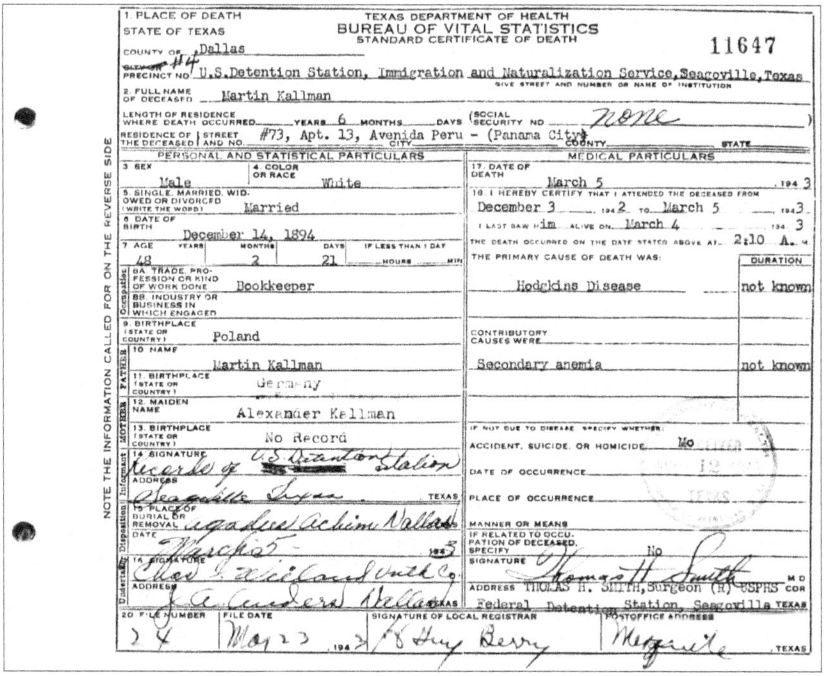

FIGURE 3.2. Death certificate for Martin Kallman, who died while interned at Camp Seagoville, Texas, in March 1943. Texas Department of State Health Services, Austin, TX.

in April aboard the *Florida* and were separated upon arrival, with Martin going east to Camp Blanding and his wife and daughter going west to Camp Seagoville.

Even though the family was reunited at Seagoville at a later date, their reunion would ultimately be short-lived. A memo dated April 17, 1943, confirms that Martin Kallman died March 5 of that year after several months of treatment for Hodgkin's disease (figure 3.2). As a result, the cases of the now widowed Lucy Kallman and her daughter were presented to Edward Ennis for reconsideration of their "dangerousness." Documents place Lucy and her daughter arriving at Camp Algiers in April 1943 and show them being released to internment at large in August, though it would take another year for them to be cleared from this last level of restriction. An April 1944 memo of their status change shows mother and daughter residing in San Francisco. Lucy Kallman was naturalized in 1952 and died in 1978.

Other cases had more fortunate outcomes but struck those deemed "alien enemies" as no less egregious than the sad story of the Kallmans. Berlin-born Fred

Kappel and his son, Werner, aged nineteen at the time of their arrest in Panama in December 1941, both made strong arguments for their loyalty to the United States. Part of the large group of Jewish detainees who arrived at Camp Algiers in early 1943, their stories nevertheless diverged from those of their camp mates with regard to certain key details. Fred Kappel, for his part, asserted that he had already lived in New York City from 1914 to 1920 and took out his first immigration papers at that time. He had later returned to Germany, where the Gestapo ordered him to leave the country in May 1938. He made his way to Denmark with his son, Werner; there the only visa he could obtain was one for Panama.

So outrageous did his December 1941 detention seem to the former US resident that "in a letter to the U.S. Army Captain in charge of the camp in which he was first interned in Panama, Kappel threatened to sue the United States for his detention," his State Department file notes.[23] An intercept of a letter he wrote from the Balboa camp in the Canal Zone dated February 2, 1942, reveals the degree to which the US government saw no apparent contradiction between being Jewish and being a Nazi, as "Possible Nazi Agent" is written at the top, and under it, "Writer is one of thirty Jewish citizens of Panama."[24]

After Kappel had been deported to the United States and was being held at Camp Blanding, the government also intercepted an April 14, 1942, letter to a Wall Street lawyer named Alfonse M. Spiegel titled "Little Germany Exists at Camp Blanding." Underneath, Kappel had written, "In Panama Prospective Internees Obtain Freedom Through Bribery." In that letter, preserved for posterity by the censors (whether it reached its original destination is not known), Kappel identifies himself as "one of nineteen Jewish internees at Camp Blanding." His portrayal of life at Camp Blanding provides background as to why the Jews from Panama and other countries were ultimately congregated at Camp Algiers in early 1943. In it Kappel explained he had been appointed as head of the group and had succeeded in getting the Jewish internees' tents separated from other groups in the camp.

> We are living amongst 350 outspoken Nazis, are shunned and boycotted in the same way as we were treated in Germany; a little funny being in "little Germany" within the boundaries of the U.S. They sing their fight songs, hold speeches for the victory of the German weapons in meetings, which of course, we do not visit, but which we can hear from our quarters. They have the "Fuehrer" principle and do all the other nonsense, only too well known to us from Nazi Germany. . . . I have to add that all the arti-

cles of the constitution were violated, we had no hearing, with the allegation, that Panama did not permit a hearing . . . everybody had another excuse, why they held us, only nobody knew and knows in fact, why.[25]

Like other Jews who had relocated from Nazi-controlled areas of Europe to Panama in the late 1930s, Kappel had worked hard to reestablish himself in his new country. After failed attempts to get ahead with a bakery and restaurant, he finally had limited success with a transportation business, acquiring three buses. When interned in December 1941, he complained that his buses were disposed of "at lamentable prices by the alien enemy custodian of Panama, leaving a very small amount in my favor." Holding fast to a moral high ground instead of resorting to bribery or other forms of corruption seems to have worked against Kappel and others. As his Department of Justice summary file notes, "He says he did not try to buy his freedom when arrested. He was never a member of any political party, but of a Jewish community in Berlin."[26]

Fred Kappel's Justice Department file also contains a censored letter that indicates the disturbing echoes he found between detention orders of the Alien Enemy Program and previous experiences in Nazi Germany: "Don't you think that this order, if applied to Jewish refugees is the greatest humiliation and discrimination possible and is just as cruel as the forced wearing in Europe of the 'Star of David'?" he asked.[27] Kappel also called government authorities to task for not seeing the clear contradiction between the continuing stigma of enemy status for declared "alien enemies" still restricted to internment at large, even as they were serving in the military: "Is it known to you that from our Jewish group from Panama of 29 men all the younger men being more than 30% (!) are in the U.S. armed forces?" Kappel even provided the servicemen's names, including that of his own son: Siegwart Fechenbach, George Karliner, Werner J. Kappel, Alberto Kohn, Max Kaufmann "(serving as military police and censor!!)," Hans J. Mueller, Willi Reichner, Werner Scholem, and Guenther Simon. As he and other family members of these servicemen languished in internment, he implored the authorities, "Are we not fighting for the human rights of mankind?"

Kappel's son, Werner, was only sixteen when he had left Germany with his father in May 1938. In his personal statement of his background dated December 12, 1942, he noted his attendance at a Jewish grade school in Berlin, at the Fasanenstrasse Synagogue—ironically a symbol of Jewish emancipation in Germany when it was built in 1912—and at the high school of Dr. Vera Lachmann, a German Jewish poet and educator who founded a private school for children expelled from public schools when Hitler assumed power in 1933. Werner noted his apprenticeship at the Jewish bakery of Louis Weinstock in Berlin and his membership in several Jewish youth organizations, such as the Bund Jüdischer Jugend, the Jüdische Sportgemeinschaft, and the Jüdischer Sport Platz.

Both father and son assumed that nothing would more emphatically demonstrate their loyalty to the United States than service in the US armed forces. When released into internment at large from Camp Algiers in August 1943, they traveled to St. Louis, where Werner landed a job as a baker's apprentice and was inducted into the US Army in December of that year. He was later seriously wounded while fighting in the Philippines, but despite being decorated as a war veteran, his early petition for citizenship was denied. In a March 1945 letter, George Lubeley of St. Louis wrote to Representative John J. Cochran in Washington, explaining,

> In August 1943, a group of 50 German refugees, mostly Semitic descent, were released from Camp Algiers, Louisiana, and their status was defined as internment at large. All in this group . . . had been forcibly sent into this country and interned at Camp Algiers. At the time of their release, 9 of the group came to St. Louis and the Jewish community here accepted sponsorship and responsibility. Recently, Kappel's father was informed by the War Department that his son had been seriously wounded on Luzon. . . . The facts and details are also known to the Jewish Social Service. It seems almost inconceivable that this boy, who has fought and bled for this country should be denied citizenship.[28]

It wasn't until June 1945 that Werner Kappel took the oath of citizenship; it would then take another six months for the government to release him from the supervision of the Alien Enemy Control Unit. In an interview he told historian Max Paul Friedman, "When you left Germany to get away from Nazism, and then you got thrown into a camp for Nazis, it was idiotic. . . . When I think about it, I get angry right now."[29] Awarded a Purple Heart for wounds sustained in the Philippines, Werner lived until 2012. His tombstone in the Sarasota National Cemetery in Florida acknowledges his military service and honors during World War II. The inscription also reads "Hope You Dance / Always in Our Hearts."

Indeed, the "Panama Jews" on Fred Kappel's list were notably active in joining the fight *against* the Nazis once they were able to do so. George Karliner, born to German parents in Poland in 1920, had been sentenced to six weeks in Buchenwald before he was released through the help of a Jewish organization in Berlin and obtained a visa for Panama. Though two uncles were able to reach the United States, Karliner's father perished at Buchenwald. After his release from Algiers, Karliner was inducted into the navy.

Max Kaufmann, born in Frankfurt in 1907, began his personal statement, written on December 12, 1942, at Camp Kenedy by expressing his concern for his mother, Sofie Kaufmann, who he believed to be detained at that moment at the Gurs Internment Camp.[30] Located in southwestern France, Camp de Gurs was constructed by the French government in 1939 primarily to house Spanish Republicans fleeing Franco, but some four thousand German Jews were also held there as enemy aliens. Kaufmann had reason to worry, as Gurs was a horrifying place plagued by starvation, typhus, and dysentery; most of the four thousand Jews held there were deported to Auschwitz and murdered there.

Kaufmann's peripatetic journey from Germany to Panama featured several years in Strasbourg, Nantes, Bordeaux, and other cities before he traveled to Paraguay with the help of a Jewish agency. He reached Panama in July 1937. Ironically, he had registered for immigration to the United States, and his quota number had come up in the summer of 1941. In the following months, having presented his affidavits, he anxiously awaited a decision from the State Department. But before that news was delivered, he too was arrested on December 9, 1941, for internment under the Alien Enemy Control Act.

Upon his internment at large, Kaufmann was inducted into the US Army at Fort Snelling, Minnesota, and rose to the rank of corporal before being honorably discharged. His file mentions work at a prisoner of war camp in Clarinda, Iowa, where his knowledge of German was a valuable asset. A letter from September 1945 notes he was eligible for immediate discharge due to his age, but "before discharging soldier, this station would, if possible, like some assurance that he can obtain an exit visa as a civilian in order that his entry into this country could be legalized," base personnel indicated.

Kaufmann's name file provides additional details from letters of affidavit submitted by relatives and even someone who had been with his mother in the Gurs Internment Camp. A cousin named Alfred Auerbacher wrote in December 1942 that he knew of Max's bar mitzvah in Kippenheim, Germany, and explained, "On account of the racial discrimination which arose in 1933 he had to leave and entered France."[31] The affidavit confirmed his movement to South America with the help of the Hebrew Immigrant Aid Society. A later letter (February 11, 1943) was from Augusta Wertheimer, who had been in the French Camp de Gurs, where Kaufmann's mother was interned. Wertheimer had been able to leave and immigrate to the United States in February 1942. "I myself am a widow," she wrote. "I have three sons, one of whom is in England and the other two of whom are serving in the United States Army. I am as happy as they are to be able to assist in wiping out the enemies of mankind."[32] The letter does not mention the fate of Kaufmann's mother.

Another name on Kappel's list of those who served in the US armed forces was Albert(o) Kohen (sometimes spelled Kohn), an army man who worked at another prisoner of war camp in Fort Jackson, South Carolina, also rising to the rank of corporal. Officials wrote that as a result of a positive review of his military service, "it is the decision of the State Department that when and if Mr. Kohen is honorably discharged from the Army of the United States, he is not to be subjected to any restraint under the Alien Enemy Act."[33] Kohen died in 1984 and is buried in the Calverton National Cemetery in Calverton, New York.

One notable figure rounded up in the second week of December 1941 was Erwin Klyszcz, who had arrived in Panama in March 1939; he was received by the INS in New Orleans on April 7, 1942, and later sent to Algiers from Camp Kenedy in March 1943 after an unspecified amount of time at Stringtown. According to a confidential memo, the State Department found "no adverse information in the file regarding Klyszcz and 3 affidavits in his favor, including one by Mr. William McCraig, formerly of the Panama Canal Administration and of the Office or Coordinator of Interamerican Affairs who states that Klyszcz is definitely anti-Nazi."[34] Klyszcz had been an interpreter for the French army in Poland in the 1920s and would do most of the interpreting for the German- and Polish-speaking Jewish refugees at New Orleans's Camp Algiers when Bell and Ickes interviewed them in the summer of 1943.

Klyszcz's Department of Justice file provides a portrait of a family diaspora that extended to several continents, with his Polish mother and two brothers then living in Brazil; several aunts, uncles, and cousins in the United States; a sister in Argentina; a brother in Shanghai; a sister who in 1941 was living in Germany but had not been heard from since; and an uncle known to have been deported to Poland. When he was released to internment at large on July 31, 1943, Klyszcz settled in the Chicago area. There, several families of internees created a tight-knit community. A few children and grandchildren of that Chicago group were still in touch with each other as of the writing of this study.

All named sponsors of the released detainees were responsible for staying in close touch with their charges and reporting frequently on the activities of those interned at large, much like a prison parole system. Herman Stryk acknowledged on paper that he would serve in that capacity for Klyszcz: "I hereby undertake to keep in close touch with him, observe his conduct and activities, and maintain knowledge of his whereabouts, to the end of assuring his compliance with the terms of parole. . . . I also agree to render a report concerning him to Alien Control Officer, Room 901, New Post Office Building, Chicago, each month."[35]

Klyszcz was one of the few Camp Algiers internees for whom I could locate a living relative in the course of this research. His daughter, Renée, and I met for lunch at the US Holocaust Memorial Museum in the summer of 2018. Renée, whose father Anglicized his surname to the more pronounceable *Klish* prior to becoming a US citizen, is a volunteer at the USHMM and participates in the effort to research looted cultural property such as artworks, antiques, and musical instruments and restore these items to their rightful owners. Like other living relatives of Camp Algiers internees I was able to contact, Renée told me her father was not forthcoming about his time in internment. In fact, much of the information I had gleaned from the files at the National Archives about him was new to her. Once again, as with experiences in internment and concentration camps in Europe and elsewhere, detainees were reluctant to recall those experiences or share them with their children, choosing to concentrate instead on the needs of the present and their dreams for a very different future.

Heavy Baggage

The negative experiences members of the Panama Jewish group described encountering in camps in the US South can be understood when placed alongside the hardships and discrimination that had driven them from their European birthplaces in the first place, compounded by their struggles to make a new life for themselves in Central America. Otto Manheimer's (sometimes Mannheimer) case is a good example.[36] He was born in Vienna in 1888, a period of "nervous splendor" in the city that boasted such compatriots as the young neuropathologist Sigmund Freud, the composer Gustav Mahler, the father of political Zionism Theodor Herzl, and the symbolist painter Gustav Klimt.[37] A confidential State Department memo in Manheimer's file states not only that he was "of Jewish descent and claims he lost his Austrian citizenship by the German decree of November 25, 1941," but also that he was "married in 1918 to a woman (presumably European-born) whom he divorced in 1939, apparently on orders of the German Government because she was Aryan and he was not." Manheimer's known arrival date in Panama of January 8, 1939, suggests that the marriage—which lasted more than two decades—was dissolved only under duress, when it became clear that he would have to leave the region.

The Manheimers apparently did not suffer retaliation or even disapprobation during the first decade and a half of their "mixed marriage." From all indications, it did not interfere with Otto Manheimer's identification with the Jewish community, as his records state he was a member of the Vienna branch of Masada, a Zionist organization, from 1905 to 1938, a period that began when he was about seventeen and ended only shortly before he left the country. Later, the Zionist youth organization IGUL would file a letter on his behalf, saying he had in fact been the president of Masada.[38] But "intermarried Jews, their partners, and their children suddenly confronted a bewildering array of Nazi regulations that had evolved gradually in Germany between 1933 and 1938."[39] At that point, unions such as that of the Manheimers were labeled *Rassenschande* or "race defilement," punishable by law.

After many attempts to leave the country, Manheimer finally secured a visa for Panama and, with the help of a nephew in the British army who financed his trip, arrived in Central America on January 8, 1939. Working first at a gas station and then a hotel, he also took part in religious services in the Canal Zone and was known to Rabbi Nathan Witkin, to whom he would send a frightened appeal upon his arrival in the United States in April 1942. By the time he was interviewed by Ickes and Bell at Camp Algiers on June 28, 1943, he was in his mid-fifties.

The dubious charges against the Viennese hotelier included possessing a picture in a photo album of "a Nazi chief" whom he reportedly described as his best friend, though "Manheimer says the picture does not show a man in uniform and thus presumably denies that the man is 'a Nazi chief.'"[40] Officials in Panama also claimed that German seamen stayed at his hotel but acknowledged it may have been the only place available to them; the seamen no doubt quickly learned they would find a German-speaking staff there. Another "intelligence source" reported that he attended Nazi meetings at a café owned by Oskar Wetterschneider. Manheimer roundly denied having attended such meetings or even knowing any had been held there, given that the Wetterschneiders were also Jews. His name file clarifies on this count: "Manheimer stated when interviewed that the first Nazis he met were those in internment camp and that he hated Hitler and his regime." Just how onerous this elbow rubbing with Nazis was for Manheimer is explored further in chapter 6.

While Manheimer's story suggests he and his wife were forced into divorcing before he left Europe alone, other Europeans decided that staying behind in Europe when spouses or children emigrated was an untenable or intolerable choice. One of the oldest members of the Panama Jewish group was Ferdinand Marcus, born in 1878 in Siegburg, Germany, and a butcher by trade who in 1937 "had to sell his sausage factory and meat market and move," due to increasing restrictions on Jewish-owned businesses and daily life.[41] Though the Marcuses subsisted for a period on family savings and the earnings of their daughter and her husband, their son-in-law Walter Wolff migrated in 1938, and his wife and child followed him soon after. In June 1939, Wolff sent immigration permits to his in-laws, and they were helped in obtaining visas to Panama by a Jewish welfare organization in Hamburg, as they by that point lacked the necessary funds to finance the trip.

Marcus is identified in 1943 paperwork as a Jewish immigrant picked up by Panamanian police on December 9, 1941. His wife, Christine, from Krefeld, was born in 1886. The couple had three daughters, one married to Walter Wolff and living in Panama, while the other two remained in Germany. When friends and associates later vouched for the Marcuses in registered affidavits, one noted, "Mrs. Marcus is Catholic, but has always followed her husband. The children were raised as Jews."[42] This suggests that in the case of both the Marcuses and the Manheimers, an interfaith marriage was not a scourge prior to the rise of Nazi state policies forbidding and punishing so-called *Rassenschande*.

The Marcuses' file makes clear there were no charges against either husband or wife, no red flag suggesting the need to detain either of them. But the couple's commitment to family ties ultimately informed their decision to opt for voluntary deportation: "He was arrested in December 1941 but was subsequently released; however, when they learned that their son-in-law was to be removed to the United States, they came along as voluntary internees." Their case strongly suggests the Jewish contingent apprehended in Panama and held at Balboa was led to believe their treatment in the United States would be different from that of other alien detainees and that their clean record would soon absolve them, triggering their release from enemy status. It also reveals that the "Jewish" group itself was by no means homogenous.

Finding strength in family and numbers, the Marcuses embarked together for the United States with their son-in-law, Walter Wolff, his wife (their daughter) Irene, and their granddaughter, Ingeborg, as well as Walter's brother, Siegfried, and the Wolff brothers' mother, Jeannette. "In a signed statement he asks to be put in the same camp as his son-in-law, Walter Wolff, in whom he seems to have utter confidence. He says he is anti-Nazi, Jewish and would defend the U.S. way of life. He wants to live here."[43] It seems, though, that the group was divided upon their arrival, at least initially, and Ferdinand Marcus wasn't reunited with his wife at Seagoville until late June of that year. Sent to Camp Kenedy soon after his arrival (as of May 2, 1942), Marcus was in detention at Seagoville as of June 23, 1942 (his wife having arrived there as of April 9 of that year), finally arriving at Algiers with his wife on February 11, 1943. A confidential memo dated March 7, 1946, notes that on August 11, 1942, Christine Marcus petitioned for nonrepatriation to Germany.

As the Marcuses were voluntary detainees, they weren't even interviewed by the Ickes-Bell team during the summer of 1943. They were interned at large as of September 30, 1943, and finally released from all proceedings relative to enemy alien status on March 15, 1946. Ferdinand Marcus died on January 25, 1949, in Chattanooga, Tennessee; his son-in-law, Walter Wolff, is listed as the "informant" on his death certificate. His name can be found on the roster of the Mizpah Congregational Cemetery in the downtown area of that city.

Strength in Numbers

German-born detainee Hans Joachim Muller left Germany for Italy in June 1933, and after several years working in various universities there, received his PhD as a statistician in January 1939. But racial legislation instituted in Italy in 1938 forced him to pack his bags once more in March 1939. "I registered for immigration to the U.S. at the U.S. Consulate General at Naples, Sept. 9th, 1938, but could not get a quota number within the time limit set by the Italian government," Muller explains in his personal account.[44]

Born in Halle in 1913 to Jewish parents, Muller was officially stateless by the end of the 1930s, but he did have an important advocate in the United States. "Muller is a nephew of [J. Robert] Oppenheimer, who got Merz to bring the subject over. Muller says that when he had to leave Italy he at first tried to gain a visa for Argentina or Australia and that his father appealed to Dr. Oppenheimer."[45] In Central America, Muller worked for the Panamanian Labor Department from June 1939 to April 1940, and in the Census Office there from May 1940 until his arrest on December 9, 1941. The arbitrary nature of his apprehension and detention is implied in the yellow summary of the Department of Justice files contained in his State Department file, which admits, "The only charge against the subject is the broad one that, like many others, he may be a pseudo German-Jewish refugee and a Nazi agent. There is little to support this idea." The Office of Naval Intelligence does mention a "suspicious" telegram Muller received from Hilfsverein, Leipzig, with the message, "Renewed efforts are being made. We are doing our best." In the midst of heightened worries that he and other Axis-born nationals in Latin America might be active Nazis or Nazi sympathizers masquerading as Jewish refugees, Muller had to explain that Hilfsverein was a Jewish organization and that the telegram in question referred to efforts to help his parents leave Europe for Panama as well—efforts that ultimately proved futile.

After he was forcibly displaced from Panama, Muller was sent to Camp Kenedy and from there to Camp Algiers in March 1943. In August of that year he was interned at large and inducted into the US Army, subsequently serving in the Pacific, where he earned the Bronze Star. After his military service, Muller spent thirty-five years as a government employee, working for the US Public Health Service and the Census Bureau as a statistician until he retired in 1981. Adam Bernstein's January 17, 2010, obituary in the *Washington Post* noted that while Muller lived to age ninety-six, his parents had died during the Holocaust, while a younger sister had survived the Nazi death camps.

Not *That* Werner Scholem

Even within the context of opposing narratives of Jewish detainees as dangerous spies on the one hand or persecuted refugees on the other, few cases seem as muddled as that of Werner Scholem.[46] His very name might have been part of the problem. *Our* Werner H. Scholem, born in Berlin in 1907, was a Jewish refugee who arrived in the Americas by a very circuitous route. In a chronology he composed of his long search for a safe haven, he first asserted his Jewish bona fides as a member of the Jüdische Gemeinde congregation in Berlin and a student of Dr. Weisse, rabbi of the Oranienburgerstrasse Synagogue, also in that city.

A flight from increasing Nazi oppression would take Scholem to several countries, internment camps and jails in four countries, and on to a stint in the US armed forces. His journey started on August 10, 1938, exactly three months before Kristallnacht, after which the Nazis' insistence that Jews emigrate hardened into more fatal policies: "I fled Germany before having been able to secure a permanent visa for any country and left for France via Switzerland." In Paris,

Scholem applied for an immigration visa to Australia and received his landing permit in July 1939. "However," he continued, "before having finished my arrangements as to my departure for this country war broke out, and I was interned in Libourne, France as a consequence of general internment measures against all people born in Germany. A hearing was given and being a Jew and a refugee from Nazi oppression I was authorized to leave France for Overseas."

Preferring to wait out the war in an American country, Scholem secured a temporary permit to enter Venezuela and traveled there in April 1940. But even there, stigma followed. "Being a Jew with a German passport stigmatized with -J-," he explained, "it was impossible for me to obtain a permanent visa for any country, and I was very glad to have secured at least temporary visas for Panama and Nicaragua which were issued to me in Caracas/Venezuela." On July 7, 1940, Scholem left Venezuela by plane, arriving the same day in Panama. But when he tried to travel to Nicaragua, he was transferred to the quarantine station at Balboa in the Canal Zone. A confidential memo in his file dated November 15, 1945, states, "The alien was jailed on suspicion of espionage, that he was accused of having been a German agent first in France, then in Venezuela. On March 12, 1941 he was interned in Balboa, Canal Zone, where he was reported awaiting passage to Yokohama from which point German authorities were to take him to Germany."[47] The FBI had been watching Scholem, and in its narrative, his time at the Libourne internment camp for being a German (at least according to his own account) became a jail term for being a spy: "An FBI report, November 14, 1941 says that he spent a term in jail in France early in 1940 for espionage, and later he was jailed in Venezuela too. He was expelled from the latter country, and he went to Panama. When he was arrested, he was trying to get to Japan and eventually to Germany."

Scholem's own account could hardly be more different from the government's version. On December 9, 1941, just days after the United States officially entered the war, Scholem was transferred from the quarantine station at Balboa to the adjacent enemy alien detention camp. Along with so many other Jewish detainees from Latin America, from that camp he was deported to the United States, traveling on the heavy-laden *Florida* in April 1942. From New Orleans, he was sent to Camp Kenedy, and from Kenedy to Stringtown, where he wrote to the legation of Switzerland explaining that as a non-Aryan, he could not be exchanged for Americans held in Germany. In mid-March, Scholem was transferred to Algiers, where he would spend only a few months before his internment at large in late July 1943. From there he traveled to Buffalo, New York.

His status changed again in May 1944, when he was released from internment at large to serve in the US armed forces.

As a soldier in the army, Scholem could expedite his naturalization application, and he was "admitted to citizenship" in a Baltimore court on February 5, 1945. In the process, he changed his name to Werner Howard Sheldon, not to be confused with his namesake, also born in Berlin, but in 1895. *That* Werner Scholem was a leftist intellectual who became a leading member of the Communist Party in Germany, despite his upbringing in a middle-class "assimilated" family. In 1917, that Scholem was arrested in his German military uniform at an antiwar demonstration on the kaiser's birthday.[48] He joined the Communist Party in 1920 and became a deputy in the Reichstag, the lower house of Germany's national legislature. As both a Communist and a Jew, the older Scholem was arrested when the Nazis came to power in 1933 and spent several years in "preventative custody" before he was deported to the Buchenwald concentration camp in 1938. He was shot to death there in 1940.[49]

Whether to further distance himself from the sad fate of his fellow Berliner or from the political ideas he espoused, which would arouse new suspicions of disloyalty in the context of the US–Soviet bloc Cold War, Werner Scholem (b. 1907) became Werner H. Sheldon. His new name appears on a memo attached to the "Military Records of Former Internees" alongside those of Max Kaufmann, Eric Rath, Wilhelm Reichner, Federico Sauter, and Gunther Simon. In fact, a letter in his file dated November 27, 1945, claims that apart from Scholem, "there are 18 alien enemies from other of the American republics who were interned at large and have been inducted into the United States armed forces."

After the Ickes-Bell team interviewed Scholem at Camp Algiers on June 20, 1943, "Ickes commented that Scholem had satisfactorily explained away the apparent adverse information about him, expressed the opinion that he was a genuine German-Jewish refugee, and recommended his release."[50] Scholem was interned at large and served in the army, from which he was honorably discharged in September 1945 after rising to the rank of corporal. He and his wife, Mary Sheldon, are both buried at the Calverton National Cemetery in Suffolk County, New York.[51]

Brotherly Love

Perhaps if Egon Wetterschneider hadn't returned to visit his brother Oskar (Oscar in some documents) in detention at Camp Balboa, he would not have been aboard the crammed *Florida* en route to New Orleans in early April 1942 along with Benno, Clara, and Steffi Ascher; Peter Bohm; Erwin Klyszcz; Ferdinand and Christine Marcus; Hans Muller; Werner Scholem; Jeannette, Walter, and Siegfried Wolff; and many others. Arrested December 9, 1941, he was released three weeks later, on January 1, 1942, for lack of evidence. According to his State Department record, "What happened thereafter is not entirely clear; according to one report he was rearrested when he went to visit his brother who was still detained."[52] As with many others in the Jewish group, the evidence against Egon Wetterschneider was superficial, but worries of being separated from family members superseded fears of being held in prisonlike conditions. As his record indicates, "There is no charge against Egon Wetterschneider except a G-2 report that the cafe in Panama owned by his brother Oskar was 'a rendezvous for Nazi sympathizers.' This is admittedly unconfirmed."

Egon was forty-three years old when the *Florida* sailed, ten years younger than his brother, Oskar, according to the ship manifest. Born in 1899 in Brunn (Bruen) when it was part of Czechoslovakia, the brothers reportedly left Austria-Hungary before the German annexation, bound for Italy. The enactment of anti-Jewish laws in Italy later led them to seek refuge in Panama. The Wetterschneider brothers were received by the INS at New Orleans on February 19, 1943, and were interned at large from Camp Algiers on August 21; Egon moved to the Minneapolis–St. Paul area, and his brother and sister-in-law went to Detroit.

In April 1943, Egon drafted a personal statement further explaining that he and his brother were living in Milan at the time of the Anschluss (Nazi annexation of Austria), but fearing Italian anti-Jewish laws, decided to emigrate. He, Oskar, and Oskar's wife, Hilda, obtained immigration visas from the Panamanian consul in Milan and arrived in that country in October 1938. Formerly the owner-operators of a famous café in Vienna, Egon and Oskar bought and ran its Central American successor, the Café Astoria, from November 1, 1938, to February 5, 1942.[53] But the fact that it was patronized by Germans led inevitably to claims it was a "Nazi hangout." When Egon was later interviewed at Algiers on June 27, 1943, he insisted the Astoria was patronized by Jewish refugees and American sailors, "but no Nazis." When it became evident Oskar would not be released, Egon "asked to accompany his brother to the U.S. and gave up the lease on the café."[54]

It is not clear from the governmental paper trail if the brothers were allowed to remain together upon their arrival in the United States, perhaps because Oskar's wife, Hilda (sometimes Hilde), accompanied him as a voluntary detainee, while Egon was single. Oskar's record shows he spent some amount of time in Fort Oglethorpe, Georgia; Camp Forrest, Tennessee; and Camp Seagoville, Texas, before arriving at Camp Algiers. The couple was interned at large in August 1945, and in March 1946, the government recommended Oskar's release from that status, as there was "no evidence of dangerousness."[55]

Egon Wetterschneider married a Minnesota-born woman in 1945 and had a child, Larry, in 1947, according to his 1954 California Naturalization Record. One of the witnesses to his US citizenship swearing-in was Salomon Lagstein, another Algiers internee, who by then was working as an accountant and boasted a Pacific Palisades address. But it seems this positive outcome was not without its anxieties, and things for Oskar were not so easy.

In September 1945, a Detroit-based lawyer named Theodore Levin wrote to Homer Ferguson, senator from Michigan, regarding the case of Oskar and Hilde Wetterschneider. A specialist in immigration and naturalization law, Levin would be nominated the following year by President Harry S. Truman to a seat on the US District Court for the Eastern District of Michigan and duly confirmed by the Senate. But in 1945 he was concerned with the situation of Oskar and Hilda Wetterschneider and another Jewish internee from Panama, Siegmund Lipschitz.

Perhaps the Wetterschneiders and Lipschitz were being considered for repatriation or were encountering difficulties in their bid for naturalization; in any case, it was no accident Levin appealed to Ferguson on their behalf. Ferguson was one of twelve senators who in 1943 cosponsored the Rescue Resolution, urging "the creation by the President of a commission of diplomatic, economic, and military experts to formulate and effectuate a plan of immediate action designed to save the surviving Jewish people of Europe from extinction at the hands of Nazi Germany," spurring Roosevelt's "first initiative to help the stricken Jews."[56]

The background Levin provided to Senator Ferguson on the case of the Jewish internees from Latin America called into question the reasons for detaining them and provided evidence of their subsequent loyalty to the United States, their sound work ethic, and their significant contributions on the military front. He noted that authorities had already investigated and cleared seventy members of the group, describing them as "attached and devoted to our form of government." Whereas they had been permitted to "be at large," engaging in gainful employment and otherwise living "normal" lives, the clients he was representing were still caught up in a bureaucratic logjam:

The Wetterschneiders and Lipschitz were part of a group of seventy-five Jews who were brought to the United States as internees for security reasons under an arrangement with other American republics. The details for the plan are set out in "Proclamation 2662, Removal of Enemy Aliens, By the President of the United States of America." Frankly, I know of no reason . . . why any of these should not also be given such relief as is possible to grant under our laws. None of us could be unmindful that we have just passed through a war, with the consequent great hardships to all classes of people, but the fact is that these particular aliens were legally admitted by other American republics for permanent residence in those respective countries, and though guilty of no wrongdoing or even wrongthinking, were taken from their homes and places of business and brought to the United States.[57]

Levin also appealed to Senator Ferguson on the basis of what had *not* been done to prevent the loss of Jewish life earlier in the war. "In view of the colossal loss," Levin wrote, "of Jewish life in Europe and the hopeless state of the survivors who are unable to be relocated, and since the Allies did relatively little to save the Jewish remnant, it would seem that our Government should at least give the benefit of the doubt to Jewish refugees of good character who find themselves in the United States and who desire to stay here rather than return to the European maelstrom." Levin noted that the names of Oskar, Hilde, and Siegmund had appeared on a March 1944 War Department list of twenty-five persons with the comment, "The following named persons, on whom no material is enclosed, were interned in the United States with very little adverse information other than that of suspicion or that of being of potential value to the enemy."

Were the applications for citizenship of Oskar and Hilda Wetterschneider rejected? Did they choose to travel in search of yet another refuge, rather than waiting out the result of their appeal? A telegram from the INS dated December 17, 1946, is the last information we have in their file; it reports their departure a few days earlier aboard the *Marine Phoenix*, bound for Australia.

Fiddler in the Camp

The story of one especially interesting Jewish refugee deported to the United States from Panama made the front page of the *New Orleans Item* on August 21, 1943, with the title "Refugee Violinist Fled from Nazis; Finds U.S. Welcomes

Self and Mother."[58] The story jumped to page 5, where a picture of the violinist, his mother, and David Fichman of the New Orleans Committee on Refugee Services appeared. The reporter, Marjorie W. Roehl, began the article on an upbeat note: "Mr. Siegfried met America this morning with music in his heart and at his fingertips. With him, her eyes glad, her earrings bobbing, went his mother." But "Mr. Siegfried's last name must remain secret," Roehl contended, as he and his mother were two of the German Jews being released to "internment at large" from the Algiers immigration detention station.

Roehl's article details "Mr. Siegfried's" background as a violinist and symphony conductor of note in Cologne, Germany, his escape from the Gestapo in 1935, and the peripatetic path that would lead him to Switzerland and finally on to Panama in 1939. Then came a series of internment camps in the United States, about which no details are provided, except that wherever he went, Mr. Siegfried faithfully practiced his violin. With the help of the New Orleans Committee for Refugee Service, affiliated with the Jewish Federation of New Orleans, the musician and conductor had now acquired work as a violinist in a US orchestra "in one of the well-known symphonies in the northern section of this country." He made his "enthusiasm evident," Roehl wrote, with the statement, "'Your America is a wonderful place,'" adding, "'We can live in quiet here where everyone is free.'"

By using the word "Welcomes" in the headline, framing the story around musical elements, and including a photo with smiling, healthy, and well-dressed internees, Roehl seems to characterize enemy alien detention at Algiers and elsewhere in the United States as a reason for celebration rather than an unjust confinement. And indeed, "Mr. Siegfried's" story has a decidedly happy outcome, so upbeat it made it into the pages of the local newspaper, prompting us to wonder just who the mystery musician might be. Fortunately, research in the National Refugee Service records revealed his last name and relationship to his brother, Walter, and mother, Jeannette.[59] His State Department name file indicates that Siegfried Wolff was born January 28, 1906, in Cologne, and like his brother, was apprehended by the Panama police in the days following Pearl Harbor, then held at Balboa before being deported to the United States. The younger of the two brothers, he was received by the INS in New Orleans and sent on to Camp Kenedy and from there to Algiers in March 1943.

A March 7, 1946, State Department memo confirms Wolff's personal narrative, in which he explains he had his own orchestra in Germany until 1935, when he was forbidden by the Reichsmusikkammer to work in Germany. A

Nazi institution that promoted "good German music" composed by Aryans and consistent with Nazi ideals while rejecting "degenerate" musical forms such as jazz and anything written by Jewish composers, the Reichsmusikkammer was founded in 1933 by Joseph Goebbels. As we shall see, Wolff's problems with the Reichsmusikkammer and with Nazi discrimination in general would ironically propel him into a new life in Panama in which his knowledge of and expertise in classical music would be set aside for gigs in tropical cabarets playing exactly the kind of music the Reichsmusikkammer denounced and banned.

After his involuntary deportation to the United States (his mother was a voluntary deportee), Siegfried Wolff was sent to Camp Kenedy, his mother to Seagoville. On December 12, 1942, he composed a personal narrative at Camp Kenedy that explained how in 1935, longtime members of his orchestra refused to work further with him for the sole reason that he was a Jew: "Therefore I was forced to dissolve my orchestra and tried immediately to get engaged as a member of another orchestra. In this capacity it happened to me several times, that I had to break up in the middle of an engagement for being found out to be a Jew. Subsequently I have been menaced by the 'Gestapo' to be placed in a concentration camp and furthermore I received a letter from the 'Reichsmusikkammer' (State's chamber of music), Berlin forbidding me officially to work within the borders of Germany."[60] Describing himself as an "all-around musician" who played seven instruments, principally violin and saxophone, Wolff worked from 1936 to 1939 in Switzerland and Luxembourg, until foreigners were later barred from receiving work permits there as well. Through his brother, Walter, who had already emigrated in 1938, he obtained a visa for Panama for himself and his mother, and on October 17, 1939, they embarked from Genoa on the *Conte Grande*. Within a week, Siegfried found work at the Kelly Ritz Cabaret. Juggling his skills as a classical and popular musician, he served as a member of the symphony orchestra, taught violin privately, and held down another job at the Happyland Cabaret in Panama City.

His Department of Justice file contains a revealing account of the events that brought Siegfried to the United States and eventually Algiers, one that resembles the experiences of others in the Panama Jewish group in many aspects. He was arrested on December 9, 1941, by the Panamanian police on the Avenida Central. Despite the fact that his cedula identified him as a German Jew, he was forced into a car with many other people, carrying only his coat and his violin. From there, he was taken to the Cárcel Modelo, where he described being placed in a cell with about thirty other people before being transferred by American

Military Police to the Balboa Quarantine Station. He further explained, "I was not able to communicate with my mother, who did not know anything about my arrest. After some days, the rumors started, that one could afford one's release through payments. Amounts from 200$ -3000$ were named. But after we Jewish Refugees saw, that even several Nazis were released, we held it for impossible, that we, the victims of Hitler Germany could be held for internment. Rabbi Witkin of the Jewish Welfare Board Balboa told my mother not to pay any money, as our release was only a matter of some days."[61] Siegfried Wolff then explains how Panamanian officials approached his mother, demanding $450 for his release, but she refused, maintaining that her son was "a despiser of Hitler Germany" and "must go free without any payment." Weeks and months passed without a hearing, as the family's rabbi, Nathan Witkin, assured them it would be advantageous to be sent to the United States, "as he had every assurance that in a very short time we would get our release." But in fact, it would take Siegfried and the other members of his nuclear and extended family until August 1943 to obtain their release from Algiers to internment at large and until 1946 to clear their names from the alien enemy rolls. Along the way, Wolff filed papers requesting nonrepatriation for both himself and his mother with the Swiss legation in June 1942 and in February 1943 wrote to Cecilia Razovsky of the National Refugee Service in New York, suggesting she contact Ernst Drucker, also from Cologne, and a violinist in one of the country's well-known symphony orchestras.[62] The full "welcome" for Siegfried and his mother that Roehl wrote about in her 1943 article in the *New Orleans Item* only came to fruition years later. An alien registration number from Siegfried Wolff's file matches a US naturalization record dated November 5, 1948, in Cleveland, Ohio. Siegfried Wolff died in 1981.

As documents examined in this study make clear, internees were not always so euphonious about their experiences as Roehl's story (and other news coverage from the era) might suggest. Many who found themselves behind barbed wire in Texas, Tennessee, Florida, and elsewhere sought in vain to obtain a hearing on their cases or even a legitimate explanation for their detention. After investigating the cases of the Latin American internees in the countries from which they were deported, Raymond Ickes concluded, "Most of these people had no more business being in detention in the United States than I had."[63] Their stories return us to the question of whether Jews in Latin America were unfairly targeted for internment or were simply subject to the same prejudices all Germans and persons from other Axis countries encountered in the US alien enemy control program. Whatever our conclusion, it is clear that they themselves found a cruel irony in protocols that lumped them together with Axis nationals of every persuasion, including some who did not consider them fully human.

Additionally, there is evidence that Jews' hoped-for deliverance from persecution and discrimination was further hampered in the United States by policies long undergirded by antisemitism. Assistant Secretary of State Breckenridge Long directed his staff to employ delay tactics for immigration requests, with the result that "90 percent of the quota places reserved for refugees from Hitler's and Mussolini's dark realms were never filled."[64] In his diary Long wrote of Jews as "lawless, scheming, defiant—and in many ways unassimilable . . . some are certainly German agents."[65] Responsible for the deportation of Germans from Latin America, as well as their repatriation, Long repeatedly blocked the investigation of the Jewish internees among that group. Even when the lack of evidence for holding the Jews became an open secret, Long warned his colleagues that releasing them would cause governmental officials embarrassment. Max Paul Friedman judges that

> Long's impact on the internees from Latin America has been as little-known as the deportation program itself, but here, too, it was of crucial importance. He and his like-minded subordinates in the Special Division helped bring Jews and other non-Nazis into the camps and ensured that they would not receive hearings or be otherwise enabled to argue their case. With security concerns and diplomatic appearances paramount in their minds and their judgment clouded by prejudice, Long and his coterie discounted the possible innocence of some internees and worried instead about the possibility of scandal that might arise from their release.[66]

Seemingly impervious to the visceral antipathy most Jews felt toward the Nazis, Long allowed Jews to remain on lists for future repatriation as late as August 1942, refusing to promise not to deport Jewish internees to Germany against their will.[67]

It seems clear that the final outcome of the enemy alien internment program was positive for many of the Jews apprehended in Panama and elsewhere: a significant majority were released to internment at large and eventually uncoupled from the status of enemy alien itself, allowing them to pursue naturalization and the establishment of a permanent home in the United States.

Personal histories, letters, and other evidence documenting the perspectives of the detainees themselves leave no doubt, though, that members of this group considered themselves to be the victims of a grave injustice. In their assessment of their experiences both during and after internment, shock, unfairness, and fear emerge as principal motifs—despite relief or celebration upon their final release from the enemy alien designation. On balance, the economic, social, and ethical costs of apprehending Jewish refugees and other anti-Nazis and interning them alongside those they identified as their worst enemies, in a sweep that at the same time spared many Nazi insiders and hardliners from that same fate, are ultimately incalculable.

CHAPTER 4

Professor, Spy, Confidant

Three Notables Interned in New Orleans

Many noteworthy individuals have a connection to the United States' Alien Enemy Control Program's operations in New Orleans, but three German-born internees capture our attention in this chapter, provoking questions regarding the impact of the World War II detention program on sociopolitical debates still at the fore today. What constitutes free speech? What is hate speech? What are the ethical or moral grounds for indefinite detention of noncitizen persons with or without a criminal record? Unlike the majority of the detainees at Camp Algiers, all three men were apprehended as part of domestic controls within the United States. The first, Professor Hermann Beyer, was a well-known archaeologist at Tulane University who had extensive experience in Mexico and other parts of Latin America. The second, Horst von der Goltz, also had a Mexican connection. He rode with Pancho Villa in the Mexican Revolution before being accused of espionage in England. The third, Kurt Ludecke, was a confidant of Adolf Hitler, with a book titled *I Knew Hitler* and pictures of himself with the führer to prove it. All three individuals' loyalty to the United States was called into question, and while the government decided that internment was warranted for all three, the outcome of this decision was different in each man's case.

Professor and Code Breaker

Born in Cologne in 1880, Hermann Beyer was a renowned archaeologist specializing in indigenous Mexico whose affiliation with the Middle American Research Institute (MARI) at Tulane University in New Orleans began in 1927 (figure 4.1).[1] Recognized for his detailed study of Mayan and other pre-Colombian hieroglyphics, he was credited with discovering elements that are crucial to contemporary understandings of Mayan writing systems. When Frans Blom, then director of MARI (1926–40), brought Beyer into the institute, he described him as "somewhat inclined to German pedantry, but with a profound knowledge of his field."[2] *Restless Blood*, a recent biography of Blom, characterizes Beyer as "the most active and probably the most intelligent" of the staff members Blom attracted to the institute.[3] From bases in Mexico and later New Orleans, Beyer established a body of pioneering research on sites such as Palenque, Chichén Itzá, Copán, and other archaeological landmarks in the Yucatán and the central valley of Mexico.

Beyer's most famous work, according to his former student and colleague Alfonso Caso, was his 1921 interpretation of the Aztec calendar, still regarded as defensible decades later. His study of pre-Columbian objects also extended beyond Mexico. In 1930, he attended a conference of Americanists in Hamburg,

FIGURE 4.1. Studio portrait of Hermann Beyer. Courtesy Tulane University Archives.

taking advantage of that opportunity to also study Mayan codices held in Dresden.[4] He had also researched the pre-Columbian Mexico collection at the Ethnographic Museum in Florence. As Caso recalled after Beyer's death, "His excellent research method, his interest not only in the foundation of any problem but also in the small details—so significant in Mayan and Mexican hieroglyphics—his reluctance to admit as true anything that had not been sufficiently proven, and—why not also mention it—his sarcastic attitude toward any theories constructed superficially without sufficient background, were for all of us a great lesson. Beyer, as a professor, knew not only how to awaken the interest of his students with the materials he presented, but also how to correct the excessive enthusiasm they provoked."[5]

Perhaps the greatest acknowledgment of Beyer's achievements and influence was the honorary doctorate in philosophy he received from the Bavarian Julius Maximilians University in Wurzburg, Germany, in recognition of his outstanding work in Mexican and Central American archaeology. According to a June 5, 1932, article in the *New Orleans States,* Dr. Rolf Jaeger, German consul in New Orleans, was to present the elaborate diploma in a ceremony at Tulane's Department of Middle American Research with "prominent local educators, leading citizens, and members of the consular corps" in attendance.[6]

In 1919, Beyer had also founded an academic journal titled *El México antiguo,* authoring dozens of the articles that appeared in its pages and personally attending to the myriad tasks related to the journal's publication. In addition, he built an impressive bibliography that in 1941 numbered 163 articles written in English, Spanish, and German, of which Caso commented, "And here it is important to praise the most salient quality of Beyer as a researcher: his scientific integrity. He never twisted an opinion distant from his own, never failed to cite a discovery, theory or idea that he used in his articles or research. He had one fundamental concern: science, knowledge, and to this concern he subordinated everything else; this is the highest praise one can give to a researcher."[7]

Despite this praise, Beyer's personal politics proved to be increasingly problematic both for him and for his colleagues as his tenure at Tulane continued. As Robert Brunhouse notes, "As the 1930s wore on, Beyer, who retained his German citizenship, began to champion Hitler and his policies. After a visit to Germany in 1938, he became more vocal."[8] Indeed, Beyer's 1938 trip to his homeland, which lasted nearly six months and was recorded on his Nazi-era German *Reisepass* or passport (figure 4.2), as well as the manifest of a ship arriving in New York harbor from Bremen, Germany, in October of that year,

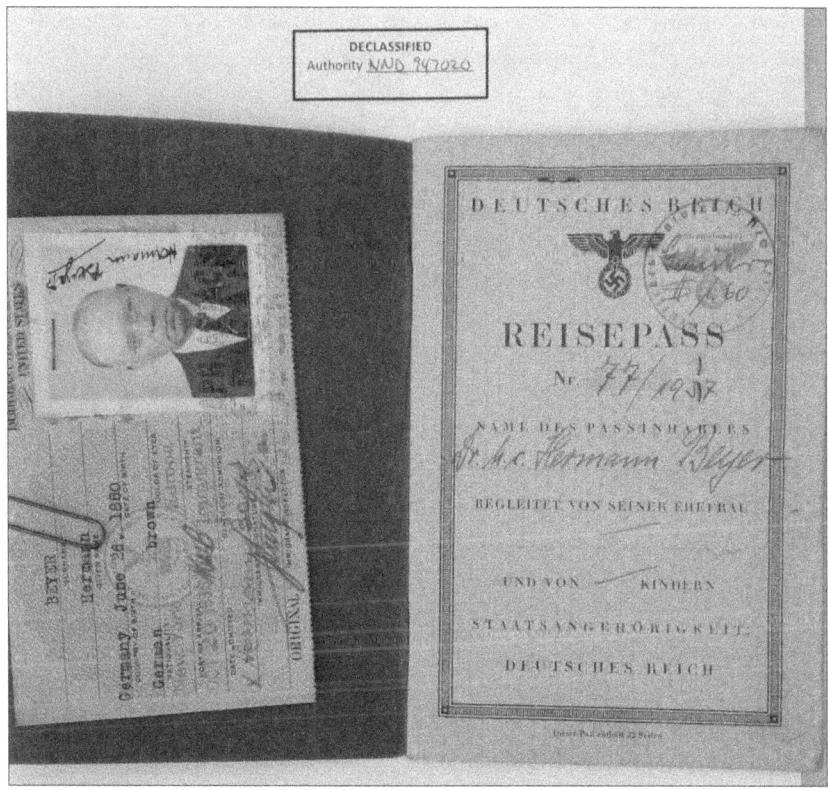

FIGURE 4.2. Hermann Beyer's Nazi-era passport. National Archives, used with permission.

convinced him that the growth of Nazism was a welcome development. An emphatic headline on page 2 of the *New Orleans Item* dated November 1, 1938, declared, "'Germany More Democratic Than Ever,' Says Tulane Scholar on Return to Work."[9]

Based on an interview with Harnett T. Kane, the piece in the *Item* opened by quoting the professor as saying, "Leaving out the question of the personal dictator, Germany under the Nazis is more democratic than it ever was" and "Germany is becoming more and more democratic because the masses are on top, and the old classes are down." By stating this opinion, the German-born archaeologist "reversed the usual custom of travelers returning from Naziland," Kane quipped. But Beyer claimed he found his compatriots "healthier than ever"; regarding the Nazi threat to the Americas, he surmised, "They don't care in Germany about America . . . but they object when America tries to meddle." With Austria and Czechoslovakia already under Nazi rule, Beyer believed Poland and Hungary would defend their autonomy. "Germany will get along with Central Europe now, but she doesn't want to conquer it," he was quoted as saying. On the subject of the Nazis' persecution of the Jews, the article stated, "He believes it is 'not against the old-time Jews but the ones that have come lately.'" As an example of this Nazi "democracy" at work, Beyer explained to his interviewer that nothing adverse happened to him when he declared on a German streetcar his lack of belief in the mental superiority of the Aryans, stating instead that he judged it a good thing for Hitler himself to have "non-Aryan" blood.

The Kane piece on Beyer ruffled some feathers, to say the least. On November 5, the *Item* ran an editorial under the title "A Democratic Demurrer" in which the editors acknowledged the troublesome issues the feature had highlighted. How strong could democracy ever have been in Germany if Beyer now found it to be at its peak in 1938? And just what was Dr. Beyer's conception of the meaning of the word "democracy"? The unnamed editorialist wrote:

> It is utterly impossible, in the face of the most unimpeachable reports from Germany, and in the teeth of the orations, proclamations, and acts of its rulers themselves, to believe that there is any democracy whatsoever in Germany—in the sense in which WE understand that term in the United States.
>
> Where no one is free to express his opinions, where newspapers are rigidly censored, where the clergy of all denominations are disciplined by the State . . . where the person is degraded in every respect by subordination to the State, and where the State itself is the Dictator—THERE can be no democracy whatsoever.[10]

While acknowledging Dr. Beyer's right to free expression of his opinions, the *Item* wondered how "any free scholar could acquire so strange a delusion" and referred to his stated opinion as a "hallucination." The editors also took issue with Beyer's position on the treatment of "old" versus "new" Jews under Hitler, insisting, "Jews who had been in Germany for centuries, who had made most illustrious careers in science, scholarship and art, have been treated in exactly the same cruel way as the latest immigrant from Poland. This extends even to Jews who risked and lost their lives for Germany on the battlefields of the World War, and to the children of such Jews." The editorial concluded, "Nazism is but a harking-back to obsolete evils that civilization had corrected many times, but must still correct again."

Rufus Harris, president of Tulane University from 1937 to 1959, was also hearing from his constituency regarding the *Item* interview. On February 7, 1938, he responded to an inquiry from Charles Rosen, a member of the board of trustees of the university for fifty years, signaling the alarm about Beyer's comments as a representative of Tulane. Harris assured him that while he wholeheartedly disagreed with the professor, "I suppose that Dr. Beyer as a citizen is entitled to hold whatever political views he wishes—no matter how much of delusion, unenlightenment, and downright obscurantism they may contain." He closed the letter, however, by saying, "I deeply regret that Mr. Beyer was willing to give publicity to views which must cause embarrassment to his colleagues and subject the institution with which he is connected to unjustified but understandable criticism."[11]

Beyer's decision to retain his German citizenship despite his long stays in Mexico and the United States would increasingly serve as a red flag to authorities building cases against resident aliens even before the United States entered the war. German noncitizens in the United States "were protected by the broad rights granted to citizens" until the European war began in 1939, but the subsequent Alien Registration Act of 1940 required all noncitizens over age fourteen to register and be photographed and fingerprinted at a post office or other government agency.[12] As James Dickerson notes in *Inside America's Concentration Camps*, "The FBI wasted no time rounding up individuals who fit its profile of an enemy alien. The agency already had spent months drawing up secret lists of people to be arrested" before Pearl Harbor, devising a classification system by which noncitizens were rated as to the threat they presented, though it became increasingly clear that this system was deeply flawed.[13] While estimates of the German population in the country at the start of the 1940s vary widely, historians concur that perhaps less than 10 percent of that population were members of pro-Nazi organizations such as the German-American Bund.[14]

Beyer's position supporting Germany and the Nazis became increasingly awkward for Tulane, not just for its president, but also for a very influential MARI colleague, Doris Stone. An archaeologist specializing in Costa Rica, Stone was the daughter of Samuel Zemurray, the famed "Sam the Banana Man" who formed the Cuyamel Fruit Company and later headed the United Fruit Company, an enterprise with extensive influence in Central America. In 1924, Zemurray had donated a library, archaeological artifacts, and an endowment that together provided for the establishment of the Department of Middle American Research, which would later become MARI. Although Stone had moved to Costa Rica with her husband, Roger Thayer Stone, in 1939, she remained closely involved in the institute and its operation. Indeed, the Zemurray and Stone family legacies have proved vital to the university and to New Orleans, as Doris and Roger Stone together founded the Roger Thayer Stone Center for Latin American Studies, and in the twenty-first century, the Zemurray Foundation endowed the Samuel Z. Stone CIPR Support Trust for the Center for Inter-American Policy and Research as well as the Doris Zemurray Stone Post-Doctoral Fellowship at the Stone Center.[15]

In June 1940, at Stone's suggestion, President Harris had written to Samuel Kirkland Lothrop in New York requesting information "about Dr. Beyer's activities in Mexico prior to and during the World War of 1917."[16] Also an accomplished archaeologist and anthropologist, Lothrop was associated with the Carnegie Institute's Historical Division, the Heye Foundation's Museum of the American Indian in New York City, and Harvard's Peabody Museum. Regarding his inquiry into Beyer's "activities" during World War I, Lothrop handwrote a short reply to Harris on a postcard-sized note stating simply,

> During the last war, the Germans maintained a propaganda bureau in Mexico known as Servicio de Informaciones Alemanes [sic] en México. One of their activities was the publication of a series entitled Disertaciones Científicas de Autores Alemanas [sic] en México, which was designed to impress on Latin Americans the great erudition of German scholars.
>
> Dr. Beyer contributed several purely scientific articles, of which there doubtless are copies in the splendid library of your Middle American Research Institute. The existence of these articles is prima facie evidence that Dr. Beyer was in contact with the German propaganda bureau in Mexico in 1918. Beyond this, however, I have no direct knowledge of his activities.[17]

Was Beyer a spy or otherwise involved in German intelligence work in Mexico during or after the First World War? For Lothrop, the "evidence" of his contact with the German propaganda bureau in the context of World War I was clear, although he claimed not to know of any activities beyond publishing some "purely scientific" articles. And combining archaeological inquiry with spy work was something Lothrop knew about from personal experience.

In *Anthropological Intelligence,* David Price shows how during World War II, American anthropologists and archaeologists worked at a variety of government agencies under the administration of the US Department of War, Department of the Interior, Department of State, and the White House. Some of that work addressed both citizen and alien detention populations directly. For example, more than a dozen anthropologists worked for the War Relocation Authority, Bureau of Sociological Research, and Japanese American Evacuation and Resettlement Study, all directed at Japanese Americans confined in domestic "relocation" sites. But the enlistment of social scientists also extended beyond US territory, just as the detention program itself reached into South and Central America. As Price notes, "The FBI's Special Intelligence Service (SIS) is shown to have used anthropologists to collect intelligence throughout Central America and South America, using archaeology as their cover for spying. These methods were a return to the tactics deployed by Samuel Lothrop."[18]

Indeed, Lothrop was both a scholar and a spy, as Price labels him in a chapter on FBI director J. Edgar Hoover's Special Intelligence Service. He accomplished "highly commendable work" in the Caribbean region using "archaeological fieldwork as a cover for espionage during the First World War" before he was identified as "well suited to work as a spy in Latin America for the SIS."[19] Together with Hoover confidant and New York socialite Victor Astor, Lothrop drew up a list of anthropologists who might be useful in foreign intelligence work, among whom Frans Blom was identified "as being particularly well informed concerning different areas of Latin America."[20] Lothrop himself would assume a leading role in this work combining spy work with archaeology. To prepare, he attended FBI espionage classes in Washington, DC, where he learned about secret codes, fictitious contact names, US mail drops and other tools of the trade. However, once installed in Lima with his wife, he worried that the lack of progress in his research would lead to the discovery of his "true work" and reported to FBI headquarters, "As regards the archaeological cover for my work in Peru, it was based on the understanding that I was to be in the country six months or less. It is wearing thin and some day somebody is going to start asking why an archaeologist spends most of his time in towns asking questions."[21]

Perhaps it is only a coincidence, but in the same month that Harris wrote to Lothrop asking about Beyer, MARI director Frans Blom wrote to Harris about a conversation he had had with Beyer in which his colleague indicated he wanted to resign from MARI, giving the following reason: "He had felt that he was shadowed and spied upon. He felt that Germans are very unpopular in New Orleans and therefore can not do his work with full peace of mind. He stated that he did not want to sever relations with our Institute, which had given him much free and full opportunity to develop his research; but at the same time, he would feel better if he were released."[22] Blom suggested to Harris that Tulane retain Beyer as a "roving" or traveling associate, paying him $150 a month. President Harris rejected the proposed arrangement. It seems he and Blom both believed Beyer would then resign of his own accord; when Harris wrote to Blom on August 5, 1940, to formally reject his proposal, he ended by saying, "Naturally, I am appreciative of the faithful and fine work which Dr. Beyer has done at Tulane, and regret his departure."[23] But President Harris's message of appreciation upon Beyer's exit was a bit premature, as the archaeologist's relationship with Tulane would not be dissolved that year—or the next.

As it turns out, Lothrop was not the only person to suggest that the specialized knowledge of the archaeologists and other scholars associated with MARI could be useful to the US government, especially during wartime. In May 1941, Doris Stone wrote a letter to her father, Sam Zemurray, making sure a copy of it reached Rufus Harris.[24] In it, she wondered if it wasn't "unimportant for the university to pay the salaries of archaeologists and linguists to dig up matters concerning dead people when there is so much that these same people could do to assist in our defense program." Stone questioned if it wouldn't be a timely move "to suggest to Norman [sic] Rockefeller's Committee—that the department with certain of its personnel are at their services for the duration of the war."[25] Enumerating the skills and knowledge of MARI's associates, Stone also judged "it would be very simple for the Government to exclude Blom and Beyer" from such work on the grounds of their status as foreigners. How Zemurray responded to Stone's idea is not clear, but Blom and Beyer would both end their affiliations with Tulane, albeit under very different circumstances.[26]

It wasn't until the following summer, in August 1941, that President Harris formally proposed that Beyer take a leave of absence until the end of the war, offering him a "reasonable monetary stipend" for the first year of that leave in view of his long and valuable service to the institute. "I hope very much that this war crisis will not involve or imperil you or your full freedom and liberty . . . and that our once happy work here someday may be resumed." Beyer accepted, but it seems his days of "full freedom and liberty" may have already ended: his paperwork in the National Archives documents his INS intake in the spring of 1941, providing few details as to the specific reason for or date of his internment or regarding his transfer from New Orleans to camps in Texas and later Oklahoma.[27]

In late January 1942, President Harris spoke of Beyer in a letter to Doris Stone, confiding, "I cannot tell you this officially, since I do not know it officially, but I understand that Dr. Beyer is being held for internment as an enemy alien."[28] On February 25, he wrote to her again, noting, "There is no further information regarding Hermann Beyer beyond that of his internment," but then adding, "I have just this minute heard that yesterday he suffered a stroke and is thought to be dying. I feel very sorry for him."[29]

Unlike the voluminous files on the other two notable internees profiled in this chapter, Beyer's government record is thin and leaves many questions hanging. It does indicate that at some point, he was transferred from New Orleans to Fort Sam Houston in San Antonio, Texas, a military base that functioned during World War II primarily as a temporary holding site for Japanese detainees from Alaska and Hawaii as well as for German and Italian nationals while permanent internment camps were being constructed.[30] His name shows up on a list of enemy aliens being held at "Fort Sam" dated May 1, 1942.[31] From Texas, he would be sent on to the Stringtown detention facility in Oklahoma in late May of that year.

As the photos on his personnel record generated at the Enemy Alien Detention Station at Algiers in 1942 suggest (figure 4.3), Beyer was not in good health when apprehended, and his condition apparently deteriorated further in detention. In a censorship intercept of a letter Beyer wrote from the Oklahoma camp in June 1942 to a Bertha Initze at a German address, he complained of the conditions at Stringtown with the sarcastic humor for which he was well known in the academic world. "Now I sit in a 'summer resort' in a former negro penitentiary. I hope that I will be exchanged soon, for Uncle Sam's somewhat miserly hospitality does not please me very much. At present I am in a hospital where there are hardly any medicines, but very many flies."[32] The mordant reference to Stringtown suggests that Beyer found it especially degrading to be detained in a facility formerly used for African Americans.[33] The reference to "exchange" strongly suggests he anticipated being repatriated to Germany in exchange for US civilians in Axis territory.

Was Beyer's description of Stringtown accurate? In his wartime memoir, Czech-born Walter Kohner recalled being posted at the Oklahoma camp shortly after being drafted into the US military. Since he was not yet a US citizen, officials decided his fluency in German would be an asset at a site then holding hundreds of German alien enemies.[34] Arriving at the camp in August 1942, Kohner recalled:

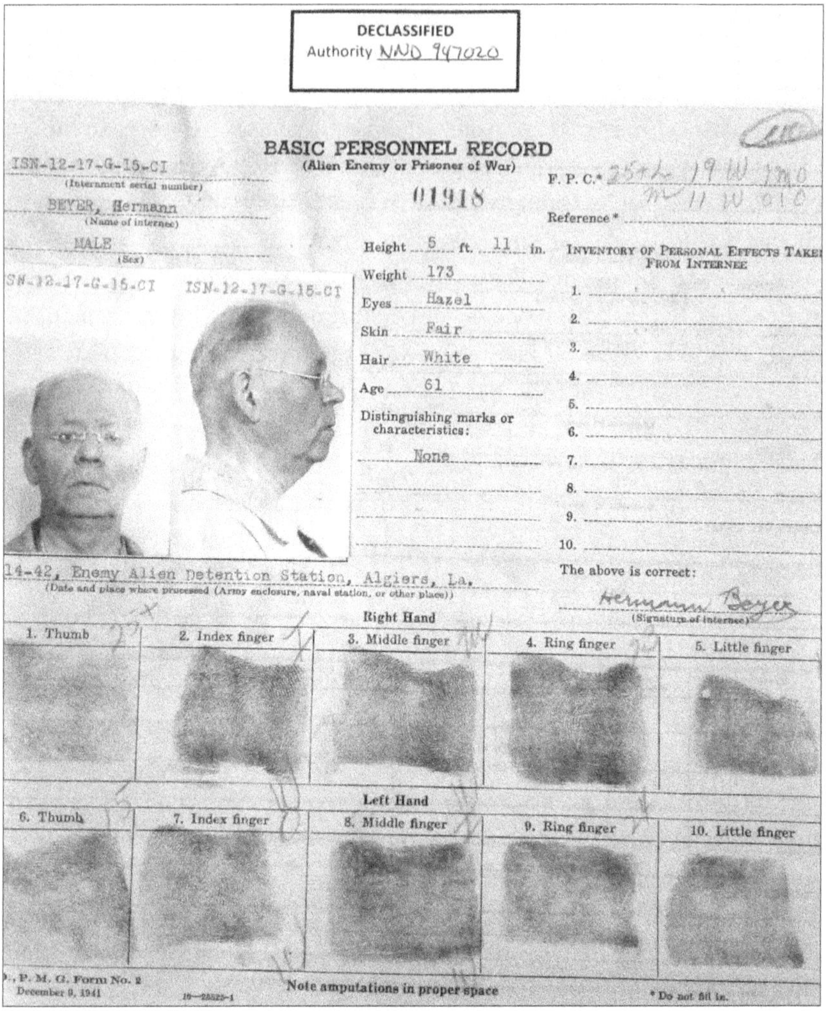
DECLASSIFIED
Authority NND 947020

BASIC PERSONNEL RECORD
(Alien Enemy or Prisoner of War)

ISN-12-17-G-15-CI
(Internment serial number)
BEYER, Hermann
(Name of internee)
MALE
(Sex)

01918

F. P. C.* 25+L 19 W IMO
M 11 W OIO
Reference *

ISN-12-17-G-15-CI ISN-12-17-G-15-CI

Height 5 ft. 11 in.
Weight 173
Eyes Hazel
Skin Fair
Hair White
Age 61
Distinguishing marks or characteristics:
None

INVENTORY OF PERSONAL EFFECTS TAKEN FROM INTERNEE
1.
2.
3.
4.
5.
6.
7.
8.
9.
10.
The above is correct:
Hermann Beyer
(Signature of internee)

14-42, Enemy Alien Detention Station, Algiers, La.
(Date and place where processed (Army enclosure, naval station, or other place))

Right Hand

1. Thumb	2. Index finger	3. Middle finger	4. Ring finger	5. Little finger

Left Hand

6. Thumb	7. Index finger	8. Middle finger	9. Ring finger	10. Little finger

P. M. G. Form No. 2
December 9, 1941
16—25525-1
Note amputations in proper space
* Do not fill in.

FIGURE 4.3. Hermann Beyer's alien enemy personnel record. National Archives, used with permission.

The internees represented a cross section of German aliens. They had not received (or even applied for) U.S. citizenship, and for various reasons were considered security risks by the FBI. Among them were farmers, businessmen, a few intellectuals and a doctor . . .

A small group was die-hard Nazis. Even though strictly forbidden, they defiantly and openly displayed swastika buttons in their lapels.

When these were confiscated by the MPS, crudely drawn swastikas and paintings of Hitler appeared on the walls of their living quarters. Many, however, were anti-Nazi and there were always conflicts between the two groups.[35]

Kohner also witnessed the arrival of a dilapidated bus carrying a large group of civilians during his time at Stringtown: "They were German-speaking Jews who had been thrown out of some Latin American country and shipped to the United States in the hope that we would grant them visitors' visas." Tasked by the internal security and intelligence officer with finding room for the new arrivals in the already crowded barracks, Kohner took issue with his superior's order:

> I explained to him that the new arrivals were Jewish refugees and could not be put into the same quarters as the Nazis. I warned him of the possible consequences if the two groups were forced to live in close proximity. He didn't seem to understand the difference between a German Jew and a German Nazi. . . . I suggested letting the refugees sleep in the camp hospital's unoccupied beds. He agreed—reluctantly.
>
> The refugees looked to me as their protector, their liberator. Most of them did not speak English, and I was besieged with anxious questions. I told them they were safe and should consider themselves lucky to have landed on American soil. They believed me. Orders arrived the next day from Washington to transfer them. They never had to confront the Nazis. The next day I accompanied the busload of refugees to the Stringtown railroad station and waved goodbye as the train pulled out.[36]

The available documentation does not bear out Kohner's contention that the German Jews who arrived at Stringtown "never had to confront the Nazis" thanks to a quick transfer, since inevitably, they encountered the same problems in subsequent camps as well. In fact, Kohner himself endured abuse as a Jewish refugee at Stringtown when the civilian German internees were sent to another site and German prisoners of war arrived to replace them. He described some in this latter group as "rabid Nazis." "My duties were still the same, but now I had to face open hostility every morning," he recounted.[37]

Beyer's own Stringtown story ended very differently. The exchange he mentioned in his censored letter never occurred. He did not return to his homeland, as he died at sixty-two on December 6, 1942, with the declared cause of death arterial nephrosclerosis and cardiac insufficiency. Stringtown administration records show he was buried at the internee cemetery, but a request to remove Beyer's remains dated October 2, 1945, was apparently granted, as his tombstone can now be found along the west wall of the Fort Reno Cemetery, about 150 miles northwest of Stringtown. Other than his name and the dates of his birth and death, the only other identifier on Beyer's headstone is the word "German."

According to Carolyn Barker's "Burials in the Fort Reno Cemetery, 1874–1948," Beyer was initially buried at Fort Sill, Oklahoma, not Stringtown. That detail would be unimportant were it not for the high visibility the former internment camp received after the US Office of Refugee Resettlement announced plans in June 2019 to house fourteen hundred unaccompanied migrant children from Latin America there, a plan considered further in the epilogue. In any case, it wasn't until February 1943 that New Orleans newspapers published news of Beyer's demise in a story with the headlines "Dr. H. Beyer Dies While Interned" and "N.O. Scholar Dies in Alien Camp." The latter of these stories, which made the front page of the *New Orleans Item* on February 25, 1943, claimed Beyer "ever since Hitler's rise to power had been an outspoken pro-Nazi."[38] Dr. Robert Wauchope, Blom's successor as Director of MARI, said he had received the news of Beyer's death in a letter from the provost marshal general of the War Department. No specific reasons for his internment were given. When Wauchope wrote his own remembrance in February 1943, published in *American Antiquity* in April of the following year, he mentioned Beyer's place of death as the Stringtown Army Internment Camp but focused primarily on his Tulane colleague as "one of the world's outstanding scholars in the field of Middle American hieroglyphic studies."[39]

More than three decades would pass before an interview of Maurice Ries—hired by Blom in 1931 to edit MARI's publications—would reveal key details regarding the FBI's decision to intern Beyer. Conducted by Thomas Niehaus, director of the Latin American Library at Tulane from 1977 to 1990, Ries explained that he and other members of the institute became increasingly concerned about Beyer after his 1938 trip to Germany. Ries claimed that Beyer "had become quite close" to Baron von Spiegel, a World War I U-boat commander who was serving as the German consul in New Orleans in the lead-up to US involvement in World War II and was a known supporter of Hitler. When prompted by Niehaus, Ries also recalled that upon returning from Germany, Beyer was suddenly absent from his office on the Tulane campus many afternoons, reportedly frequenting the city's busy wharves and observing the ship traffic there. Ries claimed he and his colleagues also noticed swastika armbands on Beyer's desk and one morning arrived at the institute to find them in use: "A few of us came early, more or less early, one morning and happened to walk up the steps together and as we entered the M.A.R.I. down at the library end where there was a large table here was Gropp, Arthur Gropp the librarian who was of Germanic extraction from Kansas, here was Gropp and Beyer with arm bands on, Nazi arm bands on, goose-stepping around this table with their arms raised in heil, heil."⁴⁰ In his interview with Niehaus, the former MARI editor referred to papers captured in North Africa after the United States had entered the war that indicated Spiegel was to "be the—the ruler of the United States" and with Spiegel was Beyer, "listed as the geopolitical advisor."

Though Ries said he "was sorry" for what had happened to Beyer, he judged the internment necessary:

> At least it was correct to pick him up. Now he was put—sent up to Oklahoma, I think it was, to a—an internment center—call it a concentration camp if you will, it—apparently it was not anything very uncomfortable and apparently everyone was very well treated and there he asked to be allowed to go on with his work. Well, the agency of the United States government which was administering this camp, this center, refused to let him have his cabinets of hieroglyphs but they did let him have his papers and books and he continued to work on—on the text at least, if he couldn't have his illustrations with his—with his drawings.⁴¹

However real a threat Beyer represented to the FBI, his subsequent death in detention at Stringtown signified a major loss for many of his fellow archaeologists in Mexico. In an issue of the Mexican journal *Boletín bibliográfico de antropología americana*, Alfonso Caso offered a remembrance of the professor in which there is no hint of the danger or peril with which the US government associated him. Caso described how he met Beyer in 1924 in Mexico, where the professor was then lecturing on archaeology at the National University; Beyer's classes were the only source of knowledge on the early cultures of Mexico inside or outside the university at that time, and Caso counted himself fortunate to have been one of his students in this still relatively new branch of study.⁴² He lamented that death had now robbed him and his colleagues of a first-class researcher in the field of Mexican archaeology, both a man of science and a friend; together they were only now realizing the magnitude of Beyer's labor in favor of the study of Mexico.

Professor Beyer had begun to publish articles on Mexico as early as 1908 in both academic publications and the local press and, according to Caso, had remained in Mexico from about 1910 until 1927, marrying a woman from the Puebla region during that period. Caso's description of his professor's detention also differs from the government's record; he laments that Beyer "had to be taken with other persons to a concentration camp, in which he died December 6 of last year, victim of a long illness from which he was already suffering when he left Mexico."[43] It may seem ironic in hindsight that Caso, who believed that the systematic study of ancient Mexican civilizations was an important way to understand Mexican cultural roots and had himself made notable discoveries in excavations at Monte Albán and in deciphering Mixtec codices, expressed no concerns whatsoever with Beyer's political leanings.[44] Carlos R. Linga also contributed to that issue of the *Boletín bibliográfico de antropología americana*, recognizing Professor Beyer's role, together with the geologist Ernesto Wittich, in one of the most important paleontological discoveries of the early twentieth century, that of the "Man of the Pedegral of San Ángel, located in the southern part of Mexico City, unearthed from more than eight meters of lava."[45]

What would happen to Beyer's formidable body of research after his death in detention? Beginning in January 1943, Robert Wauchope, the new director of MARI, began a protracted quest to recuperate elements of Beyer's research that he surmised were in the possession of the authorities, writing first to the commanding officer of the army internment camp at Stringtown and then the New Orleans office of the FBI.[46] But it was Beyer's MARI colleague Arthur Gropp, identified by Ries as being a Kansan of German extraction, who ultimately saved the day—or at least Beyer's effects. Recalling "Hermann Beyer's Last Years" in a 1959 volume of *El México antiguo* honoring the memory of the man who had founded the journal forty years earlier, Gropp wrote, "We enjoyed his friendly congeniality, his thoughtful and reserved deliberation, and his wit and humor. We came to have great respect for his scholarship and dedication to a field of study in which he excelled."[47]

The former MARI librarian remembered that after Beyer's internment, he had news of him on only two occasions, the first when he was brought from internment to New Orleans for treatment of dangerously high blood pressure and again when he was permitted to see Dr. Beyer at the Marine Hospital in

Algiers. "I left Dr. Beyer hoping that the world situation would soon be over and that he would again be able to dedicate himself to his studies. The visit had the effect of giving us increased assurance that Dr. Beyer was to have the best of medical care. This was the last time, to my knowledge, that any of his associates were privileged to see Dr. Beyer alive."[48]

Though he was living in Montevideo when he heard of Beyer's death in February 1943, it was Gropp who paid the outstanding bill on Beyer's belongings, which the OK Storage Company in New Orleans had been holding since July 1941. Gropp wrote to Wauchope, explaining that the items had been rescued in the nick of time, as they were to be sold at public auction on March 31 of that year. "The glyph materials were classified and arranged to a point where he was ready to interpret and leave his monumental life's work. I felt that if I didn't move to delay the sale of those materials . . . they might have fallen into non-appreciative hands and so would have been lost forever."[49] Recognizing the value of these materials, university officials stepped in to reimburse Gropp, and Beyer's manuscripts and other effects were moved to the MARI offices in Tulane's Dinwiddie Hall, where many remain today.

Beyer's research continued to circulate and support the mission of Tulane and MARI after his death, despite the controversies that swirled around him during the last part of his life. In 1951, the *San Antonio Express* published an article titled "Mexican Expert on Writings of Maya Indians Visits S.A.," heralding the visit of a distinguished archaeologist and professor from Mexico City named César Lizardi Ramos, who was lecturing on a document known as *The Genesis of the Maya Hieroglyphs*, written and illustrated by Dr. Hermann Beyer. The paper reported the unique document—likely the only copy of Beyer's groundbreaking findings—had been turned over to Lizardi Ramos by MARI "when it was found after being lost for several years."[50]

Beyer's careful research and findings as an archaeologist, or perhaps more specifically, as an epigrapher—someone who studies and interprets ancient inscriptions—have since been confirmed and eclipsed by later scholars, who, despite these advances, continue to recognize his contributions. For MARI director Marcello Canuto, Beyer was "the real deal," not just someone using the cover of archaeological investigation for other purposes.[51] And Beyer doesn't even merit a mention in Jeb Card's *Spooky Archaeology*, which tracks the penchant in the field for exotic artifacts, mysterious hieroglyphic inscriptions, lost continents, and extraterrestrial visitors. Beyer's case now strikes us as mysterious and eerie for other reasons.

Soldier, Spy, Pet Shop Boy

When the FBI showed up to arrest him in 1943, Horst von der Goltz had lived outside of Germany for some three decades. From age sixteen on, he had "indulged in an adventurous lifestyle that quickly brought him in conflict with the law."[52] He entered the United States for the first time through the port of New York in 1912, enlisted in the US Army, and served as a private until he deserted in 1913 in El Paso to join the Mexican army. After being named a major under Pancho Villa, he returned to Germany via Italy using a false American passport. His real name, it seems, was Franz Wachendorf. According to historian Thomas Boghardt at the International Spy Museum in Washington, "Horst von der Goltz" was a name he likely invented "to impress the Mexicans," though he listed his father's name as Francis von der Goltz on his marriage license, suggesting either that von der Goltz was authentic or that Horst was not averse to expanding the lineage of his pseudonym.[53]

Von der Goltz was also a spy. He was ostensibly en route to the United States for a second time when he was detained by the British in 1916 and found guilty of espionage. Sentenced to be shot, he confessed to British authorities his role in an earlier plot to blow up the Welland Canal on the US-Canada border, hatched with Captain Franz von Papen, the German military attaché to Washington. (Papen would later serve as vice chancellor under Adolf Hitler from 1933 to 1934.) In the course of the canal conspiracy, von der Goltz had obtained a false passport under his nom de guerre Bridgeman A. Taylor, allowing him to travel as an American citizen. He explained as much in a book he later wrote titled *My Adventures as a German Secret Service Agent,* first published by R. M. McBridge and Company in 1917.[54] In that text, von der Goltz praised German intelligence and its deep penetration of America, even if he also seemed to sympathize with a gullible population of German-born Americans:

> By the time the Great War broke out the German propaganda in America had assumed notable proportions. German newspapers were plentiful and had acquired a tremendous influence over the minds of the German-speaking folk. Many of the German societies had been consolidated into one national organisation—the German American National Alliance, with a membership of two millions. . . . And the German people of the United States had, by a long campaign of flattery and cajolery, coupled with a systematic glorification of German genius and institu-

tions, been won to attachment to the country of their origin that required only a touch to translate it into fanaticism."[55]

Von der Goltz also offered details of his apprehension as an "espionage agent" in Britain, where the canal bombing plot came to light and he feared the firing squad. Boghardt surmises that he "did great damage to the individuals implicated [in the Welland Canal conspiracy], in the process contributing significantly to the Germans' image as 'dynamiters' in the United States."[56] In exchange for his testimony, British officials returned him to North America in 1916 to turn state's evidence; having avoided the death sentence, "he was lucky to be shunted off to an internment camp on Ellis Island instead."[57] It seems from this account of his personal history, then, that von der Goltz was interned in detention facilities in the United States in the context of *both* World War I and World War II.

Despite this curiosity, what happened to von der Goltz during his first stay at Ellis Island was of little interest to the FBI or other officials engaged in determining his dangerousness in the lead-up to World War II. Much of his life story seemed remarkably benign. Von der Goltz had petitioned for naturalization as a US citizen in May 1922 and in 1925 had married Kentucky-born Margaret "Peggy" Cooper Gay. He worked in the subsequent decade and a half in a variety of jobs, including as a writer for *Field and Fancy*, as a helper to his wife in her pet shop, and as a director of folk dance events in the New York area, supported in this latter task by Daniel Cranford Smith, the founder of the New School of Social Research.[58] "Vondy," as he was nicknamed, also worked on Republican campaign committees in 1936 and 1940 and as editor in chief of the Foreign Language Press Service for an unspecified time. In January 1942, he was employed as an administrator for *Steeltrade*, a publication with a distribution to fifteen thousand subscribers in Central and South American engineering and steel companies, but by May of that same year he was on his way out over a disagreement.

After the US entry into World War II, the FBI took new interest in von der Goltz: he was reported to be an associate of Colonel William Sohier Bryant "in connection with an organization composed of the leaders of the German-American Bund, the American Destiny Party, the Christian Mobilizers, the Knights of the White Camellia and other various anti-war organizations of pro Nazi and anti-Semitic character."[59] His file claims he also expressed himself openly as pro-Hitler, pro-German, and anti-American to sources in close connection with the German-American Bund.

Hardly a household name today, William Sohier Bryant (1861–1956) was a Harvard-trained American physician and professor of medicine in New York City who served as a brigade surgeon in the Spanish American War and a lieutenant colonel in the US Army during the First World War. Bryant was also a genealogist and founding president of the American Heraldry Association, as well as a director of the College of Arms of the Noblesse in Montreal, incorporated "to register and quality [sic] the genealogies, arms, honors and privileges of the Aryan noblesse de race and to issue appropriate certificates of membership in recognition of same."[60] In a May 14, 1943, interview with the Alien Enemy Hearing Board, von der Goltz acknowledged being associated with Bryant and having attended meetings with him "whose purpose was to form a new American political party based on pro-Fascist and anti-Semitic lines."[61]

Von der Goltz's personal character was also at issue; a memo for the chief of review dated June 4, 1943, characterized him as "extremely nosy." Government officials held against him his "unwarranted" interest in the metal alloy companies in the area, his possession of a good shortwave radio, and his practice of listening "to all the reports from Berlin."[62] They also disputed his claim to have invented the first armored truck, used by Pancho Villa in the Mexican Revolution. While in retrospect such details seem colorful rather than damning, they proved sufficient to warrant the government's deep distrust.

The April 17, 1943, order to arrest von der Goltz, born in Koblenz, Germany, in 1893, came from Francis Biddle, attorney general under President Roosevelt. Von der Goltz was summarily apprehended by the FBI at his home on 51 West Fifty-Fifth Street, New York, on April 19, "pursuant to the authority of a presidential warrant." He was processed by the INS at Ellis Island; he wouldn't arrive at the Algiers Detention Station until October of that year, when he was transferred to the New Orleans facility to protect him from pro-Nazi elements.[63] While interned at Ellis Island, he wrote to his wife in a censored letter, "Those people will have to be convinced that their anxiety is not justified and that can be done only by being very patient."[64] This counsel proved misguided; whatever patience Vondy possessed proved insufficient. Though many people stepped forward to state that they knew him to be of good character, the Department of Justice concluded:

> There appears to be no alternative in this case but to recommend subject's internment, not because of any subversive activities in which he has recently engaged, but because, as the United States Attorney states, of

his activities in 1914 for which it appears he has never been punished; because he was a deserter from the United States Army in 1913, for which he was never apprehended; and because of his close connection with von Papen and other Germans and the possibility of his association with known pro-Nazis and also Bundists in the last year or two. For these reasons, and bearing in mind that the subject is an especially intelligent man, having far-flung connections and personal contacts, he may become a potential danger to the United States if released.[65]

A memo directed to Willard Kelly from Edward Ennis dated June 2, 1943, refers to a letter he received from von der Goltz's wife, warning officials that her husband was in danger because he was interned alongside individuals about whom he had furnished information to the FBI. In a later memo dated June 9, Ennis told Kelly that von der Goltz had "exposed the von Papen spy ring of the last War. She is now afraid that the Nazis on Ellis Island will conspire to injure him."[66]

Along with the distress she was feeling about her husband's situation, Peggy von der Goltz also complained in a June 15 letter to Ennis, "The publicity in this case also injured me considerably, and I don't believe anyone intended that—but the damage is done. This must be true in other cases. I earnestly hope this practice will be discontinued."[67] In fact, Peggy's insistent efforts to communicate with the government individuals and entities responsible for her husband's detention earned her one of the few records of alien enemy internment in which a woman's voice is "heard" within the bureaucratic documents. Writing again on June 22, she requested a rehearing for von der Goltz, claiming,

> I can provide proof that the book my husband had published in 1917 was almost entirely the work of ghost-writers and that the inaccuracies were theirs, not his. I can produce publisher and ghost. . . . I have been told, second-hand, that his work with the folk dance groups is under suspicion: I can satisfy anyone that his motives and behaviour were not only innocent, but that he performed a valuable work of Americanization. . . . To my mind it would be a shameful waste to lock a man up in a concentration camp to waste away his life and eat up the taxpayers' money when he really wants to help win the war.[68]

By the end of August 1943, Peggy had amassed a thick stack of papers vouching for Vondy, which she presented to Ennis with the salutation, "Dear Sir:

Here, I hope, is sufficient evidence to justify a re-hearing in my husband's case." Describing the papers she had accumulated as a "huge amount of material," she closed her letter by saying, "I cannot imagine that more evidence is necessary. But if it is, and my legs hold out, I can get you thousands of letters in support of these statements."[69] One interesting element in that portfolio was a letter from Daniel Cranford Smith related to von der Goltz's participation in the Folk Festival. He wrote, "I discovered, ten years ago, that folk dancing and singing was an instrument for breaking down divisiveness between groups of foreign born and between parents and children of foreign born. I, therefore, promoted the activity of the council; had classes formed in folk dancing and singing in the New School for Social Work; and brought about the appointment, in conjunction with Mr. Read Lewis, of von der Goltz as executive secretary of the council—a position he held for about three years."[70] But neither Smith's nor Mrs. von der Goltz's efforts had the desired consequence, as Stuart Krinsly, assistant US attorney, wrote on September 2, 1943, "In my opinion, there is nothing in the voluminous papers submitted, to justify a rehearing in this case. None of Goltz' pro-Fascist tendencies were in any way denied, nor were his associations with Dr. Bryant in any way cleared up. . . . In my opinion, petition for rehearing should be summarily denied."[71]

Weeks turned into months as von der Goltz remained in internment. In late January 1944, he refused to sign a petition for repatriation, writing, "I consider myself a citizen of Mexico and have no interest in being repatriated to Germany."[72] In March, Dorothy Waring, the director of propaganda investigation of the Anti-Nazi League, directed a letter to Thomas Cooley at the Department of Justice, wondering why von der Goltz remained in detention at Ellis Island, when another man named Fred Staudinger, whom the league considered much more dangerous, had already been released. "Our distress is induced by the prompt action given Staudinger and the delayed action in the case of Horst Von der Holtz." Assuming that von der Holtz should have already had a rehearing, Waring wrote, "The evidence against Mr. von der Goltz, in so far as we have been able to determine, does not appear to have been as derogatory as that against Mr. Staudinger."[73] Waring's letter indicates that certain nongovernmental agencies and groups found the authorities' decisions and actions regarding interned German alien enemies to be uneven, if not misguided. In April 1944, von der Goltz petitioned once more for a rehearing, and in May was again denied.

That same month, he was sent to Camp Algiers, a site that was by then serving as a warehouse for an increasing array of "problem" internees. A later report prepared for Ennis in 1945 explained that von der Goltz was known as the "Ellis Island Machiavelli" early in his stay at the New York camp and was accepted by the other Nazi prisoners. However, "because of the fact that Von der Goltz could not get along with other internees at Ellis Island, and because he had begun to claim that he was anti-Nazi, he was transferred to Algiers, Louisiana, which for some time has been used, for the most part, for the detention of persons who were difficult custodial problems for one reason or another and who claimed to be anti-Nazi."[74] According to documents in his Department of Justice file, again in September 1944, Ennis noted that von der Goltz's case was "recently reconsidered in this Unit and it was determined that no change would be made in his internment status at this time."

Von der Goltz's frustration level continued to mount. In October 1944, the internee wrote a five-page single-spaced letter to Ennis from Algiers, saying, "From here it looks as if your unit just existed to smother the cries of agony of those taken for a ride on the barbwire rail." He protested his earlier treatment at Ellis Island, where he had been "locked up in a porch-cage full of Nazis and ordinary would-be Americans who had been driven crazy by the way they had been handled and put under Nazi control." He claimed he had "quit being a German subject in mind and fact before 1916," but at Ellis Island was "kept in close proximity to about 300 highly disturbed people who had been arrested as Nazis." On the last page, he reiterated the injury to both himself and to his wife "by this entire procedure past all decency" and vowed to continue his effort to obtain US citizenship, "until the memory of what you have done to me will just be like a bad smell faintly remembered."[75]

Another letter in the Justice Department archive provides a quite distinct view of von der Goltz's loyalties, however. That same month, John Roy Carlson wrote to US attorney Thom Lord on the letterhead of a group called Friends of Democracy, requesting an address for von der Goltz at Algiers, explaining, "I knew this man personally as early as 1938, and have long known of his Nazi views." Carlson mentioned von der Goltz's association with William S. Bryant, "an elderly physician . . . who has gone in for considerable fascist propaganda." He also identified himself as the author of the book *Under Cover: My Four Years in the Nazi Underworld of America*, published in 1943 (figure 4.4).[76]

The interest in von der Goltz expressed by both the Anti-Nazi League and the Friends of Democracy points to a growing concern in the 1940s regarding the Nazi presence in certain US detention facilities, including at Camp Algiers. A February 14, 1945, issue of the *Congressional Record* carries a speech made

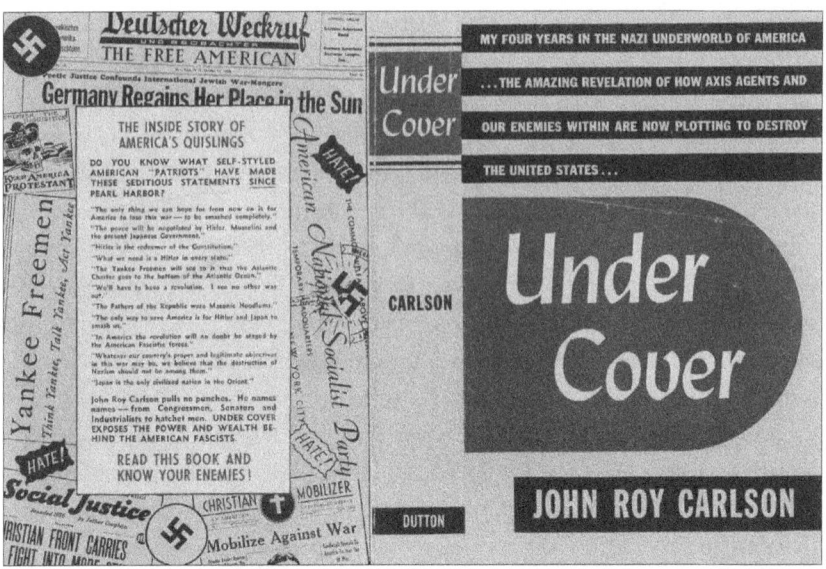

FIGURE 4.4. Jacket for John Roy Carlson's *Under Cover: My Four Years in the Nazi Underworld of America,* published in 1943. National Archives, used with permission.

by Samuel Dickstein on the floor of the House of Representatives containing allegations "by the Non-Sectarian Anti-Nazi League in connection with conditions in alien enemy internment camps operated by this service at Ellis Island, Algiers, Louisiana and Bismarck, North Dakota." The Anti-Nazi League purportedly "had positive proof of the existence of 'Gestapo' activities in the Alien Enemy internment camps" and had requested congressional investigation of conditions in the camps.[77] Dickstein argued that it was inefficient and ultimately untenable to try to guard German enemy aliens and prisoners of war in "443 prisoner camps spread all over the country": "A few days ago I received information about the fact, that in the civilian alien detention camps, a German Gestapo is functioning. In fact, I was requested to take immediate steps to end the continued existence of Nazi cells under our very noses amongst interned German nationals at Algiers, La.; Bismarck, North Dak.; and Ellis Island, N.Y." In Dickstein's address before the House of Representatives, he also referred to allegations of harassment of internees by "Nazi Elements."

Was a "Nazi cell" functioning at Camp Algiers during the period von der Goltz was interned there? It is undeniable that individuals with a prominent Nazi past were interned there, in a move that seems ironic, if not contradictory, given the fact that the detention station was hailed an "anti-Nazi" haven for the Latin American Jewish internees routed to New Orleans in February 1943 from other camps. What the concerns expressed by organizations such as Friends of Democracy or the Anti-Nazi League do seem to indicate is that—as another Algiers internee studied here would insist—there was no clear or consistent policy that guided the government's actions in the more than four hundred internment and prisoner of war camps that dotted the country.

Von der Goltz wrote to Kelly again in April 1945, once more asking for reexamination: "I do not know why I have been held a prisoner for two years and I know of no act of mine to have justified even temporary detention."[78] Raymond Bunker, the officer in charge at Algiers, wrote a memo to Ennis that same month that seemed to concur, quoting the internee as stating "that Hitler and the Nazi Party should be destroyed" and averring as well that "the United States has been my home during my entire adult life." Bunker concluded, "From my conversations with von der Goltz during his internment at this station from May 21, 1944 to the present, it is the belief of the writer that the sentiments expressed by subject in above statement, are true. His wife, to whom he has been married many years, is an American citizen and it is believed that von der Goltz, if allowed to resume residence in the United States, would conduct himself as a law-abiding person." But in May, Ennis wrote von der Goltz directly with the unwelcome news that "no change will be made at this time in your present internment status." Even after victory in Europe, the government's position did not change; on June 19, 1945, Ennis wrote to von der Goltz, "As a result of the cessation of hostilities in Europe, your case has been thoroughly reconsidered by this Department and it has been determined that no change will be made at this time in your present internment status."[79]

In July 1945, von der Goltz finally received word of a hearing on his case and requested it be held at Ellis Island instead of Algiers, perhaps to be nearer his wife or lawyers. But before he traveled to New York in October 1945, another complication arose with regard to his case. The end of the war in Europe left government officials with the predicament of "removing" from the country the same alien enemies it had detained from 1941 to 1945. Harry S. Truman, by then president of the United States, on September 8, 1945, signed Proclamation 2662, Removal of Alien Enemies, stipulating, first, that those aliens whose "continued residence in the Western Hemisphere is deemed by the Secretary of State to be prejudicial to the future security or welfare of the Americas, be subject upon the order of the Secretary of State to removal from the United States and may be required to depart therefrom in accordance with such regulations as the Secretary of State may prescribe" and second, in cases where the secretary of state had already ordered a person's removal, "thirty days shall be considered, and is hereby declared to be, a reasonable time for such alien enemy to effect the recovery, disposal, and removal of his goods and effects, and for his departure."

In Horst von der Goltz's case, a removal order seemed to many counterintuitive and counterproductive: he had not lived in Germany for three decades, had been married to an American-born wife for two of those decades, and had petitioned for nonrepatriation to Germany. Thus, in the last part of 1945, several persons, including some government employees, worked to prevent his repatriation to Germany. Malcolm Gerry wrote to the Alien Enemy Control Board on his behalf on November 23, 1945, as someone with fourteen years of experience in the US government, twelve of them in the Customs Service. In December, Stuart Krinsly, the same attorney who had dismissed the fat packet of "evidence" von der Goltz's wife, Peggy, had submitted two and a half years earlier, wrote to John F. Dailey, a Wall Street lawyer, stating, "At the present time I do not believe that this alien is harmful to the United States in any way or that his deportation would in any way serve the United States. . . . If his record as an internee is that of a loyal person, then I can see no harm in permitting him to remain in the United States."[80] Even James H. Sheldon of the Anti-Nazi League wrote a confidential memo, stating, "It is the definite belief of our office that the cause of justice would be well served by cancelling any deportation proceedings which may have been instituted against this man, and permitting him to continue in residence in the United States." Later that month, Dudley Parsons told the Hearing Board that he had invited von der Goltz to live with him and would give him a job upon his release. "He should definitely not be deported. No useful purpose will be served by further detaining a man who still wants to become an American citizen because he believes in it."[81]

Nonetheless, indecision marked the outcome of von der Goltz's hearing before the Alien Enemy Repatriation Hearing Board at Ellis Island on December 19, 1945. Ennis concluded, "On the present state of the record I am unable to decide the case." Kelly fell in line, stating, "I would like to defer making a recommendation in the case until further information, as Mr. Ennis has suggested, has been secured." Ennis's assistant, John Burling, also believed "the subject should be repatriated unless the reports of his dealings with Major Starr exculpate him from the charge of being a Fascist adventurer."[82] So in May 1946, the Repatriation Hearing Board met again. Ennis voted for repatriation; Kelly dissented.

On May 29, the attorney general ordered repatriation within thirty days, as Proclamation 2662 laid out. Various lawyers went back and forth with the Alien Enemy Control Unit, and in July, Dailey wrote, "Deportation to Germany in this case would be not only a real hardship but entail great danger to the life of Von der Goltz." He pointed out that his client had not been in Germany since 1914, was now a man of advanced years with no contacts of any character in the country of his birth—in short, someone whose return to Germany would be "disastrous." "Moreover," Dailey added, "may I recall to you the pledge of the British Government at the time of his confession and assistance to that Government and ours in 1940, that he would never be deported to a country where he might be in danger of political reprisals."[83]

Despite the outcry, von der Goltz's deportation continued to move forward. On July 11, 1946, the FBI vacated his order of internment "as he is being deported." More letters arrived, including one in August from Read Lewis, executive director of the Common Council for American Unity, a nonprofit that published a magazine promoting cultural pluralism that counted Langston Hughes, Pearl S. Buck, and Thomas Mann among the members of its editorial board. Lewis concluded his letter by stating, "If he stays here, my guess is that he will be harmless. If he is turned adrift after all these years among us, God knows what will become of him."[84]

Caught in the bureaucratic stalemate, von der Goltz surrendered to authorities at the expiration of the thirty-day parole period following his order of repatriation as stipulated in Proclamation 2662 and was interned once again. His lawyers then enlisted a chorus of voices who "would be glad to testify as to his complete loyalty to the United States," including that of Rabbi Max Felshin of Radio City Synagogue, but von der Goltz remained in internment until December 16, 1946.[85] The total period of his internment was more than three and a half years, with more than a year and a half of that time occurring after the war in Europe had ended. The last we hear of von der Goltz, at least in the government's files, is in May 1948, five years after his initial arrest, when a memo from the director of the FBI to Assistant Attorney General T. Vincent Quinn advises that von der Goltz, by then employed as a research director for the Dudley L. Parsons Company, 52 Vanderbilt Avenue in New York, was considering claiming indemnity from the US government for his wartime internment.

As we will see, von der Goltz's case bears a certain resemblance to that of Kurt Ludecke, perhaps the most controversial internee held at Camp Algiers. Both men wrote books chronicling their knowledge of German state leadership and its influence in the Americas. And both, by the time of their internment at the Algiers Detention Station in the 1940s as middle-aged men, would claim to be "cured" of any previous ideological devotion to Nazism. But while von der Goltz's change of heart may ultimately be quite convincing, especially since he claimed no proximity to the highest echelons of Nazi leadership in Germany, the true position of his compatriot and Algiers camp mate Kurt Ludecke seems more difficult to ascertain, and his professed change of heart less convincing.

Hitler's Pal

Ken Gormin's March 30, 1946, article for New Orleans's *Times-Picayune* titled "Close Pal of Hitler Held in Algiers Detention Unit" began, "One of Hitler's closest friends and confidants—a man who helped him organize the Nazi party, was in Algiers recently." He explained that the surprising proximity of Hitler's pal to the good citizens of New Orleans had been revealed the previous day, when representatives of the press were permitted to visit the camp for the first time. While he includes details as to the date the camp opened (December 1941) and the more than a thousand internees held there "from almost every European nation, most of the South American countries, and Japan," Gormin leaves out the names of the internees featured in the story, including the one alluded to in the headline as Hitler's pal, Kurt Ludecke.[86]

Born in 1890, "Herr Ludecke," as the newspapers sometimes liked to call him, claimed to have received credentials from Hitler himself on January 4, 1924, for the purpose of representing and fundraising for the Nazi Party in North America.[87] He arrived in the United States later that month and while on that initial trip, contacted Henry Ford and W. J. Cameron of the Ford Motor Company for the purpose of inducing them to support the Nazi cause. Ludecke stated that Ford's attitude on the Jewish question seemed to assure cooperation.[88] He also attempted to interest the Ku Klux Klan in the cause of the Nazi Party, because of its attitude on the Negro, Jewish, and Catholic questions. He judged both attempts to be unsuccessful, however, referring to his trip as "An Unprofitable American Begging Tour."[89]

After traveling home to Germany and working for the Nazi Party for an unspecified time, Ludecke returned to North America and in August 1927 was admitted "on the German quota" for permanent residence. Ludecke's photo ran in newspapers including the *Middletown Times Herald* on November 26, 1932, under the title "Nazi Mouthpiece"; the caption read "Kurt G. W. Ludecke, is shown in his office at Washington, D. C., where he recently opened a news and information bureau for Hitler's Fascist Party of Germany. The bureau is for the purpose of giving authentic information about the Party to the American people. Ludecke formerly headed a similar bureau in Rome." The sanguine tone of the caption suggests either that Fascism and the Nazi position had not yet been vilified in the American press or that Ludecke himself anticipated a positive response to this announcement and publicity—or perhaps both.

In fact, Ludecke's enemy alien file notes, "Several days after Hitler's rise to power in January 1933, the petitioner broadcast an appeal to Germans in the United States from Washington" in which he stated, "America too needs a Hitler or a Mussolini."[90] While hardly the only figure to espouse such ideas in the United States at that time, Ludecke was later irked when he was not made the official representative of the Nazi Party in the United States and adopted a critical attitude toward the Nazi leadership. He claimed his differences of opinion with the upper echelons of Nazi power resulted in his confinement as a political prisoner in a German concentration camp (later identified by the FBI as Oranienburg), where he remained until his escape in the spring of 1934.

In 1937, Ludecke authored a book based on these experiences provocatively titled *I Knew Hitler: The Story of a Nazi Who Escaped the Blood Purge*.[91] By no means a secret text (though it was later banned in Germany), Ludecke's story appeared in serial segments in the *Chicago Tribune*, with advertisements before its publication promising in bold face, "Hitler Exposed!" and "A Former Intimate Personal Associate Who Escaped the Blood-Purge Tells the Inside Facts!" Reviews of the book both inside and outside the United States were generally positive. The government collected these reviews in its case on Ludecke, including an opinion from Williams College Professor Frederick L. Schuman that "this work is at once a breathless story of adventure and a political document of prime importance."[92] Goronwy Rees's review for the British weekly *The Spectator* began, "Herr Ludecke has written an interesting and valuable book, though it may disappoint those who hope for sensational revelations. There are none; Herr Ludecke throws no new light on Herr Hitler's character and his book will not assist anyone who is undecided whether the Führer is an angel, a puppet or a monster."[93] Rees does refer to Ludecke's immense vanity and self-importance, characteristics that generally would not serve him in his later stint in US detention.

Thus, while Ludecke's actual proximity to Hitler was never really in question, what did spark debate was his subsequent *distancing* from the führer.

Ludecke's 1934 and 1938 applications for citizenship were denied because his political views were reportedly "not in accord with the Constitution and laws of United States." In 1939, one of the many photos of Hitler and his "pal" Ludecke included in *I Knew Hitler* ran in the news with the title "U.S. Doesn't Want This"; the caption explained, "Because of associations like this, Kurt G. W. Ludecke, shown here in a picture with Hitler, was denied the right to United States citizenship in a Detroit court. The court refused to believe Ludecke's protestations that he is a 'new man' and that his old beliefs changed after he fell out with the fuehrer and escaped the Nazi blood purge."[94]

Government officials concluded from Ludecke's book that "even after his experiences in the concentration camp, and his escape, it appears doubtful that he had completely renounced the Nazi party and given up hope of again being restored to the good graces of Hitler, as he addressed a letter to Hitler from Geneva in the spring of 1934, giving Hitler a chance to declare himself." It did not help his case that Ludecke's landlord described him as a gigolo, claiming his American wife, Mildred, worked at the Detroit Public Library and paid the rent, "and that shortly before Mildred returns to the apartment each evening, about 5:00 P.M., Ludecke begins to get busy on his typewriter."[95]

As with other figures in the enemy alien drama offering up insider information in the hopes of improving their status or securing their release (or even saving themselves from a British firing squad, as happened with von der Goltz), Ludecke's most valuable asset was also his Achilles' heel. In a December 1941 letter to Claude Bragdon, he had claimed, for example, "Extraordinary dangers, unusual situations, require extraordinary people who see clearly and act boldly. Here is a unique opportunity. No American knows as well as I do Hitler's mentality and temperament, altogether the complexity of the Hitler-Nazi-German structure; No German knows as well as I do America's purpose, American ideals and American problems within the frame of large evolutionary processes—which by the way are unknown to most Americans, so why should Hitler be aware of them?"[96] Bragdon was an architect and the author of such books as the 1933 *An Introduction to Yoga*. Why Ludecke offered his services to him is not clear, but in doing so, he claimed, "I know from unimpeachable source that Hitler still has a high opinion of me. This fact alone is invaluable in view of the general suspicion and misunderstanding. . . . In short, I could make a particularly useful and effective intermediary provided I am well prepared and supported by responsible people."

But the Department of Justice thought otherwise, and the report of a January

16, 1942, alien enemy hearing recommended interning Ludecke on the basis of *I Knew Hitler* and his inability to distance himself from Nazi ideology:

> From his answers it appeared that he has no dislike or repugnance to Hitler, and it seemed to the Board that it might well be that, if given an opportunity to bask again in the sunshine of Hitler's favor, this alien might well be susceptible. . . . The Board finds that he was an important participant in the activities of Hitler and the Nazi party; that his representations of change of heart and sentiment are not supported by anything except vague generalities, and the Board is of the opinion that if he is not in fact at the present time a Nazi agent, it would not require very much to bring him once again into its active forces, and that he is a highly intelligent and well-equipped person whose activities might be very effective and dangerous.[97]

A February 1942 assessment in the same file further clarified, "This man is a former Nazi agent, an egomaniac, a demagogue, and the organizer of a mushroom Fascist organization. He, of course, should be interned."

The FBI arrested Ludecke at the Hotel Walton in Chicago on December 8, 1941, the day after the bombing of Pearl Harbor, turning over to Immigration authorities papers, clippings, and the manuscript of a new book entitled "Through HITLER to BELLAMY." The date of April 8, 1942, was set for his internment at Fort Oglethorpe, Georgia. From there, he apparently was transferred to Camp Forrest, Tennessee, where in November he was called as a material witness in proceedings against the German-American Bund in New York. There, he would ostensibly have the opportunity to prove to the government his privileged knowledge of Nazi activities in the United States, though he later complained he was questioned regarding activities and individuals about which or whom he knew nothing. For those proceedings, Ludecke was interned at Ellis Island as of December 7, 1942, and a few days later, sent on to Fort Meade, Maryland.

It was from Fort Meade that Ludecke started a lengthy letter campaign appealing to any government employee in whom he might arouse sympathy. On January 12, 1943, he wrote to Secretary of State Cordell Hull. After invoking Providence to help him convince Hull of his "honesty of purpose" and the importance of his message, he wrote, "I propose that you arrange for me an interview with a responsible, competent, world-experienced official of the State Department, perhaps the chief of the European or German division, to whom

I can make a verbal report of certain, I emphasize, a c t u a l (not hypothetical) developments which I believe should be brought to the attention of Your Excellency and the President of the United States."⁹⁸ To his letter, Ludecke appended a short biography of himself in the third person, noting his birth in Berlin in 1890, his marriage to an American-born citizen since 1927, and from 1922 to 1933, his membership in the Nazi inner council. Besides serving as Hitler's emissary in many countries, Ludecke took credit for being the first to establish contact between the führer and Italy's Benito Mussolini and for representing the Nazi press and Party in Washington from 1932 to 1933.

Nonetheless, as Hitler's fame and influence grew, Ludecke's seemed to wane. "Back in Berlin after Hitler's rise to power he walked into a jungle of intrigues and in his fight against certain developments and personalities he was arrested by Hitler's own order to rot in Nazi concentration camps," Ludecke wrote of himself in the third person. It was following his escape from that camp that he penned the more than eight-hundred-page-long *I Knew Hitler,* which, in his modest opinion, "competent people consider to be, by a wide margin, the best and most revealing, trustworthy, and well documented account, analysis and interpretation of Hitler and the men about Hitler, Nazi mentality and Nazi politics (up to 1934), that so far has appeared in print." While Ludecke's "inner evolution" since the ordeal of his imprisonment in Germany was purportedly too long to describe in the volume, "suffice it to say that the Nazi Ludecke is dead," his letter states, and "that he has outgrown Nazism completely."⁹⁹

But Ludecke's proposition to Hull along with the assurances of his change of heart seemed to fall on deaf ears or, at the very least, skeptical ones. On May 21, 1943, he was interned at Fort Lincoln, North Dakota; from there he went to Gloucester City, New Jersey. Finally, having spent time in at least six internment facilities, he arrived at the Algiers Detention Station on October 21, 1943, after Willard Kelly, the assistant commissioner for alien control, looked into getting him private quarters to enable him to concentrate on his writing at a site where it would be possible for him to keep his manuscripts and other papers under lock and key.

Having found in Kelly an advocate, Ludecke wrote to him in November from Algiers, expressing his gratitude for his kindness, understanding and quick action in effecting the transfer, claiming, "I was very close to a nervous breakdown, so the change came just in time."¹⁰⁰ At the end of the letter, he offered to prepare a memorandum for Kelly, a project he refers to as a "memoir" in a later letter directed to Walter Miller. He hoped that document could reach Kelly without the intervention of the censors. It was also at Algiers that Ludecke signed a nonrepatriation request dated December 20, 1943. This crucial gesture was nevertheless insufficient evidence of loyalty to the United States for a man of Ludecke's antecedents, and his internment continued.

Despite his having appeared in many US newspapers in the years prior to his internment, it is likely that many other internees at Algiers were unaware of Ludecke's earlier proximity to the Nazis, especially since the majority were alien Germans, Italians, and Japanese apprehended in Latin America, who likely would not have seen news reports and photos in North America. Whatever their knowledge of his prior life and relationships, the internee population at one point elected him as their spokesperson, even when a few Jewish detainees deported from Latin America still remained in the camp.[101] Ludecke seemed to take his role as spokesman seriously, as after the visit of Walter Miller, district director of the INS to Algiers in the summer of 1944, he wrote to Miller on August 1 with several criticisms of camp operations: "Though America is already at war for 32 months, and thousands of German nationals belonging to different categories have been arrested, here and abroad, detained and interned in the United States . . . there does not seem to exist a basic policy, let alone an efficiently operating system that would do justice to a motley crowd of internees, on the basis of American principles proclaimed in the Declaration of Independence." Ludecke complained the indifference of the authorities toward German enemy alien detainees had caused "unnecessary grief and hardship" as well as unnecessary difficulties for the custodians in charge. He described those running the facilities as "subalterns" unwilling to take the initiative even in minor matters, so that "things drift month after month, year after year, and no real change for the better is in sight." Ludecke also contended that rules agreed on by Germany and the United States pertaining to the treatment of soldier prisoners of war were informing the treatment of men, women, and children detained as civilian internees. "One glance at family camps, for instance, shows that something else had to be improvised," he pointed out.[102]

Undoubtedly, there was much truth in Ludecke's descriptions of uneven and unclear policy, inefficient operations, apparent indifference on the part of some in the top brass, and the application of rules designed for prisoners of war to civilian internees. Though his requests that internees at Algiers receive the same allowance afforded those at other camps, that they have a canteen, and that they have access to meaningful work might seem petty, the closing section of the letter suggests that the atmosphere at Algiers was by then becoming increasingly toxic, and that resolving such "minor" issues might have improved morale. Speaking of one final factor that tended to disturb and intensify discontent and friction, Ludecke decried the "unfortunate development that this station has become a dumping ground for all kinds of extra abnormal cases," making it at times "a veritable madhouse." Finally, he indicated he would write to Miller regarding another important matter in a separate letter. That communication, dated the same day, focused on the fallout from a July visit by Ennis's assistant James Bell, who in openly identifying Ludecke as a Nazi in interviews with other detainees, increased disagreements among the internees and caused several to protest his role as spokesman.

Tensions between interned civilians at Algiers escalated to the point that in late September 1944, Ludecke wrote to Raymond Bunker, the officer in charge at Algiers, resigning as spokesman, noting that the arrival of new detainees had only exacerbated existing tensions and divisions. One group of internees protesting Ludecke's leadership even threatened a hunger strike, requiring Bunker to draw up an eight-page-long "Type A" report on the conduct, behavior, and attitude of Ludecke during his stint at Algiers. Beginning with the internee's background, he added several details to the government's existing profile, including the fact that Ludecke had spent 245 days in a Nazi concentration camp before escaping first to Prague and from there to Canada and the United States. Bunker claimed all the personnel at Camp Algiers found Ludecke's behavior to be "fairly satisfactory," with the exception of a few violent outbursts followed by periods of sulking. Bunker's report included a transcript of questions asked Ludecke regarding political matters and the answers he supplied, summarizing, "The subject claims to be a violent Anti-Nazi, but some of his closest friends at the station are persons who are strongly suspected of being Nazi sympathizers."[103]

Bunker's report, dated September 13, 1944, also provides other key information. When asked, "What was the reason for your arrest as an alien enemy under Presidential Warrant of Arrest?" Ludecke responded that no reason was given either at the time of his arrest or at his hearing before the Alien Enemy Hearing Board. Ludecke supplied the date of March 1, 1934, as his "complete and absolute physical as well as moral break with the Nazi Regime, the Nazi Party, and the Nazi philosophy, whatever that may be." Notwithstanding this statement, Bunker concluded that while perhaps Ludecke adamantly self-identified as "Anti-Nazi," his conversations revealed him to be "very definitely pro-German," and as such, a poor parole risk. This suggests that even Bunker, who had substantial proximity to and interaction with the internees under his charge, failed to recognize the possibility of being "pro-German" and anti-Nazi—even if this wasn't the case with Ludecke. The Alien Enemy Control Unit responded accordingly with a recommendation for his continued internment later that month.

Bunker provided Ennis with another, shorter report dated April 28, 1945, and in October of that year, Ludecke was sent to Ellis Island for a rehearing. A November 19, 1945, memo from Willard Kelly to the Pentagon, with a copy to Ennis, stated that Captain Leonard, Ludecke's interviewer, took statements confirming his offer to appear as a prosecution witness at the Nuremberg war criminal trials. Nonetheless, Ludecke's principal concern was his release from internment. In his five-page statement made for Attorney General Tom C. Clark, he stated his "moral duty to voice categorical protest against further indignities, humiliations, and violations" of his rights, and considered any further detention a "gross injustice."[104]

As was the case for his fellow internee Horst von der Goltz, Ludecke's marriage did not survive his long internment, but in November 1945, his former wife, Mildred, was still willing to sign an affidavit saying her ex-husband was no longer a Nazi. Nonetheless, in the report for a December 17 repatriation hearing held at Ellis Island just two days before a similar hearing for von der Goltz, Edward Ennis wrote, "In my opinion the subject has failed completely to establish that he rejected National Socialism. . . . I believe this is a Class I case and recommend his repatriation. It is to be noted there is no mitigation." John Burling, another member of the board, said, "I think he may be a little crazy. So was Hitler. I therefore concur in the recommendation for repatriation." Willard Kelly concluded, "To me the most significant evidence that he did not change his views was his reaction to the German breakthrough late in 1944, at which time he exalted over what he predicted was to be another Dunkirk."[105] All three men concurred on the matter of repatriation. Thus, on February 12, 1946, Ennis wrote to Ludecke informing him he was to be "removed" without any reconsideration, and he was paroled to begin disposing of his personal affairs.

Nonetheless, Ludecke was still at Ellis Island as of September 15, 1947, some seven months later, when he wrote to Charles M. Rothstein, acting director of the Alien Enemy Control Unit. In fact, he vehemently fought the order of removal through all available channels, and his case worked its way up to the Supreme Court in late 1947. Robert P. Griffin, in a 1949 essay in the *Michigan Law Review*, summarized *Ludecke v. Watkins* this way: a German alien enemy had been arrested and interned during the war by virtue of broad summary powers granted the chief executive by the Alien Enemy Act of 1798 to subject alien enemies to apprehension, detention, and deportation upon order of the president "whenever there is a declared war." It was under authority of that act that the president, on July 14, 1945, had then ordered the removal of all alien enemies "who shall be deemed by the Attorney General to be dangerous to the public peace."[106] Griffin noted the petitioner was heard before alien and repatriation boards, and on January 18, 1946, five months after cessation of actual hostilities, the attorney general had ordered his removal from the United States. Ludecke's application for writ of habeas corpus, wherein he "questioned the validity of the act and complained that he had not had a fair hearing" was denied in the district court and the circuit court of appeals.[107] Finally, the United States Supreme Court upheld the decision of the lower courts in a five-to-four vote, affirming an "alien enemy whose deportation is ordered under authority of the act is not entitled to have any court determine whether he had a fair hearing."[108] Though four justices dissented, suggesting a range of opinions on the case, Griffin concluded regarding *Ludecke v. Watkins* (US 1948) that it was "not surprising that the justices expressed no disagreement on the constitutionality of the Alien Enemy Act, for its validity, never seriously questioned, has been affirmed in an unbroken line of lower court decisions," and as of the middle of the twentieth century, "American courts have steadfastly refused to grant habeas corpus or otherwise interfere with the executive's authority under the Alien Enemy Act, considering it a legitimate exercise of the war power."[109] Ludecke would have received the news of the Supreme Court's decision back in custody at Ellis Island. His file states he was finally "removed" to Germany on the army transfer vessel *General Black* on July 8, 1948, under the attorney general's order.

Ludecke's case would leave an unsettling legacy, as law professor Stephen Vladek argued in an essay titled "Ludecke's Lengthening Shadow: The Disturbing Prospect of War without End." Published in 2006 in the context of the US "war on terrorism" following the events of September 11, 2001, Vladek maintained the Supreme Court's 1948 decision in *Ludecke v. Watkins* established a precedent in which "war"—whether against another state or against some more abstract threat such as terror or drug trafficking—does not end when the fighting stops:

> The President may continue to exercise various of his war powers until either he or Congress formally terminates hostilities, and, in some cases, even after that. *Ludecke* appears to stand for the dramatic proposition that, in determining when a war "ends" for constitutional purposes, it is irrelevant whether fighting actually has ceased. All that matters is

whether the political branches have formally acknowledged as much. At least with regard to the precise issue presented in *Ludecke*—the President's authority to detain and summarily deport German nationals under the Alien Enemy Act of 1798—the formal termination of World War II did not come until enactment of legislation on October 19, 1951, nearly six and one-half years after Germany's unconditional surrender.[110]

In other "wars against nouns" such as the war on terror and most recently, the war on immigrants from certain regions, the United States has expanded the use and breadth of alien detention for indefinite periods, often without hearings.[111] Thus, to the questions of who is an "enemy" alien and which enemy aliens should be interned and for how long, whether members of opposing factions should be interned together, whether or when an alien's loyalties to the United States might be reconsidered, and what rights detainees possess to exercise free speech opposing a detaining government while in the government's custody, was now added the question of the government's legitimate power to maintain an alien enemy in detention or insist on his or her repatriation beyond the temporal parameters of war itself. Vladek argues that Ludecke's case set a precedent for the broad expansion of those powers in the twenty-first century.

The definition of who is an alien enemy has been notably extended since Vladek wrote on Ludecke's long shadow in 2006. In its "war on terror," the Trump administration enacted the Muslim travel ban, which was upheld by the Supreme Court in June 2018 "in what may have been one of the most consequential decisions since the notorious *Korematsu* case of 1944, when the Supreme Court upheld the incarceration of Japanese-Americans during World War II."[112] In the "war on illegal immigration," noncitizen entry into the United States without proper documentation—even in the case of men, women, and children seeking asylum—also has been equated with criminal or "enemy" behavior. The Trump administration's plan to hold more than a thousand immigrant children at an Oklahoma army base that was used as an internment camp for Japanese Americans during World War II lends "even greater significance to the parallels commentators and historians have drawn between U.S. migrant detention centers and concentration camps of the past," even if the plan was later modified.[113]

As this study aims to elucidate, persons named "alien enemies" in the context of World War II represented a broad spectrum of political tenets and actions. Those who were refugees, displaced persons, or impoverished or had been separated from family members in detention or internment were especially vulnerable to wartime incarceration. But as the next chapter argues, even some individuals with royal or noble titles ended up behind the fence in the United States' enemy alien internment program, though at camps beyond the New Orleans area.

CHAPTER 5

Royals and Nobles behind Barbed Wire

The Neutral Count

Several members of European royalty or nobility were held in enemy alien detention camps in the United States during World War II. While the trio featured in this chapter have only tangential connections to New Orleans, their tales are contiguous with those of the Algiers internees, almost all of whom spent time in other internment camps as well—some surely alongside these and other titled detainees. The histories of the three individuals profiled here reveal surprising details of the wartime detention apparatus in the United States and give us a fuller sense of the range of experiences before, during, and after detention—except in cases where there was no "after," such as a death due to suicide.

Axel Georg Hans Otto Wachtmeister was born November 18, 1916, in Stockholm. A ship manifest of the SS *Drottningholm* that set sail from Gothenburg, Sweden, shows him arriving in New York harbor on January 19, 1940, and registers his profession only as "Count." Among the fourteen other passengers listed aboard the *Drottningholm* upon its arrival, four were identified as "Hebrews": one from Sweden, one from Germany, one from Poland, and one marked as "stateless."[1] Though the Jewish travelers and perhaps other shipmates were no doubt fleeing war-torn Europe, Wachtmeister would later tell the Swedish ambassador in Washington that the goals of his trip, with a stop in New York before traveling on to the Caribbean, were to improve his health and conduct research. "I left Sweden in January 1940 on my way to HAITI where I intended to accomplish some ethnographical studies and, at the same time, try to cure my chronical nose trouble (sinusitis), under a tropical sun, such as Swedish doctors had advised me to do."[2] Despite these stated intentions, it didn't take long for Wachtmeister to abandon Haiti for the Dominican Republic on the eastern side of Hispaniola. "I arrived at Port-au-Prince, via U.S.A. in the beginning of February 1940, and on the 18th of February 1940 I made up my mind to go to the neighbouring Dominican Republic, as I had found out that I could not achieve either one of my objects, nor did I find living in the Haitian Republic as agreeable as I had thought it would be," his letter to the embassy explained.

Wachtmeister stayed on in the Dominican Republic, where he was engaged primarily in sailing, fishing, and taking photographs. As a Swede, he associated with the Swedish Consul at Ciudad Trujillo, who was of German origin and thus represented a red flag to those suspicious of Count Wachtmeister's activities. This chumminess with the German carrying out the duties of the Swedish consul would haunt him, figuring in the documents as the chief reason for his "dangerous" character as an "enemy alien." On December 11, 1941, Wachtmeister was interned along with several other European-born residents at La Cumbre, a concentration camp in a mountainous region of the island. His diplomatic representative in the United States reported that he was released from that internment on January 10, 1942, "because nothing had been found against him" but was reinterned on April 6, 1942.[3]

A few weeks into his second stay at La Cumbre, Wachtmeister was ushered onto a ship bound for the United States along with several German nationals. His name appears on the manifest of the US Army transport vessel *Algonquin* entering the port of New Orleans on May 18, 1942, at which time he was delivered to US Border Patrol facilities. It's possible he spent a few days in New Orleans in immigration custody, perhaps even staying at Camp Algiers en route to his next destination. From New Orleans, Wachtmeister was sent on to Camp Kenedy, a particularly embattled environment where pro-Nazi groups held significant sway.

Just weeks before Wachtmeister arrived, Albert Greutert, the acting Swiss consul from New Orleans, and F. Van den Arend of the Special Division of the Department of State, submitted a report on a site visit to Kenedy. As of that date, there were 707 males in the camp, including 537 Germans, 156 Japanese, and 14 Italians. In the last paragraph of their summary, the visitors noted there were twenty diplomatic and consular officials being held among the group and wondered if conditions were up to par for this special category of detainees, especially as they hoped to exchange these high-profile detainees for American officials in Europe. "In view of the fact that the treatment of officials in such a situation involves the question of reciprocity, it is suggested that in connection with any future arrangements special efforts be made to avoid the possibility of again subjecting such officials to the hardships of detainee or internment camps," they concluded.[4]

Camp Kenedy would see more than thirty-five hundred declared enemy aliens pass through its gates between April 1942 and October 1944, when it ceased to function as an internment facility. Perhaps none came from such an illustrious lineage as Axel Wachtmeister, "who belonged to one of the foremost Swedish families, nobilized in Sweden in the 16th century and well-known because of its many high-ranking and prominent servants to the Crown."[5] The twentieth-century count shared the name and lineage of the seventeenth-century Axel Wachtmeister (1643–99), a count and field marshal of Estonian-Finnish-German origins who distinguished himself in the Swedish army and was a close associate of King Charles XI of Sweden.

In a Department of Justice memo recording a statement made by Wachtmeister in English on June 1, 1942, the Swede identified himself as being just twenty-six years old. Like so many other detainees from Latin America restrained in US internment camps, the count was frustrated and perplexed by why he was being held. He wrote to the Swedish ambassador in Washington, "I am at a loss to know what kind of charges, if any, have been brought against me, neither in the Dominican Republic nor in the U.S.A. In view of the foregoing, I take the liberty to humbly request Your Excellency to kindly try and obtain my liberty from the American Authorities. Once released, I shall proceed in accordance with the status the said Authorities should decide upon my person. Allow me to anticipate my sincerest thanks for whatever Your Excellency may do in my behalf."[6] When asked by Department of Justice interviewers, "By whom were you arrested in Ciudad Trujillo?" Wachtmeister responded, "By the Dominican police." To the query "Why were you arrested?" he answered, "I haven't the slightest idea." When asked, "What was your occupation in Ciudad Trujillo?" he said, "None whatsoever. That is, I was studying Spanish and trying to cure my chronic nose trouble."[7] When asked whom he associated with, Wachtmeister said he was at times with the Swedish consul, who was a German named Indoff. The interviewer clarified, for the record, that Indoff himself was being held at Kenedy as well.[8] Wachtmeister also claimed that he had a passport but was apprehended with such haste that he had not been able to retrieve it, and it was left behind in the Dominican Republic.[9]

Later that month, a letter from Edward P. Lawton, the chargé d'affaires ad interim in Ciudad Trujillo, repeated the only charges in Wachtmeister's case, namely, "He was known to be an associate of various leaders of the local National Socialist German labor party."[10] Authorities were also suspicious of the fact that he was "an inveterate photographer" and at the time of his arrest had in his possession more than three hundred photographs of various localities in the Dominican Republic. The Dominican authorities also had removed from his possession a communiqué directed to the German-owned Condor Airlines in Brazil, in which Wachtmeister offered his services as an airline pilot. "Reliable sources have stated that Wachtmeister frequented the waterfront in Ciudad Trujillo and took notes of the description of vessels in the port. Two of this gentleman's waterfront acquaintances were Erwin Kraght and Wilhelm Krost, both suspected German agents," the Lawton letter added.

Activities such as those for which Wachtmeister came under suspicion, such as taking photographs and describing the ships that came into the port at Ciudad Trujillo, were commonplace among the leisure class, as was the ready supply of cash he always had on hand, another detail that perturbed the surveillance agents. But the most damning matter against him, no doubt, was the company he kept. He himself seemed to recognize this problem of guilt by association, as the documents in his file indicate that Wachtmeister had no relations with his former acquaintances during his first stay at La Cumbre. Eric Roorda notes that at the moment Pearl Harbor was bombed, some months before the count arrived at La Cumbre, "more than 40 Germans already occupied the camp's little cabins on the crest of the cordillera, which were not unlike the shacks being inhabited by forcibly interned Japanese-Americans at desolate locations in the United States at the same time."[11] In drawing this parallel, Roorda explicitly signaled similarities between detention programs in Latin America and the United States.

The internment of Wachtmeister and other European nationals in a place like La Cumbre represented something of a swing move on the part of the country's government, as the Dominican dictator Rafael Leónidas Trujillo had shown admiration for both Hitler and Mussolini. He had also implemented a racialized immigration policy that favored Europeans and treated Haitians who lived on the same island—many of them in Dominican territory—with severely repressive measures.[12] Like the führer, he had ordered acts of genocide, the most notorious of them the 1937 massacre of thousands of Haitians living along the border between the two countries. As Roorda notes, "Although estimates of the duration of the massacre and its death toll vary widely, it seems likely that twelve thousand Haitians died during at least a week of violence throughout the country."[13] At the same time, the Dominican Republic was the first country in Latin America to declare war on the Axis, and Trujillo used the unprecedented amount of aid he received from the United States to expand his military and its control of the populace.[14] In yet another contradiction, the Dominican Republic was home to Sosúa, an agricultural colony that provided a haven for Jews fleeing Nazi-controlled Europe, at least until Trujillo cut off all immigration to the country.[15]

Despite recognizing that associating with Germans had put him in jeopardy, documents in Wachtmeister's file claim he resumed his former associations with Axis sympathizers on his second "confinement" at La Cumbre. They cite him declaring, "I might as well 'heil Hitler' myself, since there is no longer any hope."[16] Indeed, the paper trail indicates that the count became increasingly convinced that his situation would not improve, despite his protests that he was never involved in political activities and that as a Swede his official status in the war was neutral. During yet another round of questioning in the United States, he reportedly retorted that he was in the Dominican Republic to study the Arabic language, suggesting his exasperation at officials' unwillingness to accept the explanations he had already proffered in good faith.

All those at La Cumbre, including a single Japanese man and some surviving crew members of a German cargo liner that had been captured off Hispaniola, were deported to the United States in May 1942. Described by Roorda as "Nazi and Fascist sympathizers," the group included "a shady Swiss 'count,'" likely Wachtmeister himself, despite the misidentification of his country of origin and the doubts expressed regarding his noble pedigree.[17] The government continued to maintain that Wachtmeister was a dangerous Nazi sympathizer and a potential danger to the American war effort, even after his arrival at Kenedy. Like Jews' claim to "refugee" status, Wachtmeister's claim to neutrality as a Swedish citizen was treated with skepticism, if not paranoia. "Obviously, the cloak of Swedish nationality would be of assistance to him in any subversive activities which he might wish to undertake in this hemisphere," Lawton warned in his June 17, 1942, letter.

But Wollmar Boström, who served as the Swedish minister in Washington from 1925 to 1945, forcefully disputed this characterization. On August 13, 1942, several months into the count's detention at Kenedy, Boström addressed a letter to George Brandt at the State Department, repeatedly referencing Wachtmeister with his noble title and rejecting the government's unfavorable depiction of his countryman. Boström's letter provides details on his two internments in the Dominican Republic, the lack of evidence against the young man, and the minister's exasperation with the actions and omissions by both the Dominican and US governments in Wachtmeister's case. A starkly different image of the count emerges in the portrait Boström paints:

> Primo: Count Wachtmeister says in his first letter to me, copy of which is enclosed, that he was interned in the Dominican Republic on Dec. 11, 1941, released on January 10, 1942, again interned on April 6, 1942, and transferred to the United States in the latter part of May *together with a number of Germans.*
>
> Secundo: This Legation requested our representative to the Dominican Republic to give all information he had on the case. In his report it is stated that Count Wachtmeister was released (as he stated himself) because nothing had been found against him; this detention had been due to a general control of the activity of foreigners. Our representative's opinion of Count Wachtmeister is that he is perhaps a bit eccentric but that he is quite harmless and did not show interest in politics or the war.
>
> Tertio: Our representative did not succeed in getting any information about the charges against Count Wachtmeister, but only that he had been sent to the United States. Count Wachtmeister has therefore now been arrested altogether more than five months without any given reasons. I think this is a serious case, and I want to repeat my earnest request that you use pressure on the Dominican Republic to give the information about the charges against him which I have asked for.[18]

Wachtmeister's treatment in the Dominican Republic before being sent to the United States "seems to indicate that the Dominican Republic just wanted to get rid of him as well as other foreigners and that they, perhaps, doubted his Swedish nationality and title. It is also remarkable that he, a neutral, was not repatriated to Sweden at the same time as some others detained at the same camp," Boström added.

The minister's letter quickly received attention, and a few days later, FBI director J. Edgar Hoover fired off a memo to Edward Ennis at the Justice Department, stating that Wachtmeister admitted to police officials that he had obtained his release from a concentration camp by the payment of one hundred dollars. Hoover used this detail to besmirch the reputation of the Swedish diplomatic corps, insisting that reports claimed Wachtmeister had been released through the intervention of the Swedish minister in Cuba, while the count himself had admitted to German friends that money had changed hands in the arrangement for his release. This was proof for Hoover that the count was untrustworthy, though many detainees throughout the Latin American Alien Enemy Program attested to similar cases of Axis nationals avoiding detention or reducing their time detained by paying off local officials.

A letter dated the next day, sent from the secretary of state's office to the attorney general, refers to telephone conversations on August 14, 1942, between Ennis, John Burling of the Alien Enemy Control Unit, and others concerning Wachtmeister's case. Minister Boström had stated in an August 13 letter, "It would be appreciated if the Department of Justice would inform the Department of State whether it has any objection to the discharge of Count Wachtmeister under parole to the custody of the Swedish Legation for repatriation by that Legation on a Swedish tanker, which is expected to depart for Sweden within about two weeks from a Texas Port, or on a Swedish cargo ship, which is expected to leave New Orleans for Sweden on or about September 15."[19]

Thus, just as the count had come through the port of New Orleans from the Dominican Republic en route to Camp Kenedy, now the Swedish minister sought his repatriation on a voyage that would start in that same port, or perhaps a port in Texas. But that autumn, there was an interruption in the safe conduct ship traffic between the United States and Sweden, and the September target date came and went without the count's release.

By November, it appeared finally that Wachtmeister was bound for Sweden—a country that not only had sought to remain neutral throughout the war but in 1943 provided refuge to Denmark's seventy-eight hundred Jews destined for deportation to Nazi concentration camps.[20] A November 7, 1942, memo to Assistant Secretary of State Breckenridge Long, the most senior US official within the internment program, confirmed the *Balboa* was expected to sail from New Orleans for Sweden in the near future and recommended the Swedish legation book Wachtmeister's passage immediately. Long even wrote across the top of the memo, "*Put* him on this boat!"[21]

Later that month, Ennis confirmed in another memo to Willard Kelly, supervisor of the detention camps functioning under the supervision of US Customs and Border Patrol, that the State Department had consented to Wachtmeister's repatriation and advised that the count would likely sail from New Orleans or another gulf port in early December. He cautioned, "It has been agreed by this Department and the State Department that it is of utmost importance that Wachtmeister not be allowed at liberty in this country, and that he be transferred directly from detention to the vessel on which he is to be repatriated."[22]

Nonetheless, on December 9, James H. Keeley, acting chief of the State Department's Special Division, objected in writing to the repatriation, once again delaying any action. Copies of the memo and an enclosure of derogatory information circulated among officials of the Military Intelligence Division of the US Army, the FBI, the Department of Justice, and the Alien Enemy Control Unit. The "charges" against Wachtmeister were once again repeated: (1) the young count actively associated with leading Nazis in the Dominican Republic, and this was indicative of his Axis sympathies; (2) he held a pilot's license and had offered his services to the German Condor Air Lines of Brazil; (3) despite not having an occupation, he had sufficient funds to enable him to travel constantly throughout the Dominican Republic, where he frequented the waterfront and took many pictures, being an expert photographer; (4) he had been arrested in the Dominican Republic for "motivo de la guerra" and placed in La Cumbre concentration camp; and (5) by his own admission, he obtained his release from the concentration camp by the payment of money.

There was really nothing new in the memo, except perhaps that events such as his arrest and internment at La Cumbre were now being used as "evidence" of Wachtmeister's dangerous character—even though Boström's earlier letter had insisted the count had been arrested and held in the Caribbean country without any stated reasons. Describing his arrest for "motivo de la guerra" (on account of the war) suggests either that he was included in a random sweep of Axis nationals or that the agency personnel weren't sure what "motivo de la guerra" even meant, or both.

Also curious is the I-55 General Information Form that Wachtmeister completed at Kenedy on September 17, 1942. The I-55 was filled out by all alien internees held in INS facilities during the internment program. In response to question 42c, Wachtmeister stated that he served in the Swedish Air Force from June 1938 to April 1939, providing a plausible background for his experience as a pilot. And, while his I-55 corroborates the accounts of Wachtmeister's activities provided by the Swedish minister and Wachtmeister himself, what *is* strange is the frequency with which he responded, "*Supervisor of Station stated this question need not be answered.*" Did camp officials assume the Swedish national

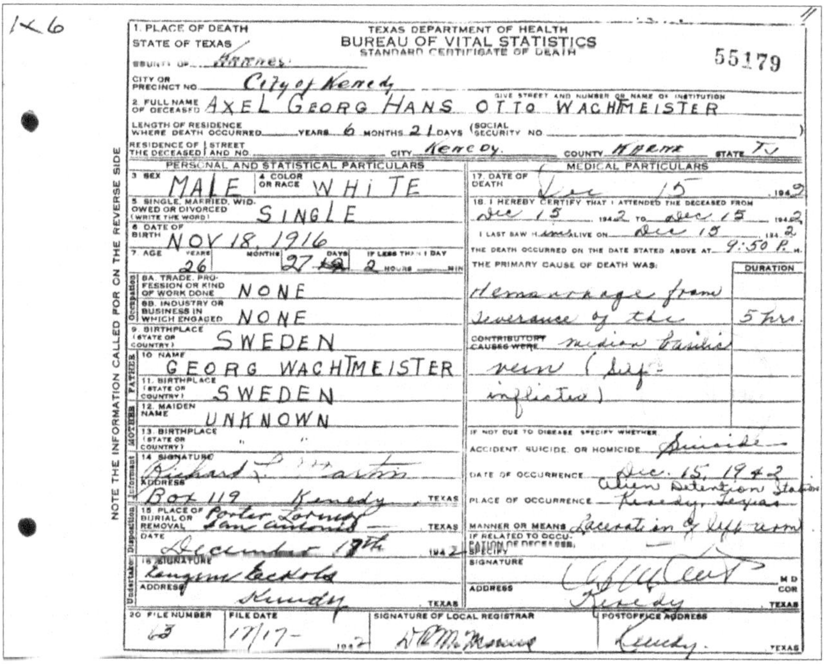

FIGURE 5.1. Death certificate for Count Axel Wachtmeister, who died of suicide at Camp Kennedy, Texas, on December 15, 1942. Image from Texas Department of State Health Services, Austin, TX.

would not be held long at Camp Kenedy? Did they believe the error of labeling a person from a neutral country an enemy alien would quickly be exposed and remedied? Did Wachtmeister even fill out his own I-55?

We may never know whether Keeley's misgivings regarding Wachtmeister's repatriation were well founded, but the obstacles he placed in the count's path undoubtedly contributed to an unexpected, tragic outcome. On December 15, 1942, as the bureaucratic back-and-forth continued, Count Wachtmeister ended his own life. A "memo of conversation" documenting a telephone call between Willard Kelly of the INS and Sidney Lafoon of the State Department's Special Division reported that Wachtmeister had been rushed to the hospital at Kenedy and had received a blood transfusion, but that he died at 9:50 p.m. that day. The death certificate from Camp Kenedy confirmed the twenty-six-year old count had died of a hemorrhage from a self-inflicted severance of the median basilic vein, a laceration to the left upper arm. Before adding his signature, the doctor noted that he attended the dying patient for five hours (figure 5.1).

The State Department, the Department of Justice, and other agencies scrambled to defend actions that had ended with a detainee taking his own life (and a detainee with a noble title at that), and they once again reiterated the black marks against him. But Minister Boström protested, laying out his position in a three-page memo that he hand-delivered to Long's office on January 4, 1943. After providing a biographical summary of Wachtmeister and the details of his internments in the Dominican Republic and the United States, Boström noted, "He seems to have had no interest in politics or in the war. His way of life is said to have been retiring and proper."[23] Reiterating that the nobility of his family stretched back four centuries, he described the count as someone "who could not be presumed willfully to do anything unlawful, and is said to be a man of good character, although maybe somewhat eccentric."

No grounds for Wachtmeister's internment had ever been established in either country, Boström maintained, and the best information Swedish diplomats could obtain indicated he was interned on the orders of Major Butler, the American military attaché in Ciudad Trujillo, who "was said to be in cooperation with the Police Department of the Dominican Republic in the supervision of foreigners." Boström also cited verbatim a crucial part of the story, one that seemingly was suppressed or censored in the official reports released by US agencies: the count's suicide note. In it—his last opportunity to clear himself of nefarious actions or associations—Wachtmeister stated,

> I have never in all my life done anything bad to anybody; neither would I harm anybody. I don't know why I am here, and why all these bad things have happened to me. From all that has been going on and is going on, I realize that you are going to "pull" something "over" me; and I won't have the intelligence to free myself from those possible charges. What's the use of living in a world filled with unjustice and where there is no fairness and humanity. I have only cared for one thing in all my life, and that was to be let alone and be able to live a quiet life, in peace. (s) A. Wachtmeister[24]

What outcome did the count so fear that he preferred to take his own life? What was it that he feared camp officials were going to "pull . . . over" him? Boström doesn't try to answer those questions, but he calls the note an explanation for Wachtmeister's "act of desperation," describing him as "an innocent and tragic victim of overzealous suspicions." He warned that the count's status as a subject of a neutral county made his detention "a rather questionable procedure," even for a diplomat such as himself who was used to operating in and negotiating with the United States. Minister Boström requested "these last greetings" of the count be given to the young man's father and Swedish authorities, along with an explanation of the actions taken: "The Legation of Sweden would therefore appreciate receiving from the Department of State as detailed an explanation as possible of the reason why he was taken from the Dominican Republic to this country to be interned here, and some indication why the circumstances pertaining to his case were considered so serious as to compel the drastic measures of internment." The minister finished the memo by stressing that Wachtmeister "affirmed emphatically that he had never occupied himself with politics or been guilty of acts against United States interests."[25]

Wachtmeister's story is unique on several counts, including his Swedish nationality, his noble lineage and the degree of despair to which he succumbed. His choice to take his own life rather than continue on "in a world filled with unjustice [sic] and where there is no fairness and humanity" might seem drastic, even amid the frustration, despair, indignation, and even fury so often expressed by internees. In fact, his despondent reaction at finding himself behind barbed wire in an internment camp in the United States was quite commonplace. Like so many others considered in these pages, he felt his detention was "unjust and unwarranted," to use Boström's phrase. He did not understand *why* he was being held, and after months without a satisfactory answer to that question, he came to distrust the motives and methods employed by the US government. If ever there was a case in which New Orleans served as a port of no return for an enemy alien deported from Latin America, that case is Wachtmeister's. Though the young count was funneled through this gateway to North America on his way to Camp Kenedy, there would be no return back through it. While the title of this study, *Port of No Return*, calls attention metaphorically to the ways in which the US internment experience irrevocably altered the lives of named enemy aliens from Latin America, whether or not they returned physically to the countries of their apprehension, for Axel Wachtmeister, the phrase is literal as well as figurative.

The Nazi Princess

Her Serene Highness Princess Stephanie von Hohenlohe-Waldenburg-Schillingsfürst of Hungary was not Hungarian and was a princess only by marriage.

But she certainly lived the life of the landed gentry—at least for a time. Apprehended on the streets of Philadelphia, Hohenlohe proceeded from there to a detention camp in New Jersey and from there to Seagoville, a family detention camp in Texas.[26] Having never passed through the port of New Orleans or the gates of Camp Algiers (to our knowledge), her case might seem unrelated to this study. Nonetheless, the story of the "Nazi princess" provides a remarkable lesson in comparisons and contrasts with that of Wachtmeister, demonstrating how differently two individuals could react to the experience of internment, even if both were titled Europeans, whether they possessed that title through blood or marriage.

Princess Stephanie's story challenges a host of stereotypes and commonplaces associated with World War II history. She exemplifies the power one woman could wield at the highest levels of political intrigue, even within the upper echelon of the Nazi Party itself, a panoply of dominant male figures. Despite her noble title, her background was that of a commoner and her lineage almost certainly Jewish. Never a passive observer, she sought out relationships that would increase her power and realm of influence; one could even argue that rather than being used by men, she used them. Undoubtedly, Hohenlohe's royal title contributed significantly to her status as a cause célèbre, both in international spy circles and within the US internment program. She associated with Adolf Hitler and his closest intimates, and in the United States, her case went before President Franklin D. Roosevelt himself. The unusual aspects of her tale and the extraordinary attention it drew help us see how the US enemy alien internment program could play out in radically different ways in individual cases.

Never resigning herself to any unsavory fate, Hohenlohe was extraordinarily adept at exerting influence on those around her, including from within the walls of her own internment. The elasticity with which she established and then changed identities and allegiances, shape-shifting from a middle-class commoner to a titled princess and castle mistress, from an outsider with cloudy Jewish origins to a Nazi insider, and finally from spending four years in US internment camps to once again hobnobbing with the rich and famous, was nothing short of remarkable. Even from the perspective of the present, her story seems more extravagant than any fiction.

Dubbed "Hitler's Spy Princess" due to her intimacy with the inner circles of the Third Reich, Princess Stephanie's character and background contrast starkly—and darkly—with those of Count Wachtmeister. Whereas the Swedish count came from a centuries-long line of noble forbears, Stephanie Richter, born in Vienna in 1891, acquired her royal status through her marriage to the German prince Friedrich Franz von Hohenlohe-Waldenburg-Schillingsfürst. Biographer Martha Schad claims not only that Richter was a commoner but that her mother, Ludmilla Kuranda, and her biological father, Max Wiener, were both Jewish, though the princess herself would never admit to this.[27]

The Hohenlohes were a "titled set who saw advantages to Hitler's rise" and were willing to overlook its unpleasant side, according to author David Talbot. Prince Maximilian Egon von Hohenlohe figured in Allen Dulles's "reign of treason as America's top spy in Nazi-occupied Europe"; the two men attempted to broker a German surrender that would leave the Reich largely intact. In fact, "The Hohenlohe family was filled with ardent Nazi admirers. Perhaps the most bizarre was Stephanie von Hohenlohe, who became known as 'Hitler's princess.' A Jew by birth, Stephanie found social position by marrying another Hohenlohe prince. In the years before the war, she became one of Hitler's most tireless promoters, helping to bring British press magnate Lord Rothermere into the Nazi fold."[28]

Raised by her mother and her mother's husband, Hans Richter, a successful lawyer, Stephanie enjoyed a rather privileged upbringing in Vienna, where she studied piano and ballet and excelled at sports. In her unpublished memoirs, Hohenlohe claimed she set a goal of marrying a prince at fifteen and by age sixteen "had something of a reputation as a beauty."[29] Her father's legal clients included Princess Franziska von Metternich, a widow who tutored Stephanie in etiquette; a wealthy aunt invited her along on travels to Venice, Berlin, Paris, Corsica, and Prague. Several months attending college in the south of England revealed Stephanie's talent for languages, and she reportedly spoke several fluently by the time she was twenty-one.[30]

At age twenty-three, though claiming she was only seventeen, Stephanie found her prince—or perhaps princes. Pregnant with a child conceived with the married Archduke Franz Salvator, Prince of Tuscany, Richter was able to convince Prince Friedrich Franz von Hohenlohe-Waldenburg-Schillingsfürst that he was the father of her unborn child or at least that the marriage would be advantageous for both parties.[31] The two married in London in May 1914, and her son, Franz Josef, who also would be held in US detention camps during World War II, was born in December of that same year in Vienna.

The Hohenlohes' marriage ended in July 1920, but rather than a setback, Stephanie seized on the divorce as an opportunity to pursue a life of pleasure and intimacy with influential men and women. She retained her married surname and continued to present herself as a Hohenlohe princess in these encounters, effectively banishing her common origins to a distant past. Notably shrewd at developing friendships with the very powerful and the very rich, by 1925 Hohenlohe had installed herself in a tony Paris apartment with a household staff of nine. When things got too slow in Paris, she would visit Monte Carlo, Nice, or Cannes, attaching herself along the way to high-stakes personalities such as the Duke of Westminster, the millionaire John Murton Gundy, and John Warden, a multimillionaire from the family that owned Standard Oil.[32]

Hohenlohe's success in these international circles earned her a reputation as many things: society gadfly, Mata Hari, mistress of Nazis, spy, even "gold digger," as she was described in an October 28, 1941, presidential memo.[33] Nonetheless, Karina Urbach argues that her preeminent role was that of go-between, serving as a conduit between key political players such as Adolf Hitler; Hermann Göring, the founder of the Gestapo; Hungarian admiral Miklós Horthy; and Harold Sidney Harmsworth, the First Viscount Rothermere, a British press baron. These central actors in the drama of the war years were not the only influential figures in her orbit, however. According to her biographer Jim Wilson, "Her contacts book was filled with a cosmopolitan list of people of influence and wealth—entrepreneurs, financiers, politicians, diplomats, statesmen and European aristocracy and royalty. This was a world in which she moved with ease, using her charm, her social skills and inevitably her title to impress and to persuade."[34]

Two of these relationships in particular furnished Hohenlohe with notoriety. The most lucrative perhaps (though arguably eclipsed by her connection to Hitler, who put a castle at her disposal) was Hohenlohe's friendship with Lord Rothermere, an Anglo-Irish press tycoon and the founder of London's *Daily Mail*. The two reportedly met in 1927 over a roulette table in Monte Carlo when Stephanie was thirty-six and Rothermere fifty-nine.[35] After he complained of a lack of good story leads for his newspaper, Stephanie convinced Rothermere she had a topic that would sell plenty of copies. He apparently could not refuse this bait and invited her to his Cap Martin villa the next day. There, the princess proceeded to passionately convince Rothermere of the injustices suffered by Hungary following World War I, when the 1920 Treaty of Trianon led to the readjustment of its boundaries and the reduction of its population from twenty-one million to eight million. Impressed with Hohenlohe's exposition of this problem, Rothermere published a series of articles in the *Daily Mail* defending Hungarian sovereignty and even suggesting the reinstatement of its monarchy. These articles won him effusive praise and a throng of followers in Hungary and elsewhere, along with the hoped-for buzz among the newspaper's readers.

The episode alerted the princess to how far her influence might reach at both the personal level and on the international stage, and in the years ahead, she would capitalize by negotiating a lucrative contract with Rothermere as his emissary in Europe, with an eye to drawing him "closer to Hitler's inner circle."[36] At the same time, she had begun to also develop her contacts in the Nazi Party. By 1930, Rothermere was quite openly pro-Nazi, portraying the führer's rise to power sympathetically in his newspapers and expressing his desire to meet Hitler.[37] Princess Stephanie served as the practical and sentimental link between the two personalities, benefitting in distinct ways from her relationship with both. In July 1932, Rothermere signed a three-year contract, which he would later renew, providing Hohenlohe with an annual retainer of £5,000, a tidy sum at that time, as well as another £2,000 each time she completed an assignment for him. In force until 1938, the contract provided the princess with an overall sum of "well over £1 million in today's money."[38]

In 1933, Lord Rothermere asked the princess to establish contact directly with Hitler. She responded by forming a relationship with Hitler's personal adjutant, Fritz Wiedemann, one that would long outlast any meeting between the führer and the British press baron. In December of that year, Hohenlohe used her association with Wiedemann to secure her own first meeting with Hitler, in which, according to her own recollection, Hitler could scarcely take his eyes off her.[39] The führer gave her a letter for Rothermere, assuring him that he was loath to provoke a war. More exchanges followed, and Rothermere met Hitler in Berlin in December 1934 in a visit that confirmed their mutual admiration for each other and their respective causes. The princess's efforts to draw Rothermere deeper into the Nazi inner circle were so successful that the two men corresponded for several years, and Lord Rothermere would later be photographed with Hitler and Princess Stephanie, along with *Daily Mail* journalist George Ward Price, Fritz Wiedemann, and Joseph Goebbels and his wife, Magda, at the Berghof, Hitler's mountain retreat.[40]

Though Princess Stephanie and her son, Franz, would both deny that she was either a trusted confidant or love interest of Nazis such as Hitler or Wiedemann, material evidence corroborated this fact. Hitler sent a large photograph of himself to Hohenlohe with the dedication "To my dear princess," a memento British intelligence found displayed in a place of honor on the desk of her London flat. But perhaps the most surprising object that marked her as a Nazi sympathizer and key player in her own right was her Golden Party Badge, which Hitler himself presented to her in June 1938 (figure 5.2). This small adornment "was a

FIGURE 5.2. Nazi Golden Party Badge. Image from Wikipedia, public domain.

badge that elevated the recipient to the level of 'Nazi royalty'"; thus recognized for her outstanding service, "the Princess, born a Jew, was now a de facto member of the Nazi Party—an 'honorary Aryan,' as Heinrich Himmler declared her."[41]

But the diminutive badge wasn't the only material proof of Princess Stephanie's position and influence in the Nazi Party. In March 1938 Hitler gave his blessing to her occupation of the sumptuous Schloss Leopoldskron, a lavish mansion in Salzburg that dated from 1736 (figure 5.3). Confiscated by the Gestapo, the palace belonged to Max Reinhardt, a prominent Jewish theater and film director who in 1933 had rejected the Nazis' offer of "honorary Aryanship."[42] Princess Stephanie was named chatelaine, or mistress of the manor, which would serve as a political salon. Learning of the favor the princess received from Hitler, Reinhardt's wife, Helene Thimig, reportedly wrote from the United States, where she and her husband had immigrated, "What a macabre joke: Reinhardt's creation—now a palace for the Nazis! And this Aryanised palace has been placed under the management of the Jewish Princess von Hohenlohe!"[43]

Remodeled at enormous expense with funds from Berlin as luxury accommodations for prominent visitors, Schloss Leopoldskron would provide the starkest possible contrast to Hohenlohe's later living conditions in detention. In fact, she would spend less time there than in the cramped quarters of camps in New Jersey and Texas. After the Allied liberation, the palace would be returned to

FIGURE 5.3. Schloss Leopoldskron, a rococo palace and national historic monument in Salzburg, Austria, was confiscated by the Gestapo and served as an event venue for elite Nazis. Hitler named Stephanie Hohenlohe chatelaine of the palace in 1938. The palace was later used as a backdrop for *The Sound of Music* (1965). Photo by Simon Bernd Kranzer, Wikimedia Commons.

the Reinhardt family and, with Thimig's blessing, become the site of the Salzburg Seminar in American Studies. It also served as the opulent backdrop for the 1965 film *The Sound of Music*. Today, fans can book the palace's hotel rooms, including the pricey "Max Reinhardt Suite," though most will likely remain unaware of Schloss Leopoldskron's role as a Nazi luxury guesthouse with Princess Stephanie presiding.

British intelligence had been aware of Hohenlohe's dealings with Nazi insiders since 1928, but Princess Stephanie's connections with the rich and powerful afforded her a level of protection that made the top brass reluctant to interfere. Her MI5 file noted she had "wormed her way into society circles in London" and formed close friendships with well-heeled figures such as Lady Ethel Snowden and Lady Emerald Cunard.[44] In 1935, invitations arrived in London for both Lady Snowden and Princess Stephanie from the führer, inviting them to the Nuremberg Nazi Party rally. This was the occasion on which Hitler announced the

ROYALS AND NOBLES BEHIND BARBED WIRE | 175

Nuremberg Laws, restricting the rights of German Jews and ultimately leading to the Shoah itself. Despite increasing noise in Hitler's orbit that Hohenlohe was herself a Jew, these origins seemed to be less important, at least at that time, than the princess's perceived value: Hitler invited her to Nazi Party rallies in 1936, 1937, and 1938.[45] Indeed, a 1938 report from British intelligence noted, "She is frequently summoned by the Führer who appreciates her intelligence and good advice. She is perhaps the only woman who can exercise any influence on him."[46]

Nonetheless, by the beginning of 1939 the fairy-tale story of the princess in her castle would come to an end when the führer discovered her ongoing relationship with family man Fritz Wiedemann. Hitler had become disgruntled with Wiedemann's military performance and had told Goebbels it was time to get rid of him. When the two men met in January 1939, the chancellor gave Wiedemann the option of serving in the United States as consul-general in San Francisco, a post he accepted. Hitler also insisted his now-former aide break off with the princess immediately, as she was "under suspicion."[47] Wiedemann's apparent refusal to do so further incensed certain members of the Nazi leadership, and the number of Hohenlohe's enemies in the party grew. Earlier that same month, Heinrich Himmler had detailed "credible evidence that for some considerable time Princess Hohenlohe had been working for British intelligence" in a report he presented to Hitler, who reacted by ordering a warrant for her arrest.[48]

In January 1939, Hohenlohe left the palace for London, where she hoped to stay out of reach of any unpleasant consequences. She did attend to one noteworthy detail before the move, though, requesting permission for her mother's sister, Olga, to come along with her and her mother to London. That request was denied, and Olga was reportedly arrested soon after. Hohenlohe's aunt died in the Theresienstadt concentration camp in September 1942.[49]

Once in London, Hohenlohe was hard pressed to improve her financial situation, since Lord Rothermere had not renewed the contract for her services. The newspaper owner continued to express approval for Hitler and his advances, lauding him in a personal letter in June 1939 for his "great and superhuman work."[50] But he no longer felt the princess was a necessary intermediary. Hohenlohe had written to him in February 1938, noting with surprising candor changes in Germany and in the Nazi leadership, as well as the consequences these changes were likely to have for the Hitler-Rothermere friendship:

> What is happening in Germany now is momentous. They are passing through their greatest crisis. Changes are taking place there, which are

of decisive importance for the future of Europe. All the conservatives are being kicked out and only the extremest extremists have or are taking their places. . . .
You will have to be very careful in the future. As a matter of fact, I can not see how you will be able to support Hitler any longer under these new conditions and at the same time serve the best interests of your own country.[51]

When Lord Rothermere refused to change his mind, the princess retaliated by suing him, planting rumors that she would publish her memoirs in the United States and cast Rothermere in an unfavorable light, alluding to his relationships with much younger women, including her. His legal counsel called this "naked blackmail."[52] And beyond the question of dalliances with younger women, Lord Rothermere was now at pains to answer for the same pro-Nazi proclivities in which Hohenlohe herself was embroiled. He insisted that throughout his correspondence with Hitler, he had been working for peace between Germany and Britain. With war now a reality, he attempted to put distance between himself and the führer, claiming he changed his stance once "Hitler had run amok."[53]

In a high-profile trial in a packed courtroom, Hohenlohe lost her suit against the press baron. Rothermere "generously" bore all the legal costs, perhaps implicitly or explicitly in exchange for her silence on certain counts. In a final desperate letter to him, she accused Rothermere of turning her life into a "horror play," while her devotion to him "was like that of a faithful dog."[54] She begged her former friend to consider her son Franz, now a young man, who she hoped to spare "from being the victim of a further sensation—his mother's suicide."[55] Hohenlohe did indeed later work up notes for a memoir, but that text was never published. As for Lord Rothermere, he died in 1940 in Bermuda after traveling there to improve his health.

Hohenlohe's highly publicized loss in the British courts might have seemed a dark and insurmountable obstacle, but the princess was never one to dwell on past defeats or bleak horizons. She decided to lose no time waiting to see if the British government would imprison her on espionage charges. In December 1939, not yet a year out from leaving the Salzburg castle, the princess and her mother, both traveling under false names, boarded the Dutch liner *Veendam* at Southampton, bound for the United States. She was not a newcomer to America, having already traveled there on several occasions with Wiedemann during the 1930s.[56] For her 1939 "visit," Hohenlohe disembarked "elegantly dressed and bedecked in her usual array of expensive jewellery," along with 106 pieces of luggage.[57] Rarely one to seek out anonymity, she was described by the *New York World Telegram* as wearing a three-quarter-length silver fox fur coat, a black silk jersey dress, and black kid Perugia sandals with very high heels and sky-blue platform soles.[58]

With all her excess baggage, in both senses, the princess apparently meant to stay in the United States, despite the fact that she only possessed a visitor's visa. Aware of her intentions, MI5 made sure the FBI was waiting for her. Ironically, as it turned out, its agents had wagered she would try to flee Britain in order to avoid internment as a Nazi agent. British intelligence instructed their American colleagues to pay especially close attention to any encounters the princess might have with Wiedemann, serving as the German consul-general in San Francisco, and described as "probably the most notorious Nazi in the country."[59] Indeed, the princess's first phone call was to Wiedemann, but she suggested they stay on opposite coasts for the time being, so as not to arouse further suspicions.

"Worse Than Ten Thousand Men"

Hohenlohe's activities in Germany, France, and England soon became known on the American side of the Atlantic. In early 1940, a *New York Times* article identified her as a star among a group of high-ranking political spies, propaganda hostesses, and "ladies of mystery" recruited by Hitler.[60] Then, on December 10, 1941, the *Times* reported on her internment as a Nazi agent and dangerous alien at a detention camp in New Jersey.

The path from Princess Stephanie's arrival in the United States to her internment and ultimate release further establishes her as someone possessing formidable resourcefulness, especially in terms of her powers of persuasion and seduction. The incredible details of that journey included: (1) defying deportation orders by a number of means, including hiring an ambulance to bring her to a court appearance and having emergency personnel wheel her into the hearing on a stretcher; (2) moving into Fritz Wiedemann's residence in San Francisco with her mother in tow, apparently with the blessing of the German consul's wife, despite common knowledge that the two were lovers; (3) seducing Lemuel B. Schofield (figure 5.4), the director of the US Immigration and Naturalization Service, when he visited her in detention; and (4) convincing a three-man board of the top brass at the INS that she was and always had been anti-Nazi.

FIGURE 5.4. (*Left to right*) Major Lemuel B. Schofield, Solicitor General Francis Biddle, and Attorney General Robert Jackson, on Schofield's appointment to the Immigration and Naturalization Service as special assistant to the attorney general, Washington, DC, June 14, 1940. National Archives, used with permission.

Not surprisingly, an October 1941 FBI memo described Hohenlohe not just as a spy but as "extremely intelligent, dangerous and clever," and "worse than ten thousand men."[61] According to the bureau, she participated with Wiedemann in a network that covered not only the United States but the whole Pacific basin, including countries in South America. Together, the princess and Hitler's former aide exercised influence and persuaded others to sympathize with the Nazi cause. Wiedemann reportedly made many trips to Mexico with the task of gaining the support of Central American countries to block the Panama Canal to American shipping in the event of a war.[62] The FBI maintained tight surveillance on the "couple," and warned that the princess was capable of resorting to any means, including bribery and seduction, to achieve the outcomes she desired.[63]

When her temporary visa expired in January 1941 after already having won a postponement, Hohenlohe wrote to President Roosevelt himself, pleading for permission to stay in the United States and asking him to extend to her the privileges of "this land of freedom" that were enjoyed by anyone not guilty of an unjust or disloyal act. "Please spare me the humiliation of having to leave this country under such oppressive circumstances, as though I were a criminal," she begged.[64]

Having been briefed by the FBI on the princess and the dangers she posed, Roosevelt was unmoved. Thus, faced with her impending deportation, Hohenlohe employed other extreme strategies. She threatened to commit suicide, claimed she was too sick to attend the deportation enforcement hearing, and was finally wheeled into the room on a stretcher, a sight that was photographed for posterity. But none of this seemed to work, and the annoyed president signed a memo to "have her put on a boat." Her lawyers countered that they could by then find no country willing to extend her a visa.

On March 8, 1941, under orders of Major Schofield, head of the US Immigration and Naturalization Service, Stephanie was arrested at her apartment and taken to the INS detention center in San Francisco. A few days later, Major Schofield, a forty-eight-year-old father of four, visited her there, and Hohenlohe, now fifty, was again able to call on her appreciable powers of persuasion and seduction. Despite Schofield's senior position, he "succumbed willingly" to the princess's wiles as other men had done before him.[65] On May 19, directly contradicting the president's orders, Schofield released the princess on $35,000 bail on the condition that she inform the INS of her whereabouts; not make contact with the German consul-general in San Francisco (Wiedemann) or any other representative of a foreign government; establish residence in a small town with no airport; and give no lectures, interviews to the press, or public declarations. Schofield dropped her deportation proceedings and told a reporter she had cooperated with the Department of Justice and provided valuable information while in custody, though he could not provide the press with specific details.

In what now seemed a familiar pattern, the princess and her mother moved across the country to the Raleigh Hotel in Washington, DC, where Schofield was also staying. In late July, Schofield wrote to US attorney general Francis Biddle, claiming that Stephanie could provide intimate details of Hitler's "treachery, his deceit, and his cunning."[66] Though purportedly "secret," FBI director J. Edgar Hoover learned of the letter and Schofield's apparent inability to claim objectivity in the case. In fact, the FBI was now keeping tabs on the Nazi princess by tailing the smitten director of the INS, who gushed to Hohenlohe in a letter: "Everything about you is new and different and gets me excited. You are the most interesting person I have ever met. You dress better than anyone else, and every time you come into a room everyone else fades out of the picture. . . . Because of you I do so many crazy things, because I am mad about you."[67] The dazzled Schofield had by the summer of 1941 set Stephanie and her mother up in a small house in Alexandria, Virginia, and was frequently seen by Hoover's employees visiting the princess there.

With the Japanese attack on Pearl Harbor on December 7, 1941, however, the status of enemy aliens in the United States changed abruptly. The very next day, Stephanie was apprehended by FBI agents in Philadelphia as she and her mother were leaving a movie theater. This time she was taken to the Gloucester Immigration Center in New Jersey, where reportedly, "overwhelmed by her current dilemma, she tried, unsuccessfully, to commit suicide by swallowing sleeping pills."[68] Across the United States and in several countries south of the border, Germans, Austrians, Italians, and Japanese were being rounded up, and many were being arrested. Despite her Hungarian passport, Hohenlohe was classified as a German and confined at the New Jersey detention camp. A few weeks later, on February 13, 1942, Attorney General Francis Biddle signed an order for her internment as "a potential danger to public security and peace in the United States." While she was interned, the FBI searched her home, finding and photographing there the Gold Party Badge that Hitler had presented to her several years earlier.[69]

As could be expected, life in the internment camp was not to the princess's liking. In melodramatic letters to her mother, she complained of the dirty, cold, damp, drafty, and smelly room to which she and her fellow female detainees were confined for long periods; of the terrible food and lack of clean linens; and of her fellow internees, who she said included prostitutes and "sluts with venereal disease."[70] Her son, Prince Franz Hohenlohe, was also arrested as an enemy alien during her stay at Gloucester, spending time first at Ellis Island and then at camps in Oklahoma and Texas. In February 1944, he would be released on parole on condition of his induction into the US Army.

Despite orders from above to discontinue his relationship with the princess, Schofield remained firmly under her spell and worked to make the detention more tolerable for her. When President Roosevelt learned of this, he wrote to J. Edgar Hoover, fuming, "Once more I have to bother you about that Hohenlohe woman. This affair verges not merely on the ridiculous but on the disgraceful." He warned: "If the immigration authorities do not stop once and for all showing favor to Hohenlohe, I will be forced to order an inquiry. The facts will not be very palatable and will go right back to her first arrest and her intimacy with Schofield. I am aware that she is interned in the Gloucester center, but by all accounts she enjoys special privileges there. To be honest, this is all turning into a scandal that requires extremely drastic and immediate action."[71] Biddle responded, transferring Hohenlohe after seven months at Gloucester to Camp Seagoville. According to Schad, even the journey between the camps was humiliating, as "four warders accompanied her, never once letting go of her wrists and ankles." Hohenlohe claimed it was the threats of morphine injections and a straightjacket that convinced her to "go quietly."[72]

Undaunted even after the angry response of the president, the smitten Schofield continued to look out for Stephanie, giving the director at Seagoville instructions to grant her special privileges, such as permission to use a telephone outside the camp and to visit with her mother outside official visiting hours. But he ultimately could not weather his superiors' reprimands and finally resigned his position, returning to a successful law practice in New York.[73] When Hohenlohe did not hear from him for a while, she turned her attentions to Hoover himself, offering him "revelations" on Schofield; seemingly, the princess was capable of turning on her closest allies and lovers in an attempt to improve her situation.[74] Fortunately for her, Schofield never learned of the proposed betrayal, and the two would not only reunite after Hohenlohe's eventual release in 1945 but also live together as a couple for several years, until Schofield died unexpectedly, purportedly of a heart attack.

In a letter to the royal Swedish legation representing Hungarian detainees, Counselor Erik de Laval wrote that on December 12, 1942, he had visited the princess at the internment camp at Seagoville, taking down "certain complaints and requests to make in connection with her internment."[75] These included "brutal" treatment on the street when she was originally arrested in Philadelphia; "undesirable" circumstances at the Immigration Station at Gloucester, New Jersey; a superficial examination by the FBI after her arrest that contained so many false statements concerning her person (name, date, place of birth, etc.) that she at first believed herself to be the victim of a case of mistaken identity; and "disagreeable" living conditions at Seagoville in the hot summer climate alongside Germans who identified as Nazis. Meanwhile, her son, Franz, was interned at Fort McAlester in Oklahoma; thus neither daughter nor grandson could look after her mother, the aged Baroness Milla de Szepessy, living in Beverly Hills, California.

Despite these grievances and pleas, Hohenlohe would not receive a hearing until March 1, 1944, some twenty-eight months from the time she was first interned at Gloucester. Nonetheless, she apparently had retained her powers of persuasion and used them in the hearing: two of the three men who constituted the Special Hearing Board in Seagoville recommended unconditional release and the third recommended parole. The majority considered the grounds justifying further supervision "quite destitute of validity"; Hohenlohe's release would allow her to reunite with her mother, "now senile," and her son, who had made bona fide efforts to enter the armed forces of our country. They concluded: "There is not a single piece of evidence that can be found based upon close observation of her speech and behavior by competent judges in the camp which raises the slightest suspicion regarding her good faith in so far as her oral protestations of loyalty are concerned. . . . Her character in terms of our internal security is in some degree established by the fact that she is unpopular with the militant Nazis in this camp who definitely view her as pro-Ally. She has been abused in camp within the limits of the militant Nazis' opportunities."[76] Once again, it appeared that Princess Stephanie had turned the tide in her favor. But others watching her case were less convinced, and two months later, on May 1, 1944, the Philadelphia board of the enemy alien program voted unanimously to "not disturb" the order of continued detention, warning, "We are firmly of the belief that the subject herein considered would sell any secret to any one who produced an amount of cash commensurate with the importance of the secret and the possibility of detection."[77]

Despite their shared status as titled Europeans detained as "Germans" in Texas detention camps, Princess Stephanie's experience at Seagoville seems very different from Count Wachtmeister's life at Kenedy. She drew on her titled status in an entirely different way. Officials wrote that she protested being placed on arrival at the camp in a house designated for Jews but when moved to the German House, was "ostracized and subjected to constant humiliation and rebuffs." Her "feelings of superiority" helped her ignore these insults and verbal persecutions, and she followed "her own patterns of living," reportedly unaware that any rules and regulations concerning internees had anything to do with her. "She makes unusual and special requests constantly. She can be very charming and courteous, but for most people, both staff and internees, she is usually contemptuous. By no one is she considered pro-German," the report concluded.[78]

But perhaps as months turned into years in internment, Princess Stephanie's level of desperation reached a high that brings to mind the ill-fated ending of the Swedish count's story. In late January 1945, Princess Stephanie's son went to visit his mother at Seagoville. Now calling himself Francis instead of Franz, he had been paroled from internment in March 1944 and released from that parole in early January, after being inducted into the US armed services. A report of their visit signed by Grace J. Hanna, the senior officer at Seagoville, advised that "Mrs. Hohenlohe's attitude as revealed from time to time is that she expects and demands her son to turn to every possible source of influence, to make any personal sacrifice necessary to achieve her release from internment. She became highly emotional and disturbed whenever he brought into the conversation any of his own plans for his furlough time."[79]

A few weeks later, Francis wrote a letter to his mother noting that he had seen Edward Ennis at the Department of Justice and found him to be "a delightful man." But when a stack of papers was brought in to Ennis regarding the mother-son visit at Seagoville, Prince Franz's delight had turned to discomfort, as "even at several thousand miles distance, you managed to embarrass the hell out of me, as usual," he wrote. It seems the princess's behavior had aroused new suspicions as the two "spoke in several languages" and she slipped him an object at some moment during their encounter. "Why does she do such abominably stupid things they all say," the prince wrote. "Far from the glamorous babe they still visualize you as, you're a sad sack in need of a good rest, complete quiet, and utter seclusion." Despite this criticism, Franz assured his mother at the end of the letter that Francis Biddle was set to revisit her case the following month.[80]

The princess never read her son's disparaging missive. A February 9, 1945, memo from Willard Kelly to Amy N. Stannard, the officer in charge at Seagoville explained: "We are withholding delivery of Private Hohenlohe's letter as the information therein contained would not seem to serve any constructive purpose, and most certainly would result in a serious emotional reaction on the Princess' part."[81] That comment seems to support a characterization of the princess's mental health as fragile and her behavior at Seagoville as volatile. For his part, Prince Hohenlohe followed up on his efforts to finally secure his mother's release, reminding Biddle in writing in early March that he had been assured by the Department of Justice that his mother's case would be reconsidered. He suggested she be allowed to join his grandmother in the baroness's small apartment in Beverly Hills and that his own parole sponsor, Harry Bennett, could serve in the same capacity with his mother as well. "It was hinted to me once or twice that my mother might harbour ideas of revenge," he wrote, but "anyone entertaining such a thought does not realise to what an extent her spirit has been broken in her three years of detention, not only her spirit, but to a great extent, her health as well."[82]

In April, just weeks before the war ended in Europe, Ennis wrote to the assistant attorney general, Herbert Weschler, noting that he had, as requested, prepared a parole order for Princess Hohenlohe. "It would relieve the Immigration Service of the constant problems she has raised in custody by threats of suicide and such conduct. My memorandum of February 1, 1945 to you points out the custodial problem raised by her threats of suicide at that time," he said.[83] Was the princess being melodramatic? Or was she indeed close to breaking under the long confinement? Whatever her state, sources concur that she was the very last detainee allowed to leave Seagoville in May 1945, following VE Day. "She had been kept locked up to until the very last moment. And that was done on the orders of President Roosevelt, who had been constantly irritated by the princess. To make matters worse, the princess had complained to the president's wife, Eleanor, about the graft and corruption in the 'Washington bureaucracy.'"[84]

Total Reinvention

Given these dark characterizations of Hohenlohe's physical and mental health toward the end of her confinement, we might expect her story of transnational drama, high-stakes negotiations, and royal bravado to end on a quiet note, once she was released to parole. Such an assumption would, however, underestimate Princess Stephanie's resilience and resourcefulness. She did not retreat in disgrace from the public eye after spending three and a half years in detention in US camps. In fact, she realigned herself with old friends and lovers, made new acquaintances with the powerful and wealthy, and entered into fresh business propositions that drew on her prodigious skills of mediation and persuasion. Jim Wilson described this process as one of "totally reinventing herself" in which she "clawed her way back into high society."[85] As part of this quest, she managed to skirt deportation orders for several years, while reinserting herself in wealthy society circles and among the political elite. Along the way, she drew the attention of a few news columnists who did not let this reappearance pass unnoticed and complained bitterly in print that the free circulation of a confirmed Nazi spy and Hitler confidante among the rich and famous in the United States was an outrage.

Like other detainees, Hohenlohe was still classified as an alien enemy upon her release and was subject to ongoing supervision by immigration authorities. But former INS director Lemuel Schofield had waited for her and now wanted her to move to New York, as he had begun divorce proceedings with his wife. On June 23, 1947, Stephanie appeared with Schofield before the immigration board in New York, expressing the impossibility of going back to Hungary, as her passport had lapsed after ten years outside the country, or to the United Kingdom, as the British government would not allow her return.[86] A series of documents that circulated between immigration officials, the Department of Justice, and the FBI show that no one was quite sure how to "solve" the problem of her deportation, so the princess remained in the United States, living for several years at Schofield's farm near Phoenixville, Pennsylvania. She even appeared in an Easter fashion parade in 1953, wearing Chanel, and was counted among the New York Dress Institute's list of Ten Best Dressed Women in America.[87] But her country idyll with Schofield ended when the attorney died suddenly in 1954.

By then in her sixties and embroiled in a scandal with the IRS due to unpaid taxes (both on her part and Schofield's, who had passed away without filing taxes for six years), Hohenlohe managed to once again talk her way out of a sticky situation. She found another pastoral outpost called Cobble Close, near Red Bank, New Jersey. A website for the property, part of which sold in 2015 for $10.9 million, describes it as "an architectural masterpiece," much of it built from dismantled European estates that were shipped to America in the 1920s.[88] Given its authentic French Norman–style buildings surrounded by fountains, old-growth trees and livestock-filled pastures, and with lawns bordered by Greco-Roman statues imported from Europe, Cobble Close was stunning proof of Princess Stephanie's ability to come full circle to the sort of life she had enjoyed as chatelaine of Schloss Leopoldskron, despite her time in internment as an enemy alien. She would spend three years there. One of her neighbors, multimillionaire Albert Monroe Greenfield, known as "the richest man in Philadelphia," reportedly became "an agreeable new lover."[89]

There were other proofs of Hohenlohe's return to the "jet set," too. In 1955, at age sixty-four, she got a job as a special correspondent for the *Washington Diplomat*, an "international society magazine" that allowed her to travel within the United States and to Europe. "The Women's Press Club of New York was proud to welcome Stephanie as a member," noted Schad.[90] Given this new role as an international journalist, the princess moved first to Manhattan and at sixty-eight returned to Europe, settling in Geneva, where her son was working in a bank. Starting in 1962, she signed lucrative contracts with several prominent publications such as *Quick* and *Stern*. And through her acquaintance with well-placed contacts, she secured interviews with world leaders and was even invited to the inauguration of President Lyndon B. Johnson on January 20, 1964. "An ex-prisoner of the United States, denounced as a danger to democracy and to American liberty, she was now an honoured guest of the President," noted Wilson.[91] During this later period, she even put her journalistic skills to good use with other members of royalty, interviewing both Grace Kelly and Queen Farah Dibah, the wife of the shah of Iran.[92]

According to her son, who under the name Prince Franz Hohenlohe published a biography of his mother titled *Steph: The Fabulous Princess*, Hohenlohe's "noble, valiant heart" stopped beating on June 13, 1972, early enough that she escaped old age.[93] In the introduction to his book, he stated, "Few people have been as much the victim of misinformation, untruths and half-truths, written and spoken, as my mother, Princess Stephanie Hohenlohe. This book is an attempt to set the record straight." The author promised readers "the factual story of a wonderful, maddening, unbelievable, loving woman of great charm who led a life which, despite some intensely black moments, can only be described as extraordinary."[94]

Princely Internment

Prince Franz Hohenlohe's own internment experience was apparently benign enough that it figured in the pages of *The G.I. Prince*, a book he wrote about himself subtitled "A pleasant assortment of narrative vignettes about some of the special people and unusual circumstances encountered in the eventful life of Prince Franz Hohenlohe." In these vignettes, he describes his arrest by the FBI in February 1942 and his first internment at Ellis Island along with an Italian movie star named Tulio Carminati and a long list of Axis nationals living in New York, including other royals such as Count Lanfranco Rassponi, Prince Girolimo Rospigliosi, the Marchese Cesare Grimaldi, and Prince Edmondo Raspoli. Though life in internment was onerous, the food was good and they had a view of the New York skyline; the prince figured his lot was better than his mother's, noting, "I never tried to take my life, whereas Steph did try it." From Ellis Island, Franz Hohenlohe was sent first to Camp Meade and then on to Camp McAlester, Oklahoma, "a bleak spot, surrounded by barbed wire and little more."[95]

The last stop on the prince's internment tour was Camp Kenedy in Texas, the same place where the Swedish noble Axel Wachtmeister had been held and had taken his own life. While on a temporary release from enemy alien internment at Kenedy, Hohenlohe even had dinner in New York with a relative of the Swede, Count Frederic Wachtmeister.[96] During that period, he also ran into Prince Boncompagni, a member of a famous Italian dynasty who was also interned at Ellis Island.[97]

These encounters featured in the younger Hohenlohe's personal memoir suggest that the count, the princess, and the prince introduced in these pages were not the only members of titled families to be apprehended and held in US internment. But perhaps Franz was the only royal to decide to serve Uncle Sam. He explained in his memoir that the decision was a difficult one: "How could I serve a government, a nation, that had treated me so badly, that had wasted years of my life, and where my own mother was still imprisoned (she was the last woman prisoner in all of America to be released, weeks after the cessation of hostilities)." But signing up for military service also meant "acceptance, and the normalization of a pretty shaken-up life."[98] Franz, by then Francis, hoped that his induction into the army would reflect favorably on the princess. Ultimately, like his mother he was able to reenter the world of the rich and famous after his internment, assuming anew his full title of Prince Franz Joseph Maximilian Rudolph Weriand Stephan Anton zu Hohenlohe Waldenburg Schillingsfürst.

Most personal stories fall somewhere in the middle of the extremes demonstrated by the titled internees profiled in this chapter. The majority of those held at Algiers and elsewhere in US internment were able to overcome the temptation to commit suicide. On the other hand, few enjoyed as full a "rehabilitation" and reintegration into a lifestyle of the rich and famous as Stephanie Hohenlohe. The lucky ones found a helping hand from a visitor or aid organization representative who was willing to hear them out and intervene on their behalf, providing improved conditions or, in the best of cases, sweet release.

CHAPTER 6

Aid Organizations, Diplomatic Efforts, and Community Allies

Internees of diverse backgrounds and political positions shared the scourge of being named "alien enemies"—a designation that some complained carried with it connotations of being pro-Hitler or pro-Nazi. Their preinternment stories, though, were unique, as were their individual reactions to the plight of internment itself. Some believed quiet discretion was the best posture to adopt, while others found it impossible to sit idly in the face of the anxiety their situations provoked and sought recourse for themselves and their families through the limited channels available to them. They wrote to the officers in charge of the camps where they found themselves, beseeched immigration officials across the country, and even directed missives to the secretary of state, the president and the president's wife. But it soon became clear that these officials and public servants, bound by the protocols and procedures of the Alien Enemy Control Program—including the secretive nature of its very existence—were often unable to provide the answers internees desperately sought.

Diplomatic units assigned to each noncitizen constituency represented one viable avenue of advocacy and defense for the interned: the Swiss legation was the primary diplomatic resource for German internees, while the Spanish embassy represented the interests of the interned Japanese in the United States, for example.[1] Nonetheless, many of those detained discovered that advocates in nongovernmental and community organizations were better positioned to provide an impartial hand. Aid organizations mentioned in the files of the internees who passed through Camp Algiers include the Joint Distribution Committee, Hebrew Immigrant Aid Society (HIAS), the Jewish Welfare Board, the YMCA, and the National Refugee Service (NRS).[2] Many of these NGOs are still active in the twenty-first century. Founded in 1914, the American Jewish Joint Distribution Committee now identifies itself as "the global Jewish 9-1-1"; it was often referred to in the World War II era simply as the "Joint." The former Hebrew Immigrant Aid Service, now just HIAS, is a nonprofit that since 1975 has provided support for refugees of all nationalities, religions, and ethnic origins, helping to resettle more than 4.5 million people, though it was founded in 1881 with the specific mission of aiding Jewish refugees.

Such organizations' multiple labors offer notable examples of humane intervention in the face of dehumanizing circumstances before, during, and after internment. They remind us that there were many efforts to provide humanitarian alternatives to the prejudices and injustices of the World War II era, efforts that in turn supply a counternarrative—and a cautionary tale—to the historical record of the breaches in human rights that occurred. Some of the internees who passed through New Orleans were lucky enough to find this aid as they clamored to leave Axis-controlled Europe; others received support in the countries to which they emigrated or once caught up in the United States' own alien enemy control program. A few, like Emanuel Gordon, got help in Europe, the Caribbean, and the United States; Gordon's case is rendered more unique by the fact that he also endeavored himself to provide help to other desperate refugees.

P(l)aying it Forward

Born in Gürzenich, Germany, in 1901, Emanuel Gordon spent time at the Buchenwald concentration camp as well as at a French internment camp before being declared an enemy alien soon after he arrived in the Dominican Republic. His record indicates he actively worked to help other Jews escape Nazi-controlled territories from his own precarious position as a refugee, despite putting himself at considerable risk in the process: "In 1938 he left Germany for Belgium where he allegedly dedicated himself to the freeing of

Jews from Germany. It is reported that he crossed and recrossed the German border many times in order to complete the necessary arrangements for bribing German officials."[3]

Gordon's subsequent internment at the St. Cyprien camp in France may have coincided with that of Felix Nussbaum, a German Jewish surrealist painter who created harrowing images based on his own experiences of camp life including *The Refugee,* painted in 1939, and perhaps his most famous work, *Self-Portrait with Jewish Identity Card,* created in 1943.[4] While Gordon finally obtained passage to the Dominican Republic in 1941 with the help of a Jewish aid organization in Geneva, Nussbaum's fate was more grim; by 1944, he and all members of his family had perished in concentration camps.

By 1941, Gordon and other Jews desperate to flee Europe had few options to choose from in terms of their destination. For him and many others, the Portuguese vessel *Serpa Pinto* (sometimes identified as *Serpa Pinta*) became a legendary "lifeboat" with up to eight hundred passengers per sailing, bearing more refugees across the Atlantic than any other Portuguese ship and leaving them in destinations such as Cuba, Jamaica, the Dominican Republic, Mexico, and the United States (figure 6.1). The Joint Distribution Committee, or "Joint," funded or shared in the financing of these trips by purchasing tickets and providing guarantees, enabling thousands to reach safety.[5] Gordon's name shows up on a list of those who sailed on the *Serpa Pinto* from Lisbon on November 17, 1941, arriving in the Dominican Republic in early December, just days before the attack on Pearl Harbor.

Disembarking in Santo Domingo, then called Ciudad Trujillo in honor of its dictator-president Rafael Leónidas Trujillo, Gordon headed to the agricultural development Sosúa, a Jewish colony heralded as a "tropical Zion," situated near Puerto Plata. Sosúa offered refuge to some eight hundred desperate German and Austrian Jews between 1940 and 1945 through an agreement between the Paris-based Jewish Colonization Association and the Trujillo government. In a dark twist of history, the same national leader who ordered the race-based murder of thousands of Haitians living in the Dominican Republic in 1937 expressed willingness in 1938 to harbor up to 100,000 Jewish refugees in the hopes of "whitening" the Dominican population. Sosúa's earliest directors shared the beliefs of the Dominican leadership in scientific racism and seized on the colony as an opportunity to "correct" the contamination of the Jewish gene pool by years of urban living.[6]

Gordon was not among the Sosúa settlers who would leave their mark on a dairy operation that continues its production in the twenty-first century,

FIGURE 6.1. The *Serpa Pinto* ferried up to eight hundred passengers per sailing across the Atlantic to Cuba, Jamaica, the Dominican Republic, Mexico, and the United States, many of its voyages supported by the US-based Joint Distribution Committee. Image courtesy United States Holocaust Memorial Museum.

however. His record states that shortly after his arrival at Sosúa he was arrested by the Dominican National Police on suspicion of Nazi activities. Then, despite his claim of Jewish descent and his previous efforts to help other Jewish refugees, he was interned with other German nationals as an enemy alien and a few months later deported to the United States. Embassy personnel would admit "there was never anything against him," and suggest that his arrest was instigated by an American named Schweitzer with whom Gordon had had a dispute.[7] The Schweitzer in question was almost certainly David Schweitzer, resident director of Sosúa at the time of Gordon's arrival.[8]

Despite his enviable luck, then, in finally securing a way out of Europe, Gordon's story demonstrates how the arrest, deportation, and internment of a German-, Japanese-, or Italian-born person in Latin America as an "alien enemy" of the United States could hinge on superficial or anecdotal evidence or even on a personal dispute such as the one that occurred at Sosúa. Gordon arrived in New Orleans from Ciudad Trujillo on May 24, 1942, aboard the *Algonquin*, whose manifest identifies him as forty-one years old, a "Hebrew," a butcher, and a speaker of German, English, and Spanish. The majority of those traveling with him were German, but the manifest also lists two Italians, a Japanese exporter named Schoichi Yokoy, a Russian, two other "Hebrews," and the Swede Axel Wachtmeister, whose story is explored earlier.

Upon their arrival in the Crescent City, Gordon and others were sent on to Camp Kenedy. It was there in December 1942 that he wrote his own personal history, recounting his time at both Buchenwald and St. Cyprien. A letter is attached to this account, directed to the attention of Mr. Bruppach at the legation of Switzerland asking him to get this history to the National Refugee Service in New York. It is likely that Cecilia Razovsky, a formidable friend to refugees and immigrants, would have read that history.

From Camp Kenedy, Gordon traveled back to New Orleans in February 1943, this time for internment with other Jews. Someone had helped him secure a spot on the *Serpa Pinto*, the "Joint" had likely supported his travel to the Dominican Republic, and the Jewish Colonization Association had probably secured him a spot at Sosúa. Now it would fall to the tireless and always-forward-moving Razovsky to provide another crucial helping hand, as she monitored conditions for Jewish internees like Gordon in the camps, pressed for hearings that would show the absurdity and error of classifying Jews as dangerous Nazi collaborators, pushed for their release to internment at large, and aided them in resettlement with the eventual goal of ridding themselves of the "alien enemy" label forever.

Razovsky, like the other individuals and organizations highlighted in this chapter, proved crucial to the internees' ability to alert advocates to violence and harassment they were experiencing in the camps, seek transfers to other camps, reunite with family members separated by internment orders, receive a hearing or interview with Immigration or Justice officials, avoid repatriation, and secure affidavits that attested to their loyalty to the United States, a necessary prerequisite to consideration for release to the intermediate status of "internment at large." Finally, such sources of aid provided essential help with acquiring sponsors who would agree to monitor and assist the internees at large in the communities where they were permitted to reside under this parole.[9]

"Identical with the Death Penalty"

The most effective advocacy work on behalf of the internees frequently involved the collective labor of community advocates, aid organizations, and government officials, though such coalitions rarely moved as quickly as those behind the fence would have liked. Along with others in his group, Otto Manheimer (introduced in chapter 3), benefitted from such combined efforts, efforts in which Cecilia Razovsky undoubtedly played a crucial role.

Manheimer was one of two drafters of a long letter, both informative and incensed, sent to HIAS on April 18, 1942, shortly after a group of Jews detained and interned in Panama for several months arrived in the United States.[10] With the permission of the officer in charge at Fort Oglethorpe, Georgia, Manheimer and coauthor Salomon Lagstein provided HIAS with their names as well as those of Peter Bohm, Dr. Richard Grunberg, Georg Karliner, Siegmund Lipschitz, Wilhelm Reichner, Alberto Kohen, and Oskar and Egon Wetterschneider, many of whose stories are explored elsewhere in this volume. They listed the nationalities of this "German" group as Polish, Austrian, German, and Czechoslovakian.

The first sentence of the letter to HIAS includes a curious linguistic detail: "29 Jewish refugees from Germany and Austria, all arrested in Panama, are today together mit nazis in internment camps in the United States. We have been driven away from our new homes and separated from our families without accusation and hearing and imprisoned under heavy guard." As in another dispatch the group would send to their rabbi in Panama two days later, the code-switch to the German *mit nazis* calls special attention to the men's concerns about finding themselves interned without their families and together with other openly pro-Nazi internees. In an effort to present the facts of their situation, Manheimer and Lagstein wrote, "In the years 1938–1939 we found a new home in Panama. With much difficulties and trouble, not able to talk the native language we have built up here a new existence, happy to have escaped Hitlers [sic] hell." They explain how many European-born men in Panama were arrested ("We do not want to talk about the cruel manner, in which this happened") and delivered to the US Army for internment at Camp Balboa in the Canal Zone, the group including "about 150 Jews from all over the countries of Europe."

The letter's authors explain that some European nationals held at the Balboa camp were released soon after their detention; it seemed, however, that *who* was released depended more on one's ability to grease an official's palm than on his or her relative danger to hemispheric security. "But to our great surprise many a leader of the fascist and nazis had been given their freedom, but poor jewish refugees remained interned." The monies that changed hands in exchange for this freedom reportedly ranged from $150 to $2,000, their family members had ascertained, and the writers acknowledged that Jews who were able to pay such sums did so.[11] But some couldn't pay and others who could chose not to, having been assured by Rabbi Nathan Witkin of the Canal Zone "that the Joint Distribution Committee has been informed about our case and will do everything upon our arrival in the States to get us free."[12]

Now it was becoming clear to the men that this promise of quick freedom upon arrival in the United States had been disingenuous or misinformed. Adding insult to injury, the detainees' wives had "sold our hosholds [sic] and business dirt-cheap" in order to voluntarily accompany their husbands, but had been separated from the men upon arrival: "We even did not have a chance to say good-by to our women and children, and we do not know their whereabouts." After about two weeks in the United States, they wrote, "our worries about our future and our families are growing bigger everyday," combined with "shame about our discrimination."

In their appeal to HIAS and by extension the "Joint," the interned men described their treatment as a "horrible insult" and a "slap in the face of the democracy and humanity." They wondered how they could be confined behind barbed wire when other more dangerous persons had been breezily freed in Panama. "We could not imagine, that it could be possible even in a perverse world like today, that the natural champions of freedom and democracy would be interned as dangerous to America."

War correspondence archived by the Jewish Welfare Board includes a second collective letter sent April 20, 1942, from Manheimer and the nine other Jews then interned at Fort Oglethorpe directly to Rabbi Witkin. Two similar concerns characterize this letter: on the one hand, the men were anxious and bewildered by their *separation* from wives, children, and other members of their group upon arriving in the United States; on the other, they were horrified to find themselves in close physical proximity to Nazis in the Georgia internment camp. The signers of the April 20, 1942, letter did not know why the group had been split, with ten men going to Oglethorpe and another nineteen German Jews going to "a place we do not know," perhaps Camp Blanding. They did not know why their wives and children, identified as "20 altogether," were also shuttled away to a distant site. But they had already discovered that other internees identified as "Nazis from U.S.A." were close at hand.[13]

Clearly, Manheimer and others were led to expect a different, better outcome upon ascending the gangplank to the *Florida* in early April of that year. Their disappointment and disillusion is almost palpable in their missive: "Up to now everything went just contrary to what we had expected, you might understand our mental conditions." Indeed, the Jewish group seems incredulous of the reality of their status as enemy aliens in detention north of the US border: "We can not believe, that our internment here with the Nazis from USA., which is identical with the death penalty for us, should be a fait accompli with no escape." How could Jewish refugees be considered dangerous to the United States? the writers wondered.

Despite the strong command of English in both these letters, the authors again found that language insufficient for expressing their extreme concern in the letter to Witkin. Before ending the typed letter with the phrase "We trust you," they pleaded with the rabbi, penciling in a phrase that incorporated Yiddish. "But, please, rabbi," they said, "*a por teg* was bearable in Balboa, because at least we could see our families, but is not here, work at high speed is the command of the hour." With an approximate meaning of "a few days," the handwritten Yiddish was included to let their rabbi know they could tolerate a few days with their Nazi antagonists but not the "internment for the duration" they now faced. The handwritten insertion suggests the need to communicate with their advocate at a level beyond the understanding of English speakers, to apprise him of their plight using their shared language as European Jews. The inclusion of Yiddish also represents a moment of privacy in a letter that would have been read and approved by censors before being sent. The syntax of the phrase also is notably foreign, but "work at high speed is the command of the hour" clearly expresses the writers' anxious concern that all haste be enlisted on every front possible to rectify the miscarriage of justice they believe characterizes their current predicament.

Four months later, Manheimer wrote again as spokesman for the Jewish detainees, this time to the Refugee Committee of the Chattanooga, Tennessee, branch of the NRS. Little if anything had changed in their situation; families were still separated:

> We are deeply depressed. . . . It is terrible that we will have to wait probably several more months, far from our families. We realize that the government cannot be pushed by Miss Razovsky, but for God's sake what has been done during 8 months? We do know positively, that Rabbi Witkin of the J.W.B. Balboa, Canal Zone, as long as February reported our situation to New York. Suppose nothing could be done until our arrival in the US. But we are already 4 months here, isn't this time enough to get on at least one step forward?[14]

Despite the evident exasperation of Manheimer and others in the Panama group after many months seeking assistance both in Central America and the United States, they need not have worried that Razovsky was twiddling her thumbs. While it would take several more months and a dedicated cadre of individuals and agencies, she would be instrumental in seeing interned men reunited with their families, effecting the transfer of the entire group of Jewish internees and their families to New Orleans's Camp Algiers, obtaining the government's cooperation in granting them interviews there in June 1943, and finally, securing the release of almost all in the Jewish group to internment at large that August.

The Grandmother of All Refugees

Cecilia Razovsky was a veritable powerhouse of immigrant and refugee activism who over the course of a long career went from teaching new immigrants in night classes to occupying prominent positions in the National Council of Jewish Women, the National Refugee Service, the United Nations Relief and Rehabilitation Administration, German-Jewish Children's Aid, the American Jewish Joint Distribution Committee, and after her "retirement," with the United Service for New Americans and as a supervisor for the Hebrew Immigrant Aid Society. In other words, Razovsky became a seemingly omnipresent specialist actively engaged in nearly every aspect (and nearly every key US-based organization) of refugee advocacy for almost a half century before her death in 1968. Indeed, in a few cases she was even able to witness the effects of her efforts into the second and third generations, as in the 1960s, when—by then in her seventies—she attended a government-sponsored resettlement program for Cuban refugees and discovered family members of persons she had met in 1924.[15]

Born to immigrant parents in St. Louis, Missouri, in 1886, Razovsky was by age twelve working to help support her family. In 1909, when she was still in her early twenties, she began teaching evening classes to foreigners through the Jewish Educational Alliance. She moved to Washington in 1917, working there as an inspector in the child labor division of the US Children's Bureau. Appointed executive secretary of the Immigrant Aid Department of the National Council of Jewish Women in 1921, she also served the rest of that decade as editor of the NCJW's journal the *Immigrant*.

Razovsky quickly realized the need for clear and cautionary information for foreigners bedazzled by tales of easy success in the United States, and in 1922 published *What Every Emigrant Should Know: A Simple Pamphlet for the Guidance and Benefit of Prospective Immigrants to the United States*. The pamphlet began by stating on the inside cover, "Attention, Friends Across The Sea, BEFORE you take any steps to break up your home; To leave relatives and friends; To give up your work on the farm or in the village; BEFORE you decide to leave your own country and begin a new life in a strange land, THINK HARD! CONSIDER LONG! DECIDE SLOWLY! and READ EVERY WORD IN THIS BOOK!!"[16]

In 1923 Razovsky traveled to several European ports to survey conditions for Jewish refugees and in 1924 visited Cuba to study circumstances there; the report she submitted after that visit helped the NCJW create a model refugee program in Havana.[17] Concerned with the specific problems of women immigrants to the United States, she published *What Every Woman Should Know about Citizenship* under the auspices of the NCJW in 1926, including an English-Yiddish version.[18] In subsequent years Razovsky visited Switzerland, Soviet Russia, Austria, Germany, and in 1937, several countries in Latin America, representing the NCJW at conferences and on committees while continuing to examine and/or monitor conditions for refugees around the world.[19] In 1938, when the National Refugee Service was created, Razovsky was named director of its Migration Department.[20]

By the 1940s, then, Razovsky was a seasoned veteran with years of service in the trenches, familiar with the range of dilemmas surrounding human displacement in the form of detention and internment, displaced persons camps, immigration, and refugee flight. She had by then weathered many policy struggles, including whether Americans should even take an active role in such efforts, especially in the context of the heated debate around the United States' appropriate role in the war itself prior to late 1941. As American Jewish leaders found themselves torn between identifying with their fellow Jews facing increasing persecution in Europe and their wish to assert their loyalty to America, many opted for a low profile, worried that protests or pressure from the Jewish community would draw accusations of being "un-American" or warmongers.[21] This posture proved lethal, in both political and literal terms, for the global Jewish community.

Cecilia Razovsky, on the other hand, was all about taking action and getting refugees the help they needed. Known for being brash and opinionated, Razovsky was an indefatigable ally for men, women, and especially children facing displacement and discrimination. She so persistently fought against immigration quotas and other regulations, she "is arguably the single individual most responsible for the 1,000 children who found a safe haven in the United States." Regarding this latter struggle, Razovsky stated, "I feel like I am fighting our entire governmental structure. I am appalled by the anti-Semitic rubbish of (Father) Coughlin and others. How can Roosevelt and his advisors fear that a few children, Jewish Children, will ruin the 'New Deal,' take food out of the mouths of others and be a burden on our society? All this happens as I know that every day more and more are sent to concentration camps and death. I cannot take even one moment to rest."[22] Such was her dedication to this work that at one point, Leo Gitlin in the Alien Enemy Control Unit of the US Justice Department wondered in a letter if Razovsky was the "grandmother of all refugees."[23] The archives confirm she corresponded regularly with figures at the top, such as Gitlin's boss, Edward Ennis, director of the AECU, as well as with those at the proverbial bottom: the stateless, the penniless, the detained. Not all her charges were unknown, though. One renowned figure Razovsky helped was the German Jewish cultural critic Walter Benjamin. In 1940, while working in the Paris office of the NRS, she was instrumental in helping Benjamin acquire a work affidavit from businessman and arts patron Milton Starr of Nashville, Tennessee, an effort Benjamin thanked her for in a letter in English.[24] Unfortunately, this aid was ultimately denied Benjamin, who in desperation took his life on the Spanish border in late September 1940 after the Spanish government canceled all transit visas and threatened to return Jewish refugees to Nazi-controlled France the next day.[25]

Many of the Algiers internees mentioned in these pages, particularly the Jewish refugees, also exchanged letters with Razovsky, anxiously checking for progress on their cases, asking for help locating family members and sponsors, and requesting she serve as a go-between with government officials and other aid agencies. Every case mattered, and Razovsky attempted to understand each one from a personal angle. After visiting internees in camps in Texas and Oklahoma in November 1942, she organized a trio of meetings with government officials in Washington that would have a lasting impact. The goal of her first meeting with Ennis was to get Jewish refugees from Latin America held at Camps McAlester (Oklahoma) and Forrest (Tennessee) reunited with others held at Camp Kenedy in Texas. She believed congregating all the Jewish internees at one site would facilitate the process of holding hearings—which had been denied to almost all those apprehended in Latin America—and securing their release. She astutely offered the aid of the NRS in compiling detailed background information on every internee prior to these hearings; Ennis confided to her that "definite and convincing proof" would be necessary to call into question the Panamanian government's characterization of these individuals as dangerous and subversive.[26]

In a second meeting with Ennis's assistant, Leo Gitlin, Razovsky campaigned for the release of stateless internees, pointing to the precedent of NRS aid to a group of 125 German Jews who had arrived in the United States in September 1941 aboard the *American Legion* (before the US entry into the war), nearly all of whom were admitted without difficulty, thanks to the guarantee of the NRS it would assume responsibility for their well-being. The special plight of a group of Jews from British Honduras interned at Camp Seagoville in Texas was the focus of the third meeting at the British embassy.[27]

In the midst of these and her other activities, Razovsky continued to serve the multiple roles of confidante, correspondent, and voice for those in US internment. Irene Wolff, still separated from her husband, Walter, in another internment camp, wrote to Razovsky in June 1942, "We are the loneliest Jewish people who are in the USA."[28] Detainees Eric Joseph and Siegwart Fechenbach wrote to "the grandmother of all refugees" in November 1942 and February 1943, respectively, asking for any news on their cases, and emphasizing their readiness to do their share by serving in the US armed forces.[29] William Reichner wrote to her in December 1942 from Camp McAlester, Oklahoma, requesting a transfer to Camp Kenedy, where other Jewish internees from Panama were detained. The address side of the required letter form indicates it contained correspondence from an "Internee of War" at the AEI (Alien Enemy Internment) Camp and had been signed and dated by a War Department censor. Two days after her husband died at Camp Seagoville, Lucy Kallman penned a note to Razovsky saying, "My poor husband is gone. He died Thursday night and was buried at the Jewish Cemetery, Dallas, Friday afternoon.—It was a hard strain I had to go through all the months and in spite of the fact that I had known my fate, I can't get it that I lost him." Razovsky responded a few days later:

> I was certainly grieved to learn of your loss. While we know that your poor husband was desperately ill, we hoped against hope that he might get better. I am sure it must have been a great comfort to him to have you with him all the time . . .
> I do hope that your future will be brighter and that it will be possible for you to build a new life with your two daughters in this country.
> Please be assured of my deepest sympathy and sincere interest.[30]

Especially sensitive to the situation of women and children like Mrs. Kallman and her daughters who had chosen voluntarily to accompany their male relative into internment, Razovsky pleaded with Ennis and Gitlin over and over on their behalf, noting that the only thing these family members were guilty of was trying to avoid separation. She wrote to Gitlin, for example, "I feel certain that it would raise the morale of the entire group if we succeed in getting these women, all of whom are able to work in the community [released], instead of remaining at the camp."[31]

Then in January 1943 a memo for Ennis enclosing a copy of a report from the officer in charge at Camp Kenedy warned of "the administrative problem which has been created by the detention in that camp of fourteen (14) Jewish aliens who were brought to the United States from the Canal Zone and Latin American countries." It noted that one of those aliens, Fred Kappel, had been able to communicate with the Swiss legation, the State and Justice Departments, and "has had the opportunity of presenting his case to Miss Razovsky of the National Refugee Service." The memo further stated, "It is hoped that the Jewish detainees at Crystal City and Seagoville can be given their hearings and their cases disposed of at an early date. If that is impracticable it would be appreciated if you would so advise in order that consideration may be given to transferring this group to our detention station at New Orleans where the danger of a serious incident between them and the German Nazis would not be so great."[32] Following this troubling description of the situation at Camp Kenedy, the JDC, NRS, Catholic groups, the ACLU, and the Jewish communities of Dallas, New Orleans, Chattanooga, and Nashville together increased their efforts to provide the Jewish detainees with a better, safer option.[33]

Finally, Razovsky wrote to Albert Abrahamson, executive director of the NRS in Dallas on February 8, 1943, with the news that

> the Department of Justice at Philadelphia has telephoned me to the effect that it has been decided to transfer the Jewish detainees now held at Camp McAllister, Oklahoma, Camp Seagoville-Texas, Camp Kenedy-Texas and Camp Forrest-Tennessee to the New Quarantine Station at New Orleans, Louisiana. Mr. Kelly of the Border Patrol Division told me that conditions at Camp Kenedy were rapidly getting worse there. He felt that it would be advisable to keep all the Jewish detainees together in New Orleans, and he hopes too because they would all be in one place, it may be possible to arrange hearings for them at an earlier date.[34]

Many of the dispersed Jewish detainees did arrive at Algiers later that month, though Mr. Kallman's poor health kept that family at Seagoville.[35] But even before the group's arrival at the "anti-Nazi" facility, Razovsky was busy advising the New Orleans NRS Committee of their arrival, and preplanning the Algiers families' future resettlements.

Even after the Jewish internees were congregated at the Algiers Detention Station, they continued to seek out Razovsky's help. Walter Wolff wrote to her from New Orleans in April 1943: "The people are desperate since they know that their release won't happen in the near future," while simultaneously assuring her, "We can take it and we will bear it as men, hoping that you now will double your efforts to get us out of this mess." Such vacillation between hope and despair is also apparent in his observation, "In our opinion, the present status of our cases is quite hopeless. Some way out will be found."[36]

But Razovsky clearly had already doubled and redoubled her efforts on behalf of the individuals and families at Camp Algiers, gathering the detailed information, personal biographies, and affidavits that were a necessary prelude to scheduling interviews to determine who might be released.[37] When Ennis had the necessary documentation, he sent twenty-nine-year-old assistant US attorney Harold Ickes to Central America to investigate the internees' cases, aided by James Bell, another lawyer who, like Ickes, was from New Mexico and fluent in Spanish.[38] Ickes's good Spanish helped smooth interactions with local police and embassy personnel, and the duo was able to both gain information on internees already deported to the United States and reduce the tide of deportation of other detainees still being held in other countries.

In June, Razovsky wrote to Joseph Beck, executive director of the NRS, that Gitlin wanted her to join him and his team in New Orleans for the hearings later that month.[39] Though she had already spearheaded efforts to secure sponsors for the released internees in New Orleans, the AECU nixed that arrangement by drawing up a short list of cities in the interior of the country where the released internees would be permitted to settle. It seems New Orleans's strategic location as a "gateway to the Americas" was a red flag for the AECU, just as the West Coast was declared off-limits to German, Italian, and Japanese enemy aliens as well as Japanese citizens in December 1941. Razovsky and her team scrambled to find new sponsors in Memphis, St. Louis, Cincinnati, Cleveland, Chicago, and other cities.

As detailed elsewhere in this volume, many of the internees at Algiers finally were granted the hearings that had been denied them throughout their entire internment experience in the final days of June 1943. For most of the Jewish internees at Algiers, the outcome would be positive, though a few would languish there until well into 1945 and a handful even until 1946. Otto Manheimer got his hearing on June 28, Emanuel Gordon on June 29. In his hearing with Ickes and Bell, Gordon told his interviewers he would like to "wring Hitler's neck."[40]

On July 6, with the exhausting process of the interviews completed, Razovsky sent an interagency memo to Beck and others at the NRS noting that fifty-four people would be recommended for release to "internment at large," with only six of the Jewish refugees (the members of the Siegfried Meyer family, Ernst Blumenthal, and Karl Kaul) "not likely to be released."[41] Noting the stipulations under which the fortunate would be paroled (all were required to register and be fingerprinted as aliens; upon reaching their destination cities, men would need to register immediately for the draft), she advised that members of the National Council of Jewish Women, under the leadership of Mrs. Isaac Heller, would help to "entrain" the parolees to their destinations. Though the Department of Justice wanted to "scatter" the internees, avoiding a concentration in any one city, Razovsky and her team even worked to honor requests from families and individuals to be paroled together, thus recognizing the friendships that had been made in internment and aiding the transition to new communities. Internees sent to Chicago from Algiers formed an especially close-knit community, and Renée Klish, daughter of Algiers internee Erwin Klyszcz, continues a friendship with Felice Kaufmann, daughter of Max Kaufmann, and remembers many others from the internee group, such as George Karliner and Isidor Rosenberg, who have passed away.

Point no. 15 of Razovsky's interagency memo brings us full circle to Emanuel Gordon, who, as it turns out, still needed her to put in a good word for him, as the "troublemaker" label had followed him from Sosúa and the Dominican Republic to Camp Algiers, and there was some question about whether he should be released. "He seems to me to be a decent fellow," Razovsky wrote. "He is very accommodating in camp, does kitchen duty night and day without complaint. The guards speak well of him (that says volumes; they are very chary of their praise). He does not speak English well. He is a good butcher." Her assessment apparently turned the tide, and Gordon was released to internment at large in August 1943 along with other Jewish internees. The final recommendation in his case was "release, on the ground that there is no evidence whatsoever of dangerousness," and on February 26, 1946, he was freed from internment at large.[42] Emanuel Gordon became a US citizen in 1950 in Los Angeles, California.[43]

The importance of Razovsky's advocacy on behalf of the New Orleans internees, both as a group and individually, perhaps cannot be overstated. But it was only one of her many accomplishments in a lifelong quest to help immigrants, refugees, and other victims of displacement and injustice. "We don't know how to thank you for helping us when in distress," wrote Grete and Leo Friedman several months after being released from Camp Seagoville. "We feel that we were still forgotten . . . without your assistance. It was a great comfort in our misery to know that there was at least one who believed our version of the story. We find it hard to get used to liberty after ten months behind iron bars."[44]

Allied Assistance

Despite Razovsky's key role in the denouement of the Camp Algiers internment drama, others in the National Refugee Service and its allied organizations were also important advocates for refugees and internees in New Orleans. In the spring of 1941, even before the United States entered the war, Arthur D. Greenleigh, assistant executive director of the NRS, wrote to New Orleans's archbishop, Joseph Rummel, after reading a copy of an address the archbishop had delivered in February to Rabbi Julian Feibelman's congregation at Temple Sinai. "I think it is one of the finest presentations of the world refugee problem which I have ever read," Greenleigh wrote. "I know I express the sentiments of the Board of Directors of the National Refugee Service in expressing gratitude for both your understanding of the refugee problem, and for the service you have rendered in behalf of the solution of that problem."[45] Remembered principally for a pastoral letter titled "Blessed Are the Peacemakers" ordering the end of segregation in the archdiocese and Catholic schools in New Orleans, Archbishop Rummel also embodied a radically different position on social issues than that of the virulent Father Coughlin. Archbishop Rummel remains a revered figure in the city's history; a Catholic high school for young men that bears his name opened in neighboring Jefferson Parish in 1962.[46]

Dr. David Fichman's appearance in a photo alongside "Mr. Siegfried" (Wolff) and his mother upon their release from Camp Algiers also provides graphic documentation of his advocacy for the detainee population, right up to the point they were boarding trains to new communities.[47] The news story accompanying the photo also mentioned the assistance of the members of the National Council of Jewish Women. Fichman had been active providing advice and assistance to local populations before Camp Algiers even opened. On December 11, 1941, just days after the Japanese bombed Pearl Harbor, triggering the US entry into World War II, Fichman wrote to Albert Abrahamson, requesting seventy-five to one hundred copies of a circular letter Abrahamson wrote after Executive Proclamation 2525 named all German noncitizens alien enemies. "We feel that if we send one of these to each member of our Committee and to the Jewish organizations where our refugees go it will have a tendency to keep people calm," he noted. The need for this calm is evident in the next paragraph: "We have been passing the word to our clients, and through them to the other refugees, that they should refrain from speaking German on the streets and should avoid congregating on the streets."[48]

Fichman continued to aid aliens and refugees during the war period in his work with the local office of the NRS, which was in turn affiliated with the Jewish Federation of New Orleans.[49] A letter from Fichman to the NRS New York office dated March 23, 1943, provides crucial information about conditions at Algiers just a few weeks after the Jewish contingents from Camps Seagoville and Kenedy had arrived there. "I have been going there quite frequently. In fact, last week I made three trips over for varying purposes. Perhaps a word as to the services we are making available is in order," he suggested, continuing,

> One of the local Rabbis is conducting a weekly afternoon religious service. A teacher in English goes out twice a week. A Committee on Personal Service from the Council of Jewish Women visits once a week and brings over sewing and knitting material for the women. Seed has been supplied for the men, who are planting a garden. The group has been provided with all sorts of games. We are making plans for Passover observance. We are allowing all but a few who do not seem to need it $1.00 a week per person for incidental expenditures. Visits are also being made by myself and the Committee from the Council of Jewish Women on six of the Detainees presently at the Marine Hospital.

Fichman also acknowledged the "splendid attitude" of the officer in charge, Raymond Bunker, who was leaving nothing undone which was in his power "to make the people under his charge happy and to build up their morale. I do not think I have ever met a Government official who has been as cooperative and has shown as humane and understanding a spirit as he." Interned civilians at Camp Algiers were thus "as well adjusted as can be expected under the circumstances," although they were, "as might also be expected, impatient and at times resentful of their long detention." Noting that he had promised internees to ask about any progress on their behalf, Fichman asked for any news regarding their possible release. He signed off, "Looking forward to your reply, which I hope will be a hopeful one for the detainees."[50] Hope, persistently sought but often exhausted throughout the internees' long confinements, was perhaps the most important aid and sustenance these advocates and organizations could provide.

Epilogue
A New War on Aliens as Enemies

World War II internment in the United States offers a crucial precedent from which to view contested questions concerning the country's relationship with noncitizen populations in our own time. Many aspects of that precedent—indefinite detention without hearings, family separation, the manipulation of detention policy and detainee populations for political purposes and economic gain, repatriation of aliens to hostile environments—are still with us in some form today.[1] The twenty-first century has brought with it new waves of displaced people and new waves of anti-alien rhetoric and policies in response to these huddled masses. The US Citizenship and Immigration Services altered its mission statement, eliminating a passage that described the United States as "a nation of immigrants" and focusing instead on "protecting Americans, securing the homeland, and honoring our values."[2] Many recent immigration policies take an even harder and more rigid view of noncitizens than those of the wartime internment program at the center of this study. Arguably, the terms "alien" and "enemy" have been equated as never before in the United States' "war" on illegal immigration. As with the evolution of the Alien and Sedition Acts themselves, the search for redress for past injustices related to internment and relocation in this country has evolved over time, constituting a lengthy chronology of legislative and personal struggle.

Japanese American survivors of relocation have been at the forefront of the battle to see the US government acknowledge the injustices it perpetrated during World War II in relation to forced displacement, though progress has been intermittent and partial throughout the last three-quarters of a century. In 1948, Congress passed the Japanese American Evacuation Claims Act, granting persons of Japanese ancestry the legal right to file claims with the government for damage to or loss of property not compensated by insurance. But "right away victims encountered problems," as they had to provide proof of those losses.[3] Receipts were hard to find in ransacked houses; the IRS had by then destroyed most prewar tax returns, and the government reviewed such claims at a snail's pace, adjudicating only 232 of 26,000 claims by 1950. The fact that the 1948 act didn't even mention German and Italian Americans who experienced internment (or, of course, alien enemies apprehended in Latin America) points to the additional prejudices and obstacles they would face in their quests for accountability and amends from the country that interned them.

After concerted insistence from the Japanese community, Congress in 1980 authorized the establishment of the Commission on Wartime Relocation and Internment of Civilians, which declared, after twenty days of hearings, testimony from 750 witnesses, and review of thousands of government and military records, that internment of Japanese Americans was the result of racism and wartime hysteria. The committee's 1983 report, titled *Personal Justice Denied,* concluded that Executive Order 9066 "was not justified by military necessity" and further averred that "the government had suppressed, altered, and destroyed evidence that showed there was no military necessity for the evacuation and relocation of Japanese Americans in the wake of the Japanese attack on Pearl Harbor."[4]

At least three American presidents would formally acknowledge the blot on national history the relocation of Japanese Americans represented.[5] On August 10, 1988, President Ronald Reagan signed the Civil Liberties Act, which called for a national apology and $20,000 in reparations for each individual American survivor, affording closure to thousands "who suffered unspeakable indignities and tremendous losses." President George H. W. Bush sent letters to survivors in 1990, and President Bill Clinton later issued an apology "for the actions that unfairly denied Japanese Americans and their families fundamental liberties during World War II."[6]

But even after these incremental gains for US citizens, "the Justice Department, under President Bill Clinton, argued that the Japanese taken from Latin America were not citizens upon their arrival on US soil and entered the country as illegal immigrants."[7] For Carmen Higa Mochizuki, the resurrection of this ruse "was as bizarre as it was false," as the Japanese, her family included, had been "abducted" by the US military, forcibly displaced to the United States on military transports, and used as hostages in US military exchanges.[8]

Besides having force in numbers, Japanese Americans were arguably successful in finally calling the government to account because they spoke from the position of wronged citizens and were appealing to their own government. Enemy aliens did not have this recourse, even though many had become citizens of the United States—and some had even fought in its military—following their release from internment. As James Dickerson noted, "Not eligible for apologies or restitution were the prisoners of Japanese ancestry who were not born in the United States or who did not obtain legal permanent residence. Also excluded were ethnic Japanese who were taken from their homes in Latin America and brought to the United States and imprisoned in concentration camps. Notably absent from the apology and restitution list were the persons of German, Italian, or Jewish ancestry who were imprisoned in the United States during the war, without regard to their citizenship status."[9] It wasn't until 1999, after the payment provision of the Civil Liberties Act had expired, that President Clinton settled a class-action lawsuit brought by Japanese Latin Americans deported to the United States with an award of $5,000 each to twelve hundred such former deportees, 80 percent of whom were from Peru.[10] And finally, on Thursday, March 19, 2009, nearly seventy years after the official implementation of the Alien Enemy Control Program, the House Subcommittee on Immigration, Citizenship, Refugees, Border Security, and International Law met for a hearing on the "Treatment of Latin Americans of Japanese Descent, European Americans, and Jewish Refugees during World War II."[11] New Orleans was mentioned three times in that hearing, once in the prepared statement of California congressman Xavier Becerra; again in the aforementioned testimony of Daniel M. Masterson, a professor of Latin American history at the Naval Academy; and lastly in the personal account of Libia Yamamoto, a Peruvian of Japanese descent who at age seven had seen her father jailed before the entire family was deported to the United States for internment.[12]

When the subcommittee's chairwoman, California congresswoman Zoe Lofgren, called the hearing to order, she explained that the hearing was a follow-up to earlier legislative efforts to expose and redress World War II internment and relocation programs. She conceded that much is now known about the confinement of over 100,000 Japanese Americans, thanks in part to the enactment of the Commission on Wartime Relocation and Internment of Civilians Act in 1980 and the subsequent Civil Liberties Act of 1988. Lofgren then called attention to the cases still largely a mystery to most Americans, namely, the mistreatment of thousands of Japanese and European Latin Americans, European Americans, and Jewish refugees prior to and during World War II. No recommendations had been made regarding the Latin American populations in earlier hearings, and they had received no apology, as had occurred with relocated Japanese, pursuant to the Civil Liberties Act. "I think it is time for this history to be fully heard and considered," Lofgren judged.[13]

This was also the goal of Congressman Becerra when he introduced HR 42, the Commission on Wartime Relocation and Internment of Latin Americans of Japanese Descent Act. "This legislation establishes a commission to investigate and review the facts relating to the abduction and internment of Japanese Latin Americans during World War II by the U.S. government," the text of the subcommittee's meeting read.[14] In short, earlier legislation was important, but it had failed to address the treatment of Latin Americans of Japanese descent, Becerra contended. The congressman argued, "Japanese Latin Americans who were unjustly abducted and interned by the U.S. continue to live with the painful memories of those lost years. Many remain hopeful they will one day be able to have their important accounts included in the official narrative." One of those individuals was Isamu "Art" Shibayama, deported with his prosperous family from Lima as a child and interned for two and a half years in a Texas camp; Shibayama later served as a corporal in the US Army and became a US citizen. Soon after the family's arrival in the United States, Art's grandparents were forcibly sent to Japan for exchange; he and his family never saw them again. "Art's experience is not uncommon," Becerra stated.

> There are hundreds of other internees from Latin America who can tell similar stories about the fear endured while being led out of their home at gunpoint, about the trauma of a 21-day boat ride from Peru to New Orleans and of the humiliation of being forced to strip naked upon arrival in the U.S. and sprayed with insecticides. Others can share vivid accounts of living in the squalor of an internment camp barrack, the emotions of being a "stateless" person facing language barriers and having to traverse the federal bureaucracy to obtain legal resident status, and about the heartbreak of being permanently separated from a family member.

Libia Yamamoto, then seventy-three years old, provided one such vivid account to those present at the hearing. She explained how her father was taken to the jail in their Peruvian town on January 6, 1943, "by the order of the United States of America," how he was later forced to board a truck to an unknown destination without the family knowing why, for how long, or if he would come back, and how all of this "was an extremely traumatic experience for me at age seven."[15] Finally, after an entire month, the family received a letter from the father, who was then in Panama. Relieved that he was alive, they later learned his passport had been confiscated and he was interned in a camp in Texas. There, he learned from other Peruvians they were going to be shipped to Japan in a prisoner exchange, which would signify indefinite separation from their families. The Department of Justice's solution was to reunite the men and their families in the internment camps. As Libia Yamamoto recalled,

> We left Peru from the Port of Callao in July 1943. Boarding the ship was horrifying because there were U.S. soldiers on board pointing their big guns at us as if we were criminals. When we got to New Orleans officials inspected our baggage and some families had precious belongings thrown into the water. The Peruvians on our ship were among the lucky ones, because I later learned from my friend that she and other women and children were let off their ship first and marched to a warehouse. They were ordered to strip and stand in line naked, and then were sprayed with insecticide.

Even after the war ended, the fate of the Japanese internees from Latin America was uncertain. "At the end of the war the U.S. government told us to leave the country because we were illegal aliens," Yamamoto stated. Her own sister and family were deported to Japan, and she herself might have suffered this fate if the arrangement had not been halted due to her father's illness. "Fortunately, we had Japanese American relatives in Berkeley who sponsored us out of camp in 1947, and we moved to Berkeley, California as parolees."

The details of Yamamoto's 2009 testimony, including the confiscation of passports and the frightening scenes of detainees forced to strip and have their bodies and luggage sprayed with DDT upon their arrival in New Orleans, are corroborated in many sources, including those of the government itself.[16] Becerra's bill died in Congress, however, and when Shibayama passed away on July 31, 2018, the *New York Times* ran a story titled "Isamu Shibayama Dies at 88, His Quest for Reparations Unfulfilled."

Detention Déjà Vu

Despite repeated setbacks, advocates such as Yamamoto have remained active in their call for accountability and redress for wartime internment. Many advocates in that struggle find close parallels between their experiences and those of noncitizens detained in the United States today, prompting warnings that history is repeating itself. Even the material structures of World War II internment seem to fulfill William Faulkner's aphorism, "The past is never dead. It's not even past." Government plans to use former internment sites for the detention of immigrants, especially children, have drawn opposition from many quarters, including from a few elderly activists who were interned in such facilities during World War II. The decision to hold children at Oklahoma's Fort Sill—which served during World War II as an internment camp for Japanese Americans and Japanese immigrants and before that as the longtime prison for Apache leader Geronimo and other Native American "prisoners of war"—sparked spirited protests from former Japanese internees such as seventy-five-year old Satsuki Ina, who said "we are here today to protest the repetition of history."[17]

The question of whether contemporary alien detention sites are concentration camps or should be compared to them has also generated an incendiary debate. Even prior to this discussion, some scholars explicitly inserted the World War II internment of "alien enemies" into the larger history of concentration camps. James Dickerson is perhaps foremost among them with his 2010 study *Inside America's Concentration Camps: Two Centuries of Internment and Torture*, which includes chapters on the origins of internment in colonial North America and in policies to remove native populations such as the Choctaw, Chickasaw, and Cherokees to reservations and other de facto forms of internment or incarceration.[18]

The "concentration camp" debate reignited after New York congresswoman Alexandria Ocasio-Cortez used that term after visiting US Customs and Border Protection facilities detaining children on the US-Mexico border in 2019. Drawing sharp criticism for allegedly demeaning the memory of those who died in the Holocaust by appropriating the term, Ocasio-Cortez also received some support from figures such as Rabbi Danya Ruttenberg, who countered with an article titled "'Never Again' Means Nothing If Holocaust Analogies Are Always Off Limits." In her perspective piece published in the *Washington Post*, Ruttenberg said such analogies should be used with caution, but that "having a historical reference point can help us understand our own moral obligations in this story." She added: "We already know that the path to atrocity can be a process, and that the Holocaust began with dehumanizing propaganda, with discriminatory laws, with roundups and deportations, and with internment. Those things are happening in our country now."[19]

In her essay "'Some Suburb of Hell': America's New Concentration Camp System," Andrea Pitzer points out that disputes over nomenclature have been a "recurrent feature in the mass detention of civilians ever since its inception, a history that long predates the Holocaust." At least as early as the late nineteenth century, Pitzer notes, the terms "*reconcentración*" and "concentration camps" have been used to name "places of forced relocation of civilians into detention on the basis of group identity."[20] "If prisons are meant for suspects convicted of crimes after a trial, a concentration camp holds those who, most often, had no real trial at all," Pitzer posits in her 2017 book *One Long Night: A Global History of Concentration Camps*. Another distinction is that "unlike prisons, camps often detain prisoners without a scheduled date of release. Where a date exists, it has generally been set arbitrarily and without warning." Other characteristics Pitzer identifies with concentration camps also suggest links between wartime internment practices and contemporary policies regarding "illegal" aliens. For example, in both cases, detention "has been framed as protective," and in both cases, "they extract people from one area to house them somewhere else. . . . Camps require the removal of a population from a society with all its accompanying rights, relationships, and connections to humanity."[21]

Many elements that connect US alien enemy internment history to contemporary policies for alien detention seem even more sinister in the present than they were during World War II. While the use of former penitentiaries, inactive military installations and other high-security sites to detain noncitizen aliens with no criminal record is an obvious holdover from the Enemy Alien Control Program, the for-profit administration of such sites has expanded exponentially. In Louisiana, where incarceration rates stand out internationally, well-meaning efforts to move away from the mass incarceration of first-time offenders or those convicted of minor crimes led to the conversion of many abruptly emptied prisons into federal immigrant detention facilities. Local municipalities often welcomed this repurposing of the prisons as a way to retain much-needed jobs and revenue in sites with limited opportunity, many of them rural. In a *Times-Picayune* article titled "Louisiana's Prisons Are Increasingly Being Used to Detain Immigrants," Jamila Johnson, a senior supervising attorney with the Southern Poverty Law Center, notes that while "it seemed that Louisiana was

EPILOGUE | 213

ready to move away from its dependence on mass incarceration . . . it's disheartening to see that it continues to rely heavily on it through its switch to the mass incarceration of civil detainees."[22]

In contrast, US government employees from the president down to Raymond Bunker, the officer in charge at Camp Algiers, routinely invoked the Geneva Convention as a guiding principle for their work in the World War II internment effort, whatever their failures and prejudices.[23] Following the war, such humanitarian obligations were reiterated in the Fourth Geneva Convention protecting civilians in 1949, as well as in the 1989 Convention on the Rights of the Child. "The twenty-first century is unraveling that response," however, as countries now are "rejecting existing obligations and meeting asylum seekers with walls and fences."[24]

A "zero tolerance" policy implemented in May 2018, under which the US Department of Justice began prosecuting all adult aliens apprehended crossing the border "illegally," with no exception for those with minor children or asylum seekers (who under existing law enter legally) also seems to have further eroded humanitarian protocols in place during the World War II enemy alien control program. Normalizing the separation of parents from children and infants at the border and routing those unaccompanied minors to separate detention facilities, these new restrictions have led to a level of family separation and fragmentation that arguably far eclipses that of wartime internment, when the government sought to avoid the "needless suffering of women and children" separated from male wage earners.[25] Secretary of State Cordell Hull's 1943 declaration that the Department of State "in principle does not approve of the separation of families" no longer undergirds policy regarding noncitizens, let alone those deemed "enemy" aliens.[26] Current policies also fall short of wartime efforts to provide detainees with adequate facilities for them to live together as families, with access to schooling, health care, child care, and other services, as it did at Crystal City, Seagoville, and other World War II–era "family" camps. Though this 2018 family separation policy drew outrage from a large cross-section of the public and spawned several legal challenges, Pitzer contends, "It never fully ended."[27]

In fact, the rising toll of the international Covid-19 pandemic in the spring of 2020 further exacerbated worries regarding the well-being of noncitizens held in detention facilities throughout the United States, including unaccompanied children. By May 2020, Covid-19 had infected hundreds of detainees in Immigration and Customs Enforcement jails, where "a long history of substandard conditions, overcrowding and unsanitary practices in some facilities, as well as the U.S. government's refusal to release many detainees at particular risk of developing complications from the disease" had led to a "rapidly escalating crisis."[28] "These facilities don't care about the people or the facts of their lives," one woman told a reporter, days after her brother died in a San Diego detention facility after living in the United States for forty years. "These are private institutions making money off of immigrants."[29]

The tale of the small contingent of Jewish refugees apprehended among thousands of World War II enemy alien internees in Latin America and later concentrated at New Orleans's Camp Algiers also bears remembering amid the debates swirling around "dangerous" alien elements today. The reluctance of government officials to acknowledge the refugee status of this group, even for those who were survivors of the Nazi camps and the Shoah itself, is echoed in the distrust of immigrants and refugees fleeing violence today. Steffani Bangel and Jessica Frankel, board members of the New Orleans Section of the National Council of Jewish Women, expressed their sense of déjà vu in an August 2019 letter published in New Orleans's remaining daily newspaper:

> The treatment of asylum-seekers at our borders feels eerily reminiscent of what Jews have seen before: people forced to hide in the shadows, afraid to leave their homes for fear of being rounded up; children torn from parents, sent to distant corners of the country with no way to communicate with each other; thousands of people denied bond and legal recourse, held in overcrowded, unsanitary, and inhumane detention centers. . . . As Jews, we are committed to keeping alive the memory of the Holocaust; we are taught Never Again—never again will our people accept the decimation of human rights that we faced in the Holocaust. We see these egregious assaults on human rights and rule of law and are reminded of the terror and genocide our ancestors faced. As Jews who are now living in freedom, we bear the responsibility to protect immigrants and refugees in our own country and ensure that history is not repeated.[30]

Were Bangel and Frankel aware that by publicly stating this opinion, they were following in the footsteps of forebears with the National Refugee Service, the Jewish Welfare Board, and their own NCJW, all of whom aided noncitizens interned at New Orleans's Camp Algiers in the 1940s? Perhaps not, but the dedicated work of these World War II–era advocates, together with the myriad efforts of those who came after them, represent a host of witnesses, spurring us to continue asking, as Judith Butler has urged, "under what conditions some human lives cease to become eligible for basic, if not universal, human rights. And how does the US government construe these conditions? And to what extent is there a racial and ethnic frame through which these imprisoned lives are viewed and judged such that they are deemed less than human?"[31]

Notes

PREFACE: *A Surprising Piece of the City's Past*

1. *TriPod* was produced in collaboration with the Historic New Orleans Collection and the Midlo Center for New Orleans Studies at the University of New Orleans. Each *TriPod* segment, including the two segments on Camp Algiers, can be accessed at WWNO.org and as podcasts on iTunes. See https://www.wwno.org/programs/tripod-new-orleans-300.

2. Friedman's *Nazis and Good Neighbors: The United States Campaign against the Germans of Latin America in World War II* and Strum's 1990 essay "Jewish Internees in the American South, 1942–1945" served as the primary source studies for this volume.

3. A photo of Edgar Reinbold's headstone can be viewed on the German American Internee Coalition website, http://gaic.info/four-internees-buried-edgewood-cemetery-crystal-city-texas/.

INTRODUCTION

1. For an overview of the program, see "World War II Enemy Alien Control Program Overview," National Archives, https://www.archives.gov/research/immigration/enemy-aliens-overview.

2. Berkin, *A Sovereign People*, 202.

3. Miller, *Crisis in Freedom*, 41. The Federalist-dominated Congress argued at the time that such bills would strengthen national security during an undeclared war with France that lasted from 1798 to 1800, but the move had serious consequences, as it connected the Federalist Party to anti-immigrant bias and efforts to suppress dissent and freedom of the press.

4. Miller, *Crisis in Freedom*, 44, 52–53.

5. Jan Jarboe Russell quotes Biddle without reference to an external source. *The Train to Crystal City*, 47.

6. The number of Japanese interned has been a matter of dispute. The figure used here represents the US government's own estimate at its website offering educator resources, "Japanese-American Internment during World War II" (https://www.archives.gov/education/lessons/japanese-relocation), claiming some 112,000 people were sent to assembly centers and then relocation centers, nearly 70,000 of them American citizens. Krammer uses the figures seventy-eight thousand US citizens and forty-two thousand Japanese citizens. *Undue Process*, 56.

7. *Personal Justice Denied*, 6.

8. Both comments by DeWitt are cited in Krammer, *Undue Process*, 56. See also "A Jap's a Jap," *Washington Post*, April 15, 1943.

9. Robinson, *By Order of the President*, 4.

10. See "World War II Enemy Alien Control Program Overview," https://www.archives.gov/research/immigration/enemy-aliens-overview. Presidential Proclamation 2525 can be accessed at https://www.foitimes.com/internment/Proc2525.html.

11. According to Karen Riley, "INS stations in the Canal Zone and New Orleans processed more than 2,000 Latin American Germans and Japanese before transporting them to camps in Texas. Of the Latin American Japanese, nearly 1,500 eventually were interned at Crystal City." *Schools behind Barbed Wire*, 36.

12. *Congressional Record*—House, May 5, 1939, quoted in Christgau, *"Enemies,"* 53. Earl Harrison, one of the architects of the internment program, would later report that the United States was once again following in the Nazis' footsteps in its administration of displaced persons camps in Europe after the war's end: "As matters now stand, we appear to be treating the Jews as the Nazis treated them except that we do not exterminate them. . . . They are in concentration camps in large number under our military guard instead of S.S. troops. One is led to wonder whether the German people, seeing this, are not supposing that we are following or at least condoning Nazi policy" (quoted in Russell, *The Train to Crystal City*, 269).

13. Quoted from National Archives, "World War II Enemy Alien Control Program Overview," https://www.archives.gov/research/immigration/enemy-aliens-overview. Regarding correct figures for the number of German alien enemies deported from Latin America and the total number of those interned in the United States, see Friedman, *Nazis and Good Neighbors*, 170n109.

14. Krammer, *Undue Process*, 1.

15. The government's overview claims that "over fifteen Latin American countries accepted the offer [to participate in the program] and eventually deported a total of over 6,600 individuals of Japanese, German, and Italian ancestry, along with some of their families, to the U.S. for internment." National Archives, "World War II Enemy Alien Control Program Overview," https://www.archives.gov/research/immigration/enemy-aliens-overview.

16. The "Good Neighbor" label for Roosevelt's policy was accidental, according to Irwin Gellman, and in fact "covered the complex totality of inter-American efforts from 1933 to 1945." Gellman devotes an entire chapter to "Nonintervention: Reality and Illusion," concluding it with the words, "No intervention was never an absolute reality—only an illusion that was valuable in popularizing the Good Neighbor principle" (*Good Neighbor Diplomacy*, 1, 39).

17. Gellman, *Good Neighbor Diplomacy*, 106.

18. On Nazi incursions in Mexico, see Krammer, *Undue Process*, 90–91.

19. See for example, Larrea, "Esvásticas, cánticos a Hitler, 'souvenirs' y dos muertos: a 80 años de la impactante celebración nazi en el Luna Park."

20.   Es latino el ejército que desfila bajo tu brazo en alto
       es la amistad de un pueblo nuestro
       es nuestra cultura romana a la defensa
       Aquí está, oh Fuhrer, para tu lucha heroica
       el fraternal apoyo de nuestra estirpe eterna.

21. Pérez, "Panama," 55. See also Strum, "Jewish Internees," 31.

22. Krammer, *Undue Process*, 89.

23. Friedman, *Nazis and Good Neighbors*, 3.

24. Leonard and Bratzel, *Latin America during World War II*, 6.

25. Masterson and Ortiz Sotelo, "Peru," 139.

26. Gellman, *Good Neighbor Diplomacy*, 112–14.

27. Leonard and Bratzel, *Latin America during World War II*, 12.

28. "Franklin D. Roosevelt's 'Navy Day Address' on the Attack on the Destroyer *Kearney*," October 27, 1941, https://www.ibiblio.org/pha/policy/1941/411027a.html.

29. Friedman, *Nazis and Good Neighbors*, 58.

30. Gellman, *Good Neighbor Diplomacy*, 115.

31. Haglund, *Latin America and the Transformation of U.S. Strategic Thought*, 182.

32. The map and the controversies surrounding it are the subject of Bratzel and Rout, "FDR and the 'Secret Map.'"

33. Friedman, *Nazis and Good Neighbors*, 3.

34. Friedman, *Nazis and Good Neighbors*, 148–49.

35. Many historians have characterized internment as incarceration, including Krammer, *Undue Process*, 8; and Christgau, "*Enemies*," 70, 180; as does repeatedly the government's own report on wartime relocation and internment of civilians, *Personal Justice Denied*.

36. Obviously, not all personnel in the cooperating countries of Latin America were corrupt, nor were Latin American officials unique in finding economic benefit in such tasks. "It is not widely recognized that the Nazi reign of terror was, in a fundamental way, a lucrative racket—an extensive criminal enterprise set up to loot the wealth of Jewish victims and exploit their labor," comments David Talbot, *The Devil's Chessboard*, 47. Parallels with Nazi Europe further call into question the efficacy of the US Latin American program as an *anti*-Nazi push.

37. Quoted in Dickerson, *Inside America's Concentration Camps*, 153.

38. J. M. Cabot, Department of State, Division of the American Republics to Messrs. Wright and Bonsal, November 15, 1943, RG 59, Special War Problems Division, Department of State, cited in Zucker, *Cecilia Razovsky*, 135–36.

39. Riley, *Schools behind Barbed Wire*, 22.

40. Zucker, *Cecilia Razovsky*, 135. Zucker lists as sources: "Memo," Cordell Hull to Roosevelt, 27 August 1942, and "Memo," State Department, 3 November and 30 December 1942, NA, RG 59 (State Department); "Memo—Regarding the Activities of the United States Government in Removing from the Other American Republics Dangerous Subversive Aliens," November 3, 1942, 3, RG 59, Subject Files, Box 180, Records of the Special War Problems Division (150n41).

41. Quoted in Friedman, *Nazis and Good Neighbors*, 197

42. Quoted in Conell, *America's Japanese Hostages*, 101.

43. Quoted in López-Calvo, *The Affinity of the Eye*, 51.

44. Gardiner, "The Latin American Japanese and World War II," 144.

45. Zucker, *Cecilia Razovsky*, 135.

46. Connell, *America's Japanese Hostages*, 81–82.

47. "H.R. 42—111th Congress: Commission on Wartime Relocation and Internment of Latin Americans of Japanese Descent Act," https://www.govtrack.us/congress/bills/111/hr42, 2009.

48. See White to Lafoon, January 30, 1946, memorandum in "Statistics," RG 59, Box 70, Special War Problems NA, http://gaic.info/wp-content/uploads/2016/02/White.Lafoonmemo.lg_.jpg.pdf.

49. Connell, *America's Japanese Hostages*, 100.

50. Friedman, *Nazis and Good Neighbors*, 134.

51. *Treatment of Latin Americans of Japanese Descent, European Americans, and Jewish Refugees in World War II*. 111th Cong., Serial no. 111–13, March 19, 2009, Hearing of the House Subcommittee on Immigration, Citizenship, Refugees, Border Security, and International Law, Committee on the Judiciary.

52. Friedman, *Nazis and Good Neighbors*, 117.

53. Quoted in Connell, *America's Japanese Hostages*, 179. Connell reports that those aboard the *Cuba* were allowed on deck only three times.

54. Connell, *America's Japanese Hostages*, 117; Higashide, *Adios to Tears*, 156–57.

55. Russell, *The Train to Crystal City*, xvii.

56. A portion of the Hartens' story can be read in English at German American Internee Coalition, "The Harten Family Story," http://gaic.info/the-harten-family-story/ Gertrude Harten's full story, and is recounted in Spanish in Sánchez and Ahlers, eds., *Gertrudis: Diarios de una mujer alemana sobre el Ecuador, 1937–1956*.

57. RG 59, 740.00115, European War (1939) / 5848 PS / MW, Box 2841, NA.

58. See Friedman, *Nazis and Good Neighbors*, 140; he notes that at Camp Stringtown, Oklahoma, eighteen Jewish internees were relegated to a steam-filled room in the basement, through which other prisoners passed on their way to bathe, tossing off insults of "Jewish swine" and "dirty Jews" along the way.

59. Friedman, *Nazis and Good Neighbors*, 156, 213–14; Krammer, *Undue Process*, 52–53; Strum, "Jewish Internees," 28, 38. One sign of this sentiment and the "unreasonable suspicion of Jewish immigrants and exiles to America" was a special billy club "invented by the founder of America First, Inc. . . . called 'The Kike-Killer,'" notes Krammer (52). I follow Deborah Lipstadt's reasoning for using *antisemitism* rather than other variants of the term. See *Antisemitism*, 12–21.

60. See the description of these two categories under "Scope of Plan" in United States, Federal Security Agency, *Policies and Procedures Governing the Administration of Services and Assistance to Enemy Aliens Affected by Governmental Action: A Handbook for State Agencies* (Washington DC: Social Security Board, 1942 page numbering not consecutive).

61. Zucker, *Cecilia Razovsky*, 131–32.

62. Krammer, *Undue Process*, 69–70.

63. Presidential Press Conferences, June 5, 1940, *Complete Presidential Press Conferences of Franklin D. Roosevelt*, 495–99, cited in Zucker, *Cecilia Razovsky*, 127.

64. Quoted in Christgau, *"Enemies,"* 50–51.

65. See the reference to Karl Lowenstein's October 1942 memorandum stating the unreliability of the Jewish spy theory in Feingold's *The Politics of Rescue*, 131.

66. Fox, *America's Invisible Gulag*, 92.

67. Christgau, *"Enemies,"* 75. For a comparative study of the British and US camps, see Pistol, *Internment during the Second World War*. The United States imposed a version of this "equal treatment for all" for the concentration camps rehabilitated as displaced person camps after the war ended in Europe in 1945. Ironically, Truman called on Harrison to oversee this operation; he visited

thirty displaced person camps in Germany and Austria in July 1945. US Army policy decreed that Jews and non-Jews live alongside each other; many Jews lived in the same camps built by the Nazis for their persecution or death, and some found themselves confined with members of the SS and Gestapo. Russell claims, "The US Army had no system in place to identify Nazis from Jews, and no recognition that Jews were the primary targets of Nazi genocide and in need of protection" (*The Train to Crystal City*, 264).

68. See Friedman, *Nazis and Good Neighbors*, 138–39.

69. Fox, *America's Invisible Gulag*, 97.

70. The remainder of the Justice Department rule reads, "Physical coercion must not be resorted to and, except in self-defense, to prevent escape or for purposes of proper search, no employee of this Service under any pretext shall invade the person of the detainee. No measures calculated to humiliate or degrade shall be undertaken." Quoted in Krammer, *Undue Process*, 49.

71. Krammer, *Undue Process*, 173.

72. See Rostow, "Our Worst Wartime Mistake."

73. Krammer, *Undue Process*, 47.

74. Lanier was also instrumental in the firing of an FBI agent who had falsified a report used in an alien's detention. See Christgau, "Enemies," 62–63.

75. Friedman, "The U.S. Internment of Families," 58.

76. See Friedman, *Nazis and Good Neighbors*, 163, who cites "Raymond W. Ickes, Memorandum to the Minister, 30 March 1943," "711.5," Costa Rica: San José Embassy Confidential File, Box 26, RG 84, NA.

77. Quoted in Russell, *The Train to Crystal City*, 39.

78. The "utter disdain" for Latin America that Friedman argued was a central part of the internment legacy (*Nazis and Good Neighbors*, 5) has arguably become open hostility in the wake of anti-immigrant legislation further criminalizing Central Americans and other Latin Americans solely on the basis of their countries of origin.

79. All living children of Camp Algiers internees that I spoke to claimed their fathers never referred to their US detention experiences and even refused to answer direct questions about them.

80. See Kachima's testimony in *Personal Justice Denied*, 298. James L. Dickerson also cites Kachima on "social amnesia" (*Inside America's Concentration Camps*, 222–23).

CHAPTER 1
NEW ORLEANS'S (MOSTLY) SECRET INTERNMENT HISTORY

1. On New Orleans's association with this term, see Arthur Carpenter's Tulane PhD dissertation, "Gateway to the Americas: New Orleans's Quest for Latin American Trade, 1900–1970," which explains that New Orleans "rested comfortably and profitably within a hemispheric economy in which North America refined or consumed Latin American commodities and in which Latin America absorbed North American manufacturing goods and investments. It lay close by the sea lanes connecting the Americas, serving as a center for U.S. trade with Latin America, especially for trade with the Caribbean Basin."

2. By February 1944, Germans from Bolivia, Columbia, Guatemala, Costa Rica, Honduras,

Nicaragua, and Haiti numbered 234 out of approximately 800 internees held at the internment camp in Crystal City, Texas, for example (Riley, *Schools behind Barbed Wire,* 36–37).

3. "Super" camps such as Crystal City and Seagoville in Texas and others elsewhere admittedly dwarfed Algiers in terms of size and numbers of internees. See, for example, Jan Jarboe Russell's *The Train to Crystal City.* In 1945, the INS produced a twenty-one-minute black-and-white film titled *Alien Enemy Detention Facility* available to the public at the National Archives Motion Picture Division, which presented a rosy picture of the Crystal City, Texas, internment camp.

4. "Thus, in one of fate's strange twists, did the fleur-de-lis, swastika, and stars and stripes once wave, overlapping in the Bayou State," notes Matthew Schott in *Bayou Stalags,* (16). In his text focusing on German prisoner of war camps elsewhere in Louisiana, Schott recounts how German POWs revisited many sites in Louisiana in 1984, "telling their own stories, and amusing audiences with tales of 'good times' in the piney woods and bayou country" (45).

5. "Kessler to Immigration Bureau 19 December 1941." Records of the Immigration and Naturalization Service, RG 85, Entry No. 9, 17W3, 11/3/6, NA.

6. Records of the Immigration and Naturalization Service, RG 85, Entry No. 9, 17W3, 11/3/6, NA.

7. Records of the Immigration and Naturalization Service, RG 85, Entry No. 9, 17W3, 11/3/6, NA. After World War II, the site served as a Border Patrol Sector Headquarters of the US Border Patrol under the Department of Homeland Security. The property functioned as an active Border Patrol station until October 23, 2018 (email from Robert Rivet, operations officer, USBP, New Orleans Sector Headquarters).

8. "Aliens Live Well at Algiers Base," *Times-Picayune,* Sunday, September 1, 1945, 13.

9. Formerly known as the Greater New Orleans Bridge, the Crescent City Connection includes the twin cantilever bridges crossing over the Mississippi River, connecting the east and west banks of Orleans Parish. The Crescent City Connection ranks as the fifth-longest cantilever bridge in the world and is the farthest downstream bridge on the Mississippi River. The Mississippi River Bridge Authority began construction on the first bridge in November 1954. See Louisiana Department of Transportation and Development, "Crescent City Connection," http://wwwsp.dotd.la.gov/Inside_LaDOTD/Divisions/Operations/ccc/Pages/default.aspx.

10. Records of the Immigration and Naturalization Service, RG 85, Entry No. 9, 17W3, 11/3/6, NA.

11. Records of the Immigration and Naturalization Service, RG 85, Entry No. 9, 17W3, 11/3/6, NA.

12. Memo to Major Lemuel B. Schofield, December 8, 1941, RG 85, Entry No. 9, 17W3, 11/3/6, NA.

13. Records of the Immigration and Naturalization Service, RG 85, Entry No. 9, 17W3, 11/3/6, NA.

14. A confidential memo from W. F. Kelly to the district director of the INS dated June 26, 1943, asked that courtesies be extended to three detectives the Chilean government had assigned to the *Aconcagua* which was expected in New Orleans in the near future with seventy Japanese aboard. Records of the Immigration and Naturalization Service, RG 85, Entry No. 9, 17W3, 11/3/6, NA.

15. Friedman, *Nazis and Good Neighbors,* 116–17.

16. "Eugene Kessler to INS Commissioner. 1 May 1942," Records of the Immigration and Naturalization Service, RG 85, Entry No. 9, 17W3, 11/3/6, NA.

17. Memo to Commissioner, INS, Philadelphia, Re: Alien enemies detained in the New Orleans District, September 25, 1942, Records of the Immigration and Naturalization Service, RG 85, Entry No. 9, 17W3, 11/3/6, NA.

18. "Eugene Kessler to INS Commissioner. 18 June 1942," Records of the Immigration and Naturalization Service. RG 85, Entry No. 9, 17W3, 11/3/6, NA.

19. Nicholson, "What's That Uniform You're Wearing?"

20. Nicholson was the *Times-Picayune*'s "amusements editor," according to an obituary for her husband, Carl Corbin, whom she married in 1948. Nicholson's grandmother, Eliza Jane Poitevent Nicholson, who wrote under the pen name Pearl Rivers, was the first woman publisher of a metropolitan daily in the United States. Her father, Yorke Nicholson, was a vice president of the Times-Picayune Publishing Company.

21. Records of the Immigration and Naturalization Service. RG 85, Entry No. 9, 17W3, 11/3/6, NA.

22. "Paul V. McNutt to Attorney General (n/d)," Military Agency Records, RG 389, Entry 459, File 255, Alien Detention Station, Algiers, Decimal File 1943–46, NA.

23. "Aliens Live Well at Algiers Base," *Times-Picayune*, Sunday, September 1, 1945, 13.

24. Friedman, *Nazis and Good Neighbors*, 137.

25. Friedman, *Nazis and Good Neighbors*, 136–37.

26. See Friedman, *Nazis and Good Neighbors*, 165, and Strum, "Jewish Internees," 36. Friedman also confirmed the use of this term in an email. In the transcript of his February 25, 1946, repatriation hearing, Camp Algiers detainee Horst von der Goltz is quoted as saying, "I was removed to Algiers because I was in danger of certain Nazi elements on Ellis Island. . . . It [Algiers] was an anti-Nazi camp." Von der Goltz also notes, "Mr. Hueper came to Camp Algiers, in Louisiana, in June, 1944. Mr. Hueper had been sent there because he had trouble with the Nazis in Camp Kenedy, Texas. He told me so himself and Mr. Bunker, the officer in charge of Camp Algiers, also told me so" (Department of Justice Enemy Alien Files, RG 60, Box 439). In 2017, Tulane University graduate students Jack Collins, Joe Hiller, and Mira Kohl made the documentary film *Camp of the Innocents* as part of Professor Justin Wolfe's seminar Historical Documentary Filmmaking. Their film is available on YouTube: https://www.youtube.com/watch?v=5x1G014XAfA.

27. Friedman, *Nazis and Good Neighbors*, 165.

28. Strum, "Jewish Internees," 39; Friedman, *Nazis and Good Neighbors*, 165.

29. Strum, "Jewish Internees," 32.

30. "Enemy Aliens Detained in Building #5," Enemy Alien Detention Station, Algiers, Louisiana, February 11, 1943, signed by Raymond E. Bunker, Officer-in-Charge, Records of the Immigration and Naturalization Service, RG 85, Entry No. 9, 17W3, 11/3/6, NA.

31. "W. W. Knopp to Commissioner, INS," March 15, 1943, and "Aliens in Detention at Alien Detention Station, Algiers, Louisiana, March 31, 1943," Records of the Immigration and Naturalization Service, RG 85, Entry No. 9, 17W3, 11/3/6, NA.

32. "W. W. Knopp to Commissioner, INS," August 21, 1943, Records of the Immigration and Naturalization Service, RG 85, Entry No. 9, 17W3, 11/3/6, NA.

33. "Freedom Soon for 50 'Enemy Alien' Refugees at Algiers," *New Orleans Item*, August 19, 1943, p. 8.

34. "50 Refugees Long Interned Here to Be Released Soon," *Times-Picayune*, August 20, 1943, 1.

35. "Democracy at Work," *New Orleans Item*, August 21, 1943, 4.

36. Roehl, "Refugee Violinist Fled from Nazis."

37. Fox, *America's Invisible Gulag*, 123.

38. Quoted in Fox, *America's Invisible Gulag*, 122.

39. Quoted in Fox, *America's Invisible Gulag*, 124.

40. Quoted in Fox, *America's Invisible Gulag*, 123. Trott became a US citizen in 1946. He died in Seattle in 1999. As of this writing, the "Trott Cabin" on Mt. Baker could be rented through Airbnb.com.

41. Quoted in Krammer, *Undue Process*, 108. Krammer notes that Meyer later worked as a physician in California.

42. "Aliens Live Well at Algiers Base," *Times-Picayune*, September 1, 1945, 13.

43. Krammer, *Undue Process*, 108. Krammer does not include Algiers on his list of World War II internment/detention camps in the United States and other countries (175–76).

44. Algiers Field Report filed by Jules Seitz, February 23, 1943, MKM 14.54 File 1130, NRS Records, American Jewish Historical Society.

45. Quoted in Algiers Field Report filed by Jules Seitz, February 23, 1943, MKM 14.54 File 1130, NRS Records, American Jewish Historical Society.

46. Fox, *America's Invisible Gulag*, 97.

47. Algiers Field Report filed by Jules Seitz, February 23, 1943, MKM 14.54 File 1130, NRS Records, American Jewish Historical Society. The Gerothwohls were being shunned by other internees because of their apparent disinterest in being freed, but Seitz, upon further inquiry, discovered "Mr. G. is a writer who has been starved and pushed around for a good part of his life. Seldom had three meals a day and a clean bed to sleep in. For the first time he is living in a 'garden spot' where he gets his food and room and doesn't have to worry about anything." Upon explaining to the Gerothwohls the commitment of the NRS to assisting refugees and assuring him "he wouldn't be left on the streets to starve if released . . . his face lit up and he changed his entire outlook."

48. Krammer, *Undue Process*, 99.

49. "Camp of Civilian Internees of Algiers visited by Mr. P. Schnyder on April 19, 1944," translation, Stamp of the International Red Cross, RG 85, Entry No. 9, 17W3, 11/3/6, NA.

50. "Albert Greutert to the Legation of Switzerland, 29 December 1944," RG 389, Entry 459, File 255, Alien Detention Station, Algiers, Decimal File 1943–46, Box 1608, NA.

51. "Dr. Friedrich Karl Kaul, et al to Raymond E. Bunker" (date illegible June 1944), Records of the Immigration and Naturalization Service, RG 85, Entry No. 9, 17W3, 11/3/6, NA.

52. The list and its viability are further explored in chapter 3.

53. "Report of Visit to Algiers Alien Detention Camp, New Orleans, Louisiana, February 6, 1945," RG 85, Entry No. 9, 17W3, 11/3/6, NA.

54. "Civilian Internees Camp at Algiers, Louisiana visited by Mr. P. Schnyder on February 6, 1945," translation, Stamp of the International Red Cross, RG 85, Entry No. 9, 17W3, 11/3/6, NA.

55. "Report of Visit to Alien Detention Station, Algiers Louisiana, May 30–31, 1945," signed by Olle Axberg, Military Agency Records, RG 389, Entry 459, File 255, Alien Detention Station, Algiers, Decimal File 1943–46, Box 1608, NA.

56. Louis Phillipp, Divisional Assistant, Department of State, to Raymond Bunker, October 31, 1945. Military Agency Records, RG 389, Entry 459, File 255, Alien Detention Station, Algiers, Decimal File 1943–46, Box 1608, NA.

57. Routh, "Distinguished Enemy Aliens N.O. Neighbors for 4 Years," *New Orleans States*, August 31, 1945, 11.

58. "Alien Enemy Detention Station, Algiers Louisiana," report signed by Van Arsdale Turner, date of visit February 25 and 26, 1946, Military Agency Records, RG 389, Entry 459, File 255, Alien Detention Station, Algiers, Decimal File 1943–46, Box 1608, NA.

59. Marjorie Roehl, "Alien Detention Camp In Algiers To Close." *New Orleans Item*, March 30, 1946, 2.

60. The Wilhelm Busch Prize is awarded annually for satirical and humorous poetry and the Wilhelm Busch Society, active since 1930, promotes Busch's works with the public. The Wilhelm Busch Museum is located in Hanover.

61. Quoted in Gilman, "The Jewish Nose," 160–61. The original text reads:

> Und der Jud mit krummer Ferse,
> Krummer Nas' und krummer Hos',
> Schlängelt sich zur hohen Börse
> Tiefverderbt und seelenlos.

62. "Friend of Hitler in Algiers Camp," *New Orleans States*, March 30, 1946, 5.

63. Ken Gormin, "Close Pal of Hitler Held in Algiers Detention Unit," *Times-Picayune*, March 30, 1946, 1.

64. See "FBI Files on Communism in Ecuador in the 1940s," Internet Archive, https://archive.org/stream/FBI-Ecuador-Communism-1940s/ecuadortoday_djvu.txt.

65. "Partmuss, Friedrich Paul. Ecuador," Name Files of Interned Enemy Aliens from Latin America, 1942–48, RG 59, Special War Problems, Box 45, NA.

66. "Aliens to Leave by Air," *New Orleans Item*, April 24, 1946, 1.

67. "Fly Ex-Foe Alien Internees to Homes," *Times-Picayune*, April 26, 1946, 15.

68. A segment of the Hartens' story can be read in English at German American Internee Coalition, "The Harten Family Story," http://gaic.info/the-harten-family-story/. Gertrude Harten's full story is recounted in Spanish in Sánchez and Ahlers, *Gertrudis: Diarios de una mujer alemana sobre el Ecuador, 1937–1956*.

69. The stated missions of Homeland Security involve antiterrorism, border security, immigration and customs, cyber security, and disaster prevention and management. It was created in November 2002 in response to the events of September 11, 2001.

CHAPTER 2
THE QUANDARIES OF CLASSIFICATION

1. Friedman quotes Long in *Nazis and Good Neighbors*, 156, and gives the source text as Breckenridge Long memo, 4 Nov 1942, 740.00115EW 939/4442, RG 59, NA.

2. Zucker, *Cecilia Razovsky*, 126.

3. Zucker, *Cecilia Razovsky*, 126–27.

4. Gushee, *The Sacredness of Human Life*, 310. The Nazis' classification system became a society-wide project enlisting everyday citizens in the exclusion and vilification of Jews and other outsiders:

> The primary but not exclusive objective of the race-based classification system the Nazis created was to exclude Germany's 500,000 "Jews" and other "Non-Aryans" from membership in society—to move them from citizens to aliens and finally from aliens to elimination. It was a project of systematic social exclusion that extended to every dimension of life—including excluding non-Aryans from voluntary associations and from public or military service, and denying them participation in the professions and the economy, citizenship status and its associated rights, and eventually any right to live in Germany. The project of exclusion after January 1933 became a society-wide endeavor, with leadership and innovation often coming from below rather than above, as leaders of every type of social and professional group in Germany raced to be the first and most creative to reject Jews and other outsiders. (Gushee, *The Sacredness of Human Life*, 309–10)

5. See Halfon, *The Polish Boxer*, 89.

6. Quoted in Williams, *American Sutra*, 36.

7. Quoted in Williams, *American Sutra*, 28, as part of his discussion of Buddhism as a national security threat, 27–32. See also Daniels, *The Politics of Prejudice*, 106–7.

8. Williams, *American Sutra*, 197.

9. Japanese aliens apprehended in Latin America or the United States were generally not held for long periods at Algiers but were quickly transferred to other detention facilities.

10. S. W. Anderson, Assistant Supervisor, Detentions Unit, Alien Enemy population at the Algiers Detention Station, to W. F. Kelly, Assistant Commissioner for Alien Control, November 8, 1944, RG 85, Entry No. 9, 17W3, 11/3/6, NA.

11. In an analysis of Friedrich Karl Kaul's partly factual, partly fantasized autobiographical novel *Es wird Zeit, dass Du nach Hause kommst,* Max Paul Friedman refers to Camp Algiers as "a separate camp for anti-Nazis" (322). In fact, as Anderson's chart confirms, a few notorious avowed Nazis such as Karl Kolb were also held there, along with some who hoped to pass themselves off as reformed Nazis, such as Horst von der Goltz and Kurt Ludecke.

12. See Friedman, "The Cold War Politics of Exile," 322.

13. S. W. Anderson, Assistant Supervisor, Detentions Unit, Alien Enemy population at the Algiers Detention Station to W. F. Kelly, Assistant Commissioner for Alien Control, November 8, 1944, RG 85, Entry No. 9, 17W3, 11/3/6, NA.

14. "Blumenthal, Ernst. Nicaragua," Name Files of Interned Enemy Aliens from Latin America, 1942–48, RG 59, Special War Problems, Box 36, NA. Ernst and his wife, Annaliese, were not released in August 1943 along with the majority of the Jewish internees, thus explaining their appearance on a list of detainees in the camp dated November 1944.

15. Quoted in Friedman, *Nazis and Good Neighbors,* 151. Friedman notes that "women whose marriages were not official, who were not German citizens or who had been expatriated by Nazi anti-Jewish laws, were ineligible for German relief payments. They were left to fend for themselves,

sometimes doubly blacklisted by the remnant pro-Nazi German community, which charged them with racial impurity, and by the U.S. Embassy and local government, which charged them with political unreliability" (*Nazis and Good Neighbors*, 151).

16. Quoted in Friedman, *Nazis and Good Neighbors*, 151.

17. Ernst Blumenthal to Legation of Switzerland, December 15, 1942, in "Blumenthal, Ernst. Nicaragua," Name Files of Interned Enemy Aliens from Latin America, 1942–48, RG 59, Special War Problems, Box 36, NA.

18. Confidential memo, January 3, 1946, "Blumenthal, Ernst. Nicaragua," Name Files of Interned Enemy Aliens from Latin America, 1942–48, RG 59, Special War Problems, Box 36, NA.

19. "Fechenbach, Siegwart. Panama," Name Files of Interned Enemy Aliens from Latin America, 1942–48, RG 59, Special War Problems, Box 39, and Class 146-13, RG 60, A1 COR 146-13, (Alien Enemy) Litigation Case File No. 14-3-2-1529, Box 753, NA.

20. "Fechenbach, Siegwart. Panama," Name Files of Interned Enemy Aliens from Latin America, 1942–48, RG 59, Special War Problems, Box 39, NA.

21. Pitt, "The Noriega Case."

22. "Fechenbach, Siegwart. Panama," Name Files of Interned Enemy Aliens from Latin America, 1942–48, RG 59, Special War Problems, Box 39, NA.

23. Jonathan Bingham to Ugo Carusi, March 15, 1946, "Fechenbach, Siegwart. Panama," Name Files of Interned Enemy Aliens from Latin America, 1942–48, RG 59, Special War Problems, Box 39, NA.

24. "Gerothwohl, Ernesto. Costa Rica," Name Files of Interned Enemy Aliens from Latin America, 1942–48, RG 59, Special War Problems, Box 39, NA. Internee names often had alternate spellings on different government documents. Certain records for both Ernesto and Clotilde spell their last name Gerothwohl, including their death notices (US Social Security Death Index).

25. Friedman, *Nazis and Good Neighbors*, 178.

26. "Gerothwohl, Ernesto. Costa Rica," Name Files of Interned Enemy Aliens from Latin America, 1942–48, RG 59, Special War Problems, Box 39, NA.

27. Airgram to the Secretary of State, December 22, 1942, "Gerothwohl, Ernesto. Costa Rica," Name Files of Interned Enemy Aliens from Latin America, 1942–48, RG 59, Special War Problems, Box 39, NA.

28. Avni, "Costa Rica and the Jews," 235. Additional background on Costa Rica's response to World War II treatment of German-born residents and even those of German descent born in Costa Rica is provided in Hernández and Solórzano, "Los archivos de la Junta de Custodia de Costa Rica durante la Segunda Guerra Mundial," which notes that the blacklists included "not only those born in the countries of the Axis, but also persons who were Costa Ricans by birth, but were born to parents of German, Japanese and Italian nationality, and Costa Rican professionals who had conducted studies in enemy countries" (263, my translation).

29. Class 146-13, RG 60, A1 COR 146-13, (Alien Enemy) Litigation Case File No. 14-3-2-1512, Box 753, NA.

30. "Hamermann, Leo. Bolivia," Name Files of Interned Enemy Aliens from Latin America, 1942–48, RG 59, Special War Problems, Box 40, NA.

31. See Friedman, *Nazis and Good Neighbors*, 133–34, 158.

32. Office of Censorship intercepted letter from Jacobo Kramer, La Paz, to Isidore Hamermann,

Cincinnati, June 16, 1944, "Hamermann, Leo. Bolivia," Name Files of Interned Enemy Aliens from Latin America, 1942–48, RG 59, Special War Problems, Box 40, NA.

33. Strum, "Jewish Internees," 43.

34. Dubois, *Danger over Panama*, 62.

35. Friedman, *Nazis and Good Neighbors*, 47–48.

36. "Heinemann, Wilhelm. Panama," Name Files of Interned Enemy Aliens from Latin America, 1942–48, RG 59, Special War Problems, Box 40, NA.

37. Censorship intercept of Willhelm Heinemann to Leo Marchowsky, May 17, 1942. "Heinemann, Wilhelm. Panama," Name Files of Interned Enemy Aliens from Latin America, 1942–48, RG 59, Special War Problems, Box 40, NA.

38. Memorandum for the Chief of Review Section of the INS, "Heinemann, Wilhelm. Panama," Name Files of Interned Enemy Aliens from Latin America, 1942–48, RG 59, Special War Problems, Box 40, NA.

39. Confidential memo, "Heinemann, Wilhelm. Panama," Name Files of Interned Enemy Aliens from Latin America, 1942–48, RG 59, Special War Problems, Box 40, NA.

40. Death notices for both Wilhelm and Marta Heinemann are located in Reports of Deaths of American Citizens Abroad, 1835–1974, Box 119, 1963–1974, HA-JZ, Ancestry.com.

41. "Kaul, Friedrich Karl. Nicaragua," Name Files of Interned Enemy Aliens from Latin America, 1942–48, RG 59, Special War Problems, Box 41, NA. A Department of Justice report in his State Department file confirmed Kaul's repatriation as of September 15, 1945.

42. Friedman, "The Cold War Politics of Exile," 306.

43. Personal statement, "Kaul, Friedrich Karl. Nicaragua," Name Files of Interned Enemy Aliens from Latin America, 1942–48, RG 59, Special War Problems, Box 41, NA.

44. "Kaul, Friedrich Karl. Nicaragua," Name Files of Interned Enemy Aliens from Latin America, 1942–48, RG 59, Special War Problems, Box 41, NA.

45. De Vita, "The Cold War in the Courtroom," 4–5.

46. De Vita, "The Cold War in the Courtroom," 2.

47. Rasmussen, "Friends of Freedom, Allies of Peace," 144.

48. "United States versus Angela Davis: Open Letter addressed by Attorney Professor Dr. Friedrich Karl Kaul to Judge Richard E. Arnason," DDR Komitee für Menschenrechte, 1972, no pagination. The context for Kaul's letter was Davis's 1970 arrest for alleged involvement in a courthouse shootout in California, at which she had not been present. See Natalia King Rasmussen's discussion of Kaul's open letter in her dissertation titled "Friends of Freedom, Allies of Peace: African Americans, the Civil Rights Movement, and East Germany, 1949–1989," 148–50.

49. See Friedman, "The Cold War Politics of Exile," 322–25.

50. Riley, *Schools behind Barbed Wire*, 57.

51. Russell, *Train to Crystal City*, 93.

52. Russell, *Train to Crystal City*, 93.

53. Russell, *The Train to Crystal City*, 94.

54. Russell, *The Train to Crystal City*, 95.

55. Russel, *The Train to Crystal City*, 115.

56. Russell, *The Train to Crystal City*, 116. See also Riley, *Schools behind Barbed Wire*, 66n22.

57. "Manzoni, Rodolfo. Nicaragua," Name Files of Interned Enemy Aliens from Latin America, 1942–48, RG 59, Special War Problems, Box 43, NA.

58. Saballos Ramírez, "70 años del ingreso de Nicaragua a la segunda guerra mundial declaración de guerra de Nicaragua a Japón, Alemania e Italia en diciembre de 1941," 94.

59. Censorship intercept of Rodolfo Manzoni to Eva Velázquez de Manzoni, October 3, 1943, "Manzoni, Rodolfo. Nicaragua," Name Files of Interned Enemy Aliens from Latin America, 1942–48, RG 59, Special War Problems, Box 43, NA.

60. W. F. Kelly to Albert Clattenburg Jr., May 13, 1944, "Manzoni, Rodolfo. Nicaragua," Name Files of Interned Enemy Aliens from Latin America, 1942–48, RG 59, Special War Problems, Box 43, NA.

61. "Europe, Registration of Foreigners and German Persecutees, 1939–1947," Arolsen Archives, International Center on Nazi Persecution, accessed through Ancestry.com.

62. "Mateju, Eugenia. Ecuador," Name Files of Interned Enemy Aliens from Latin America, 1942–48, Special War Problems, RG 59, Box 43, NA.

63. Censored letter, Eugenia Mateju to Dr. Carlos Arroyo del Río, March 21, 1944, "Mateju, Eugenia. Ecuador," Name Files of Interned Enemy Aliens from Latin America, 1942–48, RG 59, Special War Problems, Box 43, NA.

64. The full text of "FBI Files on Communism in Ecuador in the 1940s" can be accessed at Internet Archive, https://archive.org/stream/FBI-Ecuador-Communism-1940s/ecuadortoday_djvu.txt.

65. An FBI document in Mateju's file also claims, "In 1941 she was placed on the British Black List and early in 1942 was listed as one of the Axis subjects in Ecuador who should be returned to Germany."

66. Censored letter, Eugenia Mateju to Dr. Carlos Arroyo del Río, March 21, 1944, "Mateju, Eugenia. Ecuador," Name Files of Interned Enemy Aliens from Latin America, 1942–48, RG 59, Special War Problems, Box 43, NA.

67. "Mateju, Eugenia. Ecuador," Name Files of Interned Enemy Aliens from Latin America, 1942–48, RG 59, Special War Problems, Box 43, NA.

68. "Mathies, Gustavo. El Salvador," Name Files of Interned Enemy Aliens from Latin America, 1942–48, Special War Problems, RG 59, Box 43, NA.

69. Censored letter from Gustavo Mathies to Salvador Martínez, January 24, 1944, "Mathies, Gustavo. El Salvador," Name Files of Interned Enemy Aliens from Latin America, 1942–48, RG 59, Special War Problems, Box 43, NA.

70. Telegram from Gustavo Mathies, September 4, 1945, "Mathies, Gustavo. El Salvador," Name Files of Interned Enemy Aliens from Latin America, 1942–48, RG 59, Special War Problems, Box 43, NA.

71. *Converso* was a term used during the Spanish Inquisition beginning in the fifteenth century to describe a Jew who had converted to Catholicism as a requirement to continue living in Spain or Portugal, owning property there, etc. The term acquired pejorative connotations, as *conversos*—even those who reestablished themselves in the New World—were judged to be inherently dishonest and untrustworthy and were subjected to surveillance, accusation, and charges of heresy, punishable by torture and burning at the stake.

72. Confidential memo, February 21, 1946, "Meyer, Siegfried," Name Files of Interned Enemy Aliens from Latin America, 1942–48, RG 59, Special War Problems, Box 44, NA.

73. Siegfried Meyer to Legation of Switzerland, December 12, 1942, "Meyer, Siegfried," Name Files of Interned Enemy Aliens from Latin America, 1942–48, RG 59, Special War Problems, Box 44, NA.

74. Roorda, "The Dominican Republic," 86.

75. "Meyer, Siegfried," Name Files of Interned Enemy Aliens from Latin America, 1942–48, RG 59, Special War Problems, Box 44, NA.

76. Bukey, *Jews and Intermarriage in Nazi Austria*, 2–4.

77. "Meyer, Siegfried," Name Files of Interned Enemy Aliens from Latin America, 1942–48, RG 59, Special War Problems, Box 44, NA.

78. National Refugee Service letter, June 18, 1945, quoted in "Meyer, Siegfried," Name Files of Interned Enemy Aliens from Latin America, 1942–48, RG 59, Special War Problems, Box 44, NA.

79. "Meyer, Siegfried," Name Files of Interned Enemy Aliens from Latin America, 1942–48, RG 59, Special War Problems, Box 44, NA.

80. "Case of Mrs. Siegfried (Irmgard) Meyer," RG 59, Special War Problems, entry 1351, Box 16 (250/49/20/5).

81. Meyer's Justice file reveals one of the translations of this term: "In March, 1937, he was arrested by the Gestapo, charged with 'social contamination.'" Class 146-13, RG 60, A1 COR 146-13, (Alien Enemy) Litigation Case File No. 14-3-2-689, Box717, NA.

82. "Case of Mrs. Siegfried (Irmgard) Meyer," RG 59, Special War Problems, entry 1351, Box 16 (250/49/20/5).

83. "Meyer, Siegfried," Name Files of Interned Enemy Aliens from Latin America, 1942–48, RG 59, Special War Problems, Box 44, NA.

84. Bukey, *Jews and Intermarriage in Nazi Austria*, 147–65.

85. Irmgard's married name on both her naturalization documents and her tombstone is Maschler. Her date of death at age eighty-one was July 27, 1982. She is buried in Sec. 6S, Lot 182, A at Woodlawn Cemetery. State of California Marriage Records and Findagrave.com.

86. Details of Frank Meyer's reenlistment and death date are included in his US Department of Veteran Affairs BIRLS Death File, "Frank Meyer" in US Department of Veteran Affairs BIRLS Death Files, 1850–2010, accessed on Ancestry.com; see Krammer, *Undue Process*, 108, regarding Meyer's profession as a physician.

87. Friedman, "Trading Civil Liberties for National Security," 295.

88. "Mueller, Olaf," Class 146-13, RG 60, A1 COR 146-13, (Alien Enemy) Litigation Case File No. 146-13-2-2011, Box 773, NA.

89. Department of Justice summary sheet, "Mueller, Olaf," Class 146-13, RG 60, A1 COR 146-13, (Alien Enemy) Litigation Case File No. 146-13-2-2011, Box 773, NA.

90. Gerhard Rempel in "Mennonites and the Holocaust" argues that many Mennonites who had suffered the decimation of their communities under Stalin were also caught up in Nazism as an anti-Stalinist ideology and in fact participated as collaborators and even perpetrators in the Holocaust.

91. "Mueller, Olaf," Class 146-13, RG 60, A1 COR 146-13, (Alien Enemy) Litigation Case File No. 146-13-2-2011, Box 773, NA.

92. Christgau included this description in the comments he presented at the March 19, 2009, congressional hearing on the *Treatment of Latin Americans of Japanese Descent, European Americans, and Jewish Refugees*, 27.

93. Christgau, "Enemies," 60.

94. A modified version of the Crystal City film can be viewed at https://www.youtube.com/watch?v=WRfSHgdh2UA.

95. Maria's story is included in her husband Max Paschka's name file. "Paschka, Max. Costa Rica," Name Files of Interned Enemy Aliens from Latin America, 1942–48, RG 59, Special War Problems, Box 45, NA.

96. Report dated October 4, 1945,"Paschka, Max. Costa Rica," Name Files of Interned Enemy Aliens from Latin America, 1942–48, RG 59, Special War Problems, Box 45, NA.

97. Quoted in Weisaeth and Ettinger, "Research on PTSD and other Post-Traumatic Reactions." Stierlin postulated that both emotions and "unfortunate social conditions" could create a "state of lowered resistance within the nervous system which forms the basis for the development of a neurosis."

98. See Kleinberg, "Post Time."

99. S. W. Anderson, Assistant Supervisor, Detentions Unit, Alien Enemy population at the Algiers Detention Station, to W. F. Kelly, Assistant Commissioner for Alien Control, November 8. 1944, RG 85, Entry No. 9, 17W3, 11/3/6, NA.

100. Opel's letter appears in Ludecke's file. "Ludecke, Kurt," Class 146-13, RG 60, A1 COR 146-13, (Alien Enemy) Litigation Case File No. 146-13-2-37-89, Box 318, NA.

101. Ennis, "A Justice Department Attorney Comments on the Japanese-American Relocation."

102. Quoted in Kleinberg, "Post Time."

103. Nehmer, *Ford, General Motors, and the Nazis*, 281.

104. Quoted in Christgau, *"Enemies,"* 82–83.

CHAPTER 3.
INCARCERATION OR A WELCOME REFUGE? THE PANAMA JEWS AT CAMP ALGIERS

1. "Ascher, Benno. Panama," Name Files of Interned Enemy Aliens from Latin America, 1942–48, RG 59, Special War Problems, Box 35, NA.

2. Ascher may have been part of a group of Jewish German refugees who were at Stringtown only briefly. See Walter Kohner's description of this episode in chapter 4.

3. Though refugees at Fort Ontario were also locked behind a chain-link fence with barbed wire, the site represented the United States' only attempt to provide shelter to Jewish refugees during the war. In her memoir *Haven*, Ruth Gruber recalls her efforts to retain the refugees at Fort Ontario through the end of the war, even as some US government agencies suggested they should be deported to Europe.

4. Strum, "Jewish Internees," 29.

5. Jewish Telegraphic Agency, "National Refugee Service Secures Release of Jewish Internees in Texas Camp," April 15, 1943, http://www.jta.org/1943/04/15/archive/national-refugee-service-secures-release-of-jewish-internees-in-texas-camp.

6. Friedman, *Nazis and Good Neighbors*, 139, 165; Strum, "Jewish Internees," 36.

7. "Ascher, Benno. Panama," Name Files of Interned Enemy Aliens from Latin America, 1942–48, RG 59, Special War Problems, Box 35, NA.

8. "Bohm, Peter. Panama," Name Files of Interned Enemy Aliens from Latin America, 1942–48, RG 59, Special War Problems, Box 36, NA, and Class 146-13 RG 60, A1 COR 146-13, (Alien Enemy) Litigation Case File No. 146-13-2-1573, Box 754.

9. Summary of Justice File, "Bohm, Peter. Panama," Name Files of Interned Enemy Aliens from Latin America, 1942–48, RG 59, Special War Problems, Box 36, NA.

10. Form I-55, RG 60, A1 COR 146-13, (Alien Enemy) Litigation Case File No. 146-13-2-1573, Box 754.

11. Jonathan B. Bingham to Ugo Carusi, February 19, 1946, "Bohm, Peter. Panama," Name Files of Interned Enemy Aliens from Latin America, 1942–48, RG 59, Special War Problems, Box 36, NA.

12. Quoted in Erwin Fraenkel to Cordell Hull, April 16, 1943. Though the detainee signed his letter to the secretary of state "Erwin Fraenkel," most of the US government documents, including the US Social Security Death Index, list his name as "Frankel." All materials referencing Frankel come from "Fraenkel, Erwin, Dr. Panama," Name Files of Interned Enemy Aliens from Latin America, 1942–48, RG 59, Special War Problems, Box 39, and Class 146-13, RG 60, Box 718, A1 COR 146-13, (Alien Enemy) Litigation Case File No. 146-13-2-707, NA.

13. Handwritten memo from Panama police regarding Hubert Erwin Fraenkel, "Fraenkel, Erwin, Dr. Panama," Name Files of Interned Enemy Aliens from Latin America, 1942–48, RG 59, Special War Problems, Box 39, NA.

14. Report to the Director of the FBI, April 10, 1941, Class 146-13, RG 60, Box 718, A1 COR 146-13, (Alien Enemy) Litigation Case File No. 146-13-2-707, NA.

15. Besides the incalculable loss of human life associated with the false promise of a way out of Europe for his relatives, the figure of $1,226 represents over $18,000 as of 2020, adjusted for inflation, according to https://www.usinflationcalculator.com.

16. The Panama police memo in Frankel's file spells the name Westenmeier.

17. "Fraenkel, Erwin, Dr. Panama," Name Files of Interned Enemy Aliens from Latin America, 1942–48, RG 59, Special War Problems, Box 39, NA.

18. Documents referring to Toni Fraenkel, including her I-55 form, are included in her husband's file: "Fraenkel, Erwin, Dr. Panama," Name Files of Interned Enemy Aliens from Latin America, 1942–48, RG 59, Special War Problems, Box 39, NA.

19. "Fraenkel, Erwin, Dr. Panama," Name Files of Interned Enemy Aliens from Latin America, 1942–48, RG 59, Special War Problems, Box 39, NA.

20. Memorandum from R. H. Robinson to T. B. Shoemaker, Class 146-13, RG 60, Box 718, A1 COR 146-13, (Alien Enemy) Litigation Case File No. 146-13-2-707, NA.

21. Thomas M. Cooley II to Director of the Alien Enemy Control Unit [Edward Ennis], July 31, 1946, Class 146-13, RG 60, Box 718, A1 COR 146-13, (Alien Enemy) Litigation Case File No. 146-13-2-707, NA.

22. "Kallman, Martin. Panama," Name Files of Interned Enemy Aliens from Latin America, 1942–48, RG 59, Special War Problems, Box 41, NA.

23. "Kappel, Fred. Panama," Name Files of Interned Enemy Aliens from Latin America, 1942–48, RG 59, Special War Problems, Box 41, NA.

24. Department of State intercept of letter from Fred Kappel to Alice Kassel, February 2, 1942, "Kappel, Fred. Panama," Name Files of Interned Enemy Aliens from Latin America, 1942–48, Special War Problems, RG 59, Box 41, NA.

25. Department of State intercept of letter from Fred Kappel to Alphonse M. Spiegel, April 14, 1942, "Kappel, Fred. Panama," Name Files of Interned Enemy Aliens from Latin America, 1942–48, RG 59, Special War Problems, Box 41, NA.

26. "Kappel, Fred. Panama," Name Files of Interned Enemy Aliens from Latin America, 1942–48, RG 59, Special War Problems, Box 41, NA.

27. Class 146-13, RG 60, Box 718, A1 COR 146-13, (Alien Enemy) Litigation Case File No. 146-13-2-2702, NA.

28. "Kappel, Werner. Panama," Name Files of Interned Enemy Aliens from Latin America, 1942–48, RG 59, Special War Problems, Box 41, NA.

29. Friedman, *Nazis and Good Neighbors*, x.

30. "Kaufmann, Max. Panama," Name Files of Interned Enemy Aliens from Latin America, 1942–48, RG 59, Special War Problems, Box 41, NA.

31. Alfred Auerbacher, December 27, 1942, Class 146-13, RG 60, A1 COR 146-13, (Alien Enemy) Litigation Case File No. 146-13-2-703, Box 718, NA.

32. Augusta Wertheimer, February 11, 1943, Class 146-13, RG 60, A1 COR 146-13, (Alien Enemy) Litigation Case File No. 146-13-2-703, Box 718, NA.

33. "Kohen, Albert(o). Panama." Name Files of Interned Enemy Aliens from Latin America, 1942–48, RG 59, Special War Problems, Box 42, NA.

34. "Klyszcz, Erwin. Panama," Name Files of Interned Enemy Aliens from Latin America, 1942–48, RG 59, Special War Problems, Box 42, NA.

35. Quoted in "Klyszcz, Erwin. Panama," Name Files of Interned Enemy Aliens from Latin America, 1942–48, RG 59, Special War Problems, Box 42, NA.

36. "Mannheimer, Otto. Panama," Name Files of Interned Enemy Aliens from Latin America, 1942–48, RG 59, Special War Problems, Box 44, NA.

37. See Morton, *A Nervous Splendor*.

38. Manheimer's activities with the student group Masada are also mentioned in Gregor Gatscher-Reidl, "Eine vergessene Facette der österreichischen Studentengeschichte."

39. Bukey, *Jews and Intermarriage in Nazi Austria*, 4.

40. State Department confidential memo, March 6, 1946, "Mannheimer, Otto. Panama," Name Files of Interned Enemy Aliens from Latin America, 1942–48, RG 59, Special War Problems, Box 44, NA.

41. "Marcus, Ferdinand. Panama," Name Files of Interned Enemy Aliens from Latin America, 1942–48, RG 59, Special War Problems, Box 43, NA.

42. Quoted in "Marcus, Ferdinand. Panama," Name Files of Interned Enemy Aliens from Latin America, 1942–48, RG 59, Special War Problems, Box 43, NA.

43. "Marcus, Ferdinand. Panama," Name Files of Interned Enemy Aliens from Latin America, 1942–48, RG 59, Special War Problems, Box 43, NA.

44. "Muller, (Mueller) Hans Joachim. Panama." Name Files of Interned Enemy Aliens from Latin America, 1942–48, RG 59, Special War Problems, Box 44, NA.

45. Oppenheimer was an American-born theoretical physicist and scientist who directed the Los Alamos National Laboratory during the development of the atomic bomb and, later, the Institute for Advanced Study at Princeton.

46. "Scholem, Werner. Panama," Name Files of Interned Enemy Aliens from Latin America, 1942–48, RG 59, Special War Problems, Box 47, NA.

47. Confidential memo, November 15, 1945, "Scholem, Werner. Panama," Name Files of Interned Enemy Aliens from Latin America, 1942–48, RG 59, Special War Problems, Box 47, NA.

48. Bolbrinker, *Between Utopia and Counter Revolution*.

49. See Triendl-Zadoff, *Werner Scholem*, and Hoffrogge, *A Jewish Communist in Weimar Germany*, presenting different perspectives on Scholem's (b. 1895) life, as well as Geller, *The Scholems*.

50. Confidential memo, March 12, 1946, "Scholem, Werner. Panama," Name Files of Interned Enemy Aliens from Latin America, 1942–48, RG 59, Special War Problems, Box 47, NA.

51. "Calverton National Cemetery, Calverton, Suffolk County, New York: Surnames Sha–She," Interment.net, http://www.interment.net/data/us/ny/suffolk/calverton/calverton-national-cemetery-records-sha-she.htm.

52. "Wetterschneider, Egon. Panama," Name Files of Interned Enemy Aliens from Latin America, 1942–48, RG 59, Special War Problems, Box 50, NA.

53. As of July 2020, there is an Astoria Café Restaurante Bar y Café located on Avenida B in Panama City.

54. Summary of Department of Justice File in "Wetterschneider, Egon. Panama," Name Files of Interned Enemy Aliens from Latin America, 1942–48, RG 59, Special War Problems, Box 50, NA.

55. "Wetterschneider, Oskar. Panama," Name Files of Interned Enemy Aliens from Latin America, 1942–48, RG 59, Special War Problems, Box 50, NA.

56. Rapoport, *Shake Heaven and Earth*, 127.

57. Theodore Levin to Homer Ferguson, September 21, 1945, in "Wetterschneider, Oskar. Panama," Name Files of Interned Enemy Aliens from Latin America, 1942–48, RG 59, Special War Problems, Box 50, NA.

58. Roehl, "Refugee Violinist Fled from Nazis."

59. "Internees Released from Internment in Camp Algiers and Camp Seagoville." National Refugee Services, American Jewish Historial Society Records.

60. "Wolff, Siegfried. Panama," Name Files of Interned Enemy Aliens from Latin America, 1942–48, RG 59, Special War Problems, Box 50, NA.

61. Class 146-13, RG 60, A1 COR 146-13, (Alien Enemy) Litigation Case File No. 146-13-2-732, RG 60, Box 721, NA.

62. Razovsky responded to Siegfried Wolff's February 1, 1943, letter on February 16, assuring him she would contact Druker and ask him to provide an affidavit for Wolff and his mother. Cecilia Razovsky to Siegfried Wolff, February 16, 1943, Razovsky Papers, American Jewish Historical Society Records.

63. Quoted in Friedman, *Nazis and Good Neighbors*, 161.

64. Talbot, *The Devil's Chessboard*, 45.

65. Quoted in Friedman, *Nazis and Good Neighbors*, 156.

66. Friedman, *Nazis and Good Neighbors*, 157–58.

67. Long to Mohler, September 24, 1942, Folder "W," Name Files of Interned Enemy Aliens from Latin America, 1942–48, RG 59, Box 35, NA, cited by Zucker, *Cecilia Razovsky*, 137.

CHAPTER 4.
PROFESSOR, SPY, CONFIDANT: THREE NOTABLES INTERNED IN NEW ORLEANS

1. Records of the Enemy Alien Information Bureau, Office of the Provost Marshal General, RG 389, Box 9, NA.

2. Brunhouse, *Frans Blom*, 85.

3. Leifer et al., *Restless Blood*, 156.

4. Caso, "Hermann Beyer," 31. In Beyer's era, the term "Americanist" referred to someone working in the Americas with a focus on ancient cultures and civilizations.

5. Caso, "Hermann Beyer," 31. Caso's remembrance was published in the *Boletín bibliográfico de antropología americana* 6 (1942): 29–34 and reprinted in other journals. My translation.

6. "Dr. Beyer Given Foreign Tribute," *New Orleans States,* June 5, 1932, 8.

7. Caso, "Hermann Beyer," 33.

8. Brunhouse, *Frans Blom,* 86–87.

9. Kane, "'Germany More Democratic Than Ever,'" 2.

10. "A Democratic Demurrer," *New Orleans Item,* November 4, 1938, p. 4.

11. Rufus C. Harris to Charles Rosen, February 7, 1938, Presidents Record Group: Rufus C. Harris Papers, University Archives, Special Collections, Howard-Tilton Memorial Library, Tulane University, New Orleans, Middle American Research Institute (M.A.R.I.): 1939–1940, Indexed Correspondence.

12. Krammer, *Undue Process,* 4.

13. Dickerson, *Inside America's Concentration Camps,* 149.

14. See Krammer on the wildly disparate figures on the German population in the United States at the start of the war and membership numbers in the German-American Bund (*Undue Process,* 4–5).

15. After the death of Roger Stone in 1983, Doris Stone served as the president of the Zemurray Foundation. She died in 1994.

16. Rufus Harris, letter to Samuel K. Lothrop, June 27, 1940, Presidents Record Group: Rufus C. Harris Papers, University Archives, Special Collections, Howard-Tilton Memorial Library, Tulane University, New Orleans, Middle American Research Institute (M.A.R.I.): 1939–1940, Indexed Correspondence.

17. S. K. Lothrop, postcard to Rufus Harris, July 1, 1940, Presidents Record Group: Rufus C. Harris Papers, University Archives, Special Collections, Howard-Tilton Memorial Library, Tulane University, New Orleans, Middle American Research Institute (M.A.R.I.): 1939–1940, Indexed Correspondence. Lothrop's grammatical errors in the Spanish terms suggest an imperfect command of the language.

18. Price, *Anthropological Intelligence,* xvii.

19. Price, *Anthropological Intelligence,* 203.

20. Price, *Anthropological Intelligence,* 203. Roger Stone, Doris Stone's husband, was also identified as well informed and potentially useful (Price, *Anthropological Intelligence,* 306n6).

21. Price, *Anthropological Intelligence,* 204–5.

22. Frans Blom, letter to Rufus Harris, July 22, 1940, Presidents Record Group: Rufus C. Harris Papers, University Archives, Special Collections, Howard-Tilton Memorial Library, Tulane University, New Orleans, Middle American Research Institute (M.A.R.I.): 1939–1940, Indexed Correspondence.

23. Rufus Harris, letter to Frans Blom, August 5, 1940, Presidents Record Group: Rufus C. Harris Papers, University Archives, Special Collections, Howard-Tilton Memorial Library, Tulane University, New Orleans, Middle American Research Institute (M.A.R.I.): 1939–1940, Indexed Correspondence.

24. Doris Stone, letter to Samuel Zemurray, May 12, 1941 (copy), Presidents Record Group: Rufus C. Harris Papers, University Archives, Special Collections, Howard-Tilton Memorial Library,

Tulane University, New Orleans, Middle American Research Institute (M.A.R.I.): 1939–1940, Indexed Correspondence.

25. Stone was no doubt speaking of Nelson Rockefeller and the Office of the Coordinator for Inter-American Affairs, a US government agency promoting inter-American cooperation, especially in economic and business arenas during the 1940s. Roosevelt had appointed Rockefeller as coordinator of inter-American affairs. The agency's purpose was to counter German and Italian propaganda in the Americas through the distribution of news, films, and advertising. In 1945, the agency was renamed the Office of Inter-American Affairs.

26. Leifer et al., *Restless Blood*, provides a chronology of Blom's demise as the director of MARI:

> During 1940 Frans's drinking and indifference towards M.A.R.I. reached new heights and finally, after they had let him have a long leash for a long time, the board at Tulane intervened. On November 14, 1940, the letter which Frans must long have suspected was on its way finally arrived: Blom had been suspended as director of the institute and Ries and the librarian Arthur Gropp were to take over until further notice. Frans was allowed to keep a position as a member of the archaeological staff, and it was still hoped "that when this period is over Mr. Blom may be able to undertake his duties as Director once more and carry them on as he used to do." But the problems had only just begun. A short time after Ries and Gropp had taken over the management at M.A.R.I. they discovered that the institute had accumulated a debt amounting to the astronomical sum of $50,000 and, even worse, that the university administration had never been informed of this debt. It seems that Frans had been even worse at controlling the finances than his predecessor Gates. Tulane's president Harris had to ask for help from Samuel Zemurray, who responded by donating the large amount to the bankrupt institute. Ries and Gropp also initiated a major clean-up in the library and in the collections of artifacts, partly in order to find out what might perhaps belong to Frans Blom personally, and once again they encountered a mess which was embarrassingly similar to that which Blom had taken over from Gates. . . . In the spring of 1941, Frans was back in New Orleans—still an alcoholic and still in desperate need of money. He therefore began to make claims on the archaeological artifacts in M.A.R.I's collections which he maintained belonged to him. This led to an investigation which later that same year ended in a minor scandal. (193)

27. Rufus Harris, letter to Hermann Beyer, August 16, 1941, and Hermann Beyer, letter to Rufus Harris, September 6, 1941, Presidents Record Group: Rufus C. Harris Papers, University Archives, Special Collections, Howard-Tilton Memorial Library, Tulane University, New Orleans, Middle American Research Institute (M.A.R.I.): 1939–1940, Indexed Correspondence.

28. Rufus Harris, letter to Doris Stone, January 29, 1942, Presidents Record Group: Rufus C. Harris Papers, University Archives, Special Collections, Howard-Tilton Memorial Library, Tulane University, New Orleans, Middle American Research Institute (M.A.R.I.): 1939–1940, Indexed Correspondence. Harris had heard that Beyer had been "abusive" of him and other Tulane colleagues, believing the president to be responsible for encouraging the authorities to investigate and ultimately arrest Beyer: "He believes this because I warned him last summer when the German consulates were closed that it might be well for him to leave the country and return

to Germany and the Hitler he espoused while he could do so." Harris also shared with Stone his efforts to resolve problems regarding Frans Blom's departure from the university, reportedly due to chronic alcoholism.

29. Rufus Harris, letter to Doris Stone, February 25, 1942, Presidents Record Group: Rufus C. Harris Papers, University Archives, Special Collections, Howard-Tilton Memorial Library, Tulane University, New Orleans, Middle American Research Institute (M.A.R.I.): 1939–1940, Indexed Correspondence.

30. "Fort Sam Houston (detention facility)," Densho Encyclopedia.

31. See "Ft. Sam Houston Census 1942" at German American Internee Coalition, https://gaic.info/wp-content/uploads/2015/10/Ft.-Sam-Houston-census-1942.pdf.

32. Censorship intercept of Hermann Beyer to Bertha Initze, June 29, 1942, Records of the Enemy Alien Information Bureau, Office of the Provost Marshal General, RG 389, Box 9, NA.

33. I could not locate a reference to Stringtown as a "Negro penitentiary," but did discover some of its history: "A Correctional Center has stood in Stringtown since the early 1930s; at various times it has been a venereal disease hospital, a prisoner-of-war camp, and a vocational training school" (Simpson, *The Mammoth Book of Prison Breaks*, 120).

34. Walter Kohner worked alongside his brother, Paul Kohner, a Hollywood talent agent and producer who managed the careers of Ingrid Bergman, Maurice Chevalier, Greta Garbo, Marlene Dietrich, Jon Huston, Liv Ullman, and other European actors who came to the United States prior to World War II. Kohner's wife, Hanna, was the first noncelebrity featured on the television program *This Is Your Life* in 1953; she spoke in that episode of her experience in concentration and death camps during the Holocaust.

35. Kohner and Kohner, *Hanna and Walter*, 60.

36. Kohner and Kohner, *Hanna and Walter*, 61.

37. Kohner and Kohner, *Hanna and Walter*, 62. Kohner's account of conditions for internees at Stringtown varies significantly from Beyer's, as Kohner described the camp hospital as "outfitted with the latest modern therapeutic equipment and x-ray machines" (*Hanna and Walter*, 63).

38. *Times Picayune*, February 26, 1943, 2, and *New Orleans Item*, February 25, 1943, 1.

39. Wauchope, "Hermann Beyer," 439.

40. Transcript of Thomas Niehaus, oral history interview of Maurice Ries, September 21, 1978, Collection 63, MARI Series, folder 8, Latin American Library, Tulane University.

41. Transcript of Thomas Niehaus, oral history interview of Maurice Ries, September 21, 1978, Collection 63, MARI Series, folder 8, Latin American Library, Tulane University.

42. Caso, "Hermann Beyer," 29.

43. Caso, "Hermann Beyer," 30.

44. Alfonso Caso y Andrade also served as the rector of the Universidad Nacional Autónoma de México from 1944 to 1945.

45. Linga, "Hermann Beyer," 34. The same issue of the *Boletín* contains articles or notices on the establishment of the African-American Studies Group in Mexico in 1943, the death of Bronislaw Malinowski, known as the founder of social anthropology, and the work of Frank Boas in Mexico, as well as a slew of book reviews on topics in general and physical anthropology, linguistics, folklore, ethnology, and archaeology.

46. Beyer's alien enemy name file at the National Archives includes an envelope from the

War Department with his name that contains a trunk key and the date May 3, 1943. Regarding Wauchope's efforts, see Robert Wauchope, letter to R. A. Guerin, February 5, 1943, and to Office of Alien Property Custodian, Francis J. McNamara, July 8, 1943, Presidents Record Group: Rufus C. Harris Papers, University Archives, Special Collections, Howard-Tilton Memorial Library, Tulane University, New Orleans, Middle American Research Institute (M.A.R.I.): 1939–1940, Indexed Correspondence.

47. Gropp, "Hermann Beyer's Last Years," 35.

48. Gropp, "Hermann Beyer's Last Years," 36.

49. Gropp, "Hermann Beyer's Last Years," 38.

50. "Mexican Expert on Writings of Maya Indians Visits S.A.," *San Antonio Express*, May 17, 1951, 1B.

51. Phone conversation and personal interview with Marcello Canuto, July 29, 2019, MARI.

52. Boghardt, *Spies of the Kaiser*, 132.

53. Boghardt, *Spies of the Kaiser*, 123. Von der Goltz married for a second time on November 24, 1948, to Else M. Hartman, in Wilmington, Delaware. Delaware Marriage Records, 1944–1949.

54. Von der Goltz, *My Adventures as a German Secret Service Agent*, 153. A digitized copy of a 1918 edition of the book published by Cassell is available at https://ia600205.us.archive.org/30/items/myadventuresasgeoogoltrich/myadventuresasgeoogoltrich.pdf.

55. Von der Goltz, *My Adventures as a German Secret Service Agent*, 205–6.

56. Von der Goltz, *My Adventures as a German Secret Service Agent*, 126.

57. Boghardt, *Spies of the Kaiser*, 126.

58. Von der Goltz's file includes a letter Dorothy Wisoff and Eugene Perkin sent him on February 23, 1939, on letterhead of the New York City Region of Young Judaea praising him for his ability to "unite many organizations into one evening, without any political red tape attached to it." Identifying themselves explicitly as a Zionist youth organization in the letter, they concluded, "Wishing you the best of luck in this noble undertaking of giving an opportunity to all races in order to bring out the high lights of their existence and their contribution to American Democracy in a form of Pageantry and Folk Dance." RG 60 COR 146-13, Enemy Alien Files 230/25/23/4, Box 439, NA.

59. RG 60 COR 146-13, Enemy Alien Files 230/25/23/4, Box 439, NA.

60. Drolet, "The Aryan Order of America," 63.

61. Memo for the Alien Enemy Hearing Board, May 14, 1943, RG 60 COR 146-13, Enemy Alien Files 230/25/23/4, Box 439, NA.

62. Memo for the Chief of Review, June 4, 1943, RG 60 COR 146-13, Enemy Alien Files 230/25/23/4, Box 439, NA.

63. RG 60 COR 146-13, Enemy Alien Files 230/25/23/4, Box 439, NA. The State Department name file (RG 59, Box 539, NA) offers additional details on von der Goltz's case,

64. Horst von der Goltz to Margaret (Peggy) Cooper Gay von der Goltz, undated. RG 60 COR 146-13, Enemy Alien Files 230/25/23/4, RG 60, Box 439, NA

65. Memo for the Chief of Review, June 4, 1943, RG 60 COR 146-13, Enemy Alien Files 230/25/23/4, RG 60, Box 439, NA.

66. Edward Ennis to Willard Kelly, June 2, 1943, RG 60 COR 146-13, Enemy Alien Files 230/25/23/4, Box 439, NA.

67. Margaret (Peggy) von der Goltz to Edward Ennis, June 15, 1943, in RG 60 COR 146-13, Enemy Alien Files 230/25/23/4, Box 439, NA.

68. Margaret (Peggy) Cooper Gay von der Goltz to Edward Ennis, June 22, 1943, in RG 60 COR 146-13, Enemy Alien Files 230/25/23/4, Box 439, NA.

69. Margaret (Peggy) Cooper Gay von der Goltz to Edward Ennis, August 30, 1943, in RG 60 COR 146-13, Enemy Alien Files 230/25/23/4, Box 439, NA.

70. Daniel Cranford Smith, July 3, 1943, in RG 60 COR 146-13, Enemy Alien Files 230/25/23/4, Box 439, NA.

71. Quoted in RG 60 COR 146-13, Enemy Alien Files 230/25/23/4, Box 439, NA.

72. RG 60 COR 146-13, Enemy Alien Files 230/25/23/4, Box 439, NA.

73. Dorothy Waring to Thomas Cooley, March 20, 1944, RG 60 COR 146-13, Enemy Alien Files 230/25/23/4, Box 439, NA.

74. Report for Edward Ennis, February 16, 1945, RG 60 COR 146-13, Enemy Alien Files 230/25/23/4, Box 439, NA.

75. Horst von der Goltz to Edward Ennis, October 6, 1944, RG 60 COR 146-13, Enemy Alien Files 230/25/23/4, Box 439, NA.

76. John Ray Carlson to Thom Lord, October 9, 1944, RG 60 COR 146-13, Enemy Alien Files 230/25/23/4, Box 439, NA. Von der Goltz's Justice file includes a Friends of Democracy pamphlet that warns the public not to be taken in by figures such as Father Charles Coughlin, a Roman Catholic priest who in the 1930s had a weekly radio broadcast that reached an audience of some thirty million listeners, described as "a variation of the Fascist agenda applied to American culture" (DiStasi, *Excerpts from Una Storia Segreta*, 163). Initially a supporter of Franklin Roosevelt and his New Deal policy, Father Coughlin later became a harsh critic and formed his own National Union for Social Justice. The program was eventually forced off the air in 1939 due to its pro-Fascist and antisemitic rhetoric. See Hilmes, *Only Connect*, 144–46.

77. *Congressional Record*—House, February 14, 1945, 1104, https://www.govinfo.gov/content/pkg/GPO-CRECB-1945-pt1/pdf/GPO-CRECB-1945-pt1-28-1.pdf.

78. Horst von der Goltz to Willard Kelly, April 15, 1945, RG 60 COR 146-13, Enemy Alien Files 230/25/23/4, Box 439, NA

79. Raymond Bunker to Edward Ennis, April 28, 1945, and Edward Ennis to Horst von der Goltz, May 3, 1945, RG 60 COR 146-13, Enemy Alien Files 230/25/23/4, Box 439, NA.

80. Stuart Krinsly to John F. Dailey Jr., December 15, 1945, RG 60 COR 146-13, Enemy Alien Files 230/25/23/4, Box 439, NA.

81. James Sheldon's confidential memo of December 18, 1945 and Dudley Parsons's December 20, 1945 letter to the Hearing Board are included in RG 60 COR 146-13, Enemy Alien Files 230/25/23/4, Box 439, NA.

82. Comments of Edward Ennis, Willard Kelly, and John Burling are included in an excerpt of the Alien Enemy Repatriation Hearing Board held at Ellis Island, December 19, 1945, RG 60 COR 146-13, Enemy Alien Files 230/25/23/4, Box 439, NA.

83. John Dailey to Thomas M. Cooley II, June 5, 1946, RG 60 COR 146-13, Enemy Alien Files 230/25/23/4, Box 439, NA.

84. Read Lewis to Department of Justice, August 8, 1946, RG 60 COR 146-13, Enemy Alien Files 230/25/23/4, Box 439, NA.

85. John Dailey to Thomas M. Cooley II, August 23, 1946. RG 60 COR 146-13, Enemy Alien Files 230/25/23/4, Box 439, NA

86. Gormin, "Close Pal of Hitler Held in Algiers Detention Unit," *Times-Picayune*, March 30, 1946, 1.

87. Ludecke, *I Knew Hitler*, 190.

88. Ludecke, *I Knew Hitler*, 193.

89. Ludecke, *I Knew Hitler*, 213.

90. RG 60 COR 146-13, Enemy Alien Files, Box 318, NA. Other details on Ludecke's case are drawn from RG 59, file 740.00115, European War 1939/5819, Box 2841, NA.

91. Also known as the Röhm Purge, the Night of the Long Knives, and Operation Hummingbird, the 1934 Blood Purge marked the summary execution of many members of the Nazi paramilitary formation the Sturmabteilungen (Storm Troopers, or SA) between June 30 and July 2 of that year. On the order of Nazi Party leader and Reich Chancellor Adolf Hitler, SA Chief of Staff Ernst Röhm and other political enemies on the German nationalist right were executed, enabling Hitler to proclaim himself führer of National Socialist Germany and to claim absolute power. Kurt von Schleicher, the last chancellor of the Weimar Republic, and his wife were also killed in the purge. Recent scholarship on this transition is compiled in Beck and Jones, *From Weimar to Hitler*.

92. Quoted in RG 60 COR 146-13, Enemy Alien Files, Box 318, NA. Schuman was author of *The Nazi Dictatorship: A Study in Social Pathology and the Politics of Fascism*. He reviewed *I Knew Hitler* in *New York Herald Tribune Books* on November 14, 1937, according to documents in his Justice file.

93. *Spectator*, March 4, 1938, 374.

94. *Coshocton Tribune*, December 20, 1939, 8.

95. FBI Form 1, File number 54-291, May 8, 1940, in RG 60 COR 146-13, Enemy Alien Files, Box 318, NA.

96. Kurt Ludecke to Claude Bragdon, December 2, 1941, in RG 60 COR 146-13, Enemy Alien Files, Box 318, NA.

97. Department of Justice Alien Enemy Hearing Board Report regarding January 16, 1942, hearing, RG 60 COR 146-13, Enemy Alien Files, Box 318, NA

98. Kurt Ludecke to Cordell Hull, January 12, 1943, RG 59, 740.00115, European War 1939 / 5819, Box 2841, NA.

99. Both quotes are from Ludecke's narrative about himself in the autobiographical sketch that accompanied his letter to Secretary of State Cordell Hull, January 12, 1943, RG 59, 740.00115, European War 1939 / 5819, Box 2841, NA.

100. Kurt Ludecke to W. F. Kelly, November 17, 1943, RG 60 COR 146-13, Enemy Alien Files, Box 318, NA.

101. It is no small irony that Ludecke was finally interned at Algiers, where a large group of Jewish internees from Latin America had been released in the summer of 1943. According to Arthur Smith, he had a substantial history of antisemitic activity and at one point had even "launched an anti-Semitic monthly publication he called the 'American Guard,' but succeeded in publishing only one issue before his funds ran out" (Smith, "Kurt Ludecke," 599).

102. Kurt Ludecke to Walter F. Miller, August 1, 1944, RG 60 COR 146-13, Enemy Alien Files, Box 318, NA.

103. Raymond E. Bunker to Edward J. Ennis, September 13, 1944, RG 60 COR 146-13, Enemy Alien Files, Box 318, NA.

104. Willard Kelly to Pentagon, November 19, 1945. RG 60 COR 146-13, Enemy Alien Files, Box 318, NA.

105. Kelly was presumably referring to the "Battle of the Bulge," also known as the Ardennes Counteroffensive, which occurred from December 16, 1944, to January 25, 1945. It was the last important German offensive on the western front of World War II. Comments of Edward Ennis, Willard Kelly, and John Burling are included in the excerpt of the Alien Enemy Repatriation Hearing Board held at Ellis Island, December 17, 1945.

106. Quoted in Griffin, "Constitutional Law," 404.

107. Griffin, "Constitutional Law," 404.

108. Griffin, "Constitutional Law," 404–5.

109. Griffin, "Constitutional Law," 405.

110. Vladek, "Ludecke's Lengthening Shadow," 54–55.

111. See, for example, Maria Clark's "Louisiana's Prisons Are Increasingly Being Used to Detain Immigrants," *Times-Picayune,* May 8, 2019. Cokie and Steve Roberts argued in a May 15, 2019, column titled "Trump Makes War on Legal Immigration" that "Trump has waged a ruthless scorched earth campaign against many forms of legal immigration," despite employing rhetoric claiming to only oppose undocumented immigrants. *Advocate,* May 15, 2019, 7B.

112. 'Arafa, "Donald Trump's Muslim Travel Ban," Jurist.org, https://www.jurist.org/commentary/2019/04/mohamed-arafa-donald-trumps-travel-ban/.

113. See Johnson, "'This Is Sick,'" *Common Dreams,* June 12, 2019, https://www.commondreams.org/news/2019/06/12/sick-horror-trump-administration-plans-detain-migrant-children-former-japanese and Del Valle, "Survivors of Japanese Internment," *Vice News,* June 14, 2019, https://news.vice.com/en_us/article/vb9qzj/survivors-of-japanese-internment-are-horrified-trump-is-using-a-former-facility-to-detain-migrant-kids. Del Valle cites Japanese-American psychotherapist Satsuki Ina, who grew up in the Tule Lake Segregation Center, a World War II internment camp in Newell City, California, and has studied the effects of detention on migrant children: "I know what's happening to these children will have a lasting impact on their mental health. Indefinite detention is a form of torture."

CHAPTER 5.
ROYALS AND NOBLES BEHIND BARBED WIRE

1. Given the 1940 date, it is likely that the "Hebrews" from Germany and Poland were technically stateless as well, since the Nazi government did not recognize non-Aryan persons as citizens after November 1939.

2. "Wachtmeister, Axel. Dominican Republic," RG 60, Class 146-13, Enemy Alien File 146-13-2-245, Box 688, NA.

3. RG 59, R740.00115 European War (1939) / 5960 PS /EPM, Box 2841, NA.

4. Special War Problems, Reports on War Relocation Centers, 1942–1946, RG 59, Box 20, NA.

5. RG 59, R740.00115 European War (1939) / 5960 PS /EPM, Box 2841, NA.

6. Axel Wachtmeister to Swedish Embassy, May 30, 1942, "Wachtmeister, Axel. Dominican Republic," RG 60, Class 146-13, Enemy Alien File 146-13-2-245, Box 688, NA.

7. "Wachtmeister, Axel. Dominican Republic," RG 60, Class 146-13, Enemy Alien File 146-13-

2-245, Box 688, NA. Santo Domingo was referred to as Ciudad Trujillo from 1936 to 1961, during the dictatorship of Rafael Trujillo.

8. Indoff's name does not appear on an October 31 list of German detainees at Camp Kenedy, however, suggesting he had been released before that date ("List of Detainees at Camp Kenedy, Texas, Oct. 31, 1942," RG 389, Box 3, Records of the Alien Enemy Information Bureau, NA, http://gaic.info/wp-content/uploads/2016/10/31-Oct-1940-Kenedy-census.pdf).

9. "Wachtmeister, Axel. Dominican Republic," RG 60, Class 146-13, Enemy Alien File 146-13-2-245, Box 688, NA.

10. Edward P. Lawton to Department of Justice, June 17, 1942, "Wachtmeister, Axel. Dominican Republic," RG 60, Class 146-13, Enemy Alien File 146-13-2-245, Box 688, NA.

11. Roorda, "The Dominican Republic," 87.

12. See for example, Mayes, *The Mulatto Republic*.

13. Between 1937 and 1987, more than fifty estimates of the number of Haitians killed were put forward, ranging from five hundred to thirty-five thousand, according to Roorda. "Genocide Next Door," 301. In 2015, Greg Grandin ("Concentration Camps in the Dominican Republic?") and others questioned whether the Dominican Republic was rehabilitating the concentration camp model as Dominicans of Haitian descent faced persistent threats of deportation and detention.

14. The Lend-Lease Act, passed in March 1941, authorized Franklin D. Roosevelt to provide military equipment to countries the United States argued were vital to US defense.

15. Roorda, "The Dominican Republic," 79.

16. Quoted in Edward P. Lawton to Department of Justice, June 17, 1942, "Wachtmeister, Axel. Dominican Republic," RG 60, Class 146-13, Enemy Alien File 146-13-2-245, Box 688, NA.

17. Roorda, "The Dominican Republic," 82.

18. RG 59, R740.00115 European War (1939) / 5960 PS /EPM, Box 2841, NA.

19. Quoted in RG 60, Class 146-13, Enemy Alien File 146-13-2-245, Box 688, NA.

20. Historians have debated the neutrality of Sweden and other countries that claimed to be neutral. See, for example, Hagglof, "A Test of Neutrality."

21. RG 59, R740.00115 European War (1939) / 5957 PS /EPM, Box 2841, NA.

22. Edward Ennis to Willard Kelly, November 28, 1942, RG 60, Class 146-13, Enemy Alien File 146-13-2-245, Box 688, NA.

23. Wollmar Bolström to Breckenridge Long, January 4, 1943. RG 59, R740.00115 European War (1939) / 5962, Box 2841, NA.

24. Quoted in Wollmar Bolström to Breckenridge Long, January 4, 1943, RG 59, R740.00115 European War (1939) / 5962, Box 2841, NA.

25. Wollmar Bolström to Breckenridge Long, January 4, 1943, RG 59, R740.00115 European War (1939) / 5962, Box 2841, NA.

26. "Hohenlohe (Waldenburg), Stephanie von," RG 60, A1COR 146-13, File 146-13-2-62-4, Box 653, NA.

27. Schad, *Hitler's Spy Princess*, 2.

28. Talbot, *The Devil's Chessboard*, 31–33. Talbot also confirms details of Stephanie Hohenlohe's relationship with Hitler's adjutant Fritz Wiedemann and the death of her aunt in a concentration camp.

29. Princess Stephanie Hohenlohe Papers, Hoover Institution Archives, Box 5.

30. Wilson, *Nazi Princess*, 30.

31. Jim Wilson surmises that Prince Hohenlohe had financial motives for the marriage. *Nazi Princess*, 31.

32. Wilson, *Nazi Princess*, 32.

33. "Memorandum re: Princess Stephanie Von Hohenlohe Waldenburg, with Aliases," October 28, 1941, FDR Library, Safe Files Box 3, http://docs.fdrlibrary.marist.edu/PSF/BOX3/a31a01.html.

34. Wilson, *Nazi Princess*, 28.

35. Wilson, *Nazi Princess*, 33.

36. Wilson, *Nazi Princess*, 40.

37. Urbach notes that Rothermere's biographer did not attribute to Lord Rothermere a "genuine interest in the Nazi ideology" but rather portrayed him as a "good appeaser" who could lead Hitler on, so that Britain could build its air force. Urbach considers this interpretation of his actions as "rather generous," however. His pro-Nazi article "Youth Triumphant" was received enthusiastically at Nazi Party headquarters and was the spur for the Hitler-Rothermere correspondence that began in 1933. *Go-Betweens for Hitler*, 233–235.

38. Schad, *Hitler's Spy Princess*, 22.

39. Wilson, *Nazi Princess*, 49.

40. See Simkin, "Stephanie von Hohenlohe."

41. Wilson, *Nazi Princess*, 76.

42. Wilson, *Nazi Princess*, 125.

43. Quoted in Schad, *Hitler's Spy Princess*, 92. Hohenlohe herself may have recognized certain injustices in this arrangement, as with the help of her son Franz, she sent "a quantity of books, china, silver, furniture, etc." to Reinhardt in California, though "admittedly it was only junk" (Schad, *Hitler's Spy Princess*, 94–95).

44. Urbach, *Go-Betweens for Hitler*, 244.

45. Wilson, *Nazi Princess*, 34.

46. This characterization can be found in British Intelligence Public Record Office file PRO KV2/1696.

47. Schad, *Hitler's Spy Princess*, 104–5.

48. Schad, *Hitler's Spy Princess*, 106.

49. Schad, *Hitler's Spy Princess*, 112; Wilson, *Nazi Princess*, 133.

50. Wilson, *Nazi Princess*, 135.

51. Exhibit no. 40, RG 60, A1COR 146-13, Box 653, NA.

52. Wilson, *Nazi Princess*, 136.

53. Wilson, *Nazi Princess*, 143.

54. Quoted in Bahney, *Betrayer's Waltz*, 171.

55. Schad, *Hitler's Spy Princess*, 118–19.

56. For example, in November 1937, the couple had been received in New York by the German consul-general, but a hostile crowd was also on the dock, some bearing the message "Out with Wiedemann, the Nazy spy." See Wilson, *Nazi Princess*, 117.

57. Wilson, *Nazi Princess*, 152.

58. Schad, *Hitler's Spy Princess*, 122.

59. Wilson, *Nazi Princess*, 145, 153.

60. Wilson, *Nazi Princess*, 153.
61. Quoted in Bahney, *Betrayer's Waltz*, 174.
62. Wilson, *Nazi Princess*, 155–56.
63. "Memorandum re: Princess Stephanie von Hohenlohe, with Aliases."
64. Schad, *Hitler's Spy Princess*, 144.
65. Wilson, *Nazi Princess*, 160–61.
66. Wilson, *Nazi Princess*, 161.
67. Quoted in Schad, *Hitler's Spy Princess*, 151.
68. Krammer, *Undue Process*, 41.
69. Schad, *Hitler's Spy Princess*, 152.
70. Quoted in Schad, *Hitler's Spy Princess*, 152.
71. Franklin D Roosevelt to J. Edgar Hoover, June 17, 1942, "Hohenlohe (Waldenburg), Stephanie von," RG 60, A1COR 146-13, File 146-13-2-62-4, Box 653, NA.
72. Schad, *Hitler's Spy Princess*, 157.
73. Wilson, *Nazi Princess*, 166.
74. Schad, *Hitler's Spy Princess*, 160.
75. File 740.00115, European War 1939/5830, RG 59, Box 2841, NA.
76. RG 60, A1COR 146-13, Box 653, NA.
77. "Hohenlohe (Waldenburg), Stephanie von," RG 60, A1COR 146-13, File 146-13-2-62-4, Box 653, NA.
78. Comments of the special hearing board that convened at Seagoville showed a substantial disparity of opinion regarding Hohenlohe's bid for release but agreed on the whole that her unpopularity with other German internees was evidence of her being anti-Nazi. "Hohenlohe (Waldenburg), Stephanie von," RG 60, A1COR 146-13 File 146-13-2-62-4, Box 653, NA.
79. Report by Grace J. Hanna, "Hohenlohe (Waldenburg), Stephanie von," RG 60, A1COR 146-13 File 146-13-2-62-4, Box 653, NA.
80. A copy of Francis Hohenlohe's letter to his mother dated February 1, 1945, and marked "Confidential" is included in her Department of Justice file, "Hohenlohe (Waldenburg), Stephanie von," RG 60, A1COR 146-13 File 146-13-2-62-4, Box 653, NA.
81. W. F. Kelly to Amy N. Stannard, February 9, 1945, "Hohenlohe (Waldenburg), Stephanie von," RG 60, A1COR 146-13 File 146-13-2-62-4, Box 653, NA.
82. Francis Hohenlohe to Francis Bidle, March 3, 1945, "Hohenlohe (Waldenburg), Stephanie von," RG 60, A1COR 146-13 File 146-13-2-62-4, Box 653, NA.
83. Edward J. Ennis to Herbert Weschler, April 28, 1945, "Hohenlohe (Waldenburg), Stephanie von," RG 60, A1COR 146-13 File 146-13-2-62-4, Box 653, NA.
84. Schad, *Hitler's Spy Princess*, 161.
85. Wilson, *Nazi Princess*, 172.
86. Schad, *Hitler's Spy Princess*, 161.
87. Wilson, *Nazi Princess*, 173; Schad, *Hitler's Spy Princess*, 164.
88. A description and photos of the property can be found at https://www.cobbleclose.com/.
89. Schad, *Hitler's Spy Princess*, 165.
90. Schad, *Hitler's Spy Princess*, 166.
91. Wilson, *Nazi Princess*, 175.

92. Schad, *Hitler's Spy Princess*, 167–69.
93. Hohenlohe, *Steph*, 205.
94. Hohenlohe, *Steph*, 5.
95. Hohenlohe, *Steph*, 165.
96. Hohenlohe, *The G.I. Prince*, 177.
97. Hohenlohe, *The G.I. Prince*, 186.
98. Hohenlohe, *The G.I. Prince*, 195.

CHAPTER 6.
AID ORGANIZATIONS, DIPLOMATIC EFFORTS, AND COMMUNITY ALLIES

1. Axel Wachtmeister's case (chapter 5) shows that other diplomatic personnel, such as Wollmar Boström, who served as the Swedish minister in Washington from 1925 to 1945, were also instrumental in representing certain internees.

2. Many German Jewish internees also received financial assistance that permitted their emigration to the Americas from the Judischer Hilfsverein (Aid Association of German Jews). See Shoah Resource Center, "Hilfsverein der Deutschen Juden," https://www.yadvashem.org/odot_pdf/Microsoft%20Word%20-%206371.pdf.

3. "Gordon, Emanuel. Dominican Republic," Name Files of Interned Enemy Aliens from Latin America, 1942–48, RG 59, Special War Problems, Box 40, NA.

4. Images of this work and others by Nussbaum can be viewed in the Yad Vashem digital archive. See the "Art from the Holocaust" collection, https://www.yadvashem.org/yv/en/exhibitions/art/index.asp, and https://www.yadvashem.org/articles/general/felix-nussbaum.html. For a biographical synopsis of Nussbaum, see https://www.yadvashem.org/yv/en/exhibitions/art/nussbaum.asp.

5. Many related documents in the JDC Archives are available digitally at https://archives.jdc.org/.

6. Wells, *Tropical Zion*, 51–53.

7. "Gordon, Emanuel. Dominican Republic," Name Files of Interned Enemy Aliens from Latin America, 1942–48, RG 59, Special War Problems, Box 40, NA.

8. For more details on the operation of Sosúa, see Kaplan, *Dominican Haven*.

9. Internment officials generally sought to avoid using the term "parole" due to its association with incarceration or imprisonment.

10. Both the April 18 and April 20 letters bearing Manheimer's name are archived in Jewish Welfare Board War Correspondence, 1917–1954, Series 04: Corps Areas (1941–1949), Tennessee Camp Forest [sic], Ancestry.com. Original data: National Jewish Welfare Board, Army-Navy Division Records, I-180, American Jewish Historical Society, New York.

11. The sum of $2,000 (1942) would be equivalent to about $31,190 in 2019 dollars, according to consumer price index calculations (https://www.officialdata.org/).

12. Otto Manheimer and Salomon Lagstein to HIAS, April 18, 1942, Jewish Welfare Board War Correspondence, 1917–1954, Series 04: Corps Areas (1941–1949), Tennessee Camp Forest [sic], Ancestry.com. Original data: National Jewish Welfare Board, Army-Navy Division Records, I-180, American Jewish Historical Society, New York, accessed on Ancestry.com.

13. Peter Bohm et al., to Rabbi Nathan Witkins, April 20, 1942, Jewish Welfare Board War

Correspondence, 1917–1954, Series 04: Corps Areas (1941–1949), Tennessee Camp Forest [sic], Ancestry.com. Original data: National Jewish Welfare Board, Army-Navy Division Records, I-180, American Jewish Historical Society, New York, accessed on Ancestry.com.

14. Otto Manheimer to George Berke, Chairman, Refugee Committee, Chattanooga, Tenn., 5 August 1943, Razovsky Papers, Box 3, Folder: NRS: Jews Interned at Detentions Centers in Southwest US, 1941–1943, American Jewish Historical Society Archives, New York. Quoted in Zucker, *Cecilia Razovsky*, 141–42.

15. Zucker, *Cecilia Razovsky*, 178–79.

16. Razovsky's *What Every Emigrant Should Know: A Simple Pamphlet for the Guidance and Benefit of Prospective Immigrants to the United States* (1922) and *What Every Woman Should Know about Citizenship* (1926) are available online at https://alexanderstreet.com/. *What Every Emigrant Should Know* is also available in an interactive archive at Internet Archive, https://archive.org.

17. Razovsky was also involved in the unsuccessful efforts to avert the tragedy of the SS *St. Louis*, a ship that sailed in May 1939 from Europe with 937 passengers aboard, most of them Jews fleeing persecution, only to find that officials in their destination city of Havana refused to allow them to land, sparking a desperate and failed attempt to find safe harbor in the United States and Canada before returning to Europe, where many of the passengers ultimately perished in concentration camps. See Zucker, *Cecilia Razovsky*, 110–13.

18. Cecilia Razovsky, *Vos Yede Froy Darf Visen Vegen Birgershaft*, or *What Every Woman Should Know about Citizenship* (New York: Department of Immigrant Aid, National Council of Jewish Women, 1926). The Cable Act of 1922 (ch. 411, 42 Stat. 1021, "Married Women's Independent Nationality Act"), also known as the Married Women's Citizenship Act or the Women's Citizenship Act, granted women independent female citizenship but only for those who were married to an "alien eligible to naturalization." At the time of the law's passage, for example, Asian aliens were not considered to be racially eligible for US citizenship.

19. "She negotiated with representatives of, among others, Cuba, Panama, Trinidad, the Dominican Republic, Costa Rica, Venezuela, British Honduras, Guatemala, Peru, Bolivia and Chile. Her primary objective was to persuade the governments of these countries to allow the entrance of Jewish refugees from Europe" (Zucker, *Cecilia Razovsky*, 106).

20. Zucker provides a more lengthy chronology of Razovsky's work with refugees, as well as a list of her memberships. *Cecilia Razovsky*, 175–79.

21. Philip Roth's 2004 novel *The Plot against America* dramatizes this fear by imagining the election of the pro-Nazi Charles Lindberg in 1940 rather than Franklin D. Roosevelt, leading to an alliance of the United States with the Third Reich and Fascist projects on the domestic front, such as the construction of concentration camps in the state of Montana by the Department of the Interior (56).

22. See the profile of Razovsky on the "One Thousand Children" page at Yivo.org, https://onethousandandchildren.yivo.org/Cecilia-Razovsky.

23. Ann S. Petluck to Joseph E. Beck, December 3, 1943, Razovsky Papers, MKM 123.26, file 542, American Jewish Historical Society Archives.

24. See Benjamin, *Selected Writings*. 422n34.

25. Hannah Arendt includes the details of Benjamin's suicide in her introduction to Benjamin's *Illuminations*, 17–18.

26. Quoted in Zucker, *Cecilia Razovsky,* 139.

27. See Zucker, *Cecilia Razovsky,* 139–40, for details on Razovsky's negotiations with government officials in late 1942.

28. "Irene Wolff to Cecilia Razovsky, 5 June 1942," Chamberlain Papers, Folder 49, American Jewish Historical Society Archives, cited in Zucker, *Cecilia Razovsky,* 143, 152n82.

29. "Eric Joseph, Camp Forrest, Tenn., to Razovsky, 9 November 1942," and "Siegwart Fechenbach, Camp Forrest, Tenn., to Razovsky, 4 February, 1943," NRS Records, Folder 537, American Jewish Historical Society Archives.

30. "Lucy Kallman to Cecilia Razovsky, 7 March, 1943," and "Cecilia Razovsky to Lucy Kallman, 15 March, 1943," NRS Records, MKM 13.26, American Jewish Historical Society Archives.

31. "Cecilia Razovsky to Leo Gitlin, Enemy Alien Control Unit, 28 April 1943," Razovsky Papers, Box 3, Folder: Treatment of Enemy Aliens in Wartime, n.d., American Jewish Historical Society Archives, cited in Zucker, *Cecilia Razovsky,* 145.

32. RG 85, Entry 9, 17W3, 11/3/6, Immigration and Naturalization Service Records, NA.

33. It took all these groups' efforts "to untangle the bureaucratic red tape and combat the antisemitism that caused the incarceration of eighty one Jews from Latin American in hostile enemy internment camps in the United States," writes Zucker, *Cecilia Razovsky,* 145.

34. "Cecilia Razovsky to Albert Abrahamson, 8 February 1943," MKM 13.26, NRS Records, American Jewish Historical Society Archives.

35. NRS representative Jules Seitz's Field Report dated February 25, 1943, indicates the Jewish internees from Camp Kenedy had yet to arrive at Algiers. See more on the contents of this report in chapter 1.

36. "Walter Wolff, Camp Algiers, Louisiana, to Razovsky, 17 April 1943," NRS Records, Folder: Jews Interned at Detention Centers in Southwest US, 1941–1943, American Jewish Historical Society Archives, cited in Zucker, *Cecilia Razovsky,* 142.

37. An April 12 memo included Wolff's name among those whose documents had been turned over to the AECU, along with a shorter list of those whose preinterview portfolios still needed work. "Cecilia Razovsky to Augusta Myerson, 12 April 1943," NRS Records, American Jewish Historical Society Archives.

38. Friedman, *Nazis and Good Neighbors,* 161.

39. "Cecilia Razovsky to Joseph Beck, 17 June, 1943," NRS Records, American Jewish Historical Society Archives.

40. Summary of Department of Justice files in "Gordon, Emanuel. Dominican Republic," Name Files of Interned Enemy Aliens from Latin America, 1942–48, RG 59, Special War Problems, Box 40, NA.

41. "Cecilia Razovsky to Joseph Beck, E. Gomberg, Dorothy Kahn, Augusta Myerson, Dorothy Spielburg, 6 July 1943," NRS Records, MKM 13.26, File 542, American Jewish Historical Society Archives.

42. "Gordon, Emanuel. Dominican Republic," Name Files of Interned Enemy Aliens from Latin America, 1942–48, RG 59, Special War Problems, Box 40, NA.

43. "Emanuel Gordon, 14 Jul 1950," Citizenship Records, US Naturalization Record Indexes, 1771–1992 (indexed in World Archives Project).

44. "Grete and Leo Friedmann to Cecilia Razovsky, 11 April 1943," Razovsky Papers, Box 3,

Folder: Detainees in Internment Camps in the South, American Jewish Historical Society Archives, cited in Zucker, *Cecilia Razovsky*, 148, 153n100.

45. "Arthur D. Greenleigh to His Excellency, the Archbishop of New Orleans [Joseph Rummel], April 7, 1941," NRS Records, American Jewish Historical Society Archives. Arthur Greenleigh also occupied other important posts on the War Manpower Commission, supervising the rebuilding of Pearl Harbor, spearheading the JDC's efforts to help refugees in Italy and France, and as the executive director of the United Service for New Americans and its successor, United HIAS Service, which helped resettle Jewish survivors of the Holocaust. He was also an adviser to Presidents Harry S. Truman and Dwight D. Eisenhower on immigration issues at a moment when thousands of refugees were being turned away, and he advised the United Nations as the chairman of the International Conference of Non-governmental Organizations Interested in Migration.

46. On Rummel's contributions, see Mark Newman's 2018 study, *Desegregating Dixie: The Catholic Church in the South and Desegregation, 1945–1992*.

47. The title "On Way to New Life" ran with the photo. *New Orleans Item*, August 21, 1943, 5.

48. David Fichman to Albert Abrahamson, December 11, 1941, NRS Records, MGM 13.54, File 1129, American Jewish Historical Society Archives. Of course, the NRS was active throughout the country and in the international effort to help refugees. Eddie Friedman, a German Jew apprehended as an alien enemy in San Francisco, wrote to the NRS from his internment at Fort Lincoln, North Dakota, "I refrained up till now from asking your help because I thought you might be bothered enough with people's troubles. Now I am in such a jam that I have to ask for your kindly help" (quoted in Zucker, *Cecilia Razovsky*, 18). Fichman also wrote to Jules Seitz at the NRS office in New York, noting that the *Magallanes* had docked in New Orleans on October 2, 1942, with ten Jewish passengers aboard, of whom six had been detained. "We have been so far unable to ascertain from the Immigration Authorities the reasons for their detention," he wrote. David Fichman to Jules Seitz, October 6, 1942, NRS Records, MGM 13.54, American Jewish Historical Society Archives.

49. On the work of the New Orleans branch of the National Council of Jewish Women, especially its Service to Foreign Born Division, which came into existence during World War II, see Lawrence Powell's chapter "New Americans" in *Troubled Memory: Anne Levy, the Holocaust, and David Duke's Louisiana* (2019). Powell notes that the Displaced Persons Act of 1948 "required that Jews alone show proof of employment and housing before receiving visas" (365).

50. "David Fichman to the National Refugee Service, March 21, 1943," NRS Records, American Jewish Historical Society Archives.

EPILOGUE A New War on Aliens and Enemies

1. Rallying cries for the reimplementation and expansion of World War II–style detention and internment programs increased during the campaign and early administration of President Donald Trump, but there was substantial defense for them even before 2016. See, for example, Michelle Malkin's *In Defense of Internment: The Case for "Racial Profiling" in World War II and the War on Terror* (2004).

2. Gonzales, Richard. "America No Longer a 'Nation Of Immigrants,' USCIS Says."

3. Dickerson, *Inside America's Concentration Camps*, 217.

4. Dickerson, *Inside America's Concentration Camps*, 227–28.

5. See, for example Robinson, *A Tragedy of Democracy*.

6. An image of Bill Clinton, Presidential Letter of Apology, October 1, 1993, is available at https://www.pbs.org/childofcamp/history/clinton.html.

7. Russell, *The Train to Crystal City*, 320.

8. Quoted in Russell, *The Train to Crystal City*, 320.

9. Dickerson, *Inside America's Concentration Camps,* 229. He contends that "there are sociological, political, and practical reasons for those groups [German internees, Italian internees, and Jewish refugees] being overlooked for an apology and reparations, but the main reason is that Japanese Americans were rounded up and interned in such large numbers that it was impossible to ignore them for long" (231).

10. Dickerson, *Inside America's Concentration Camps*, 229.

11. The proceedings of the House hearing on *Treatment of Latin Americans of Japanese Descent, European Americans, and Jewish Refugees during World War II* are available at https://www.govinfo.gov/content/pkg/CHRG-111hhrg48322/html/CHRG-111hhrg48322.htm.

12. On the illegality of the enemy alien control program with regard to Japanese Peruvians in particular, see Saito, "Justice Held Hostage."

13. "The 1980 commission did detail the mistreatment of Japanese, German, and Italian Latin Americans, but only in the appendix of the report," she explained. "It also included one chapter, 13, on the mistreatment of German and Italian Americans in the United States," Lofgren clarified.

14. House of Representatives, Subcommittee on Immigration, Citizenship, Refugees, Border Security, and International Law, Committee on the Judiciary, Washington, DC, March 19, 2009, https://www.govinfo.gov/content/pkg/CHRG-111hhrg48322/html/CHRG-111hhrg48322.htm.

15. Testimony of Lidia Yamamoto in proceedings of the House of Representatives, Subcommittee on Immigration, Citizenship, Refugees, Border Security, and International Law. Committee on the Judiciary. Washington, DC, March 19, 2009, https://www.govinfo.gov/content/pkg/CHRG-111hhrg48322/html/CHRG-111hhrg48322.htm. On March 30, 2019, Yamamoto spoke before the Crystal City Pilgrimage Committee, which met at the site of the former Crystal City detention camp in Texas, where thousands of Japanese Latin Americans, Japanese Americans, and persons of German and Italian ancestry were confined by the US government during World War II. On the same day, the CCPC and Grassroots Leadership of Austin, Texas, staged a protest at the Dilley, Texas, immigration detention center, the largest migrant detention center for children and women in the United States, holding as many as twenty-five hundred people, including children under the age of one. "The March 30 actions were significant in that at least seven Japanese American former child detainees at Crystal City and several from other detention camps led both the remembrance of the Crystal City camp and also the protest of the unjust present-day detention of immigrants and separation of families at Dilley," according to John Ota of the CCPC. The group was planning other pilgrimages with the theme "Crystal City Hidden History, Justice Denied." Crystal City was the last World War II "concentration camp" to shut down, according to James Dickerson (*Inside America's Concentration Camps*, 214). It closed its doors on November 1, 1947. See John Ota, "Crystal City: Review of March Action and Plan for Return in November," https://www.rafu.com/2019/06/crystal-city-review-of-march-action-and-plan-for-return-in-november/.

16. See for example, "Bannerman to Fitch. 28 March 1944. USAT Cuba Memo; Box 71, Subject Files, 1939–1954, Box 7; Accession Job No. N3-59-87-15, Records of the Special War Problems Division, Department of State, NA—arrival and treatment of Latin Americans in Algiers, LA," in which Bannerman detailed the procedures taken with 540 Japanese and German internees from Latin America who arrived March 17, 1944, aboard the US Army transport *Cuba*. https://gaic.info/wp-content/uploads/2019/08/Bannerman-to-Fitch.pdf.

17. Brockell, "Geronimo and the Japanese Were Imprisoned There." See press release dated June 26, 2019, and titled "San Francisco Japantown Community Denounces Trump Concentration Camps" at https://www.facebook.com/sfjacl/posts/2393711337380285. A July 28, 2019, AP story reported the US Department of Health and Human Services said it had halted plans to house unaccompanied minors at the Oklahoma base, due to a drop in numbers: "Plan Halted to House Migrant Kids at Okla. Base," *New Orleans Advocate*, Sunday, July 28, 2019, 11A.

18. Andrea Pitzer locates the "world's first concentration camps" in Cuba, created by Spain in the lead-up to the island's independence as a Spanish colony (*One Long Night*, 3–4).

19. Danya Ruttenberg, "'Never Again' Means Nothing If Holocaust Analogies Are Always Off Limits."

20. Pitzer, "'Some Suburb of Hell.'"

21. Pitzer, *One Long Night*, 5–6.

22. Maria Clark, "Louisiana's Prisons Are Increasingly Being Used to Detain Immigrants," *Times-Picayune*, May 8, 2019, https://www.nola.com/news/article_9110ce70-bb2f-54e1-b4e1-54140b7a0559.html. On Louisiana's high incarceration rates, which include thousands of people who have not been convicted of a crime, see Louisiana's profile at the Prison Policy Initiative website, https://www.prisonpolicy.org/profiles/LA.html.

23. On Bunker's use of this term at Camp Algiers, see Nicholson, "What's That Uniform You're Wearing?"

24. Pitzer, "'Some Suburb of Hell.'"

25. The Department of Justice claimed its "policy represented a change in the level of enforcement of an existing statute rather than a change in statute or regulation. Prior Administrations prosecuted illegal border crossings relatively infrequently." A summary of the policy can be found in Congressional Research Service, "The Trump Administration's 'Zero Tolerance, Immigration Enforcement Policy," February 26, 2019, https://fas.org/sgp/crs/homesec/R45266.pdf.

26. RG 59, 740.00115 European War (1939) / 5848 PS /MW, Box 2841, NA. During World War II, the US government allowed spouses and children to join their family member deported from Latin America as "voluntary detainees"; it also established certain facilities as family camps and provided schooling, child care, and other services directed at family living.

27. Pitzer, "'Some Suburb of Hell.'"

28. Levin, "He Lived in the US for 40 Years."

29. Levin, "He Lived in the US for 40 Years."

30. Bangel and Frankel, "Trump Shouldn't Reject Refugees Seeking Safety."

31. Butler, *Precarious Life*, 57.

Selected Bibliography

ARCHIVES

American Jewish Historical Society Archives
    National Refugee Services Records
    Razovsky Papers

Historic New Orleans Collection

National Archives (NA)

College Park, MD
    RG 59 State Department
        Special War Problems Division
    RG 60 Justice Department
        Alien Enemy Control Unit—Closed Legal Case Files
    RG 389 Provost Marshal General
        Alien Enemy Information Bureau
Washington, DC
    RG 85 Records of the Immigration and Naturalization Service.

New Orleans Public Library
    New Orleans Newspapers Historical and Current, Newsbank Database

Tulane University Archives
    Louisiana Research Collection
        National Council of Jewish Women

DIGITAL RESOURCES

Ancestry.com
Densho Encyclopedia
German American Internee Coalition

BOOKS, ARTICLES, FILM AND RADIO, DISSERTATIONS

'Arafa, Mohamed. "Donald Trump's Muslim Travel Ban: The United States' Political, Legal, and Moral Responsibility," Jurist Legal News & Research, April 30, 2019. https://www.jurist.org/commentary/2019/04/mohamed-arafa-donald-trumps-travel-ban/.

Avni, Haim. "Costa Rica and the Jews during the Holocaust." *Judaica Latinoamericana* 7 (2013): 215–36.

Bahney, Jennifer Bowers. *Betrayer's Waltz: The Unlikely Bond between Marie Valerie of Austria and Hitler's Princess-Spy.* Jefferson, NC: McFarland, 2017.

Bangel, Steffani, and Jessica Frankel. "Trump Shouldn't Reject Refugees Seeking Safety." *Times-Picayune / New Orleans Advocate,* August 10, 2019, 4B.

Barker, Carolyn. "Burials in the Fort Reno Cemetery, 1874–1948." USGenWeb Archives, 2000. Accessed June 29, 2019. http://files.usgwarchives.net/ok/canadian/cemetery/ftreno.txt.

Beck, Hermann, and Larry Eugene Jones, eds. *From Weimar to Hitler: Studies in the Dissolution of the Weimar Republic and the Establishment of the Third Reich, 1932–1934.* New York: Berghahn Books, 2019.

Benjamin, Walter. *Illuminations.* Edited with an introduction by Hannah Arendt. New York: Schocken Books, 1986.

———. *Selected Writings.* Vol. 4, *1938–1940.* Edited by Marcus Bullock and Michael W. Jennings. Cambridge, MA: Belknap Press of Harvard University Press, 1996.

Berkin, Carol. *A Sovereign People: The Crises of the 1790s and the Birth of American Nationalism.* New York: Basic Books, 2017.

Bernstein, Adam. "Hans Mueller." *Washington Post,* January 17, 2010.

Biddle, Francis. "Americans of Italian Origin." Address delivered at the Columbus Day Celebration, Carnegie Hall, New York, October 12, 1942. https://www.justice.gov/sites/default/files/ag/legacy/2011/09/16/10-12-1942.pdf.

Bolbrinker, Niels, dir. *Between Utopia and Counter Revolution*. Documentary film. German with English subtitles. 2014. https://www.youtube.com/watch?v=TQv-ieP7D2k&index=1&list=PL386363754EF67D7A.

Boghardt, Thomas. *Spies of the Kaiser: German Covert Operations in Great Britain during the First World War Era*. Houndmills: Palgrave Macmillan, in Association with St. Antony's College, 2004.

Bratzel, John F., and Leslie B. Rout. "FDR and the 'Secret Map.'" *Wilson Quarterly* 9, no. 1 (1985):167–73.

Brockell, Gillian. "Geronimo and the Japanese Were Imprisoned There. Now Fort Sill Will Hold Migrant Children Again, Sparking Protests." *Washington Post*, June 23, 2019.

Brunhouse, Robert L. *Frans Blom, Maya Explorer*. Albuquerque: University of New Mexico Press, 1976.

Bukey, Evan Burr. *Jews and Intermarriage in Nazi Austria*. Cambridge: Cambridge University Press, 2011.

Busch, Wilhelm. *Hypocritical Helena, Plus a Plenty of Other Pleasures*. New York: Dover, 1962.

———. *Max Und Moritz: Eine Bubengeschichte in Sieben Streichen*. Munich: Braun and Schneider, 1900.

———. *Neues Wilhelm Busch Album: Sammlung Lustiger Bildergeschichten. Mit 1500 zum Teil Farbigen Bildern*. Leipzig: H. Klemm, 1923.

Butler, Judith. *Precarious Life: The Powers of Mourning and Violence*. New York: Verso, 2004.

Card, Jeb J. *Spooky Archaeology: Myth and the Science of the Past*. Albuquerque: University of New Mexico Press, 2018.

Carlson, John Roy. *Under Cover: My Four Years in the Nazi Underworld of America—the Amazing Revelation of How Axis Agents and Our Enemies within Are Now Plotting to Destroy the United States*. Philadelphia: Blakiston, distributed by E. P. Dutton, 1943.

Carpenter, Arthur E. "Gateway to the Americas: New Orleans's Quest for Latin American Trade, 1900–1970." PhD diss., Tulane University, 1987.

Caso, Alfonso. "Hermann Beyer." *Boletín bibliográfico de antropología americana* 6 (1942): 29–34.

Christgau, John. *"Enemies": World War II Alien Internment*. Ames: Iowa State University Press, 1985.

Civil Liberties Act of 1988. Enacted by the United States Congress, August 10, 1988. At PBS, Children of the Camps: Internment History. https://www.pbs.org/childofcamp/history/civilact.html.

Clark, Maria. "Louisiana's Prisons Are Increasingly Being Used to Detain Immigrants." *Times-Picayune,* May 8, 2019. https://www.nola.com/news/article_9110ce70-bb2f-54e1-b4e1-54140b7a0559.html.

Connell, Thomas. *America's Japanese Hostages: The World War II Plan for a Japanese Free Latin America.* Westport, CT: Praeger, 2002.

———. "The Internment of Latin American Japanese in the United States during World War Two: The Peruvian Japanese Experience." PhD diss., Florida State University, 1995.

Crane, Harnett T. "'Germany More Democratic Than Ever,' Says Tulane Scholar on Return to Work." *New Orleans Item,* November 1, 1938, 2.

Cuvi Sánchez, María, and Karin Harten Ahlers, eds. *Gertrudis: Diarios de una mujer alemana sobre el Ecuador, 1937–1956.* Quito: Abya-Yala, 2014.

Daniels, Roger. *The Politics of Prejudice: The Anti-Japanese Movement in California and the Struggle for Japanese Exclusion.* University of California Publications in History, vol. 71. Berkeley: University of California Press, 1962.

De Vita, L. "The Cold War in the Courtroom: Friedrich Karl Kaul in Jerusalem." *Histoire@Politique* 35 (2018).

Del Valle, Gaby. "Survivors of Japanese Internment Are Horrified Trump Is Using a Former Facility to Detain Migrant Kids." *Vice News,* June 14, 2019. https://news.vice.com/en_us/article/vb9qzj/survivors-of-japanese-internment-are-horrified-trump-is-using-a-former-facility-to-detain-migrant-kids.

"A Democratic Demurrer." *New Orleans Item,* November 5, 1938, 4.

Dickerson, James L. *Inside America's Concentration Camps: Two Centuries of Internment and Torture.* Chicago: Lawrence Hill Books, 2010.

DiStasi, Lawrence. *Excerpts from Una Storia Segreta: The Secret History of Italian American Evacuation and Internment during World War II.* Berkeley, CA: Heyday Books, 2001.

Drolet, Yves. "The Aryan Order of America and the College of Arms of Canada 1880–1937." Self-published study. http://pnaf.us/pdfs/aryan-order-of-america.pdf.

Dubois, Jules. *Danger over Panama.* Indianapolis: Bobbs-Merrill, 1964.

Ennis, Edward J. "A Justice Department Attorney Comments on the Japanese-American Relocation." Interview by Miriam Feingold. In *Japanese-American Relocation Reviewed,* vol. 1, *Decision and Exodus.* Earl Warren Oral History Project. Regents of the University of California, 1976. https://oac.cdlib.org/ark:/13030/ft667nb2x8/?brand=oac4.

Fallon, Joseph E. "The Censored History of Internment." Foitimes.com. Reprinted from *Chronicles: A Magazine of American Culture,* February 1998.

Feingold, Henry L. *The Politics of Rescue: The Roosevelt Administration and the Holocaust, 1938–1945.* New Brunswick, NJ: Rutgers University Press, 1970.

Fox, Stephen. *America's Invisible Gulag: A Biography of German American Internment & Exclusion in World War II; Memory and History.* New York: Peter Lang, 2000.

———. "The Deportation of Latin American Germans, 1941–1947: Fresh Legs for Mr. Monroe's Doctrine." *Yearbook of German-American Studies* (1997): 117–44.

Friedman, Max Paul. "The Cold War Politics of Exile, Return, and the Search for a Usable Past in Friedrich Karl Kaul's *Es wird Zeit, dass Du nach Hause kommst*." *German Life and Letters* 58, no. 3 (2005): 306–25.

———. *Nazis and Good Neighbors: The United States Campaign against the Germans of Latin America in World War II*. Cambridge: Cambridge University Press, 2003.

———. "Trading Civil Liberties for National Security: Warnings from a World War II Internment Program." *Journal of Policy History* 17, no. 3 (2005): 294–307.

———. "The U.S. Internment of Families from Latin America in World War II." *DEP* 9 (2008): 57–73. http://www.unive.it/media/allegato/dep/n9-2008/Saggi/Friedman-saggio.pdf.

Gardiner, C. Harvey. "The Latin American Japanese and World War II." In *Japanese Americans: from Relocation to Redress*, rev. ed., edited by Roger Daniels, Sandra C. Taylor, and Harry H. L. Kitano, 142–45. Seattle: University of Washington Press, 1991.

———. *Pawns in a Triangle of Hate: The Peruvian Japanese and the United States*. Seattle: University of Washington Press, 1981.

Gatscher-Reidl, Gregor. "Eine vergessene Facette der österreichischen Studentengeschichte." *David kultur* 118 (September 2018). http://davidkultur.at/artikel/eine-vergessene-facette-der-oesterreichischen-studentengeschichte.

Geller, Jay Howard. *The Scholems: A Story of the German-Jewish Bourgeoisie from Emancipation to Destruction*. Ithaca, NY: Cornell University Press, 2019.

Gellman, Irwin F. *Good Neighbor Diplomacy: United States Policies in Latin America, 1933–1945*. Baltimore: Johns Hopkins University Press, 1979.

Gilman, Sander. "The Jewish Nose: Are Jews White? Or, The History of the Nose Job." In *Encountering the Other(s): Studies in Literature, History, and Culture*, edited by Gisela Brinker-Gabler. Albany: SUNY Press, 1995, 149-182.

Gonzales, Richard. "America No Longer a 'Nation Of Immigrants,' USCIS Says." National Public Radio, February 22, 2018.

Grandin, Greg. "Concentration Camps in the Dominican Republic?" *Nation*, June 15, 2015.

Griffin, Robert P. "Constitutional Law: Due Process: Right of Alien Enemy to Judicial Review of Deportation Proceeding." *Michigan Law Review* 47, no. 3 (1949): 404–6.

Gropp, Arthur E. "Hermann Beyer's Last Years." "Homenaje al Dr. Hermann Beyer." Special issue, *El México antiguo*. 9 (1959): 35–38.

Gruber, Ruth. *Haven: The Dramatic Story of 1000 World War II Refugees and How They Came to America*. New York: Three Rivers, 2000.

Gushee, David. *The Sacredness of Human Life*. Grand Rapids, MI: William B. Eerdmans, 2013.

Hagglof, M. Gunnar. "A Test of Neutrality: Sweden in the Second World War." *International Affairs* 36, no. 2 (1960):153–67.

Haglund, David G. *Latin America and the Transformation of U.S. Strategic Thought, 1936–1940*. Albuquerque: University of New Mexico Press, 1984.

Halfon, Eduardo. *The Polish Boxer*. Translated by Daniel Hahn, Ollie Brock, Lisa Dillman, Thomas Bunstead, and Anne McLean. New York: Bellevue Literary Press, 2012.

Higashide, Seiichi. *Adios to Tears: The Memoirs of a Japanese-Peruvian Internee in U.S. Concentration Camps*. Honolulu: E & E Kudo, 1993.

Hilmes, Michele. *Only Connect: A Cultural History of Broadcasting in the United States*. 3rd ed. Boston: Wadsworth, 2011.

Hoffrogge, Ralf. *A Jewish Communist in Weimar Germany: The Life of Werner Scholem (1895–1940)*. Leiden; Boston: Brill, 2017.

Hohenlohe, Prince Franz. *The G.I. Prince*. Desert Hot Springs, CA: Event Horizon, 1995.

———. *Steph: The Fabulous Princess*. London: New English Library, 1976.

"H.R. 42—111th Congress: Commission on Wartime Relocation and Internment of Latin Americans of Japanese Descent Act." 2009. https://www.govtrack.us/congress/bills/111/hr42.

"Jews, Nazis Fight in U.S. Internment Camps; Separation Asked by Jewish Internees." Jewish Telegraphic Agency Archive, vol. 2, no. 190, August 18, 1942.

Johnson, Jake. "'This Is Sick': Horror as Trump Administration Plans to Detain Migrant Children at Former Japanese Internment Camp." *Common Dreams*, June 12, 2019. https://www.commondreams.org/news/2019/06/12/sick-horror-trump-administration-plans-detain-migrant-children-former-japanese.

Kane, Harnett T. "'Germany More Democratic Than Ever,' Says Tulane Scholar on Return to Work." *New Orleans Item*, November 1, 1938, 2.

Kaplan, Marion J. *Dominican Haven: The Jewish Refugee Settlement in Sosúa, 1940–1945*. New York: Museum of Jewish Heritage, 2008.

Kaplan-Levenson, Laine. "The World War II Internment Camp, 'Camp Algiers,' Part I." WWNO, *Tripod: New Orleans at 300*, January 12, 2017. http://wwno.org/post/wwii-internment-camp-camp-algiers-part-i.

Kaul, Karl Friedrich. *Es wird Zeit, dass Du nach Hause kommst*. Berlin: Verlag Das Neue Berlin, 1959.

———. *Iba siendo hora de que volvieras a casa*. Translated by Paula Sánchez de Muniain Cidranes. Madrid: Antonio Machado Libros, 2015.

Kleinberg, Eliot. "Post Time: The World War II Palm Beach Take-Down of Baron Von Opel." *Palm Beach Post*, September 27, 2017.

Kohner, Hanna, and Walter Kohner, with Frederick Kohner. *Hanna and Walter: A Love Story*. New York: Random House, 1984.

Krammer, Arnold. *Undue Process: The Untold Story of America's German Alien Internees.* London: Rowman and Littlefield, 1997.

La *"quinta columna" en las dos Américas: La conquista de la América Latina es el objectivo final de Hitler.* N.p.: n.p. 1940.

Larrea, Agustina. "Esvásticas, cánticos a Hitler, 'souvenirs' y dos muertos: a 80 años de la impactante celebración nazi en el Luna Park." *Infobae,* April 22, 2018.

Leifer, Tore, Jesper Nielsen, Reunert T. Sellner, and Knub J. Nehammer. *Restless Blood: Frans Bloom, Explorer and Maya Archaeologist.* New Orleans: Middle American Research Institute, 2017.

Leonard, Thomas M., and John F. Bratzel. *Latin America during World War II.* Lanham, MD.: Rowman and Littlefield, 2007.

Levin, Sam. "He Lived in the US for 40 Years. Then He Became the First to Die from Covid-19 in Immigration Jail." *Guardian,* May 12, 2020. https://www.theguardian.com/us-news/2020/may/12/first-ice-detainee-dies-coronavirus-immigration carlos-ernesto-escobar-mejia.

Linga, Carlos. "Hermann Beyer." *Boletín bibliográfico de antropología americana* 6 (1942): 34–35.

Lipstadt, Deborah E. *Antisemitism: Here and Now.* New York: Schocken, 2019.

"List of Detainees at Camp Kenedy, Texas, Oct. 31, 1942." RG 389, Box 3, Records of the Alien Enemy Information Bureau, National Archives. http://gaic.info/wp-content/uploads/2016/10/31-Oct-1940-Kenedy-census.pdf.

López-Calvo, Ignacio. *The Affinity of the Eye: Writing Nikkei in Peru.* Tucson: University of Arizona Press, 2013.

Ludecke, Kurt Georg Wilhelm. *I Knew Hitler: The Story of a Nazi Who Escaped the Blood Purge.* New York: C. Scribner's Sons, 1937.

Malkin, Michelle. *In Defense of Internment: The Case for "Racial Profiling" in World War II and the War on Terror.* Washington, DC: Regnery; Lanham, MD: Distributed to the Trade by National Book Network, 2004.

Masterson, Daniel M., and Jorge Ortiz Sotelo. "Peru: International Developments and Local Realities." In Leonard and Bratzel, *Latin America during World War II,* 126–43.

Mayes, April J. *The Mulatto Republic: Class, Race, and Dominican National Identity.* Gainesville: University Press of Florida, 2014.

Miller, John Chester. *Crisis in Freedom: The Alien and Sedition Acts.* Boston: Little, Brown, 1951.

Miller, Marilyn. "Lessons for the Present from the Alien Enemy Act and the Deportation of Latin Americans to the United States during World War II" / "Lecciones para el presente que deja la Ley del Extranjero Enemigo y la deportación de latinoamericanos a Estados Unidos durante la Segunda Guerra Mundial." *Tabula rasa* 33 (2020): 201–24.

Morton, Frederic. *A Nervous Splendor: Vienna, 1888/1889.* Boston: Little, Brown, 1979.

"The Nazis in Latin America." *Spectator,* July 25, 1941, 74.

Nehmer, Scott. *Ford, General Motors, and the Nazis: Marxist Myths about Production, Patriotism, and Philosophies.* Bloomington, IN: AuthorHouse, 2013.

Newman, Mark. *Desegregating Dixie: The Catholic Church in the South and Desegregation, 1945–1992.* Jackson: University Press of Mississippi, 2018.

Nicholson, Eleanor. "What's That Uniform You're Wearing?" *Times-Picayune/New Orleans States,* Sunday, March 25, 1945, sect. 2, p. 10.

Pérez, Orlando. J. "Panama: Nationalism and the Challenge to Canal Security." In Leonard and Bratzel, *Latin America during World War II,* 54–74.

Personal Justice Denied: Report of the Commission on Wartime Relocation and Internment of Civilians. Washington, DC: Civil Liberties Public Education Fund; Seattle: University of Washington Press, 1997.

Pistol, Rachel. *Internment during the Second World War.* London: Bloomsbury, 2017.

Pitt, David E. "The Noriega Case: Noriega's Outcasts; For Panama's Inmates, a Prison Like Devil's Island." *New York Times,* Jan. 7, 1990.

Pitzer, Andrea. *One Long Night: A Global History of Concentration Camps.* Boston: Little, Brown, 2017.

———. "'Some Suburb of Hell': America's New Concentration Camp System." *NYR Daily,* June 21, 2019. https://www.nybooks.com/daily/2019/06/21/some-suburb-of-hell-americas-new-concentration-camp-system/.

Powell, Lawrence N. *Troubled Memory: Anne Levy, the Holocaust, and David Duke's Louisiana.* 2d ed. Chapel Hill: University of North Carolina Press, 2019.

Price, David H. *Anthropological Intelligence: The Deployment and Neglect of American Anthropology in the Second World War.* Durham, NC: Duke University Press, 2008.

Rapoport, Louis. *Shake Heaven and Earth. Peter Bergson and the Struggle to Rescue the Jews of Europe.* Jerusalem: Gefen, 1999.

Rasmussen, Natalia King. "Friends of Freedom, Allies of Peace: African Americans, the Civil Rights Movement, and East Germany, 1949–1989." PhD diss., Boston College, 2014.

Razovsky, Cecilia. *What Every Emigrant Should Know: A Simple Pamphlet for the Guidance and Benefit of Prospective Immigrants to the United States.* New York: Department of Immigrant Aid, National Council of Jewish Women, 1922.

———. *What Every Woman Should Know about Citizenship.* New York: Department of Immigrant Aid, National Council of Jewish Women, 1926.

Rempel, Gerhard. "Mennonites and the Holocaust." *Mennonite Quarterly Review* 84, no. 4 (2010): 507–49.

Riley, Karen Lea. *Schools behind Barbed Wire: The Untold Story of Wartime Internment and the Children of Arrested Enemy Aliens.* Lanham, MD: Rowman and Littlefield, 2002.

Roberts, Cokie, and Steve Roberts. "Trump Makes War on Legal Immigration." *Advocate*, May 15, 2019, 7B.

Roberts, Sam. "Isamu Shibayama Dies at 88, His Quest for Reparations Unfulfilled." *New York Times*, August 17, 2018. https://www.nytimes.com/2018/08/17/obituaries/isamu-shibayama-dies-at-88-his-quest-for-reparations-unfulfilled.html.

Robinson, Greg. *By Order of the President: FDR and the Internment of Japanese Americans*. Cambridge, MA: Harvard University Press, 2001.

———. *A Tragedy of Democracy: Japanese Confinement in North America*. New York: Columbia University Press, 2009.

Roehl, Marjorie H. "Refugee Violinist Fled from Nazis; Finds U.S. Welcomes Self and Mother." *New Orleans Item*, August 21, 1943, 1, 5.

Roorda, Eric Paul. "The Dominican Republic: The Axis, the Allies, and the Trujillo Dictatorship." In Leonard and Bratzel, *Latin America during World War II*, 75–91.

———. "Genocide Next Door: The Good Neighbor Policy, the Trujillo Regime, and the Haitian Massacre of 1937." *Diplomatic History* 20, no. 3 (1996): 301–19.

Roosevelt, Franklin D. *Complete Presidential Press Conferences of Franklin D. Roosevelt*. New York: Da Capo, 1972.

Rostow, Eugene. "Our Worst Wartime Mistake." *Harper's Magazine* 191, no. 1144 (1945): 193.

Roth, Philip. *The Plot against America*. Boston: Houghton Mifflin, 2004.

Russell, Jan Jarboe. *The Train to Crystal City: FDR's Secret Prisoner Exchange Program and America's Only Family Internment Camp during World War II*. New York: Scribner, 2015.

Ruttenberg, Danya. "'Never Again' Means Nothing If Holcaust Analogies Are Always Off Limits." *Washington Post*, June 19, 2019. https://www.washingtonpost.com/outlook/2019/06/19/never-again-means-nothing-if-holocaust-analogies-are-always-off-limits/.

Saballos Ramírez, Marvin. "70 años del ingreso de Nicaragua a la segunda guerra mundial declaración de guerra de Nicaragua a Japón, Alemania e Italia en diciembre de 1941." *Revista de temas Nicaragüenses* 44 (2011): 72–104.

Saito, Natsu Taylor. "Justice Held Hostage: U.S. Disregard for International Law in the World War II Internment of Japanese Peruvians—A Case Study." *Boston College Law Review* 40, no. 1 (1998): 275–348.

Schad, Martha. *Hitler's Spy Princess: The Extraordinary Life of Stephanie von Hohenlohe*. Stroud: Sutton, 2004.

Schott, Matthew J. *Bayou Stalags: German Prisoners of War in Louisiana*. Lafayette: University of Southwestern Louisiana, 1981.

Schuman, Frederick L. *The Nazi Dictatorship: A Study in Social Pathology and the Politics of Fascism*. 2d ed., rev. New York: Knopf, 1936.

Simkin, John. "Stephanie von Hohenlohe." Spartacus Educational. http://spartacus-educational.com/Stephanie_von_Hohenlohe.htm.
Simpson, Paul. *The Mammoth Book of Prison Breaks.* London: Robinson, 2013.
Slack, Charles. *Liberty's First Crisis: Adams, Jefferson, and the Misfits Who Saved Free Speech,* New York: Atlantic Monthly Press, 2015.
Smith, Arthur L., Jr. "Kurt Ludecke: The Man Who Knew Hitler." *German Studies Review* 26, no. 3 (2003): 597–606.
Strum, Harvey. "Jewish Internees in the American South, 1942–1945." *American Jewish Archives* 42, no. 1 (1990): 27–48.
Talbot, David. *The Devil's Chessboard: Allen Dulles, the CIA, and the Rise of America's Secret Government.* New York: Harper Collins, 2015.
Tejera, Adolfo. *Penetración nazi en América Latina.* Montevideo: Editorial Nueva America, 1938.
Torres Hernández, Margarita, and Gertrud Peters Solórzano. "Los archivos de la Junta de Custodia de Costa Rica durante la Segunda Guerra Mundial: Ciudadanos y empresas en las diferentes listas construidas por los gobiernos británico, estadounidense y costarricense." *Revista Historia* 46 (2002): 261–307.
Treatment of Latin Americans of Japanese Descent, European Americans, and Jewish Refugees in World War II. 111th Cong., Serial no. 111–13, March 19, 2009, Hearing of the House Subcommittee on Immigration, Citizenship, Refugees, Border Security, and International Law, Committee on the Judiciary. https://www.govinfo.gov/content/pkg/CHRG-111hhrg48322/html/CHRG-111hhrg48322.htm. Video available at https://www.youtube.com/watch?v=Mf_ATQL9NOE.
Triendl-Zadoff, Mirjam. *Werner Scholem: A German Life.* Translated by Dona Geyer. Philadelphia: University of Pennsylvania Press, 2018.
US Federal Security Agency. *Policies and Procedures Governing the Administration of Services and Assistance to Enemy Aliens Affected by Governmental Action: A Handbook for State Agencies.* Washington, DC: Social Security Board, 1942.
Urbach, Karina. *Go-Betweens for Hitler.* Oxford: Oxford University Press, 2015.
Vladek, Stephen. "Ludecke's Lengthening Shadow: The Disturbing Prospect of War without End." *Journal of National Security Law and Policy* 2 (2006): 53–110.
Von der Goltz, Horst. *My Adventures as a German Secret Service Agent.* London: Cassell, 1918. https://ia600205.us.archive.org/30/items/myadventuresasgeoogoltrich/myadventuresasgeoogoltrich.pdf.
Wauchope, Robert. "Hermann Beyer." *American Antiquity* 9, no. 4 (1944): 439.
Wells, Allen. *Tropical Zion: General Trujillo, FDR, and the Jews of Sosúa.* Durham, NC: Duke University Press, 2009.
Weisaeth, Lars, and Leo Ettinger. "Research on PTSD and other Post-Traumatic Reactions: European Literature." *PTSD Research Quarterly* 2, No. 2 (Spring 1991).

https://pdfs.semanticscholar.org/2d9e/f203f00ec95c7bce9ae6502857c3c1f4e287.pdf.

Williams, Duncan RyĐken. *American Sutra: A Story of Faith and Freedom in the Second World War*. Cambridge, MA: Harvard University Press, 2019.

Wilson, Jim. *Nazi Princess: Hitler, Lord Rothermere and Princess Stephanie Von Hohenlohe*. Stroud: History Press, 2011.

"World War II Enemy Alien Control Program Overview." National Archives. https://www.archives.gov/research/immigration/enemy-aliens-overview.

Wyman, David. *The Abandonment of the Jews: America and the Holocaust, 1941–1945*. New York: Pantheon Books, 1984.

Zucker, Bat-Ami. *Cecilia Razovsky and the American Jewish Women's Rescue Operations in the Second World War*. London: Vallentine Mitchell, 2008.

Index

Note: Page numbers in *italics* refer to illustrations; those followed by "n" indicate endnotes.

Abrahamson, Albert, 201, 205
Acadia, 14, 30
Algiers, Louisiana (New Orleans neighborhood), ix, 25, 27, 39
Alien and Sedition Acts (1798), 1–2, 24, 155–6, 207
Alien Registration Act (1940), 2, 127
Anderson, S. W., 57–59
Anti-Nazi League, 142–46
antisemitism, 19, 120, 199, 240n101
Argentina, 6, 7
Arias, Arnulfo, 7
Ascher, Benno, 89–90, 92–94, 231n2
Ascher, Clara, 89–90, 93–94
Astor, Victor, 129
Axberg, Olle, 43–44

Bangel, Steffani, 215
Becerra, Xavier, 209–10
Beck, Joseph, 202–3
Belize, 20
Bell, James: Frankel case and, 98; investigations in Central America, 23, 202–3; Jewish refugees and, 100; Ludecke case and, 154; Manheimer case and, 108; Meyer case and, 80
Benjamin, Walter, 199
Bennett, Harry, 184
Berkin, Carol, 1
Beyer, Hermann, *123*; career of, 123–24, 136–37; death of, 133–34, 135–37; FBI decision to intern, 134–36; *The Genesis of the Maya Hieroglyphs*, 137; inquiry into activities of, 128–30; internment at Stringtown, 130–34; personal politics and *New Orleans Item* piece on, 124–28; personnel record, *132*
Biddle, Francis, *179*; on Alien Registration Act, 2; classification and, 88; Hohenlohe case (Stephanie) and, 180–82, 184; Jewish release and, 34; levelheadedness of, 22; stateless refugees and, 19; von der Goltz case and, 139
Bingham, Jonathan, 95
Blom, Frans, 123, 129–30, 236n26
Blumenthal, Anneliese, 44, 59–60, 226n14
Blumenthal, Ernst, 44, 59–60, 203, 226n14
Boghardt, Thomas, 138–39
Bohm, Peter, 94–95, 194
Border Patrol, US, 31–32, 50–51
Boström, Wollmar, 163–65, 168–69, 245n1
Bragdon, Claude, 150

263

Brandt, George, 163–64
Bratzel, John, 8–9
Brazil: Bohm case, 94; Klyszcz case, 106; Wachtmeister and Condor Airlines, 162, 166
bribery in Latin America, 11–12, 98–99, 165, 194–95
Brunhouse, Robert, 124
Bryant, William Sohier, 139
Buchenwald concentration camp, 190, 193
Bukey, Evan, 78
Bunker, Raymond: on Blumenthal (Ernst), 60; on camp administration and details, 27, 32; Camp Algiers closure and, 45–48; Camp Algiers living conditions and, 38–44; Fichman on, 205; Geneva Convention and, 214; Ludecke, reports on, 154–55; von der Goltz case and, 145; von Opel case and, 86
Burling, John, 146, 155, 165
Busch, Wilhelm, 47, 225n60
Bush, George H. W., 208
Butler, Judith, 216

Cable Act of 1922 (Married Women's Citizenship Act), 246n18
Cabot, John Moors, 12
Camp Algiers, New Orleans: about, 18; Border Patrol operation of, 31–32; as "Camp of the Innocent" or "anti-Nazi" camp, 21–22, 34–36, 40–42, 47, 58, 92; closure, repatriation, and reverse deportations, 44–50; floor plans, 27, 33; Japanese aliens at, 226n9; living conditions at, 38–44, 205–6; Ludecke as camp spokesman at, 42–43, 86, 153–54; Nazi cell, possibility of, 144–45; opening and early use of, 29–34; post-war fate of site, 28, 50–51; quarantine station site, 25, 26, 27–29, 28; Razovsky and transfer of Jews to, 201–2; release of Jewish detainees (1943), 34–36; Trott hearing at, 36–38. *See also* classification of detainees; Jewish refugees and detainees; Panama Jews; *specific internees by name*
Camp Balboa, Canal Zone, 7, 194–95, 196
Camp Blanding, Florida, 97, 102–3, 195
Camp Empire, Canal Zone, 11
Camp Forrest, Tennessee: Fechenbach case, 247n29; Ludecke case, 151; Razovsky attempt to reunited Jews at, 199–201; Trott case, 37; Wetterschneider case (Oskar), 115
Camp Kenedy, Texas: about, 21; Blumenthal case, 59; Gordon case, 193; Hohenlohe case (Franz), 187–88; Kaufmann case, 105; Kaul case, 68–69; Marcus case, 110; Meyer case, 77; Mueller (Olaf) case, 83–84; Mueller/Muller (Hans) case, 111; Razovsky attempt to reunite Jews at, 199–200; Scholem case, 112; transfer of Jewish internees to Algiers, 21, 35, 39, 201–2; Wachtmeister case, 160–61, 163–67; Wolff case (Siegfried), 118
Camp McAlester, Oklahoma, 39, 182, 187, 199–202
Camp Seagoville, Texas: Ascher case, 90; Frankel case, 97; Heinemann case, 66–67; Hohenlohe case (Stephanie), 170, 182–85; Jewish refugees, 39, 40, 92, 204; Kallman case, 101; Klemm and Levigon cases, 29–30; Manzoni case, 72; Marcus case, 110; Razovsky and transfer of Jews from, 201–2; as supercamp, 222n3
Camp Stringtown, Oklahoma: Ascher case, 89–90, 231n2; Beyer case, 131–34; descriptions of, 131–33, 237n37; Frankel case, 97; Heinemann case, 66; history of, 237n33; Jewish refugees at, 133, 220n58; Scholem case, 112
Canuto, Marcello, 137
Carlson, John Roy, 143
Carpenter, Arthur, 221n1
Caso y Andrade, Alfonso, 123–24, 135–36, 237n44
Chile, 222n14

INDEX | 264

citizenship: Ascher case, 94; document confiscation and, 53; German, loss of, 54; Ludecke case, 150; Scholem case, 113; stateless refugees, 19, 61, 93; Wetterschneider case, 115–16
Civil Liberties Act (1988), 208–10
Clark, Tom C., 155
classification of detainees: about, 52–53; Ennis on criteria for, 87; Fechenbach case, 61–62; German nationality, questions of, 73–76; Gerothwohl case, 62–64; Hamermann case, 64–65; Heinemann case, 65–67; Kaul case, 68–70; Kolb case, 70–71; Manzoni case, 71–73; Mateju case, 73–75; Mathies case, 75–76; Meyer case, 77–83; Mueller case, 83–84; Nazi system of, 226n4; Paschka case, 84–85; pro-Nazi vs. anti-Nazi vs. Jew, 56–62, 57; religion and race, 53; religious identification and, 76–83; on ship manifests, 52, 54, 55; speaking out against Nazism as backfiring, 62–64; stereotypes and racial discrimination, 53–56; suffering due to, 83–85; von Opel case, 85–88
Clinton, Bill, 208
Colombia: Blumenthal case, 59; deportations on the *Acadia*, 30; Fechenbach case, 61–62; Kaul case, 68
Commission on Wartime Relocation and Internment of Civilians, 208, 209
Commission on Wartime Relocation and Internment of Latin Americans of Japanese Descent Act (HR 42), 210–11
Common Council for American Unity, 147
"concentration camp" debate, 212–13
Convention on the Rights of the Child, 214
conversos, contemporary, 76, 229n71
Cooley, Thomas M., II, 100
Costa Rica: blacklist, 227n28; Fechenbach case, 61; Gerothwohl case, 39, 62–64; Paschka case, 84–85; Sauter case, 21; Stone (Doris) as archaeologist in, 127–28
Coughlin, Charles, 199, 204, 239n76

Crystal City detention camp (Texas): demographics, 221n2; as family camp, 214; film on, 84; Jewish detainees at, 201; Nazis at, 34; news report on repatriations from, 49; Paschka case, 84–85; pro-Nazi detainees at, 70–71; as supercamp, 222n3
Crystal City Pilgrimage Committee, 249n15
Cuba: early concentration camps in, 250n18; Grunberg in, 98; Heinemann case, 67; Isle of Pines camp, 11; Razovsky and Cuban refugees, 197–98; Wachtmeister case, 165
Cuba, SS, 15–16, 20, 55, 84, 220n53
Cunard, Emerald, 175

Dailey, John F., 146–47
Davalos, Ignacio, 74
Davis, Angela, 69–70
DDT, 16–17, 210–11
de Laval, Erik, 182
deportations: dubious, 64–65; from Latin America, 12–13, 14; reverse, 44–50. See also *specific cases by name*
"detention," definition of, 33
De Witt, John, 4
Dickerson, James, 127, 209, 212, 249n9
Dickstein, Samuel, 144
Dix, George G., 80
documents, confiscation of, 15, 53, 211
Dominican Republic: Gordon case, 190–92; La Cumbre camp, 160, 162–63, 166; Meyer case, 77–80; Sosúa Jewish colony, 191–92; Wachtmeister case, 99, 160–64, 167, 168
Drottningholm, SS, 159
Drucker, Ernst, 119
Dubois, Jules, 65
Dulles, Allen, 171

Eckardt, Ted, 11
Ecuador: deportations on the *Acadia*, 30; "FBI Files on Communism in Ecuador in the 1940s," 48, 74; Harten case, 16; Lisken case, 34; Mateju case, 73–75; Partmuss

INDEX | 265

Ecuador *(continued)*
    case, 48–49; reverse deportations, acceptance of, 50; von Opel case, 48
Eichmann, Adolf, 68, 69
Ellis Island, New York: Hohenlohe case (Franz), 181, 187–88; Ludecke case, 151, 155–56; von der Goltz case, 139, 143–47
El Salvador: Mathies case, 75–76; Mueller case, 83–84
Emmerson, John K., 13
emotional illness or distress, 82, 84–85, 184
Enemy Alien Control Program: "alien enemy," 21st-century extensions of, 157–58, 213; assessments and consequences of, 22–24; "detention," definition of, 33; INS responsibility for, 26; Japanese American internment and, 3–5; Jewish detainees under, 18–22; New Orleans traffic and processing, 14–17; as precedent, 207; roots of, 1–2; secrecy of, 44–45; secret map and fear of Nazi fifth column and, 9–14, *10*; security purpose of, 5–9; similarities to Hitler policy, 5, 54–56, 103, 218n12; wives and children, 15, 16–17. *See also* classification of detainees; Japanese American internment; Jewish refugees and detainees; Panama Jews; *specific camps by name*
Ennis, Edward: on classification criteria, 87; Hohenlohe case (Stephanie) and, 184–85; Kallman case and, 101; Ludecke case and, 155; Mateju case and, 75; Mueller case and, 84; Razovsky and, 199–202; Trott case and, 37; von der Goltz case and, 141–43, 145–46; von Opel case and, 87; Wachtmeister case and, 164–66
Evangeline, 67
exchanges of prisoners or hostages, 12–13, 66–67, 112
Executive Order 9066 (1942), 3–4, 45

family separations: in 21st-century war on illegal immigrants, 214; about, 16–17; Hull's declaration on, 214; Jewish Welfare Board and concerns about, 195–96. *See also specific cases by name*
Faulkner, William, 212
Fechenbach, Siegwart, 61–62, 103, 200
Federal Bureau of Investigation (FBI): Alien Registration Act and, 127; Beyer case, 134–36; Biddle directive on classification system, 88; Blumenthal case, 59; detentions in Latin America and, 6; failure to recognize Jews as anti-Nazi, 61; "FBI Files on Communism in Ecuador in the 1940s," 48, 74; Frankel case, 97–99; Friedman case, 20; Hohenlohe case (Stephanie), 178–82, 186; Japanese Americans, suspicions of, 56; Ludecke case, 151; Mateju case, 74, 229n65; overzealousness of, 22–23, 221n74; Partmuss case, 48; Scholem case, 112; Special Intelligence Service (SIS) and use of anthropologists, 129; Trott case, 37; von der Goltz case, 138–41, 147; von Opel case, 85; Wachtmeister case, 164–66; wartime internment as precedent for, 22. *See also* Hoover, J. Edgar
Feibelman, Julian, 204
Feingold, Miriam, 87
Felshin, Max, 147
"fence sickness" *(Gitterkrankheit)*, 84–85
Ferguson, Homer, 115–16
Fichman, David, 36, 40, 117, 204–6, 248n48
fifth column, 6–10, 56
flag controversy at Crystal City, 70–71
Florida, SS: Ascher case, 89; Frankel case, 97; Hamermann case, 64; Heinemann case, 66; Kallman case, 101; Klemm and Levigon cases, 30; Manheimer case, 195; manifest, 52, *54;* in New Orleans, 15; Paschka case, 84–85; Scholem case, 112; Wetterschneider case, 114
Ford, Henry, 148
Fort Lincoln, North Dakota, 152, 248n48
Fort (Camp) Meade, Maryland, 151, 187
Fort Oglethorpe, Georgia, 151, 194–97

Fort Ontario, New York, 91, 231n3
Fort Sill, Oklahoma, 134, 212
Fox, Stephen, 39
Frankel, Erwin, 96–100
Frankel, Jessica, 215
Frankel, Toni, 99
Friedman, Eddie, 20, 84, 248n48
Friedman, Leo, 204
Friedman, Max Paul, 8, 30, 70, 83, 92, 104, 120, 226n11
Friends of Democracy, 143–45, 239n76

Gellman, Irwin, 218n16
Geneva Convention, 214
George Washington, SS, 73
German-American Bund, 127, 139, 141, 151
German Democratic Republic (East Germany), 69
German detainees, numbers of, 14, 91. *See also* classification of detainees; Jewish refugees and detainees; Nazi detainees; *specific camps and cases by name*
Geronimo, 212
Gerothwohl, Clotilde, 39, 62–63, 224n47
Gerothwohl, Ernst (Ernesto), 39, 62–64, 224n47
Gerry, Malcolm, 146
Gitlin, Leo, 199–202
Gitterkrankheit ("fence sickness"), 84–85
Gloucester internment center, New Jersey, 152, 181–82
Gnadenschuss (shot to the back of the neck), 55
Goebbels, Joseph, 118, 173, 176
Good Neighbor Policy, 6, 12, 23, 96
Gordon, Emanuel, 190–93, 203
Göring, Hermann, 172
Gormin, Ken, 48
Greenfield, Albert Monroe, 186
Greenleigh, Arthur D., 204, 248n45
Greutert, Albert, 41–42, 160–61
Griffin, Robert P., 155–56
Gripsholm, 14

Gropp, Arthur, 135, 136–37, 236n26
Gruber, Ruth, 231n3
Grunberg, Henry, 98
Grunberg, Richard, 194
Guatemala, 66
Gunther, Simon, 39
Gurs Internment Camp, France, 105–6
Gushee, David, 55

Haglund, David, 10
Halfon, Eduardo, 226n5
Hamermann, Leo, 64–65
Harris, Rufus, 127, 128–31, 236n26, 236n28
Harrison, Earl, 22, 23, 40, 71, 218n12
Harten, Gertrude, 16–17, 17, 49–50
Hebrew Immigrant Aid Society (HIAS), 190, 194–96, 197
Heinemann, Marta, 66–67
Heinemann, Wilhelm, 65–67
Heller, Mrs. Isaac, 203
Henkin, Louis, 80
Hersey, Evelyn, 96
Hertel, Karl, 78, 79, 81
Higashide, Seechi, 16
Himmler, Heinrich, 174, 176
Hitler, Adolf: Beyer and, 124–26; birthday of, 34, 70; Blood Purge (Night of the Long Knives) (1934), 149, 240n91; Gordon on, 203; Hohenlohe (Stephanie) and, 170, 172–78, 180–81; Latin American celebrations of, 6–7, 7; Ludecke and, 48, 122, 148–52; Meyer on, 81; Nuremburg Laws, 175–76; Rothermere and, 176–77, 243n37; secret map and, 9; US policies compared to, 5, 96; von der Goltz and, 138; von Opel and, 86, 88; von Papen and, 138
Hobbs Bill (1939), 5
Hohenlohe, Franz (Francis), 171, 177, 181–85, 187–88
Hohenlohe, Prince Friedrich Franz von, 171
Hohenlohe, Princess Stephanie von: arrival in US, 177–78; background, 169–70; at Cobble Close estate (New Jersey), 186;

Hohenlohe, Princess Stephanie von (cont.)
  death of, 187; deportation hearing, arrest, and release, 180; FBI view of, 179–81; at Gloucester, 181–82; Golden Party Badge, 173, *174*, 181; Hitler, Nazi Party, and, 170, 173–76; as international journalist, 186–87; Jewish lineage of, 170; in London, 175–76; marriage and divorce, 171–72; reinventing herself on parole, 185–86; Rothermere and, 172–73, 176–77; at Schloss Leopoldskron, 174–76, *175*; Schofield and, 178, 180–82, 186; at Seagoville, 182–85; suicide threats, 181, 185; Wachtmeister compared with, 171, 183, 188; Wiedemann and, 173, 176–80
Holocaust (Shoa): analogies, question of, 212–13; definition of Holocaust survivor, 95; Eichmann and, 69; Memphis memorial, 95; Mennonites and, 230n90; Muller and, 111; "never again," 212, 215; Nuremburg Laws, 19, 54, 62–63, 175–76; US Holocaust Memorial Museum, 95, 107; US parallels to, 54–55, 215
Hoover, J. Edgar, 56, 74, 88, 129, 164–65, 180–82
Horthy, Miklós, 172
House Subcommittee on Immigration, Citizenship, Refugees, Border Security, and International Law, 209–11
Hull, Cordell, 12, 13, 17, 96–97, 151–52, 214
Huper, Wilhelm, 43

I-55 General Information Form, 166–67
Ickes, Raymond: Frankel case and, 98; on internment, 23, 119; investigations in Central America, 23, 202–3; Jewish refugees and, 100; Manheimer case and, 108; Scholem case and, 113
Immigration and Naturalization Service (INS): *Alien Enemy Detention Facility* (film), 222n3; Beyer case, 130; Bohm case, 95; Camp Algiers and, 26, 30–33, 47–48; flag issue at Crystal City, 71; Frankel case, 99; Hamermann case, 65; Heinemann case, 67; Hohenlohe case (Stephanie), 178, 180; I-55 form and, 166; Kaul case, 68–69; Klyszcz case, 106; Kolb case, 71; Ludecke case, 153; Manzoni case, 72–73; Mateju case, 73, 75; Meyer case, 77, 79; processing at New Orleans, 15–17, 218n11; responsibility for enemy alien detention, 26; von der Goltz case and, 140; Wetterschneider case, 114, 116; Wolff case, 117. *See also* Kelly, Willard
Ina, Satsuki, 212, 241n113
Indoff, Mr. (Swedish consul), 160, 161, 242n8
insecticide decontamination, 16–17, 210–11
internment at large (parole-like): affidavits of loyalty and, 193; Fechenbach and, 62; Gerothwohl and, 63–64; Jews and, 21, 34–35; Wolff (Siegfried) and, 44
Isle of Pines camp, Cuba, 11
Italian detainees, 14, 19, 31, 91

Jackson, Robert, *179*
Jaeger, Rolf, 124
Japanese American Evacuation Claims Act (1948), 208
Japanese American internment: about, 3–5; at Algiers, 226n9; children, effects on, 241n113; efforts for acknowledgment and reparations, 207–11; hostage exchanges and, 13; *Korematsu* case, 157; numbers, 14, 91, 217n6; religion-based discrimination, 56
Jewish Colonization Association, 191, 193
Jewish refugees and detainees: antisemitism, 19, 120, 199, 240n101; Camp Algiers as "Camp of the Innocent" or "anti-Nazi" camp, 21–22, 34–36, 40–42, 47, 58, 92; at Camp Stringtown, 133, 220n58; classification of pro-Nazi vs. anti-Nazi vs. Jew, 56–62, *57*; *conversos*, contemporary, 76, 229n71; Fort Ontario refugee camp, 91, 231n3; German classification and exclusion of, 194–96, 226n4; "Holo-

caust survivor," definition of, 95; *Mischlinge* ("mixed-race" children), 82; Nazis detainees and, 18–21, 34, 102–3; number from Latin America, 91; *Rassenschande* ("mixed" marriages) and, 71–72, 78, 81, 108–9; Razovsky attempt to reunite Jews, at Kenedy, 199–200; release of (1943), 34–36; as stateless refugees, 19, 61, 93, 200; suspected as spies, 20. *See also* Holocaust; Panama Jews
Jewish Welfare Board, 190, 195–96, 215
Johnson, Jamila, 213–14
Johnson, Lyndon B., 187
Joint Distribution Committee (JDC), 65, 92, 190, 191, 195, 201, 248n45
Joseph, Eric, 200
Judischer Hilfsverein (Aid Association of German Jews), 111, 245n2

Kachima, Tetsuden, 24
Kallman, Lucy, 100–101, 200–202
Kallman, Martin, 100–101
Kane, Harnett T., 125–26
Kappel, Fred, 101–4, 201
Kappel, Werner, 103–4
Karliner, George, 103, 104–5, 194, 203
Kaufmann, Felice, 203
Kaufmann, Max, 103, 105–6, 203
Kaufmann, Sophie, 105–6
Kaul, Friedrich Karl, 40–43, 58, 68–70, 203, 226n11
Keeley, James H., 166–67
Kelly, Willard: on *Acadia* security, 30; Anderson's classification and, 57–58; Hohenlohe case (Stephanie) and, 184; Jewish detainees and, 35; Ludecke case and, 152–53, 155; Manzoni case and, 72–73; Mueller case and, 84; Seitz report and, 40; von der Goltz case and, 141, 145–47; Wachtmeister case and, 165–66, 167
Kessler, Eugene, 26, 29–31
Klemm, Alicia, 29–30
Klish, Renée, 203

Klyszcz, Erwin, 106–7, 203
Kohen/Kohn, Albert or Alberto, 103, 106, 194
Kohner, Hanna, 237n34
Kohner, Paul, 237n34
Kohner, Walter, 131–33, 237n34, 237n37
Kolb, Karl, 70–71, 226n11
Kraght, Erwin, 162
Kramer, Jacobo, 64–65
Krammer, Arnold, 5, 22, 38, 217n6
Krinsly, Stuart, 142, 146
Krost, Wilhelm, 162

La Cumbre concentration camp, Dominican Republic, 160, 162–63, 166
Lafoon, Sidney, 167
Lagstein, Salomon, 115, 194–95
Lauler, P. W., 23, 221n74
Latin America: bribery and corruption in, 11–12; deportation and hostage exchange plans, 12–13; Good Neighbor Policy toward, 6, 12, 23, 96; Nazi sympathies in, 6–9; numbers deported from, 14, 91. *See also* Panama Jews; *specific countries*
Lawton, Edward P., 162, 163
Lend-Lease Act (1941), 242n14
Leonard, Thomas, 8–9
Levigon, Elida, 29–30
Levin, Theodore, 115–16
Levy, Edmund, 43
Lewis, Read, 147
Linga, Carlos R., 136
Lipschitz, Siegmund, 115–16, 194
Lisken, Gunter, 34
Lizardi Ramos, César, 137
Loewenthal, Joan, 35
Lofgren, Zoe, 209–10
Long, Breckenridge, 53, 120, 165, 168
Lothrop, Samuel Kirkland, 128–29
loyalty to US, affidavits of, 193
Lubeley, George, 104
Ludecke, Kurt: antisemitic activity, history of, 240n101; arrest and internment, 151–52; arrival at Camp Algiers, 40, 152–53;

Ludecke, Kurt (cont.)
  Bunder's report on, 154–55; as camp spokesman at Algiers, 42–43, 86, 153–54; citizenship applications, 150; Hitler and, 148–52; *I Knew Hitler*, 86, 122, 149–52; Nazi allegiance of, 46–47, 58, 148–52; in news reports, 48, 148–49; repatriation hearing and order of removal, 155–56; von der Goltz compared to, 147–48; von Opel and, 86
Ludecke, Mildred, 150, 155
Ludecke v. Watkins, 155–57

Maier, Julius, 20
Mangione, Jetre, 23
Manheimer/Mannheimer, Otto, 107–9, 194–97, 203
Manzoni, Rodolfo, 71–73
map, secret, 9–10, *10*
Marcus, Christine, 109–10
Marcus, Ferdinand, 109–10
marriages, "mixed" (*Rassenschande*), 71–72, 78, 81, 108
Married Women's Citizenship Act (Cable Act of 1922), 246n18
Masterson, Daniel, 9, 15, 209
Mateju, Eugenia, 73–75
Mathies, Gustavo, 75–76
Matsuda, Kunikichi, 15–16
McCraig, William, 106
McNutt, Paul V., 32–33
Mennonites, 83, 230n90
Mexico: Beyer and pre-Columbian research in, 123–24, 128, 135–37; children detained on US-Mexico border (2019), 212; German propaganda bureau in, 128; von der Goltz, Pancho Villa, and Mexican Revolution, 122, 138, 140; Weidemann and, 179
Meyer, Frank, 38, 80, 82–83
Meyer, Irmgard, 78–83
Meyer, Siegfried, 77–83, 203
Middle American Research Institute (MARI),

Tulane University, 123–24, 127–30, 134–37, 236n26
military service. *See* US Army, detainees inducted into
Miller, John, 1–2
Miller, Walter, 152–54
Mischlinge ("mixed-race" children), 82
Mochizuki, Carmen Higa, 208–9
Mueller/Muller, Hans, 103, 110–11
Mueller, Olaf, 83–84
Muslim travel ban, 157
Mussolini, Benito, 7

National Council of Jewish Women (NCJW), 197–98, 203, 215
National Refugee Service (NRS): Camp Algiers and, 36, 40, 92; Fichman case and, 248n48; legacy of, 215; Manheimer case and, 196; Razovsky, work of, 198–206; Wolff case (Siegfried) and, 117, 119
national security, 5–9, 23
Native American "prisoners of war," 212
Nazi detainees: Camp Algiers as "anti-Nazi" camp, 21–22, 34–36, 40–42, 47, 58, 92; as camp spokesmen, 42–43; concerns about Nazi cells in camps, 144–45; at Crystal City, 70–71; Jewish detainees and, 18–21, 34, 102–3, 194–96; Kaul on, 41; liberties given to, 34; Ludecke and questions of allegiance, 46–47, 58, 148–52; political arguments and, 47. *See also* classification of detainees
Nazi Party in Germany, 173–76
New Orleans: Algiers neighborhood, ix, 25, 27, 39; Crescent City Connection, 27, 222n9; as "Gateway to the Americas," 25, 202; as port of entry and departure, 14–17, 25, 30. *See also* Camp Algiers, New Orleans
New Orleans Committee for Refugee Services, 35, 117
Nicholson, Eleanor, 31–32, 223n20
Niehaus, Thomas, 134–35

Nuremburg Laws, 19, 54, 62–63, 175–76
Nussbaum, Felix, 191

Ocasio-Cortez, Alexandria, 212
O'Day, Caroline, 5
Office of Strategic Services (OSS), 8
Office of the Coordinator for Inter-American Affairs, 236n25
Okihiro, Gary, 56
Opel, Fritz von ("Rocket Fritz"), 48, 85–88
Oppenheimer, J. Robert, 110, 233n45
O'Rourke, Joseph, 71
Ortiz Sotelo, Jorge, 9

Panama: Camp Balboa, Canal Zone, 7, 194–95, 196; Camp Empire, Canal Zone, 11; Canal Zone and Enemy Alien Control Program, 6; deportation and property confiscation, 11; Fechenbach case, 61; Gunther case, 39; Harten case, 16, 50; Heinemann case, 65–67; Nazism in, 7; secret map and, 9
Panama Jews: about, 90–92, 119–21; Ascher case, 89–90, 92–94; Bohm case, 94–95; bribery and, 98–99; at Camp Balboa, Canal Zone, 194–95, 196; Frankel case, 96–100; Kallman case, 100–101; Kappel case, 101–4; Karliner case, 104–5; Kaufmann case, 105–6; Klyszcz case, 106–7; Lipschitz case, 115–16; Manheimer case, 107–9, 194–95; Marcus case, 109–10; Muller case, 110–11; Razovsky and, 197, 199–200; Scholem case, 111–13; Wetterschneider case, 108, 113–16; Wolff case, 116–19
Papen, Franz von, 138, 141
Parsons, Dudley, 146
Partmuss, Friedrich Paul (Federico Pablo), 48–49
Paschka, María (Emma Marie), 84–85
Paschka, Max Richard, 84–85
Paulsen, Jakob Christian, 43
Pepper, Claude, 87–88

Perkin, Eugene, 238n58
Peru: Japanese detainees from, 13–16, 209–11; Lothrop as spy in, 129
pesticide decontamination, 16–17, 210–11
Phillipp, Louis, 44
Pitzer, Andrea, 213–14
Plath, August Wilhelm, 59
Plath, Humberto, 58–59
Pomeroy, Allan, 37
Price, David, 129
Price, George Ward, 173
prisoner exchanges, 12–13, 66–67, 112
prisons, repurposing of, 213–14
Proclamation 2525 (1941), 4, 205
Proclamation 2526 (1941), 4
Proclamation 2527 (1941), 4
Proclamation 2662 (Removal of Alien Enemies) (1945), 116, 145–47

Quinn, T. Vincent, 147

Rassenschande ("race defilement" or mixed marriages), 71–72, 78, 81, 108–9
Razovsky, Cecilia, 119, 193, 194, 196–204
Reagan, Ronald, 208
Rees, Goronwy, 149
refugee camps vs. internment camps, 91
Reichner, Wilhelm, 103, 194, 200
Reinhardt, Max, 174–75, 243n43
religion: Buddhists and Shintoists, 56; classification and, 53; *conversos*, contemporary, 76, 229n71; discrimination based on, 56; Mennonites, 83, 230n90
repatriation: classification and, 59–60; closure of Camp Algiers and, 45–50; Jewish fears of, 97; Kaul case, 68; Ludecke case and *Ludecke v. Watkins*, 155–57; Truman proclamation on (1945), 45–46; Proclamation 2662 (1945), 116, 145–47; "Routine Inquiry Concerning Wish to Be Repatriated" forms, 82; Wachtmeister case, 165–66
Rescue Resolution (1943), 115

Richter, Hans, 171
Richter, Ludmilla (mother of Stephanie von Hohenlohe, later Baroness de Szepessy), 171, 176–78, 180–83
Ries, Maurice, 134–35, 136, 236n26
Riley, Karen, 12
Robinson, Greg, 4
Rockefeller, Nelson, 130, 236n25
Roehl, Marjorie, 46, 117
Röhm, Ernst, 240n91
Roorda, Eric, 162–63
Roosevelt, Franklin D.: antisemitism and, 199; Enemy Alien Control Program and, 1, 5–6; Executive Order 9066 (1942), 3–4, 45; "fifth column" and, 9; Hohenlohe case (Stephanie) and, 170, 180–82, 185; Japanese internment and, 56; Jewish refugees and, 19, 20; Lend-Lease Act and, 242n14; Rescue Resolution and, 115; secret map and National Defense Day address, 9–10, 10
Rosenberg, Isidor, 203
Rostow, Eugene, 22
Roth, Philip, 246n21
Rothermere, Harold Sidney Harmsworth, First Viscount, 172–73, 176–77, 243n37
Rothstein, Charles M., 155
Routh, Cope, 45
Rucker, Hans, 44
Rummel, Joseph, 204
Russell, Jan Jarboe, 71
Ruttenberg, Danya, 212–13

Sauter, Fritz, 21
Savoretti, Joseph, 27–28
Schad, Martha, 171, 182
Schloss Leopoldskron, Salzburg, 174–76, 175
Schnyder, Paul, 40–43
Schofield, Lemuel B., 28, 178, 179, 180–82, 186
Scholem, Werner (leftist intellectual), 113
Scholem, Werner H. (detainee, later Werner H. Sheldon), 103, 111–13
Schott, Matthew, 222n4

Schuman, Frederick L., 149
Schweitzer, David, 192
Seitz, Jules, 39–40, 248n48
Sellnick, Margot, 85–87
Serpa Pinto, 191, *192*, 193
Sheldon, James H., 146
Shibayama, Isamu "Art," 210–11
ship manifests, 52, *54, 55*
Slack, Charles, 2
Smith, Daniel Cranford, 142
Smith, Richard E., 98
Snowden, Ethel, 175
Sosúa Jewish colony, Dominican Republic, 191–92
Spiegel, Baron von, 134–35
sponsors, 193, 211
Stannard, Amy N., 184
Starr, Milton, 199
stateless refugees, 19, 61, 93, 200
Staudinger, Fred, 142
St. Cyprien camp, France, 190–91, 193
stereotypes and classification, 53–56
Stierlin, Eduard, 85, 231n97
St. Louis, SS, 246n17
Stoltzfus, Frank, 42
Stone, Doris, 127–28, 130–31, 235n15
Stone, Roger Thayer, 128, 235n15, 235n20
Strum, Harvey, 65, 91–92
Stryk, Herman, 107
suicide, 167–69, 181, 185
Swiss legation, 59, 70–71, 77, 119, 189–90, 201
Szepessy, Baroness Milla de. *See* Richter, Ludmilla

Talbot, David, 219n36, 242n28
Tenney, Daniel G., 80
Thimig, Helene, 174–75
Trott, Otto, 36–38
Trujillo, Rafael Leónidas, 162–63, 191
Trump, Donald, 157, 241n111, 248n1
Tulane University, 123–24, 127–30, 134–37, 236n26
Turner, Van Arsdale, 46

Urbach, Karina, 172, 243n37
US Army, detainees inducted into, 103–4, 105, 113, 181, 188
US Citizenship and Immigration Services, 207
US Quarantine Station–New Orleans, 25, 26, 27–29, 50–51

Van den Arend, F., 160–61
Velázquez, Eva, 71–73
Venezuela, 112
Villa, Pancho, 122, 138
Vladek, Stephen, 156–57
von der Goltz, Horst: at Algiers, 40, 142–43; on "anti-Nazi camp," 223n26; Anti-Nazi League and the Friends of Democracy, concerns of, 142–46; on committee of spokesmen, 43; at Ellis Island, 139, 140, 143; investigation, arrest order, and letters on behalf of, 139–42; life of, 138–39; Ludecke compared to, 147–48; *My Adventures as a German Secret Service Agent*, 138–39; no hearing, claim of, 44; repatriation hearing, 145–47
von der Goltz, Peggy, 139, 141–42, 146

Wachtmeister, Axel, Count: background, 159–60; at Camp Kenedy, 160–61, 163–67; charges against, 161–63; Condor Airlines and, 162, 166; in Dominican Republic and La Cumbre camp, 99, 160–64, 167, 168; Hohenlohe (Stephanic) compared with, 170–71, 183, 188; I-55 General Information Form, 166–67; repatriation plans, 167–68; suicide and death certificate, 167, 167–69
Waring, Dorothy, 142
war on terror and war on illegal immigration, 157, 207, 214
Wauchope, Robert, 134, 136–37
Weschler, Herbert, 185
Westermeier, Carl, 98
Wetterschneider, Egon, 113–16, 194
Wetterschneider, Hilda (Hilde), 114–16
Wetterschneider, Oskar, 108, 113–16, 194
Wiedemann, Fritz, 173, 176–80, 243n56
Wiener, Max, 171
Williams, Duncan Ryōken, 56
Wilson, Jim, 172, 185, 187, 243n31
Wisoff, Dorothy, 238n58
Witkin, Nathan, 108, 119, 195, 196
Wolff, Irene, 200
Wolff, Jeanette, 35, 109, 117–18
Wolff, Siegfried, 44, 94, 109, 116–19, 204
Wolff, Walter, 94, 109–10, 117–18, 202
World War I, 48, 56, 128–29, 134, 139–40, 172

Yamamoto, Libia, 209–11
Yiddish, 194, 196
Yokoy, Schoichi, 193

Zehnder, Max, 42
Zemurray, Samuel, 127–28, 130, 236n26
Zucker, Bat-Ami, 12

CPSIA information can be obtained
at www.ICGtesting.com
Printed in the USA
LVHW090035220521
688148LV00007B/283